Indian Freedom

The Cause of Bartolomé de las Casas, 1484-1566

A Reader

Translations and Notes
by
Francis Patrick Sullivan, S.J.

Sheed & Ward

Sheed & Ward™ is a service of The National Catholic Reporter Publishing Company.

———————————◆———————————

Library of Congress Cataloguing-in-Publication Data

Casas, Bartolomé de las, 1474-1566.
    [Selections. English. 1995]
    Indian freedom : the cause of Bartolomé de las Casas, 1484-1566 :
a reader / translations and notes by Francis Patrick Sullivan.
        p.   cm.
    Translated from Spanish and Latin.
    Includes bibliographical references and index.
    ISBN 1-55612-717-0 (acid-free paper)
    1. Indians, Treatment of—Latin America. 2. Indians—Legal status,
laws, etc. 3. Spain—Colonies—America. I. Sullivan, Francis, 1929- .
II. Title.
F1411.C47645213   1995
970.01'6—dc20   94-32961
                                               CIP

———————————◆———————————

Published by: Sheed & Ward
                  115 E. Armour Blvd.
                  P.O. Box 419492
                  Kansas City, MO 64141

To order, call: (800) 333-7373

Cover design by Emil Antonucci.

Cover illustration is taken from the titlepage drawing of Las Casas' *Destruction of the Indies*. Used by permission of the William L. Clements Library, University of Michigan, Ann Arbor, Michigan.

Contents

Part III.
Creating Pro-Indian Law

Part IV.
Defending Pro-Indian Law

Introduction

The Indians of the New World, conquered by Spain in the 16th century, were deprived of voice from the start, so they could not plead their own innocence before any human court or human conscience. Thus argued Bartolomé de las Casas during that lethal period. Indians had no standing as human beings in the eyes of the conquistador. Somebody had to become a voice for them, somebody who recognized their innocence, their human reality, and could awaken the conscience of the King of Spain and those who acted in the New World in the King's name. It took time for people to appear inside the Spanish system, people who recognized the appeal to conscience right within the Indian reality, and recognized all the laws of belief and behavior on the Spanish side that required submission to that Indian reality. In all justice, they must be restored to their freedom, or those who hold them must suffer eternal consequences, a living death before God.

How credible to the modern world is this overall assessment of the Conquest by Las Casas? In the recent Quincentenary celebration of Columbus' voyage and its aftermath, issues of right and justice were rarely raised, or were mentioned as disputations in the schools of Spain. Mainly, the impression was left that the devastation of the New World resulted from sheer happenstance—disease, for example. When Las Casas and his view of events were mentioned, the focus was mainly on his passion, his exaggeration of facts as a means he justified by the end he had in view, preservation of the Indians. No one called attention to the unique experience the man had, no one knew enough about his life to realize he had to be taken as a primary witness to, a primary force in that whole period.

He was born in Seville in 1484, into a family that was involved both in farming and merchandising.[1] He first saw Columbus and his captive Indians

---

[1] See Helen Rand Parish, with Harold E. Weidman. "The Correct Birthdate of Bartolomé de las Casas." *Hispanic American Historical Review* 56 (1976): 385-403. The biographical sketch that follows is due mainly to the scholarly work of Helen Rand Parish. See *Bartolomé de las Casas: The Only Way*, ed. Helen Rand Parish, trans. Francis Patrick Sullivan, S.J. (Mahwah: Paulist Press, 1992), Introduction, pp. 9-58 [hereafter, *The Only Way*]. For a close reading of the ideas of

in that city the day the Discoverer, just home from his First Voyage, took part in the Palm Sunday procession, March, 1493. Las Casas' father and uncle signed up for the Second Voyage and went out within months. The boy continued his studies, in classics and canon law, but he heard stories over the next few years—they were all around Spain—of how cruel Columbus was, how harsh in his rule overseas. He would remember these stories when he came later to write the life of the Discoverer as part of his *History of the Indies*. They would help him understand. Columbus was indeed harsh, he had to rule violent men. But Las Casas' father and uncle were intensely loyal to Columbus, so the youngster was introduced to a contradiction it took him years to resolve. Columbus could command loyalty because of his good intentions; his actions, however, towards Spaniards, could arouse bitter opposition. They were a fierce bunch and resented the foreigner placed over them. And his actions towards the Indians would lead Bartolomé de las Casas later to judge him severely as someone blinded to the truth of Indian freedom because of his own purposes—to gain wealth for the Kings of Spain so they would continue to back his voyages of discovery.

It was in 1502 that Las Casas went out to the New World, to work for his father and himself with holdings of land and Indians on the island of Hispaniola (Haiti/Dominican Republic). Columbus was on his way back to Spain in shackles, so much had the Spaniards on the island fallen to fighting one another and ravaging the Indians and blaming their rebellion on Columbus. A new governor, as bad as any Spaniard on Hispaniola, had been sent out to replace him in 1500, and had believed the rebels against Columbus, seized him and his brothers, stashed the three on a vessel and summarily sent them off. A second governor, Ovando, was on his way in 1502—the Kings thought the first replacement had acted too harshly—and Las Casas was in that governor's fleet. When Las Casas' ship arrived in the port of Santo Domingo, settlers ran down to the river bank and shouted, "What's new, Spain okay?" "Spain okay," was the shout back, "what's new with you?" "Found a big hunk of gold," was the answer from shore, "and there's a great war going on, get us a lot of slaves! Great stuff!" That was Las Casas' introduction to the island, and the beginning of his disenchantment as he later recalls it.

He spent the next five years running his own holdings and traveling the island as a provisioner to the Spanish soldiery. But he was trying to be a good man in a bad system. He presumed things about Spain and Christianity he should not have, presumed things about himself he had to unlearn, and his later writings on behalf of the Indians show the process of his awakening. He began to see the useless waste of Indian life during his first five years on

Las Casas, their sources, and the counter-positions of those he argued against, see Gustavo Gutiérrez, *Las Casas: In Search of the Poor of Jesus Christ*, tr. by Robert R. Barr (Maryknoll: Orbis Books, 1993).

Hispaniola, and more, the useless waste of Indian spirit, so he went back to Spain in 1506 to resume studies and seek ordination to the priesthood, then return to the island as a more religiously oriented person. He was ordained actually in Rome in 1507, he had gone there as an assistant to Bartholomew Columbus, Christopher's brother, in order to help Bartholomew get papal backing for a new voyage which would finally reach Cathay, the great and rich kingdom Christopher had been seeking all along. Christopher had died in 1506.

After ordination, Las Casas studied canon law in Spain for two years, then sailed to the New World in 1509 with the Second Admiral, Diego Columbus. There he took up his task as Indian catechist, but also as a holder of Indians and property. His conscience could not sustain this position much longer. He says he tried to go to confession to a Dominican—Dominicans had come in 1510, and within a year or so judged that everything Spain was doing in the New World was mortal sin. There was the great scene in Santo Domingo when one of them, Antón Montesino, speaking for the others, denounced the Spanish islanders for their tyranny. There was an uproar, and a demand on the Dominicans that they reverse their preaching the next week. Their Superior and remarkable man, Pedro de Córdoba—Las Casas describes him in terms reserved for a saint—had his preacher mount the pulpit the next week in the hut of a church and intensify the denunciation. This was in Advent, 1511, and Las Casas is the only one to record it, though he may not have been in attendance. His Dominican confessor was only willing to absolve him if he changed the pattern of his life—no holding Indians—which Las Casas was reluctant still to do.

It was three years later that the full truth burst through on Las Casas. He had been asked to go to Cuba as part of a pacifying expedition led by a friend, Diego Velásquez. Velásquez knew how good Las Casas was with the Indians—if anyone could approach them peaceably it was this "white behique," someone the Indians recognized as a spiritual person. But in that process of "pacification," Las Casas saw a horrible massacre happen one day at Caonao. The Spanish soldiery had come to a stream with good flint rocks in it, excellent for sharpening their swords, which they did, then looked for people to use them on, and there were some thousands of Indians nearby, seated and waiting to receive the Spanish party which they knew was coming. The soldiers ran amok and killed in a frenzy everyone in reach of their newly sharpened swords. Las Casas tried to stop the slaughter, but the Captain in charge was heartless. Soon after, when Las Casas had to preach a sermon for Pentecost 1514, he had to face a text that tore him wide open and allowed the conscience that had been mounting in him to clear his heart and mind: *"Unclean is the offering sacrificed by an oppressor. [Such] mockeries of the unjust are not pleasing [to God]. The Lord is pleased only by those who keep to the way of truth and justice. . . The one whose*

sacrifice comes from the goods of the poor is like one who kills his neighbor.
The one who sheds blood and the one who defrauds the laborer are kin and
kind. "(Ecclesiasticus 34:18 ff.)[2]

The next thing was to surrender all his holdings, give land and Indians
back to Governor Velázquez, which he did, though he knew the Indians
might well be wiped out by some other owner. Then Las Casas preached, as
the Dominicans had done, but that was not enough and he knew it. So he
began in 1514 to imagine how Spaniards and Indians could live together in
mutual creativity in the situation as it existed. His first memorial on how to
do so found its way to Flanders in 1516, to Adrian of Utrecht, co-Regent of
Spain, then through him to Erasmus, the tutor of Charles I, who in turn gave
it to Thomas More who was influenced by it to write *Utopia*.[3] But Las
Casas' memorial didn't succeed otherwise, nor his return to Spain and
attempt to influence the powers in charge of the Indies. His good ideas were
accepted, but then subverted by other motivations than concern for the
Indians and the Indies. In the early 1520's he tried himself a peaceful
settlement scheme on the north coast of South America at Cumaná, one that
would have a minimum of force and a maximum of persuasion to allow
Spaniards to live in fruitful peace with Indian peoples. That too failed
because of greed for slaving in the party he had assembled. Las Casas saw
he had compromised his duty to be the Protector of the Indians, so, in deep
discouragement, he left his work and entered the Dominican Order on the
island of Hispaniola. The time was 1522.

The monastic life, however, only sharpened his recognition of the
destruction of the Indians and the corruption of the Spanish soul. He was
already deeply schooled in canon law from two stays at Salamanca, Spain,
earlier in his life. He now added more theology to his knowledge, then he
was made Prior of a house on the north coast of Hispaniola. There he saw
some of the Indian slaves brought in from the Bahamas, the ones who had
fallen sick during transportation. They were left to die on the beaches. He
said later the slave ships needed no navigator, the helmsmen simply
followed the line of corpses thrown overboard. So he began to write reports
informing authorities in Spain and on the island. These were effective, and
by the late 1520's a law suppressing slavery was passed, but did not stay
passed long. Someone, another Dominican missionary, defamed the Indians
to Spanish authority, calling them near animals whose sufferings were a just

---

[2] See *The Only Way*, Addendum I, pp. 185-96, for a translation of the passages from
Bartolomé de las Casas, *Historia de las Indias*. Introd. by Lewis Hanke, transcription
and index by Agustín Millares Carlo. 3 vols. (Mexico City: Fondo de Cultura
Económica, 1951), lib. 3, cap. 78-9 [hereafter, *History*].

[3] See Victor N. Baptiste, *Bartolomé de las Casas and Thomas More's Utopia:*
Connections and Similarities (Culver City, CA: Labyrinthos, 1990, pp. 1-10
[hereafter, *Utopia*].

punishment from God for their past sins. The defamation brought about revocation of the anti-slavery law. Las Casas preached against this revocation and was silenced for what he said, and told to stay behind his monastery walls and keep shut. The time was the early 1530's.

Then something remarkable happened which brought Las Casas out into the struggle again, and gave him a vision of what now to do. The vision was provided by an Indian guerrilla chief, up in the inaccessible mountains of Hispaniola. Enriquillo, as the Spaniards called this Indian, had been raised as a Christian child in a Franciscan convent back in the early years of the century. He was the son of a cacique (chief), and was expected to head his tribe when he became an adult. The cacique's role was to guarantee work forces of Indians for the Spanish mines and cassava fields. In the two work places, the Indians died in droves. When Enriquillo married, his wife was taken that first night and raped by the Spanish encomendero who owned the Indians of the area. Enriquillo went to Spanish justice to gain redress, but received further humiliation instead, and no redress for his wife. So at a point, he took his family and people and went up into the rugged mountains where he eluded Spanish pursuit for the next fifteen years. He proved to be a superb tactician, fending off the Spaniards, killing only as a last resort, mostly capturing, disarming, and dismissing the troops hunting him. This hunt was costing Spain enormous amounts of money. One time, Enriquillo was on the opposite side of a crevasse from a Spanish captain. That captain had been empowered to make peace. The two talked across the crevasse, agreed to meet on a day down at the shore, then Enriquillo could settle his people in peace wherever they wished. On the day, more Spaniards showed up for the meeting than were agreed upon, and a man-o-war stood just offshore. Enriquillo suspected a trap, so he hid again.

Las Casas heard about this. He got permission to go up into the mountains unarmed, with just one companion, to try and talk with Enriquillo and ask him to bring his people out and settle. Enriquillo welcomed him because he knew Las Casas wanted no power over him, no gold from him, that Las Casas was coming with respect for him and his people, and was motivated only by the charity Enriquillo had learned as a youngster was the soul of Christianity. Las Casas was overwhelmed by the belief he found. It was true and living, quite the opposite to that of the settiers. So, on a second trip, he brought Enriquillo and his people out of the mountains and located them in an area where they could live. Las Casas had learned how to approach anyone in the New World—unarmed, with their permission, through peace and truth. That was the only way. He wrote this up in a short tract, and with that tract left the island to become a missionary in the true sense of the word. The time is 1534. Behind him, on Hispaniola, a tragic betrayal was in the making. Word was sent from Spain to seize Enriquillo and ship him back there as a prisoner where he would be disposed of permanently. But Enriquillo died of natural causes beforehand.[4]

Las Casas filled the next few years with great activity, as a missionary in Central America first, then as a powerful figure in the Mexican ecclesiastical conferences of 1535 and 1536. He won those conferences over to his doctrine of peaceful conversion. As a result, representatives were sent to Rome bearing the recommendations of the conference of 1536, where they were accepted as the doctrine of the whole church by Pope Paul III, who then issued a Bull, "Sublimis Deus," making the rights of Indian peoples church law—"The Indians we speak of, and all other peoples who later come to the knowledge of Christians, outside the faith though they be, are not to be deprived of their liberty or the right to their property. They are to have, to hold, to enjoy both liberty and dominion, freely, lawfully. They must not be enslaved. Should anything different be done, it is void, invalid, of no force, no worth. And those Indians and other peoples are to be invited into the faith of Christ by the preaching of God's word and the example of a good life."[5] But those rights were blocked a year later by other decisions of both the Pope and the King of Spain. So Las Casas knew he had to carry the struggle to court if Indian rights were ever to be preserved. He had his chance in 1540 when the Dominican Order sent him back as Dominican representative for the New World.

What he achieved at court was no less than New Laws for the good government of the Indies. Those New Laws were really the start of international law as we know it today, and are remarkably similar in purpose to the United Nations Declaration of Universal Human Rights. During 1542, Las Casas wrote and presented to the King and the Reform Commission some documents that are staggering in their power and intensity. First was his indictment of the deliberate policy of terror practiced out in the Indies against the Indians—there was not one whit of justification for that policy. He told a series of horror stories, a condensation of which appeared later in a famous book called *Brief Account of the Decimation of the Indies*. People couldn't breathe listening to him read his material. Next, he indicted the encomienda system, the one that gave Spaniards the right to hold Indians "in order to bring them up in the faith." A mockery if there ever was one, Las Casas argued. And then he argued what good relationship could have been, could still be. That did it, the conscience of the King, Charles I of Spain, was moved, the Reform Commission was moved, and over the intervening months laws were drafted which went a long way towards redressing Indian

---

[4] See *History*, Bk. 3, cap. 125.

[5] See *The Only Way*, p. 114-15, for full text. See also Helen Rand Parish, *Las Casas en México: Historia y obra desconocidas* (Mexico City: Fondo de Cultura Económica, 1992), 1ª Parte. 1ª Parte details Las Casas' origination of Church policy towards Indian peoples.

wrongs and protecting Indian rights—e.g., "ITEM, We ordain and command that from henceforward for no cause of war nor any other whatsoever, though it be under the title of rebellion, nor by ransom nor in other manner can an Indian be made a slave, and we will that they be treated as our vassals of the Crown of Castile since such they are."[6]

Las Casas wrote one other piece, an anti-slavery tract, the only one written in that century, at the request of the Commission, and he left it with the same. In those days, everyone, from the Pope on down, accepted slavery if it resulted from capture in a just war. The tract is a devastating attack on the "just war" moral norm for Indian enslavement, the norm that had been used since Columbus' time. There was no just war in the Indies. The tract kept the anti-slavery law from being revoked. Some years later, in 1552, Las Casas learned there was no just war on the African Guinea coast. He was chagrined that he did not recognize this earlier, and he denounced Black African enslavement and sale by the Portugese as equally immoral.[7]

After 1542, Las Casas' life was filled with struggles to save his two major achievements, the Church doctrine of the peaceful, truthful presentation of Christianity, and the civil doctrine of the rights of Indian peoples in the face of Spanish (or any) power. He accepted to become a bishop in Chiapa, Mexico, so he could practice his mission theory in a poor area. The time was 1544-5. But in that area he ran into fierce opposition from Spanish settlers. There was the threat of violence. So he wrote a manual of rules and regulations for confessors. The latter were to refuse deathbed absolution to anyone who kept profiting from Indian life and land. Las Casas had to leave his diocese in 1546, he was simply persona non grata. The manual became known and raised a political as well as an ecclesiastical storm. Meantime, back in Spain, some laws protecting the Indians were being revoked. Las Casas knew his real fight was back there, on constant watch, so he returned in 1546 and ran smack into another controversy.

A humanist, Juan Ginés de Sepúlveda had acted on an earlier defamation of the Indians and was now, in a second book, defending Spain's right to conquer and civilize barbaric peoples such as the Indians of the New World. Las Casas undertook a refutation of Sepúlveda, before an advisory commission appointed by the King. It was not a debate, it was a hearing of arguments by a group of learned men who voted to reject Sepúlveda's position

---

[6] Charles V, *The New Laws of the Indies for the Good Treatment and Preservation of the Indians, promulgated by the Emperor Charles the Fifth, 1542-1543:* Facsimile of original Spanish first edition, literal English translation, and Introd. by Henry Stevens and Fred W. Lucas. (London: Chiswick Press, 1893), [#21].

[7] See *The Only Way*, Addendum III, pp. 201-8, "Las Casas' Condemnation of African Slavery," for 1) Parish's treatment of the accusation against Las Casas that he originated the importation of Black slaves to the New World, 2) translations of the relevant passages in the *History*. They are reprinted below under B.7.

and renew the laws against conquest and slavery. At this time, apart from writing up the refutation of Sepúlveda, Las Casas also composed a massive *Defense of Indian Civilization* which revealed his knowledge of, and respect for, the humanity of all the Indians he had known or had been informed about. At this same time, he worked on his *History of the Indies*, especially the "Life of Columbus" section, in order to point out to Spain's king and people what had caused the awful conquest. He did this so Spain could change its ways, save its soul, and allow the Indians to save theirs. This was all done in the early and middle 1550's. Las Casas was in constant danger from royal power during this challenge he mounted against royal policy. But he had written, in the late 1540's, a piece that showed how the rights of conscience were not subject either to royal or papal power. And he knew Church doctrine and civil law so well that no one dared touch him openly.

He needed all his skill in the late 1550's because a new disaster loomed. The owners [*encomenderos*] of Indians and land in Peru knew that the king of Spain, now Philip II, was in desperate debt. So, in 1555, they offered him a huge sum of money if he would grant them perpetual rights over the Indians, i.e., a right to keep the Indians practically enslaved forever. Las Casas caught wind of this and began a counter-movement. He contacted missionaries and, through them, Indian leaders in the New World. Together they presented a proposal to the king—they would pay more for Indian freedom than the *encomenderos* would pay for Indian slavery. The king took the bait and sent a commission out to Peru to investigate the power the Indians had to pay. Clearly that power meant the fabulous treasure hidden in the tombs of the ancient kings. Many, many such tombs had been discovered and plundered during the period of the 1550's. So the King knew that Las Casas and the Indians could come up with the money. The whole affair of the offer and counter-offer came to nothing because the royal commission ended up in such a state of corruption and fraud that the king halted it.

Something happened after this, in 1564, which brought out in Las Casas a full appreciation of all the principles he had used for over fifty years to try and free the Indians and set right the conscience of Spain. He was asked to solve twelve problems confessors in Peru needed answered so they could deal with their penitents' sins. Las Casas had, a short time before, written a major tract concerning the treasures of Peru, and the problem of the true ownership of such treasure. The Incas owned it, not the Spaniards. So when the twelve problems were proposed to him, he wrote up the story behind each one, outlined the principles of solution, then proceeded to apply those principles. All Spanish sovereignty in Peru was based on the murder of the Inca king, Atabaliba, by the conquistadors. What followed was tyrannical conquest, enslavement, seizure of property, plundering of tombs. Not one bit of Peruvian wealth belonged to Spain, Las Casas said, or to its king, or to its church, or to Spanish people at home or abroad. Every house, every church had been set on stolen ground, the income of all monasteries and priests was ill-gotten, all authority was usurped. Therefore Spain was obliged to total restoration, restitution, if it wished to save its collective soul.

Las Casas proved every single one of his positions from canon law, from civil law, from gospel principles, from sheer human compassion. And the document, called *Twelve Doubts*, stands even today as the very best of European culture's ability to see and understand and preserve the integrity of innocent, non-European peoples. Las Casas knew that the natives of the New World had acted towards the Spaniards in human, civilized ways. They had their own sense of social integrity, however well or ill they lived up to their ideal. He was haunted by what could have resulted by a marriage between the ideals instead of the murder that did occur.

His Last Will and Testament, written a few years before he died on July 18, 1566, sums up well the meaning of his whole life:

> "I testify that it was God in his goodness and mercy who chose me as his minister . . . on behalf of all those people out in what we call the Indies, the true possessors of those kingdoms . . . so as to restore them to the original liberty they were lawlessly deprived of, and get them free of death by violence. . . . For almost fifty years I have done this work, back and forth between the Indies and Castile . . . often, since 1514. . . . And I have done it . . . out of compassion at seeing the deaths of so many human beings. . . . All that the Spaniards perpetrated against those [Indian] peoples . . . was in violation of the holy and spotless law of Jesus Christ . . . of the whole natural law, and a terrible blot on the name of Christ and the Christian faith. . . . And I think that God shall have to pour out his fury and anger on Spain. . . . For the whole of Spain has shared in the blood-soaked riches . . . and all must pay unless Spain does a mighty penance. . . . I fear it will do so too late or not at all, because there is a blindness . . . which is not even today aware that . . . such devastation, such genocide of populations, have been sins, monumental injustices!"[8]

It is one thing to read a biographical sketch of the importance of Las Casas to the issues of 16th century Spain, it is another to read the man

---

[8] See Nicolás Sanchez Albornoz, "La población de las Indias en Las Casas y en la historia," *En el quinto centenario de Bartolomé las Casas* (Madrid: Ediciones Cultura Hispánica, ICI, 1986), pp. 85-92. He establishes that Las Casas' figures on Indian deaths are not exaggerated.

himself speaking from within that life and sensing in the experiences he underwent the issues pressing on him for solution, then to read the solutions themselves, their originality, their long-lasting effects. In the selections that follow, I have tried to present Las Casas describing *what* happened in the aftermath of the "Discovery" by Columbus, and *why* it did—the *why* for him being crucial, or events simply escaped human responsibility, fate was at work, and no one need repair the damage and restore Indian integrity, or worry about the loss of their souls. Las Casas' written texts come from the period 1527-1564, with concentrations in the 1542-1546 period, and the period from 1550-1564. But his collation of basic principles come from 1542, with some refinements at later dates, 1552, 1564. So the writings are of a mature man who has thought long and hard about the Indies and Spain, he is the one who stretches back in memory to the beginnings, who supports what he says by compelling documentation as well as personal experience, who discerns the issues at play from this later vantage point, though it took him time when he was young to realize them, who invents a way of life together for Spain and for the Indies, who recognizes, finally, the lethal consequences that will follow, for both conquered and conquerors, if Spain does not restore Indian freedom.

Part I.
The Destructive Pattern

- 1 -

Las Casas' Prologue:
"The Lie Has Many Friends"

Prenote

The gist of Las Casas' Prologue to the History of the Indies *is that the truth is an instrument of freedom, the lie is an instrument of enslavement.*[9] *The truth about the Indies and Indians is that they were always free, there was never a justifying reason for the removal of that freedom by Spain in the aftermath of Columbus and 1492. The lie about the Indies and the Indians is that they lost their right to freedom because they were savages who needed civilization imposed; they were idolaters who needed Christianity imposed; they were loafers who needed discipline imposed; they were actually subjects of Spain, given by the Pope, so they had to be brought to heel.*

The truth about Indian freedom can be known by a close examination of events as met with in primary sources—participants, eyewitnesses both Indian and Spaniard, documents, letters, sworn testimony, personal experience. And those sources are to be made available to the reader so the judgment of the historian—Las Casas, in this case—can itself be judged. And the principles of judgment the historian uses—natural law, divine law,

---

[9] For a description of the *History*, see Henry Raup Wagner and Helen Rand Parish, *The Life and Writings of Bartolomé de las Casas* (Albuquerque: University of New Mexico Press, 1967), Catalogue no. 65, pp. 290-2 [hereafter, Wagner-Parish]. Parish establishes the dates of composition, the structure used, the subsequent influence of this most important work of Las Casas: it was written between 1527-1561 in free periods; it included material later separated into the *Apologética historia sumaria*; the manuscript was to be sequestered for 40 years after Las Casas' death by his own wish; it was borrowed from heavily by Herrera in late 16th century with scant notice; it was used by later historians who borrowed from Herrera, e.g., Washington Irving.

*law of nations—must also be laid out, and their origin in tradition clearly
indicated. The historian's motivation in doing the work must also be made
clear, again so the reader can judge how the evidence is being handled.
Motivation can prompt a truth search as well as propaganda play. Las
Casas is motivated by two loves, one of the Indians he came to know, the
other of Spain he already knew. He sought the truth about the Indies in
order to set both free, the one from devastation in this world, the other from
devastation in the next.*

. . . My one motive in dictating this book [*The History of the Indies*]
was that I saw Spain had an urgent, a mortal need to have the truth, the light
of the truth shed on Indian affairs, a long-standing need, and at every level
of society.[10] For lack of that truth, or the meagerness of it, what huge
calamities occurred out in the Indies, what violence, what slaughter of whole
peoples, what losses of soul, dead in this life and in the life to come, what
massive injustice! And here in the realm of Castile, what frequent and
unforgiveable sins have been committed, what blindness and stifling of
conscience, what pitiful damage was done, is done every day, as a result of
what I just described. What happened will never be revealed as it ought, I
am certain, never weighed, assessed, bewailed as it ought, until that last
fearsome day of strict and accurate divine judgment. . .

I know some people have written about Indian affairs, not from
what they witnessed, but secondhand and poorly heard (though they don't
admit it), and have done deep damage to the truth. . . So the seed they sowed
was bad, erratic, fruitless, it came from self-seeking, worldly instincts, it
ended producing a greater and greater crop of that choking weed in people,
increasingly—knowledge that was shockingly false and conscience that was
twisted. To such an extent that the Christian faith itself has suffered
irreparable damage, and the long-standing moral values of the Church
universal as well, and of almost the whole human race. . .

We are to believe that God has chosen for salvation some from
among every single group of human beings and has determined the time of
their calling, their conversion, their glorification. But we do not know who
they are, those chosen. So we have to think and feel and judge and act and
be helpful toward every human being, as if we wanted them to be the saved,
and wanted with our works to help effect their salvation insofar as we could,
and we were sure that everyone was called. . . [11]

I have thought long and hard and often about the defects, the errors
laid out above and the manifest, the harmful things that happened and still

---

[10] See *History*, Bk. 1, "Prologo," pp. 12-3.

[11] *History*, p. 14.

happen as a result. And thought how justice has its birth, its roots in the presentation of the truth—so the canon lawyers say. So I decided to write about the major events of the Indies, some of which I saw done, saw happen right before my eyes during my sixty and some years of life—for I was there present, in various areas, realms, provinces, lands—and write also about things public and notorious, not just those over and done with, but also the very many that go on all the time. No one can rightfully refuse to admit that there are done today, in the year 1552, the same deadly things that were done back in earlier years, no more than one can refuse to admit the sun shines bright at noonday in a cloudless sky. If I record some deeds I did not see with my own eyes, or saw but do not recall well, or things that I heard, but which were told to me by different people and in different ways, I will interpret them in terms of the very large experience I have of the totality. That is more likely to gain me the truth, I think. . .

Though I have much else to do, I wanted to undertake this major task, first and foremost, for the honor and glory of God, to make evident God's unfathomable designs, to act in accord with God's divine and unfailing justice, and to do some good for God's whole Church.

Secondly, for the good that can come of it, spiritual and temporal, for those countless peoples over there, if they are not destroyed first, before this history can be completed.

Thirdly, not to please, not to flatter, not to praise the Kings. Instead, to defend the royal honor and reputation of the illustrious sovereigns of Castile. . .

Fourthly, for the good of the whole of Spain, to help it, because I think once it understands what good or evil affected the Indies, it will understand what good or evil affects the whole of itself.

Fifthly, to provide clarity and certainty to readers about what happened back in the beginning when that part of the world was discovered. The material will be very informative to those who read it. And I thoroughly affirm the following: I am the only man living who can describe in any detail how things occurred, and much else that few have written about—or they have, but not with the fidelity to truth they should have had, maybe because they didn't know the facts, or didn't understand them, or were more afraid than they ought, or had as informants people who distorted things—one or the other is the reason why we find today in their writings so many unbearable mistakes.

Sixthly, to free my Spanish nation from error, the deep, wicked lie it lived in, still lives in. It thinks those peoples overseas are not human beings. It makes them out to be brute beasts, intractable, unteachable. It corrupts what good they have, it intensifies what evil—as if for centuries they have been savage and lost peoples and incapable of any help to prevent their remaining as they are, ruined, beaten flat—and all this due to the false, false opinion held about them.

Seventhly, to temper the arrogance, the public pretense of many, and reveal the injustice of many who glory in their vicious, their detestable wickedness, pretending—as if they could—to be heroic men of daring deeds. And I write for the sake of those to come, so they may be able to tell the difference between what was good and what evil, what was virtue and what hideous, horrible sin and vice.

No one should be surprised that I condemn, I abhor the wrong things the Spaniards did, nor should call my attitude bitter or depraved. Should not for this reason—as Polybius expresses it in his History of the Romans—: "Whoever assumes the role of historian must sometimes heap high praise on an enemy if the worth of the deeds they do merits it, and must at other times blame friends bitterly and condemn them when the wrongs they do are worthy of blame and condemnation."

Eighthly, and lastly, to make known—but following a different tack than others—the amazing feats accomplished out there, feats we think are not matched by anything ever done in the long gone past.[12]

---

[12] *History*, p. 19-20.

- 2 -

From the Life of Columbus

Prenote

The behavior of Christopher Columbus towards the Indians of the New World set a destructive pattern going which Spaniards then followed. He seized sovereign territory without warrant, subjugated free peoples without cause, enslaved many of them unjustly, forced the rest to pay tribute, then to serve Spaniards as masters. This caused Indians to die in large numbers.[13] Las Casas knew the pattern from the writings of Columbus himself—the logs of the voyages, letters, royal documents, books—found in the Columbus library Las Casas had access to in 1544 and 1552. Then there were eyewitness accounts, Indian sources, and his own personal knowledge of people who sailed with the Admiral, his father and uncle among them. A large amount of what Columbus wrote is preserved only in Las Casas who faithfully copied what he found.[14] So Las Casas reveals Columbus and what he did from the man's own mouth, or the mouths of those with him, or of those who backed him, or of those who opposed him. And Las Casas' narrative offers readers a chance to check his judgment for themselves. The selections which follow were chosen to reveal Las Casas' art of historical narration, his sense that Columbus was an extraordinary, a heroic man who was blinded to what he actually did by what he thought he was doing. He thought he was glorifying Spain and Christendom. He was actually destroying free peoples, the lands they lived in, and any respect they might ever have for Castile or Christendom. And the selections

---

[13] See *Las Casas' Life of Columbus*, trans. by Francis Patrick Sullivan, with Introduction by Helen Rand Parish (Berkeley: University of California Press, 1995 (in preparation). See especially the flagging of the destructive pattern throughout the text, plus the flagging of what might have been the creative pattern. The sections here are printed with permission of the University of California Press.

[14] See Consuelo Varela, *Cristóbal Colón: Textos y documentos completos* (Madrid: Alianza Editorial, 2nd ed. 1989), Intro. p. ix.

will also reveal Las Casas' sense that the Indians were remarkable human beings who could not withstand the armed might of the conquistadors, and their remarkable humanity was thereby lost to the world at large.

The first selection, "SHIPWRECK CHRISTMAS EVE," reveals the humanity and generosity of the Indians, as Columbus records it and eyewitnesses tell of it. The time is 1492. Within a year, Columbus will violate that humanity and generosity. The second selection, "STORM HOMEWARD BOUND," records the dramatic finish to the First Voyage and demonstrates the courage and genius of the Discoverer. The third selection, "UNCOVERING DISASTER," shows the lawless behavior of the Spaniards left on the island half-way through the First Voyage due to the loss of the flagship. Columbus finds them dead when he returns on the Second Voyage, 1493. The fourth selection, "GOLD TOWN NIGHTMARE," reveals the illusion that gripped Spaniards who came out on that Second Voyage and on subsequent ones—gold and spices were to be found ready and crated on the beaches, to be hauled home to Spain where life would then be rich beyond imagining. Las Casas includes a Hamlet-like legend at the end of the story, as if to say the souls of the damned must haunt the place of their damnation. The fifth selection, "PROPHETIC ENCOUNTER," demonstrates the spirituality of an Indian in contrast to the worldliness of the Admiral, a point Las Casas constantly makes about other Indians and other Spaniards throughout the rest of the History.

The sixth selection, "PALM SUNDAY UPSIDE DOWN," shows by way of reverse image how Bartholomew Columbus was welcomed by the Indians as Jesus was welcomed into Jerusalem. Bartholomew came in the guise of a savior, but was in reality a destroyer. For Las Casas, this is a symbol of the whole Spanish approach to the New World. Christopher, meanwhile, was back in Spain, 1496-98, answering charges against him made by his own people. The seventh selection, "THE ADMIRAL ENCHAINED," symbolizes for Las Casas the enchainment of Spain because of its immoral behavior. For the Admiral, and for Spain, the enchainment was brought about by God to force both to a consciousness of their immorality, but the lesson was lost. The year was 1500, the end of the Third Voyage. The eighth selection, "CRITIQUE," is Las Casas' summary description of the destructive pattern established by Columbus and his replacement governor up to the beginning of the Fourth Voyage in 1502. Las Casas' condemnation of what happened is the clearest that can be found in any of his writings. The ninth selection, "FIASCO AT BELEN," shows Spanish unconsciousness of Indian rights to self-defense, but also Indian courage and ingenuity in the face of aggression. The fiasco occurs during the Fourth Voyage, 1502. The tenth selection, "MOON TRICK," symbolizes best for Las Casas the Spanish betrayal of scientific knowledge and religious belief for utterly selfish purposes. Columbus has no scruples in this episode. The eleventh selection, "LAST STRUGGLE," reveals Columbus still judging himself on his intentions, not his actions. The time is 1506, the year Columbus died. Again, for Las Casas, this symbolizes Spain's blindness, a blindness he knew affected him also at one time.

Las Casas' Life of Columbus, within the History of the Indies, *is massively documented. The documentation can be verified to the letter. And Las Casas' judgment is open for inspection within the text he provides, the remarkable narratives that reveal people right to the root of their motivation and responsibility.*

a. Shipwreck Christmas Eve

He sailed that day, Monday, and a part of the night we call Nochebuena de Navidad [Christmas Eve, 1492], though it was full of trouble for the Admiral, that night, one in which God began to spoil the pleasures, the joys He was giving him by the hour there, they must surely have been boundless, seeing himself discover blessed lands and peoples fortunate in their very nature—fortunate if we had found a way to know and deal with them rightly, or else we fortunate that God does not damn us [for what we did]—from lands and people the Admiral could readily anticipate and expect the very greatest and amplest spiritual and temporal goods.[15] Anyway, he sailed that day and part of that night with little wind, it was almost calm, until he came to within a league or league and a half of the village of king Guacaganarí who deeply desired to see him, and he had no less an eager desire to see the king.

They were off a certain point of land, near the end of the first watch, which would be 11 at night, and the Admiral had been on watch continually, and since he saw they made no headway and the sea was calm as if in a bowl, he decided to go and sleep because of sheer exhaustion, it had been two days and one night that he had gone without rest. When the sailor at the helm saw the Admiral lie down for a sleep, he gave the helm to a young cabin boy and went for one himself, an action the Admiral had always forbidden during the whole voyage—the sailors were not to give the helm to cabin boys, whether it was calm or windy weather. Every sailor did the same when they saw that the Admiral was resting and the sea was smooth. The Admiral slept because he was sure he was safe from shoals and reefs. The previous Sunday, when he had sent the ships' boats to king Guacaganarí, the crews had examined the entire shore, where the shoals were, and where one could steer from that point of land to the village of the king, something they had not done so far on the entire trip. It pleased God that at 12 midnight the sea currents carried the ship onto a bar without the boy at the tiller being aware of it happening,

---

[15] *History*, bk 1, caps. 59-60.

even though the shoals were loud enough, he could have heard them a league away.

The boy felt the tiller ground on the bar, and heard the sound of the surf, and he shouted. At the shout, the Admiral was the first up since it was he who was always the most alert, and he moved very quickly, before anyone was aware they had run aground. The ship's master was up next, it was his watch. The Admiral instantly ordered him and his whole crew to haul in the ship's boat which they towed astern, to take an anchor and drop it aft, that way they could pull the ship off using the capstan. The master and crew jumped aboard the ship's boat, but frightened by the danger, they made a noisy exit and fled for the caravel which was windward of them, which means up wind, half a league away. The Admiral, thinking they had done what he had ordered, was sure the maneuver would soon have them free. But however badly the men in the boat behaved, the men aboard the caravel behaved well, they were faithful and courageous, they would not take the others on board, they forbade them entry. And then, quickly, the caravel's men jumped into their own boat and came to rescue the Admiral and save his ship. The others followed later in disarray and shame.

Before either the one or the other arrived, the Admiral, once he saw that his own had fled, leaving him in great peril, and that the tide was dropping, and that the ship was broadside to the waves, not having any other recourse left, ordered the mast cut and the ship lightened as much as they could, lightened to see if they could free it. But since the water was dropping swiftly, the ship was higher and drier by the minute, so they could not save it, it was broadside to the sea. Though the surf was small because the sea was calm, the seams sprang with it all—seams are the spaces running rib to rib—but the ship did not break open. Had there been wind or wave, the Admiral would not have escaped, nor a man of the crew still aboard with him. But if the ship's master and the others had done what he had ordered them to do, drop the anchor off the stern, he would have freed the ship for certain, because experience shows constantly that this is the solution for such a crisis.

Immediately, the Admiral sent Diego Arana de Córdoba—bailiff for the fleet—and Pero Gutiérrez—a steward of the royal household—in the boat to inform king Guacanagarí, who had invited him to come, of the disaster, the bad luck that had happened to him. The Admiral shifted to the caravel so as to bring the flagship's crew to safety. Since the wind had now risen, and they had still to pass a large part of the night, and he did not know how far the shoal stretched, he decided to ply to windward until daylight. The village of Guacanagarí was a league and a half from where the ship was lost. After the Christians arrived and told the king of the accident, they say he showed great sorrow, he almost wept, then quickly ordered everyone to get in what canoes he had, large and small, and go help the Admiral and the Christians, which they did with remarkable energy. Canoes and a host of people came to the ship; they worked at such speed that in a very short time they had unloaded it. As the Admiral says, the help, the aid the king supplied was remarkable and timely, both in the unloading of the flagship and in the guarding of everything hauled out and set ashore, so not the head of a pin was missing, not a thing great or small was lost. He personally, he and his brothers, stood guard over what was off-loaded, ordering all his people to do as he did.

From time to time he sent someone, a relative or a councillor, to express sorrow and console the Admiral, and to say the king begged him not to yield to grief or anger, he, the king, would give him whatever he possessed. The Admiral at this point writes the following to the Sovereigns: "I assure Your Highnesses that nowhere in Castile could a guard so good be set over things so as not to lose even a needle." The king ordered all the off-loaded things to be set near the houses, while the ones he had ordered emptied were being cleared so the things could all be put inside and watched. He likewise ordered men armed with their kind of weapons—bows and arrows—to surround all the matériel and to stand watch throughout the night. He and the whole village wept, says the Admiral:

"They are such a loving people, not at all greedy, so ready
to do anything, that I assure your Highnesses I think there
is no better people in the world, nor is there a better land.
They love their neighbors as themselves, their speech is
the softest, the gentlest anywhere, they speak always with
a smile. They go around mother-naked, both men and
women. Your Highnesses should understand that they
have fine ways of dealing with one another, and the king
has a marvelous bearing, in a way very, very dignified, it
is a delight to see all of this, and the memory they have,
and the desires they have to see, to ask, what's this?
What's it for?"

Next day, 26 December, St. Stephen's, a Wednesday, the king Guacanagarí, deeply saddened almost to the point of tears, came to see the Admiral who was aboard the Niña. The king's look was calming, his way of consoling gentle, insofar as he could make himself understood with words and gestures. He told the Admiral not to feel bad, he would give him all he possessed, and that he had already given the Christians who were ashore with the offloaded cargo, two large houses in which to store and guard it, and he would provide more space if need be, and sufficient canoes for loading and unloading the ship, and as many men as he wanted. And the day before, he had ordered a strict safety watch over everything, so no one would dare touch a biscuit crumb, let alone anything else. That is how loyal they are, the Admiral says, they are not covetous of another's goods. The king was the most virtuous of them all. This is the way the Admiral puts it.

While the king was talking to the Admiral, a different canoe from a different place arrived, it carried some pieces of gold intended as swap for a small hawkbell, they wanted nothing else so much. The reason being that the Indians of this island, and every island in the Indies, have a penchant for dancing a great deal, it is their custom. To accompany them in the words and songs they sing, the music they make while dancing, they have certain very thin rattles, made of wood most ingeniously, having small pebbles inside, they play these, but seldom and with a harsh sound. They see our hawkbells as large and shiny and melodious, so they want them more than anything, and to have them are willing to give whatever anyone wants or whatever they have. They came in close to the caravel, held up the pieces of gold and shouted, "Chuque, chuque, hawkbells," which means, "Take these, give us hawkbells."

Even though the incident I am going to tell did not happen at that time— it happened later, when the Admiral came to colonize the island on his second voyage—I want to tell it here because it fits. An Indian came to barter with the Christians for a hawkbell. He had worked some mines and gotten from friends upwards of half a mark of gold—worth twenty-five gold castellanos or pesos—which he carried wrapped in a few leaves or in a cotton cloth, and when he came to the Christians, he said they should give him a hawkbell and he would give them the gold he brought for it. When offered a hawkbell by one of the Christians, the Indian, holding his gold in his left hand, not wanting to give first, said: "Give me the bell," putting out his right; it was given him, and once he had it, he gave over his half mark of gold, spun around, and raced off like a horse, often looking back over his shoulder, afraid someone was after him because he had fooled the man who gave him the hawkbell for a half mark of gold. Spaniards back then wanted to be fooled like that every day, and I even think Spaniards of today would not be loath.

To resume, when the canoes from other villages had to return home, they asked the Admiral to order a hawkbell saved for them until the next day—they were afraid, it seems, that there would be none left after the rush—when they would bring four hunks of gold as big as a hand. The Admiral was happy to hear them, and the chagrin he felt about his adversity he tempered with the hope he could recoup himself due to the news he would get so much gold. Later a seaman came, one who had carried the clothing ashore, and he told the Admiral it was magnificent to see the pieces of gold the Christians got, who were ashore with the clothing, for practically nothing, how for a leather strap, for a segment of strap, the Indians gave them nuggets worth more than two castellanos, and what the men ashore had was nothing compared to what they hoped to get in a month's time more. Anything made of brass the Indians prized most of all. To get it, a segment of leather strap, they gave whatever they held in their hands. They called brass "turey," a thing from heaven, because they called heaven "turey." They smelled it as if in the smelling they could tell it came from there. So they found in brass the kind of odor they considered very precious. They find the same in a kind of low-grade gold which has a somewhat purplish color, they call it "guanin." It is by the smell they know it is special and more to be valued.

Since king Guacanagarí saw that the Admiral brightened from his sadness at the sight of the gold and at the news of it they brought him, he was pleased and told the Admiral through words and signs that he knew where a lot of gold was, nearby, that the Admiral should cheer up, he would have as much gold brought as the Admiral could want. He got it across, they say, that there was a great amount especially in Cibao, which shows that the Indians have no use for it and it is to be found right in their land. Whenever the Admiral heard about Cibao, his heart grew happier, he thought it was Japan, the island marked on his map . . . He did not understand that "nearby" meant an area of this island, but thought it was an island apart.

The king ate aboard the caravel with the Admiral, and afterwards he asked the Admiral to come ashore with him, to see his house, his people, his land. They went, and the king had him received with great honor, took him to his house, and ordered him given a meal of two or three kinds of fruit, of fish, game, and other foods they had, and of their bread which they call cassava. He took him to see some fields and lovely groves next to the houses, and a good thousand Indians went along with him, all naked. The king wore the shirt and gloves the Admiral had given him, and it was for the gloves he was happiest, he celebrated them most. He showed his nobility, the Admiral says, in the way he ate, in his integrity, dignity, neatness.

After they ate, and they ate for a long time, the Indians brought the Admiral herbs with which to rub his hands thoroughly—the Admiral thought it was to soften them—and then gave him water for washing. Once the meal was over, he took the Admiral to the beach, and the Admiral sent for a turkish bow and a handful of arrows he had brought from Castile, then had a man of his group who could do it well shoot some. The king, since he did not know weapons—he and his people have none, use none—thought this marvelous. So the Admiral tells it. Talk then turned to the cannibals who infested the region, at which time the Admiral let the king know through signs that the Kings of Castile were mighty powerful and they had ordered their men to destroy the cannibals and bring them back captive. The Admiral commanded a cannon fired, and a musket, or "espingarda" as it was then called, and the King was astonished at the effect of their fire, and at what they pierced, while the people, hearing the boom of the shots, dropped to the ground in fright.

The natives brought a great mask for the Admiral, it had large hunks of gold on the ears, in the eyes, on the rest of it. The king gave it to him along with other gold jewelry, and the king himself placed the gifts on the Admiral's head and chest, and he gave the Christians who were with him many things made of gold. The delight the Admiral took in these things he saw was beyond words, happiness, consolation, joy, he thanked God intensely for all that had happened and the anxiety he felt at the loss of the ship was draining away. He saw that Our Lord had done him a favor in having the ship run aground in that place, and that he should set up a station here. So many things fell into his hands, he says, that they led him to the decision, because it was surely not a disaster, the shipwreck, it was great good luck—

"It is certain," he says, "that if I had not run aground, I would have kept going and not stopped at this place, because it is set at the back of a large bay in which there are two or three barrier shoals. Nor would I, on this voyage, have left people here, and even if I had wanted to leave them, I could not have given them a better location, nor as many supplies or necessaries or materials for a fort.

"It is indeed true that a lot of people who came out here with me asked me if I would be willing to give them permission to remain behind. I have now ordered a tower and fortress built, built solidly, and a big trench, not that I think either is necessary for these men—I take it for granted that with the ones I brought I could conquer this whole island and I think it to be larger than Portugal and to have more people, twice as many, but the Indians are naked and unarmed and cowards beyond redemption. It is prudent to build the fortification and have it be as it should be, since we are at such a distance from Your Majesties, so that the natives here know how smart your people are, and what they can construct, and thus obey them out of both fear and love."

It seems that the will of God effected all this, allowing the ship's master and crew to pull off the treachery of leaving the Admiral in peril and not taking the anchor abaft as he had ordered, for if they had done what he had ordered, he would have freed and saved the vessel, and consequently not gotten to know the land, he says, as he did during the few days he was there, because he had no intention of stopping anywhere, he wanted to press on with the exploration. And the wrecked ship, they say, was not right for exploring, it was too sluggish, that was the fault of the people of Palos, they did not keep their promise to the King, which was to provide ships fit for exploring and they had not done so. The Admiral concludes that he lost nothing of what was on board, not a strap, not a plank, not a nail, but all was as intact as when he set out. He further says that he hopes in God that on the return voyage he intends to make from Castile, he will find a ton of gold waiting, acquired by those he purposes to leave behind, and that they will have found the source of gold and spices, and in such quantity that three years hence the Kings can order an expedition mounted to go and recover the Holy House. "For I solemnly promised Your Majesties," he says, "that all profit from my undertaking would be spent on the conquest of Jerusalem, and Your Majesties laughed and said that would please them, but they wanted the conquest anyway." He says also he saw some copper, but not much.

b. Home Bound

Wednesday, 16 January [1493], he left the gulf he named Golfo de las Flechas, the wind was off the land, and later, with a west wind, he set his prow eastward, a quarter northeast, with the intention of looking at some islands, not just the one he saw, which he says is the one now called Sant Juan, but others also which the Indians had told him of, especially Matinino.[16] Since he thought the islands lay along the route to Castile, judging from the many the Indians informed him of by name, and judging from what he saw of their locations and the directions of their mountains, and judging by the sea grass similar to what he encountered outbound, there was a lot of it in this Golfo de las Flechas and he thought it grew only in shallow water, he concluded that there were many islands and lands due eastward, straight ahead of where he first hit the sea grass, and he therefore argued that the land of these Indies was less than 400 leagues from the Canaries.

He was not wrong by much, that's sure, instead his guess was remarkably close, because there is a string of islands that runs from Sant

---

[16] *History*, bk. 1, caps. 68-9.

Juan, which is 25 to 30 leagues from Hispaniola, all the way to Trinidad which is almost attached to the mainland at Paria, a 300 league stretch, thus someone traveling by ship along it could shelter each night at a different island; so, there are 400 leagues, very few more or very few less, from where he was to the Canaries. After he had sailed what he reckoned were 64 miles—16 leagues—the Indians made signs to him that the island—either Sant Juan or Matinino or Carib—lay to the southeast. It is said that the Indians all fear that island greatly because its people eat people. It is two quarters off the wind, right of the course he was maintaining, so he decided to change course in that direction and ordered sails trimmed. After he sailed two leagues, the wind intensified, a good one for heading home to Castile, and he notes that the Spaniards became glum, they must have begun muttering about his course change from the direct route to Spain because there was danger since both caravels were taking a lot of water, and there was no remedy for that but the grace of God. The situation affected him, he decided to shift course from the islands and go directly to Spain, northeast, a quarter east, one wind direction to the left of east. He followed that course until sundown—48 miles, 12 leagues—making good time, so he lost sight of the cape or promontory which forms the Bahía or Golfo de las Flechas, which cape he named Cabo Sant Iheramo, it's the one we call today Cabo del Engaño, the furthermost point of Higuey province. . .

Sunday, 10 February . . . Aboard the Admiral's caravel a course charting session—checking the points marked on the chart, the course directions, counting the leagues covered—with Vicente Yañez and Sancho Ruiz and Peralonso Niño, pilots, and Roldán who lived a lot of years later in the city of Santo Domingo on Hispaniola. . . All the pilots who had made plottings placed themselves much beyond the Azores, further east according to their charts—they had reckoned more leagues than the caravels had actually made—so if they sailed north to gain the Azores, no one would touch the island of Sancta Maria, the easternmost of the islands, they would be five leagues off and would fetch up near the island of Madera or Puerto Sancto. But the Admiral reckoned they were much short of them, and off their original course, since he knew better how to count the leagues they had covered because of his greater judgment, his memory, his experience of navigation, so the others were 150 leagues ahead of themselves. He says that once they see land, by the grace of God, they will know whose plot was more correct. He says further that on the outward voyage of discovery, he sailed 263 leagues beyond the island of Hierro before he spotted the first seagrass. That night he sailed 39 leagues, and during the whole of Monday, 11 February, 16 and 1/2 leagues, a total of 55 and 1/2 leagues for day and night. He saw a lot of birds, so he reckoned he was close to land. He made

18 leagues that night, and on Tuesday, 12 February, the sea began to roughen, to kick up a storm, the kind in which he would fear sinking if the caravel he sailed on was not a good and manageable ship.

At this point in the voyage, God Our Lord, in his mysterious decisions, began to cut with the water of great fear, anxiety, sorrow, harsh adversity, and hour by hour, the wine of the Admiral's great joy and happiness, a wine he had elated the Admiral with often in ways without measure, again, again, in the discovery, especially the discovery of Hispaniola. This will become clear in the present and following sections.

Tuesday, during the day, he ran 12 leagues in desperate struggle and danger; that whole night, on into Wednesday morning, heavy storm winds turned up, heavy seas, lightning showed to the north northeast, three times; a sign of a mighty storm, he writes, coming down from that quarter, or up from its opposite. He rode with bare masts most of the night, then put on some sail, little, and made 13 leagues. The wind lessened a while, but shortly after stiffened again and the sea became wild and fearful, the waves crisscrossed and tore at the ships—that is, a wave from one side hit a wave from the other catching the ships between, a mortal danger for them. He made 13 and 1/2 leagues. Wednesday, during the night, the wind heightened, the waves were terrifying, one crashing against the other as just described, they broke aboard, the ship could not escape from between them. He carried some sail, but very short—the mainsail, stripped of its added canvas—to keep way and get out free of the waves. He ran for three hours this way, leaving 20 miles astern, 5 leagues. Wind and wave intensified even more, and recognizing that he was in terrible danger, be began to run before the wind, whatever the direction it took him, he had no other choice. The caravel Pinta of Martín Alonso ran headlong also, and disappeared, the Admiral fearing it had foundered, because all that night long he ran with a signal aloft, a lamp with a light, and the Pinta answered with a light of its own, until it must not have been able any longer due to the ferocity of the storm. The Admiral sailed 13 leagues that night, direction northeast, a quarter east.

Thursday, 14 February, daybreak, the wind fiercer, the waves every which way, each hour they feared sinking, and they were quite desolate at the disappearance of the Pinta because when several ships run together there is somewhat more chance of rescue, if one is lost or springs a leak, the other can often save its crew. And so he sailed 7 leagues or more. The danger was so great, he ordered that someone be chosen to make a pilgrimage to Nuestra Señora de Guadalupe, and carry a candle made of five pounds of wax, and every man should swear that if the lot fell to him, he would make that pilgrimage—this is the kind of panic-vow mariners make whenever they think they are imperiled by a storm, and often, due to the vow, Our Lord frees them from death, but they do it more to humble themselves and, fearing death, to repent their sins and promise to amend their lives. So then the Admiral ordered brought as many peas as there were crew aboard, ordered one marked with a knife in a cross, and all placed in a hat and shaken well. The Admiral was the first to put in his hand, and he drew the pea marked with the cross, so the task fell to him, and from that moment he accepted it as his duty to make the pilgrimage.

He decided to cast lots again, to send someone on pilgrimage to Sancta María de Loreto, which is in the Marches of Ancona, the Holy House of Our Lady Saint Mary, where many great miracles occur, from what is told. This time the lot fell to a sailor from Puerto de Sancta María, 3 leagues from San Lucar de Barrameda, a sailor named Pedro de Villa. The Admiral promised he would give him the money to pay the costs. And since the storm tormented and threatened them even more, he ordered lots cast for another pilgrimage, a one night vigil at Sancta Clara de Moguer, and a mass to be said, because that also is a place sailors have devotion to, especially ones from Condado. The peas were thrown in the hat, one marked with a cross, and the Admiral drew it, so he was obligated now twice to go make the designated pilgrimages.

And next, since fear and worry about the sea was draining them, the Admiral and the whole crew made a vow that if they ever reached land, the first one they did, they would go ashore on it, in shirtsleeves and in procession, to pray and give thanks at a church dedicated to the name of Our Lady, the Virgin Mary. The storm kept growing fiercer and no one expected to live, so beyond the vows in common, each one made private vows, according to the devotion God gave them. The danger and fear were made the more because the ship was sailing without ballast—the heavy stones placed as weights in the hold so the ship does not capsize—and it went along light as a gourd and that is a most dangerous thing for those aboard. The lightness of the ship was partly caused by the lessening of cargo, the food was consumed, the drink, the water, the wine, and [partly by] the Admiral who was overly eager to take advantage of the prosperous wind that blew between the islands, so he did not order ballast aboard, stone weights for the caravels, since he intended to do so when they reached the neighborhood of the Islands of Women where he wanted to go. Mention has been made of this. He writes some pitiable things at this crisis point: he notes some reasons why he is afraid that Our Lord wants him to perish right there, then other reasons why he hopes God will bring him to safety, so that the news, the remarkable news he carries to the Kings, should not perish in this storm.

It seemed to him that the great desire he had to report back his unique story, and show he was right in what he had said he would discover, caused him to fear greatly that he would not succeed in doing so, and he feared every little thing, he says, that could stand in the way and block him, attributing this fear to his lack of faith, his lack of trust in divine providence. On the other hand, the graces God gave him in achieving such a triumph in the discovery he had made, thus fulfilling all his desires, comfort him, for in Castile he had faced enormous difficulties over his project, huge ones. And just as then he had placed before God his goal, his purpose and project, and God had heard his prayer, and in the end granted all he had asked for, [so now] he ought to trust that God would bring to completion the goods and graces He had given him initially—especially for having saved him on the outward voyage, when he had greater reason to fear, in the struggles he had with the sailors and with the civilians on board. They were all, with one voice, determined to turn back, to mutiny against him, they were in constant protest against him, but God eternal gave him strength and power against them all, and there were other marvelous things God had made manifest to him, for him, concerning that voyage, beyond what Their Highnesses knew from members of their household.

These are all the Admiral words, though some in his simple, unpretentious style, which testify to his goodness. So he blames himself for fearing the storm, though he has many, many reasons for confidence, "but exhaustion and worry," he says, "do not let me calm my soul." He goes on to say that he is greatly worried about the two sons he has at school in Córdoba, they will be orphaned of father and mother and in a foreign land, and the Kings would never know the deeds he had done for them due to this voyage, and the bountiful news he was bringing, so they would be moved to help the children.

For this, and in order that Their Majesties would know how Our Lord had let him succeed in all that he had desired to discover about the Indies, and would know that the Indies were storm free—he says one can know that from the grass and trees which take root and grow even in the water—and would know about the [return] voyage in case he was lost in the storm, he used the following strategem: he took parchment and wrote down on it all he could about the discovery he had made, asking urgently the one who found the parchment to bring it to the Kings of Castile. He wrapped it in an oilskin cloth, tightly tied, and ordered a large wooden cask brought and put the parchment inside—no one knew what was on it, but all thought it was one more devotion—and he ordered the cask pitched into the sea. Then, in a swirl of rain squalls, the wind shifted west, and he ran before it with only a jib, for five hours in savage seas, making 13 leagues that Thursday night.

It is something worth noting, the difference in the voyage, outbound to the Indies the weather was so fair that everyone thought there could never be a storm in such a sea, and some were afraid there would be no winds for sailing back to Castile. The Admiral did not speak of or experience such a nice voyage on his fourth trip when he discovered Veragua, as I will narrate if God gives me life, because among the fiercest storms that can conceivably occur on any ocean in the world, are those that occur in those islands and along the mainland, as those who sail it know and feel every day. Marvelous are the things of God, in sum, and the order and providence God has for his works. Because if those volatile mariners Columbus had with him had run into and experienced on the way out the storms that usually arise, they would have had much less patience extending the voyage, so new, so long, as he made them do. Instead, at the first storm to hit them, there is no doubt they would have turned back, and the Admiral would have been in greater danger of his life if he ever dared to stop them. But God arranged things to happen as He planned and brought the Spaniards to discover and explore those lands as if they were sailing down a river.

c. Uncovering Disaster

Friday, November 22 [1493], the Admiral caught sight of the eastern end of Hispaniola, off to the north, and the western end of Sant Juan, fifteen leagues distant from it.[17] At Hispaniola, he sent ashore one of the Indians he had brought back from Castile, giving him the task of bringing all the people of his own region—it was the province of Samaná, near where they halted—to cherish the Christians, and tell them of the greatness of the Kings of Castile, the remarkable things found in their realm. The Indian had offered to do it quite willingly. No one ever heard of that Indian again, it was thought he must have died.

The Admiral headed on, and he reached a Cape—which he had named Cape Angel when he discovered it on his first voyage—where some Indians came out to the ships in canoes, they had food and things, in order to barter with the Christians, and after the fleet anchored at Monte-Christi, a boat went shorewards, towards a river there, it saw two dead men, one young, one old, judging by appearances, and the old man had a Castilian grass rope around his throat, his arms, his hands were tied to a beam as if to a cross. The shore-party could not tell if the dead were Indian or Christian, and right then the Admiral began to suspect that the thirty-nine Christians were dead, or some of them.

Next day, Tuesday, 26 November, the Admiral again sent men ashore in various directions to get some information about the ones [left behind] in the fort. A lot of Indians came to talk to the Christians, they

---

[17] *History*, bk. 1, caps. 85-7.

approached them very calmly, with no fear, and touched them on their jackets and shirts saying "jacket," "shirt," showing that they knew the names of those things. Because of this lack of fear in the Indians, of this use of Spanish words, the Admiral felt somewhat reassured that the men of the fort would not be dead.

At the entrance to the port of Navidad, he anchored his fleet. It was Wednesday, 27 November. Near midnight, a full canoe of Indians came out to the flagship and called out for him, "Admiral! Admiral!" The crew answered they were to climb aboard, he was there, but they refused until the Admiral appeared at the rail, but once they recognized him—he was quite recognizable from the dignity of his person—two of them did climb on board, and presented him with lovely masks they call guaycas, beautifully made, partially gold . . . , presenting them for King Guacaganarí with his deepest respects, expressed to the best of their abilities. When the Admiral asked them about the Christians—that is what weighed on him—they answered that some were dead due to sickness, others had vanished inland along with their women, many many women. They have to be all dead, the Admiral thought, but kept his thoughts to himself for the moment, and sent them back, giving them a present of brass bowls which the Indians prized so highly, and other things sure to please the Lord Guacaganarí, and he gave the messengers presents also, and they went away happy, that very night.

He entered the port of Navidad, on Thursday, 28 November, in the afternoon, with the whole fleet, and right near the place he had built the fort. He saw that it was burned to the ground, and that produced a heavy sadness in him because he saw sure evidence of the death of all thirty nine Christians he had left behind in it, and for that whole day, no one showed. Next day, in the morning, the Admiral went ashore, sad, troubled, to see the fort burned and not a soul of those he had left behind to everyone's joy and happiness. There was some debris behind from the Christians, broken bows, plates, things they call throws, farmers put them on the table. Since the Admiral saw no one he could ask, he went up a river close by with a few boats, and he left the others orders to clean out the well dug for the fort to see if the Christians had hidden any gold in it, but none was found. The Admiral still found no one to ask, because the Indians had all fled their houses. In the houses, however, he noticed some clothing Christians wore, so he turned back. Near the fort they discovered buried seven or eight people, and a little further out in the fields, another three, and they recognized they were Christians because clothed, they seemed to have died about a month earlier, maybe a little more. As he was searching the area for writings or other things that might give him a clue to what happened, a brother of King Guacanagarí arrived with some Indians who could speak and understand Spanish a bit, and they named by name each of the Christians who had stayed behind in the fort. And they told the story of the whole disaster also through the language of those Indians the Admiral had brought back from Castile—of one especially, who had been given the name "Diego Colón," I knew him well later.

The Indians said that no sooner had the Admiral left the Christians than they started to fight each other, to get in quarrels, to knife each other, to seize women, each man the one he wanted, and the gold he could get, and to split into factions. Then Pero Gutiérrez and Escobedo killed one Jacomé, and the two killers, along with nine others, took off, with their equipment and the women they had seized, for the territory of a chief called Canabo who ruled over the mines. (The spelling is wrong, the name should be Caonabo, the Lord, the powerful King of Maguana, about whom I will have a lot to say later.) Caonabo killed all ten or eleven. The Indians said more, that after many days, chief Caonabo came with a large group to the fort, but in it were only Diego de Arana, its commander, and five others who chose to remain with him to defend the place, because the rest had scattered throughout the island. Caonabo set fire to the fort at night, and to the houses where the Christians lived, because, as it happened, they were not in the fort. They ran for the sea and were drowned. Chief Guacanagarí came out to fight chief Caonabo in defense of the Christians. He was badly wounded, and had not yet recovered.

This account agreed totally with the accounts brought back by the men the Admiral had sent out around to learn what happened to the thirty-nine Christians. They had reached the main village of Guacanagarí, they had seen he was in bad shape from being wounded, as just described, and for that reason he was sorry he was not able to come and greet the Admiral and relate to him what had happened after he sailed for Castile, and how the men had died. They died because, as soon as the Admiral left, they started to quarrel and fight with one another, they seized women from their husbands, children from their parents, and they went on a hunt for gold, every man for himself. Some Biscayans formed a group against the others, and thus [in groups] they roamed the landscape, where the Indians killed them for their blameworthy and wicked deeds. But this is sure: if they had stayed together as a group within Guacanagarí's territory and under his protection, and if they had not enraged the natives of the place by seizing their wives and daughters—that is what most injures and enrages the Indians, and anyone anywhere—they would never have perished.

d. Gold Town Nightmare

Saturday, 29 March [1494], the Admiral reached Isabela where he found everyone exhausted, very few escaped sickness or death, and those few who stayed healthy were weak from lack of nourishment and constantly afraid of falling sick like the others.[18] And for those who didn't fall, just the sorrow, the fellow suffering they felt at seeing almost everyone else in such dire straits, such pain, was itself a sad thing, sorrowful and hopeless. Increasingly, people sickened and died as the food supply dropped, and the rationing of it got stricter, stricter by the day, because when they had unloaded the ships they found much food damaged or rotten. The Admiral laid the blame for this mainly on the skippers of each vessel, on their carelessness, their negligence. And the food that was good, it stayed good without spoiling less long than in Castile, due to the heat and humidity of the new land. Since biscuit was running out, and there was no flour, only grain, the Admiral decided to build a dam across the large river at Isabela, for a water run and some mills, but no place good enough for them was found within a league's distance. And because the laborers and skilled workmen were among the sickest, the weakest, the hungriest, and could do little because they lacked the strength, the gentlemen had to pitch in also, and the people from the Palace, people of dignity who were hungry and miserable too. And both types considered it a death sentence to have to work with their hands, especially in their starved state. So the Admiral had to add clout to his order, and by the threat of punishment, had to force both types so that suitable public works could be constructed.

The result of this could only be that he was hated by everyone, great and small, and this decision was at the root of his being slandered before the Kings and throughout Spain as a cruel man who hated Spaniards, one incapable of governing at all, and his reputation went downhill from then on, he had not one day of peace the rest of his life, and ultimately from this seed grew his downfall. This had to be the reason why the priest was furious with the Admiral, Fray Buil, of the Order of St. Benedict, who was supposedly there as a legate, or, since he was an exempt prelate, he reprehended the Admiral for the punishments he imposed on the men, or maybe for the tight-fisted way he rationed out food—tighter than need be, in Padre Buil's judgment—or maybe because the Admiral did not give him and his attendants the larger rations they had demanded.

Thus he was hateful to all or most for the reasons given, hateful especially to the purser, Bernal de Pisa, and must have been also to other officials and gentry, who presumed to authority they did not have—they were

---

[18] *History*, lib. 1, cap. 92.

all angered mainly by the rationing of food, I think, as is evident from the disclaimers in the letters the Admiral brought of his own accord to the Kings—i.e., many people from Castile had begged him to take them along on the trip, and they took more servants than they could sustain; he did not hand out rations to those servants as amply as they would wish; he had to cross them on this matter, since he was responsible for everyone.

Another element entered to make his position more awkward, i.e., he was a foreigner and had no influence in Castile. So for this, among the Spaniards, especially the people of quality who are haughty by nature, he was of little worth since they had no esteem for him, and this, plus the discontent of Padre Fray Buil, had to have a very damaging effect, and from then on his influence would shrink. And frankly, judging on what I myself know of the affair, and on what others from that period have told me, and people I asked a bit about it, and on what reason forces me to conclude, I do not know what harm, in such a short time the Admiral could have done to the Spaniards he brought out with him, to have him incur, with any reason, such bad repute and blame, unless divine judgment was secretely at work—because not three months had gone by, and the hardships, the fix they were in, were no one's fault, they came from the climate, the newness of the venture and of the land.

But back to the plight of the Christians there, it got worse day by day, hour by hour, since all support and nourishment were running low, and not just the food the sick and those gravely afflicted needed—for purges, they were down to a chicken's egg and a pot of boiled chickpeas for every five sick men—but low also on the necessaries to keep the still healthy alive, and the same with cures and medicines, even though the Admiral had brought some along, but not in the quantity or kind needed for so many people, nor suited to the different illnesses. But on top of this, there was no one to nurse the sick, so they had to cook their own food, when they had some, though because they had none, cooking was the least of their concerns, and finally, whatever needed doing, they had to do for themselves.

And what made the desperate situation of those people back then even more pitiful and pitiable was that they saw themselves dying far, far from any help or solace—dying of hunger, mainly, with no one to bring them a cup of water, dying loaded with bitter complaints—this caused them greater suffering than the hunger and lack of nourishment for the sick, and distance was the worst suffering for anyone else who got sick and died later, anywhere out in the Indies—I will speak of this further on, God willing. So, because they were beset by every kind of affliction, and because many were nobility or high-class servants who had never been in such straits, maybe they had never passed a bad day in their whole lives, so for them, the smallest pain they suffered was intolerable to them, they died, many of them, utterly resistant and, it is to be feared, totally desperate.

For this reason, many times on the island of Hispaniola, many people held it as gospel that no one dared, without fear and danger, pass through Isabela after it was abandoned, because those who chose to, those who had to, i.e., people hunting wild pigs—there were a lot of pigs there later—and people who lived in the area, let it be known they saw things, heard things, day and night, voices, many, terror-stricken, horrible, and those who heard them, never dared go back again. The story was also public—at least it was told and affirmed as true by ordinary people—that one time, as one or two men were passing through the site at Isabela, two ranks of men appeared in the street, like two male choirs, and all seemed to be nobility, palace nobility, well dressed, swords strapped on, wearing travel hats, the kind fashionable in Spain back then, and they were amazed, the man or men who saw this sight, at how such new and well-dressed people were able to come here and the island know nothing about it, so they greeted them and asked when and where they came from, and the ranks answered with silence. They just raised their hats with their hands in salutation back and their heads lifted from their bodies with their hats and they stood there headless, then they vanished, and those who saw this frightening apparition were like dead men, and for days they were dark and numb.

e. Prophetic Encounter

On 7 July [1494], the Admiral went ashore [on Cuba] to hear Mass, and while he was attending it, an old man, a cacique, arrived, he seemed to be ruler of the entire region or province.[19] As he watched all the rites and ceremonies performed by the priest, and the signs of adoration and reverence and humility made by the Christians, and as he saw the sign of peace given to the Admiral, the respect shown him by those under him, saw the commanding nature of his person, the cacique knew that the Admiral must be the one whom everyone else obeyed, so the cacique offered him a pot of the kind the islanders call hiburas—they used them as bowls—filled with a certain fruit of the earth, and he squatted on his haunches next to the Admiral, for that is the way Indians sit when they have no *duhos*, i.e., low chairs, and he began the following discourse:

> "You have come in great might to lands you never saw be-
> fore, and by your arrival, you have caused a great fear
> throughout the villages and their peoples. I will have you
> know what we here feel, that there are two places in the

---

[19] *History*, bk. 1, cap. 96.

next life where souls which have left their bodies go. One place is evil and full of darkness, it is watched over by those who trouble, who afflict humankind; the other is happy and good. They are to abide there who, while they live here, love the peace and quiet of peoples. Therefore, if you know that you are mortal, and that everyone, once above, will be rewarded according to what they did below, you will do no evil or harm to anyone who does you no evil or harm. And the rite you have just performed is very good because it seems to me to be a way of thanking God."

The story is that he said more, how he had been on the island of Hispaniola and of Jamaica, and he had gone down along Cuba westward, and the ruler there went around dressed as a priest. This all is what the Admiral understood, interpreted as could be by the Indians the Admiral had brought from Hispaniola, especially "Diego Colón," whom he had taken to Castile then back again. The Admiral, amazed at the wise presentation by the old Indian—it was loftier, for sure, than what a pagan philosopher could give, someone without faith, though deeply schooled in philosophy—replied to the cacique that he had known well, and for a long time, what the cacique had said to him, that souls live forever after this life, and the evil ones go to the evil place, called Hell, the good ones go to the good place, called Heaven by the Christians. And it delighted him greatly to know that the cacique and the people of that region had such a good knowledge of the other world, something he never knew until then that they did. And he gave the cacique to understand that he was sent by kings, his kings, who were great, rich, powerful, lords of the realm of Castile, to discover and explore these lands, for no other purpose but to find out if there were people who inflicted evil on other people, since he had heard it said that there were such out in these oceans who were called cannibals or caribes and did inflict evil on others, and he was to stop them, keep them from doing this. He was to respect and defend good people, and try to bring it about that everyone should live at peace, to the detriment of no one. The wise elder heard the Admiral out with tears in his eyes and deep happiness, saying that if he did not have a wife and children, he would go with the Admiral to Castile. And after he received from the Admiral some trinkets, he knelt, making gestures of great respect, asking over and over if the place where such people were born was in heaven or on earth.[20]

---

[20] This incident points up the tragedy of the Christians missing the meaning of their own doctrine whereas the native peoples grasped it. Las Casas uses many such incidents in his writings to point out there could really have been a marriage not a murder.

I have taken this incident in substance from what Don Hernando Colón wrote—the first Admiral's son—and from the Décadas of Pedro Mártir, who describes it much more fully than Don Hernando, because the latter was just a boy at the time, and Pedro Mártir could have gotten the story from the Admiral himself since he wrote a lot of detail—Pedro Mártir, at the time, was resident in Court and a great favorite of the kings.[21]

It is not strange that the old man should tell the Admiral such things about the afterlife, because the Indians in the Indies nearly all think that souls do not die, Indians on Cuba especially, and please God, in the proper place, I will have things to say about views they hold.

f. Palm Sunday Upside Down

Bartholomew Columbus left the Hocama river [1497], what we now call the Santo Domingo, his men with him, and after a thirty league march, he reached a powerful river, the Neyba, as the Indians named it, as we do also today, where he ran into an army of Indians, a host of them with bows and arrows and the look of war about them, though they were stark naked—and note what kind of war they were capable of with bare bellies for bucklers![22] It seems that because King Behechio got news that the Christians were coming, and he had heard of the kinds of things they had done to King Caonabo and his country, he sent his army—or he himself came—with plaything weapons to stop them. . . When the Christians saw the army, Don Bartholomew signaled that he came to do them no harm, but to visit them, spend time among them, and he wanted to see King Behechio and his country. The Indians relaxed, as if they had gotten great pledges from the Christians, and it would be impossible for them to fail in their word. So messengers went flying off to King Behechio, or, if he was already there, he sent orders that his whole court and all his people, plus his sister Anacaona, a remarkable and gracious woman, should go out and welcome the Christians, and that they should put on all the festivities usually done for their own rulers, the full panoply of their traditional celebrations. The Indians and the Christians went a further thirty leagues to reach the city of Xaragua because it is some sixty leagues from Santo Domingo. A whole host of people, including many chiefs and nobles, came out to meet them, a gathering of the entire region with King Behechio and Queen Anacaona, his sister, singing their songs, dancing their dances, which they call "areitos," a happy, happy

---

[21] See Hernando Colón, *Vida del Almirante*, trans. and ed. by Ramon Iglesia (Mexico: Fondo de Cultura Económica, 1947), cap. 58 [hereafter, *Vida*]; and Pedro Mártir de Anglería, *Decades de orbe novo* (Alcalá, 1530).

[22] *History*, bk. 1, cap. 114.

thing to see, especially when performed jointly by large numbers. Thirty women led the procession, the wives of King Behechio, they were stark naked except their lower bodies were covered with short cotton skirts, white skirts beautifully woven which they called naguas, and which covered them from waist to thigh. They carried green branches in their hands, and they sang and danced and leaped with grace in a womanly way, expressing great, great delight, excitement, and festival joy. The women danced up to Bartholomew Columbus, sank to the ground on their knees, and with great respect, presented him with the palm branches they carried. The rest of the people, a huge, huge number, all danced in jubilation, and in that festive, celebratory fashion—almost beyond description—they led Bartholomew Columbus to the royal house, the palace of King Behechio, where a huge feast was ready and waiting, of native foods, i.e., cassava bread, rodents—rabbit-like creatures of the island—roasted or stewed, and all sorts of fresh and salt water fish that run in that area. After the feast, the Spaniards went, in threes and fours, to quarters the Indians assigned to them, the beds there already prepared, hammocks woven of cotton, beautiful things, and rich for what they were. Don Bartholomew and some half dozen Christians stayed in the house of King Behechio. Next day, the Indians gathered in the town plaza to offer further and varied festivities, so they brought Don Bartholomew and the Christians to watch. During the events, two troops of men, armed with bows and arrows, naked otherwise, suddenly appeared and started to skirmish in a war game, one against the other. At first, it was like wooden-sword fights in Spain, but little by little the men got heated up, then it was as if they were battling their worst enemies, so much so that they wounded each other and severely, four were soon dead and many quite hurt. And this was done with all the exhilaration and zest and enthusiasm in the world, making no more of the wounded or a dead than if someone had flicked them in the face. The bash would have kept up and many more died if King Behechio, at the request of Don Bartholomew and the Christians, had not ordered a halt to it. . . Anacaona was a very remarkable woman, very prudent, very gracious and cultured in her speech, in crafts, in relationships, and very friendly towards the Christians. She was, as well, Queen of Maguana, because she was the wife of King Caonabo. . .

When the festivities were over, Don Bartholomew told King Behechio and her ladyship, Anacaona, that his own brother, the Admiral, had been sent by the Kings of Castile—they were mighty lords and rulers, they had a huge realm and many people under their sovereignty—and the Admiral had gone back to Castile to see them and inform them that already many lords, many people on this island were paying tribute, and how much they were paying. And that was the reason why he, Don Bartholomew, had come to King Behechio and his country, to have the King pay tribute also, and accept the Kings of Castile as overlords, a sign of which would be payment to them in suitable things. . . The King answered: "How can I pay tribute, because neither in the whole of my kingdom, nor in any part or place thereof, is gold formed or gathered, and my people do not know what it is!" He thought, with good reason, that the Christians sought gold, they came there for no other purpose than to bring gold back to their Kings and Lords. Don Bartholomew replied in turn: "It is not our desire, not our intent to impose on anyone a tribute to be paid in goods they do not have on their own ground, [but] goods they can well afford to pay. With what we know you do have in abundance in your region and realm, cotton in plenty, cassava bread, we wish you pay the tribute, and with what you have the most of here, not with what you do not have." The King, when he heard this, was greatly relieved and said that whenever Don Bartholomew wanted, he would fill him to satiety with the local goods. He immediately sent messengers with orders to all chiefs and people, his subjects, that they should plant plenty of cotton in their gardens and fields so there would be a large surplus of it, because the King had to pay it as tribute to the Kings of Castile, whose servant and envoy the Admiral was, as was his brother who had just arrived and was staying with the King. . .

The other thing we ought to stop and notice at this point is how perversely, how outrageously Don Bartholomew made his entry into the realm of Xaragua, first announcing to untutored pagans the grandeur and dignity of the Kings of Castile, rather than, first, the true God, then weighting them down first with tribute payment, rather than giving them something that would profit and promote them—there was no other legitimate reason for the Christians to enter those realms, those countries, except one, to offer those peoples the knowledge of the one, true God, and of Jesus Christ, His Son, the Redeemer of all. It seems clear that those peoples must have thought the Kings of Castile were gods, since what was preached before all else to them were the dignity and power of the Kings of Castile, and what was owed to them from other kings over great lands and peoples such as [the Indians' own] was recognition of their sovereignty, and tribute money. Or those peoples must have thought the goal the Christians had, a goal they prized more than anything, was their own welfare, and to haul back home, from other people's goods, gold and tribute. The exact opposite to the way Christ taught his apostles to win the entire world over to Him—they were to preach God first and foremost, and not only did [the Apostles] not ask for payment, nor take anything from anyone, they did great good, they gave their lives, they died to win over and save those to whom they preached, as the Son of God gave his life to save all. But Don Bartholomew came in and took the same route as that taken by his brother from the start, certainly deceived I do not know by what, or maybe I do: an absolutely inexcusable—no excuse for anyone—ignorance of divine and natural law.

g. The Admiral Enchained

When the Admiral learned of the arrival of Bobadilla [1500], and what he had started to do in Sancto Domingo, the decrees he displayed, the taking of the fort and the rest—because his brother Don Diego informed him immediately about it all—he could not believe the Kings would have sanctioned such things, it was as if they wanted to undo him totally, without his having offended them anew in any respect, rather, he put them more in his debt with his new efforts and services—the discovery of mainland, of pearls at Paria, of other islands, and he guessed it was not some kind of fake on the part of Bobadilla, as it had been in the case of Hojeda who, in order to turn the men against the Admiral, had pretended he had powers from the Kings to co-govern with him and force him to pay the salaries of those who were due them from the Kings. . .[23]

Certainly, the situation was disturbing, a bitter shock to the Admiral—it would be also to anyone else, wise as he might be—because the Admiral had done so many new services, had not misbehaved up to then since the time Juan Aguado had alerted the Kings—Aguado had brought as many complaints as he could about the grief people said the Admiral had given the Christians up to a point in time. It was an extremely horrible, painful thing for the Admiral to see himself stripped, dispossessed abso-lutely of his position, without a hearing or defense, by the Most Catholic Kings whom he had put under such obligation, but, as I said earlier. . . , it was not really the Kings' power at work, rather it was divinely and mercifully ordained for the Admiral's own good.

But because he suspected it was perhaps a machination like Hoje-da's, he alerted, they say, the caciques and leading Indians, they were to ready their warriors for when he should summon them, since he had little confidence in the Christians, the most of them—he was out hunting many of them down for having rebelled, and every day he was afraid some more would do the same, for the uprising of Roldán was still fresh, one that had gone on and on.

Finally, he decided to come in closer to Sancto Domingo, so he shifted to Bonao, ten leagues nearer than Vega where he was staying. Some Christians were there as settlers, they had fields nearby which they had taken from the Indians, and other fields they had forced the Indians to create,

---

[23] *History*, bk. 1, caps. 176-80.

though it was sheer hardship on them, and the village was already being called Bonao. Commandant Bobadilla—he was now Governor and people addressed him openly as such—sent an official deputy inland with his powers and copies of the decrees, and had him show them to the Admiral and anyone else he might run into there. The official met the Admiral just arrived at Bonao. The Commandant had sent no letter advising the Admiral of his arrival. (Whereas the Admiral had written him to say welcome and never got a reply, which was a great discourtesy and a sign that he was intent on something bad against the Admiral.) And worse than that, Bobadilla wrote to Francisco Roldán who was in Xaragua, and maybe to others of the rebels, to which the Admiral objected very much.

Once he was notified of the royal decrees, the Admiral answered—so people said—that he was Viceroy and Governor General, and that the decrees, the powers the Commandant brought were only for what touched on the administration of justice, and therefore he required the very official the Commandant had sent, plus all the men at Bonao, to submit to him, the Admiral, and obey him in things general, and obey the Commandant in that which pertained to him as judge and administrator of justice. The Admiral's entire response was sent in writing. After a few days, there arrived Fray Juan de Trasierra, a Franciscan, and Juan Velázquez, a treasurer for the Kings, with whom the Commandant sent a letter from the Kings which said the following . . . : "Don Christopher Columbus, Our Admiral of the Ocean Sea: We have ordered Commandant Francisco de Bobadilla, the bearer of this letter, to speak to you and tell you some things on our behalf. We ask that you give him your trust and credence, and act upon what he says. I, the King. I, the Queen. And by their command, Miguel Pérez de Almazán." After he received the letter, and after he had long talks between himself and the friar and the treasurer, he decided to return with them to Sancto Domingo.

Meantime, the Commandant conducted an investigation in depth, a hearing of witnesses, concerning treasure that belonged to the Kings, who was in charge of it, and what belonged to the Admiral, from whom he took the coffers and all the wealth the Admiral had in gold and silver and precious stones and household furnishings, he even set himself up in the Admiral's house, took possession of it, and everything of the Admiral's in it. He seized certain goldish stones which were like "mother-of-gold," because over time, they turn into gold completely . . . He took as his own also the mares, the stallions, everything else he found, including all books, all writings, personal and public, which the Admiral kept in the coffers—that pained the Admiral more than the rest—and the Commandant was unwilling to return a single one. He took all this, he said, in order to pay the salaries owed to people who were the Admiral's responsibility, and on the basis of the clauses that came with the powers detailed above.

At that time every Spaniard who could, from Vega and Bonao and elsewhere around, descended on Sancto Domingo to get a look at the governor and revel in the new situation. To win all of them over to himself, the Commandant ordered announced an exemption for gold, i.e., everyone who wanted could mine it and not pay the Kings more than a tenth for twenty years to come, but that announcement cost him dearly . . . He granted the same exemption to the tithes then paid the crown. He announced also that he came to pay the salaries owed them by the Kings, and to force the Admiral to pay those in his employ. At such news the Spaniards would damn, would double-damn their own parents.

The Commandant came up with a cute tactic. Since almost all the Spaniards were discontented and angry, angry at the Admiral and his brothers, and since they saw him fallen from his governorship and high position, and they would come to the governor with their complaints and accusations and make their injuries known, he, by virtue of his office, launched a secret investigation of the Admiral and his brothers, for which he found everyone willing and quite ready. And because, as Boethius says, the first thing that deserts the misfortunate is good repute, and disrepute follows, and shunning, and opposition, when the Commandant began hearing witnesses, the stones began to cry out against the Admiral and his brothers. "Whence it happens that good repute is the first thing of all to abandon the victim. Who must now suffer recalling the applause of the people as raucous and fickle condemnation. I would say only this: the heaviest burden the victim must bear is that during the time some crime is imputed to him, he is thought to deserve what he suffers."[24]

. . . A very apt statement when applied to the luckless, maligned Admiral, because once the inquiry began, not only the secret one but the open one also, he was accused, slandered, his defects were broadcast loudly, people deemed him fit for the worst of punishments. They accused him of inflicting evil, cruel treatment on the Christians in Isabela when, by forcing men to work without giving them food—sick and weak men—he attempted to build a fortress, and his house, and mills, and a sluice, and other structures, then do the same for the fort in the Vega, which was at Concepción, and in other locations. [And said] many men died of hunger and exhaustion and disease because he did not feed them what each one needed to survive, and that he ordered men whipped, humiliated for trivial

---

[24] *Boethii Consolationis Philosophiae Quinque Libri*, E. Gegenschatz and O. Gigon, eds. (Zurich: Artemis Verlag, 1949), p. 24.

things, because, for example, they stole a peck of wheat when famished to death, or went scrounging for food. [And said] some men went searching for food in a place reserved for some Christian officers, and this after having asked permission and he denied it, but they were unable to bear the hunger, and he ordered them hung. He hung many for this and for other causes, all unjust. [And said] he did not permit the clerics and friars to baptize the Indians they wished, because he preferred to have slaves rather than Christians—though he could have blocked this justly if the clerics and friars wished to baptize without instruction first, because it was a great sacrilege to baptize someone who did not know what he was getting. They accused him of making war on the Indians, or provoking wars unjustly, and making many slaves in order to send them back to Castile. And they further accused him of not wanting to give licenses for mining gold so he could control the riches of the island and the Indies in order to rebel with those riches, with the backing of some other Christian king. The falsity of this latter accusation is obvious for many reasons noted earlier and referred to later, from which it is clear that he would rather die, and that he made every effort to send the Kings news of rich mines, and send them gold to pay for their expenses on his behalf. And that was his main purpose and occupation, because he saw that all who opposed him to the Kings pointed to no other reason than that the Kings spent money and got no return for it, and this way the enterprise of the Indies was defamed and respect for it fell—all the evil done to him, all the harm, came from this cause, so the above accusation they made against him does not have the ring of truth to it.

They further accused him of ordering many armed Indians to gather for the purpose of fighting the Commandant and forcing him to go back to Castile, and accused him of committing many other faults, injustices, cruelties against the Spaniards. But no one questioned the honesty of his character, nor said anything against him personally, because they had nothing on him, and those who accused him took very little trouble to mention what they themselves had committed—and he in ordering it—in the unjust wars, in the wicked and harsh treatment they meted out to the Indians. And the same general insensitivity and brutality affected all the judges who came out and had the duty of assessing, investigating other judges in the Indies, they never considered as chargeable crimes the deaths, the oppressions, the cruelties inflicted on the Indians—until some very few years ago, until some religious people went and raised a cry in Castile—these judges only considered [chargeable] the trivial aggravations one Spaniard inflicted on another, and other things, grave and grievous as they may have been, were in reality thin as air and the merest of accidents when compared to the smallest Indian sufferings, sufferings so substantial they decimated the place, as they later decimated the whole Indies. Many of the same charges, and others also, were laid against the Admiral's brothers. I saw the records, the investigation, saw the witnesses who made the above accusations, knew them for many years. God only knows which accusations were true, and what was the motive, the purpose for which they were taken and given. Though I am sure the Admiral and his brothers were not modest and discreet in their rule over Spaniards, which they should have been. And they had many failings in the rationing out of food to the men—they were harsh and partial—because the Kings gave them provisions destined for everyone, they were to distribute food according to the needs, the requirements each one had, so all the Spaniards harbored a great enmity against them . . .

When the Commandant knew that the Admiral was coming to Sancto Domingo, he ordered Don Diego, the brother, seized, and put shackled aboard one of the caravels he had brought out, without giving Don Diego a why or a wherefore, giving him no charge, no term, no prospect of release. The Admiral arrived, went to see the Commandant, and the welcome the Commandant gave was to order him shackled and imprisoned in the fort, where the Commandant did not visit him after that, did not speak to him, nor would he allow anyone else to do so either. It was clearly something utterly absurd, insulting, despicable altogether, pitiful and pitiable, to have a man who rose to such dignity as to be Viceroy and Governor in perpetuity over a whole region of the world, who was by merit called the Admiral of the Ocean Sea, who had gained those titles through enormous efforts, through storm and strife, who was especially chosen by God for the task, a man who had revealed to the world another world hidden from it for ages—so it must be said—and had obligated the Kings and realm of Castile in a special way to an everlasting gratitude by an untouchable bond, a bond based on natural reason, treated so inhumanely, so insultingly, so dishonorably, something that was surely unworthy of right reason, something more than monstrous.

The Lieutenant, still in Xaragua, and Francisco Roldán, held some captives from among the recently rebelled—I think I heard it said back then that there were sixteen—held in a pit or well, and about to be hung. The Commandant sent word to the Admiral that he was to write and tell the Lieutenant not to touch those men for anything in the world, and to summon the Lieutenant back, and this he did, telling the Lieutenant to come in peace, obedient to royal commands, and not to resist the Admiral's capture, they would both go to Castile and the Kings would right the wrongs done them. When the Lieutenant arrived in Sancto Domingo, he found in the Commandant the same hospitality given to the Admiral.

Once the Admiral and his two brothers were prisoners, in chains, aboard the caravels, those who most wished them evil took this occasion to get revenge on them, because it wasn't revenge enough to see them suffering under great disgrace and humiliation, but in speech, in writing, day and night, they kept after them, posting wicked libels on every corner, reading them openly, to blame, to ridicule, to curse the brothers, and it was hardest on them that some of those who were doing this so boldly, so shamelessly, had eaten their bread and accepted their pay and were their servants. And this [next] cannot be said without the great grief and sorrow that befits it: when the shackles were to be put on the Admiral, no one of those present would do it, out of reverence and compassion, rather it was a cook of his, a nobody, a shameless man, who so bare-facedly shackled him, as if bringing him some plates of new and delicious food. I knew that cook very well, his name was Espinosa, if I have not forgotten. The Admiral kept those chains, he ordered them buried with his bones, as a witness to the way the world often pays those who work for it. And that is well worth a lot of thought, so people will not rely on duty done or heroic deeds, will not expect to be safe because princes or kings are obligated to them for the same, because ultimately, princes and kings are human and mutable—the more the royal soul is under pressure, the more mutable—and seldom do they match their rewards fully to what services to them really merit, and they often undo the rewards they granted with negative treatment, with gratitude that is dead and gone. . .

Though the Catholic Kings were very grateful for the services the Admiral rendered, and though the capture and maltreatment of him and his brothers by the Commandant grieved them (more on this later), yet the fact is that so extensive and unconditional were the powers they gave the Commandant, so great was the confidence they placed in him, that if he had done worse than he did, treated the Admiral and his brothers worse, it would seem from the powers he was given that he had the right so to order it. And it is clear the Kings ought to have stipulated that he not touch the person of the Admiral, but I think that since touching the person of the Admiral was obviously not included in the powers granted, sound reason said not to, the rules of law said not to, the Kings forgot to make that exception. . .

The Kings did not order his eyes out [as Justinian did the eyes of Belisarius], nor do I think they ordered his arrest, and though the Commandant arrested him, and sent him back in deep disgrace and in shackles, deprived of his rank, his honor, his possessions, brothers, friends and servants, as the Admiral would have done to Francisco Roldán or any other of those base and fractious men who had rebelled with him, never, while he lived, did the Kings compensate him for his lost rank, honor, possessions, instead, after he made further remarkable efforts and underwent further severe dangers in new explorations in order to serve the Kings, he died at the end in dire straits, out of favor and a pauper, as the next book will show. And there is something he felt as more bitter, more painful than having his eyes out—and his feelings were right—it was the shock, the panic that hit him when they were taking him from the fort to put him aboard ship, he thinking they were going to behead him. So when Alonso de Vallejo, a gentleman and a respected person—more about him later—came to remove the Admiral and take him out to the ship, the Admiral, his face downcast and in deep distress—and that shows the intensity of his fear—asked him, "Vallejo, where are you taking me?" Vallejo answered, "My Lord, your Lordship is going to be put aboard ship for embarkation." But the Admiral, in doubtful tones, asked again, "Vallejo, is this the truth?" Vallejo answered, "On your Lordship's life, it is the truth, you are going aboard ship." The answer revived the Admiral, almost from death to life. Could anyone suffer greater anxiety? Could anything cause him greater panic? He would have thought having his eyes out like Belisarius a light punishment, if Vallejo had affirmed death for him. He was a man suddenly unseated from the dignity of being Viceroy—who ruled and governed everyone—without having committed any new faults, the kind mentioned earlier—I speak with reference to the Spaniards, and what they thought were faults, and the reason they maltreated him. And it was the other way round, after he returned he was the object of offense, disobedience, great damage—and he had no charge placed against him, no way of freeing himself from such a wretched, helpless position, and he feared he would be judged by one man, by a single judge, so all this had to be for him grounds, unique grounds for anxiety and bitterness and frightful panic.

As to Francisco Roldán, the author of all the ruckuses and rebellions in the past, and to Don Hernando de Guevara who rebelled more recently, as to the rest on the brink of being hanged, I do not know that the Commandant punished them or penalized them in any way. I saw them safe and sound a short time after this, when I arrived on the island, and much better off than the Admiral and his brothers, if one can call the life they led better instead of worse.

So when the Admiral and his brothers were on board in chains, the Commandant gave charge of them over to a man he named captain of the two ships he had brought out, Alonso de Vallejo, ordering Vallejo to take the prisoners, chains and all, with the records of the inquiry the Commandant had made, and hand them over to Bishop Don Juan de Fonseca upon arrival at Cadiz. This Alonso de Vallejo was a prudent person—as I said before—a gentleman, well respected, a very good friend of mine, was the servant of a gentleman named Gonzalo Gómez de Cervantes, uncle of the Bishop Don Juan, so it is said, and that explains why the Commandant Bobadilla chose to give him the task of taking the Admiral back prisoner, it was to please the Bishop. The suspicion was then very strong that the Commandant had meted out such awful, such bad treatment to the Admiral with the backing and for the sake of the said Bishop Don Juan, and if that was true, the lord Bishop did not have to take the consequences.

h. Critique

After the departure of the two caravels aboard which Commandant Bobadilla put the Admiral and his brothers as prisoners, the Commandant then tried to mollify as much as he could the Spaniards who were there, upwards of three hundred men in all, for that was the number the Admiral had earlier informed the Kings was sufficient to keep Hispaniola and its peoples subject.[25] So the Kings had ordered those three hundred men to maintain themselves partly at the Kings' expense, partly at the Admiral's. They were enough, more than enough, to keep the Indians quiet—much fewer would do—if that was the approach they wanted to take, but enough also to conquer and kill the Indians all, as kill them all they finally did. For with twenty or thirty horses, they had enough to hack the Indians to pieces. And further, they had trained their dogs, so that with a dog, a Spaniard moved with as much safety as if he had fifty, a hundred Christians along. . .

. . . The Commandant first decided quickly the cases of those who [had been sentenced by the Admiral] to be hung, then those of Francisco Roldán and the men who had rebelled with him [against the Admiral]. I saw them, not long after, safe and sound, as if they had done nothing, living happy and respectable lives. I never knew or heard he had punished them in any way, because at that time I was not after such knowledge and made no effort to gain it. To go with the exemptions, the favors Commandant Bobadilla had given the three hundred Spaniards—they were to pay but eleven pesos apiece for the gold they acquired, and they had no thought of going and digging it themselves—they asked him to give them Indians to do the digging and to till the casssava fields. He ordered (or urged) them to group two by two, in order to share estates and the profits gained. To do this he assigned them the people of this or that cacique or lord, and he mollified them thus, much to their pleasure.

Here you saw brutish men, men who had been whipped, had had their ears cut off in Castile, men deported to Hispaniola because they were murderous and murderers, who were there to work off their crimes, lord it

---

[25] *History*, bk. 2, cap. 1.

over native kings and rulers, possess them as the lowest and meanest of servants, even lower. And those caciques, rulers, had daughters or sisters or women relatives in their households. These were taken right away, by force or by concession, for the purpose of concubinage. So all three hundred gentlemen Spaniards lived in concubinage for some years in the state of mortal sin associated with that evil, not to speak of the awful sins they were committing every hour of every day being tyrant oppressors of the Indians. They called the women they had as concubines their servants. Thus the shameless custom they had in each other's presence of saying my servant so-and-so, or so-and-so's servant, as if they were saying my wife or his wife. The Commandant had almost no concern about this, to avoid or cure the situation. He often told them, "Enrich yourselves as much as you can, you know not how long the time for it will last." He had almost no regard for the sweat, the toil, the sufferings, the deaths of the Indians. The Spaniards, for these favors, the help, the energy, the counsel, adored him, he was their very favorite. They recognized the large liberty they now had to live the law of life they had chosen, so much larger than under the Admiral, for the sad thing about the Admiral was that he was the cause of great and irreparable harm to the Indians, but through blindness, and through an anxiety to please the Kings. However, even if he ignored certain damages the Spaniards did, and even if he licensed and designated Francisco Roldán or someone else to have some cacique and land and his people work his estate, or some Indians dig gold for him, that rarely, rarely occurred, and was the result almost of force, when the Admiral felt constrained to satisfy some men in the light of past rebellions. But their brutish sins, and the loose and lawless life they led, those who called themselves Christian, he never ceased to abhor. And because a man who sins, a people steeped in one or more sins, cannot stop at just those, but the force of sin twists them into greater and more numerous sins, so the Spaniards, for many years, had not a thought, not a scruple, over missing Lent, Fridays, Saturdays—the fasting, the abstinence required—no more than over the days of Easter. They saw themselves as lords of lords and chieftains, saw themselves served and feared by all the peoples great and small, for the Indians quaked in the Spaniards' presence, an effect of the cruelties inflicted in past wars, and when they irritated the Spaniards, the cruelties were brought up to date. And if the Spaniard had taken as his servant the wife, the daughter or sister of the chieftain—who thought that according to Spanish custom they were then married—he grew daily in self-delusion, in arrogance, vanity, indulgence, disdain for these simple people. As exalted beings, the Spaniards scorned to go anywhere on foot, though they had no horses or mules. It was on the backs of the beaten Indians, if they were in a hurry, or in a litter, i.e., slung in a hammock, if they were not, and the Indians who carried them worked in shifts, and this way, the Spaniards flew along. In the same party were Indians who carried large leaves from trees to shade them, and others with goose wings to cool them. I saw droves of Indians loaded with cassava headed for the mines, under a donkey's load, and often their backs and shoulders were galled like beasts. Wherever the Spaniards went, in any Indian village, they ate in a day what would more than suffice for fifty Indians. The cacique and all the villagers had to bring out what they had and dance it before them. And these were not the only displays of mightiness and empty pomp. They had other women besides the main one, with titles, Madame Stewardess, Madame Chef, and such like. I knew a carpenter by trade, a maker of organs, one from back in that time period, who had women with such designations.

The Spaniards had two kinds of servants. One, all those Indians—mostly boys and girls—they took when they roamed the island robbing and killing their parents. This kind they kept for constant use in the house by day, by night, and they called them naborias, which means servant in the island language. The other kind is the Indian who works the fields or digs gold for periods of time, then goes back to his village afterwards half starved, exhausted, weak and worn. It was a laughable thing to see the Spaniards' presumption, their regal vanity as they preened and puffed themselves up, because they had not the fine shirt of Castilian linen to put on, nor the cape, nor the sash, nor the hose. They had but a cotton shirt over another one from Castile, if they could obtain it, and if not, then just a cotton shirt, and legs bare, and instead of boots or shoes, some rope sandals, some stockings.

The treatment, the thanks, the Spaniards handed out consistently to the pitiful Indians, as a return for their constant attendance and labor, were blows and beatings. The Indians heard only the word "dog" come from the Spaniard's mouths, no other, and would to God they treated them as they treated their dogs, because they would not kill a dog for a thousand castellanos, they who think nothing of killing ten to twenty Indians when the Indians irritate them, slashing away at them, or, for recreation, testing the temper or sharpness of their swords, as if they were killing cats. One time it happened among such like that two Indian boys each brought parrots, and the ones who call themselves Christian took the parrots and just for the fun of it cut the heads off the two boys. One tyrant Spaniard, angry at a cacique for not having brought or given him what he demanded, hanged twelve of the cacique's subjects. Another hanged eighteen, all in one house. Another shot an Indian with an arrow in a public ceremony, announcing he sentenced him to death for not delivering fast enough a letter sent the Spaniard. Cases, incidents of this type, and no end to their number, have been the glorious expressions of our Christian people. The Indians of the island suffered these and other afflictions as I just described them, not afflictions caused by men, but by devils incarnate. The Indians are gentle people, humble, extraordinarily patient, and once they could do no more to defend themselves—they had tried warfare, they had run for it, mainly to the mountains, they had found out there was no place to hide from the Christians—suffered and died in the mines and at other labors, like people who are numb, deadened, frightened, giving up and letting themselves perish, mute in their desperation, there was no one anywhere to whom they could protest, no one to feel for them. The next step was this: soulless men gone blind, brutal, unable to recognize in themselves unforgiveable sins, lacking utterly any love or fear of God or humankind which could check them, killed without scruple, never thought it a sin. And they also made perverse use of the patience of those peoples, their natural simplicity, goodness, obedience, meekness, made perverse use of their services, day and night, without let up. Instead of admiring them, pitying them, being ashamed, softening their cruel treatment, the Spaniards cheapened them, degraded them so much they tagged them as mindless beasts, by their nature, before the whole world, and thus the Spaniards caused a doubt to arise, in those who had never seen them, about whether they were human or subhuman. Then the next step was a worse error, a pitiful blindness: someone said they were incapable of Christian faith. That is brutal heresy, and hellfire awaits the one who holds such a view obstinately. And other bad things followed: the view that they needed caring for as children do, because they could not govern themselves, for if they were left to themselves, they would not work, and hence had to die of hunger. All these views were concocted so power over the Indians would not be taken from the Spaniards. And there was never anyone to take the Indian side, to protest on their behalf. Instead, everyone drank their blood and ate their flesh. The wicked characterization of the Indians was set going so shrewdly that for a long time the Kings of Castile and their counsellors and people of all kind took the Indians as described, deemed them and dealt with them as subhuman. Until God had someone—as we will later see—reveal to the Kings, to the world, the illusion, the judgment gone stupid, the manifest untruth. And the truth was not obscure, it needed no new miracle or supernatural illumination to be gotten at. There is not a lout from Loutland unable to know it, and no one could brag that he taught it to others. It was just a matter of discovering that the cause of what happened is, was, violent and blind and uncontrollable greed. From it all harm came, all evil. Then a matter of recognizing the numbing fear caused by the first tyrants, then by all those who came later in the same self-damnation, who solidified the situation by the exact same wicked deeds, and took away any hope that the situation would ever be different. Is there any one with the least knowledge who does not know that even the wisest of souls, the most noble of human beings, degenerate, become weak, timid, fearful, if they are pressed into harsh and constant servitude, if they are crushed, cruelly treated, threatened, tortured, battered every which way, to such a degree that they forget they are human beings and cannot concentrate their thoughts on anything except the wretched, pitiful, bitter life they lead? And that is the main policy all tyrants use to keep themselves in power in captured kingdoms: oppress, harrass without let up the most powerful, the most intelligent. For if they are caught up in bemoaning their miserable state, they have no time, no heart for thinking about their freedom. Thus they turn into cowards, into weaklings. . .[26] So if wise, if very intelligent people—even Greeks and Romans, history is full of examples—often, often feared this bad situation for the very same reason, if they knew by experience, if many other peoples knew by experience, if philosophers spoke of it, what are we to expect of these gentle Indian nations, these meek and kind and naked nations, who have suffered such great torment, fear, trembling, enslavement, death and disappearance? What expect but an immense passivity, a bottomless discouragement, a total loss of their human sense of themselves? In doubt, perplexity about themselves, were they human beings or cats? And equally, is there anyone, even a lout from Loutland, who would not judge it utter and absolute malice in those who had the gall to defame those countless peoples, then spread the defamation, saying they need guardians for they cannot govern themselves? Even though they have their own kings, own governors, own villages, own homes, each area, each person their own, even a small group, relating to one another in human ways, economic as well as political, people to people, and living ordered lives, in harmony, in complete peace? He has little or no brains who does not recognize that it takes justice, order, peace, for a large group to live together, and there are countless Indians. Finally, there is an argument that reveals the wicked design of those who invent and thus mock the truth—those who claim that the Indians need guardians to make them work so they do not die of hunger. It would be good to ask those who claim this if, during the thousands of years the Indies have been populated, Spaniards had sent them their food from overseas? Likewise if, when we came there at the propitious time, we found them weak and waning, we gave them the skill whereby to eat—because they lived without eating and we brought them food from Castile, and filled them? Or rather were they the ones who killed

---

[26] Omitted here, a cross reference by Las Casas: "I spoke about this at length in my other book, *Historia Apologética*, in chapters 27 and 36."

our hunger, kept us from death a thousand times, giving us not only the food necessary, but food in abundance, food overflowing? From them, therefore, from the first wreckers of this island, came the deceitful and devastating slander against these multitudes of Adam's descendants, a slander that spread across the world. There was no basis for it, no cause. They took the goodness, the meekness, the obedience, the natural simplicity of these people, which ought to have moved them to love and prize the Indians, even learn these natural virtues from them, and used these qualities instead as a means, an excuse to cheapen them, to describe them as animals, to rob them, afflict them, oppress them, annihilate them, to consider them as no more than dung in the streets. This suffices to give some idea, some knowledge of the state of the island during Commandant Bobadilla's time, after he sent the Admiral off in chains to Castile.

i. Pitched Battle

Back to the story as Don Hernando relates it, saying it was to guarantee the security of those who decided to stay in the settlement—the Lieutenant and seventy-four men—that on 30 March [1503], the Lieutenant went to the village of Veragua, whose houses were not grouped but scattered as in Biscay.[27] Once King Quibia knew the Lieutenant was nearby, he sent to tell him not to approach his house which was built on a rise above the river Veragua. The Lieutenant paid no heed to what he was told, and so that the king would not be frightened into fleeing him, he decided to proceed with only five men, leaving orders with the rest to get in close, at intervals, two by two, and at hearing a gun fired—an arquebus they now call it—in a sweep they were to surround the house so no one escaped or fled. Here one will see whether or not the king was preparing to kill the Spaniards, because the Lieutenant, with the five men, walked in and did what he did unopposed. This way: when the Lieutenant got near the house, the cacique Quibia sent another messenger telling him not to enter, instead he would come out, though he was wounded—they say the Indians do this so the visitors do not see their women, they are very jealous about them. So the cacique came to the door, seated himself, and said only the Lieutenant should approach, which the Lieutenant did, after leaving orders that when his men saw him seize the cacique by the arm, they were to attack. And when he reached the cacique, he began to talk, asking him about his wound and about other things concerning the land, interpreted through an Indian the Spaniards had taken, back up the coast, and it seemed to the Spaniards that they understood something. The Lieutenant, pretending he was pointing to the cacique's

---

[27] *History*, bk. 2, caps. 27-9.

wound, seized him by the wrist. Both men were very strong, but the Lieutenant held the cacique long enough for the four Spaniards to rush in and the
fifth to fire the gun, and then all the rest came out from cover, reached and
entered the house where there were fifty people, adults and children, most
of whom were captured, among them, the wives and children of the king
himself, Quibia, and of other important people. They offered great riches,
saying that on a mountain or in a certain place, they kept their treasure and
they would give it all to ransom themselves. This was one heroic deed the
Lieutenant accomplished there back then, and there were more.

In order to prevent word spreading throughout the region, he hurried his unjust catch of innocents off to the ships. He stayed, and most of his
men, in order to hunt down and capture the remaining relatives and subjects
who had escaped his violent hands. When he was discussing with the men
he had with him who would take their catch in a boat back to the ships, a
navigator volunteered, a man thought to be very careful. They gave him the
king bound hand and foot, and when they warned him to keep a sharp look
that the king did not jump for it, the navigator said he accepted responsibility for him, and they could pluck out his beard if the king got away. After he
set off down river with the king and the rest, and there was no more than half
a league to its mouth and the sea, the king began to complain strongly about
his tied hands, and the navigator, out of pity, untied him from the seat in the
boat he was lashed to, but kept him carefully on a rope. Just a bit later the
cacique made a sudden jump into the water. The navigator, unable to hold
onto the rope—it meant being dragged in after—chose to let it go and the
cacique escaped his clutches. Due to it being already dark, and due to the
noise and commotion on the boat, the navigator could neither see nor hear
where the cacique got ashore, so the Spaniards never found a trace of him.
And to prevent any further escape from happening among the other captives,
the Spaniards decided not to stop until they reached the ships, they were very
chagrined that the cacique had fooled them.

The next day, it would be 1 March, the Lieutenant recognizing that
further pursuit and capture through mountainous territory, as this was, would
be too difficult, decided to return to the ships, quite happy with his exploit,
with the spoils he had hoisted from King Quibia's house, something on the
order of three hundred ducats worth in mirrors, eaglets, bugling, like beads
of gold strung on thread and worn on arms and legs, plus circlets of gold
Indians wear around their heads like crowns, all of which the Lieutenant
presented to the Admiral. Once he had set aside a fifth for their Majesties,
he split the remainder among those who went on the raid, as if it were a good
war, a preached crusade against the Turks. And funny thing, Don Hernando
adds that in recognition of that remarkable victory, a crown was given the

Lieutenant. What was remarkable back then was the blindness—coming to those lands and treating those peoples as if they were lands and peoples of Africa—that was engendered, first in the Admiral then in the others.[28] Would to God that blindness had been halted in past centuries, and the world today was not ruined by it.

Then God sent a great rain, the river rose and freed the channel so the ships could make it out to sea. Consequently, the Admiral decided to return to Castile with three of the ships, leaving one for his brother and the group that was going to remain with him in the settlement they had decided to make in Veragua. But he thought to go by way of the island of Hispaniola, and from there to send what help he could. He sailed out of the river into the sea, after saying goodbye to his brother and company, and dropped anchor a league from the mouth, waiting for a good wind to make up so he could head off on his voyage. The wait provided the chance for him to send a boat back in to go up river and pick up water and bring other things the Admiral wanted to provide for his brother.

Now King Quibia, who had escaped into the river when the Spaniards were taking him a prisoner out to the ships, was mightily offended by his capture, and the capture of his wife and children and others of his household, and by other injuries as well, and he saw the three ships had sailed with the Admiral, or maybe he didn't wait for them to sail, rather, when he had enough men grouped and ready, he came down on the Spaniard's settlement, right at the moment the boat arrived there, and he crept in so quietly he was not noticed until within ten feet of the settlement, the mountain growth was that thick around it, and he attacked with such ferocity and shouting, the shouts seemed to crack the air. Since the Spaniards were off guard—they should not have been, because they knew the serious harm they had done to someone who had in no way harmed them, rather had entertained them, and they should have been aware that the injured were not going to ignore it—and since the huts were covered with rushes or leaves, the Indians hurled their spears—fire hardened poles pointed with fish bone—which went right through the walls of the huts, in one, out the other, so in a short time some Spaniards were badly hurt. The Lieutenant was a brave and spirited man, and with seven or eight Spaniards who formed around him, he put up a manly show, urging on his men in such way that they drove the Indians back until they sought cover on a hill said to be nearby. The Indians launched further attacks from there, hurling their spears and then retreating, the way our people act in war games. . . The pitiful, naked,

---

[28] Las Casas once again sees the pattern of greed at work, the seed, the poison, stemming from the Admiral and devastating the New World.

and poorly armed Indians got the worst of the fight, as they always do. . .
the Spaniards cut into them with their swords, so the Indians lost legs,
bellies, heads, arms. And the Indians fled, especially from a hound dog
which the Spaniards had, one that went after them viciously and bit them
open—flight is the Indians' best weapon—but leaving one Spaniard dead
and seven or eight wounded, while the Indians, one can well guess, were
badly mauled. One of the Spaniards hurt was the Lieutenant, wounded in the
chest by a spear, but it did not harm him much after all.

    The men aboard the boat halted to watch the battle, refusing to land
and help though they were right close to the riverbank—the boat chief
answered the men who blamed him for this that he was afraid those who
were on land and wanted to escape in the boat would swamp it, then
everyone would be lost, and what was more, the boat was from the Admiral's
ship, and if it were lost, the Admiral was going to be in great danger out at
sea where he was anchored, the surf inshore was so severe. And truly, any
ship or vessel without its boat runs risks that are great and certain, so the
man said he intended to do nothing else than what the Admiral ordered him,
which was to get water. The boat chief, bent on doing that, then going back
quickly so as to bring news of what happened to the Admiral, went up river
to where the salt water does not reach and mix with the fresh, though some
people warned him not to proceed due to the danger there was from the
Indian canoes. He replied he had no fear of that danger, because he had
come for water, sent by the only one who could give him commands. So he
rowed on up river, a river walled in on either side by hills and thick growth
right down to the water's edge, though there are some narrow paths the
Indians had made to come down and fish, and where they keep their canoes
out of sight. When the Indians noticed the boat a half league up river from
the settlement, they darted out from the thickest undergrowth on either bank
in many canoes, light, light things, shouting, blowing conchs, sure of
themselves, and began circling the boat, which had only seven or eight
oarsmen, the boat chief, and two or three extras. They could not defend
themselves against the rain of spears the Indians hurled at them. With these,
the Indians wounded them, almost all, the boat chief too, he received many
wounds, but wounded though he was, he kept urging his men on valiantly.
But since they were under attack from all sides, and were unable to deploy
or use the small cannons they had aboard, the strength, the strategy of the
boat chief, the combined efforts of them all proved useless. Finally the
Indians drove a spear right through the eye of the boat chief and he fell dead,
and the rest died there too, their luck run out. Only one man made it to
shore—in the heat of the fight he fell into the water and escaped by
swimming under it, so the Indians did not notice him, and he brought back

to the settlement the news of the boat disaster.

A great discouragement, a dismay came over the men there, seeing themselves so few, and most wounded, the men in the boat dead, and the Admiral beyond, at sea, without a boat, in danger of not being able to reach a place from whence he could help them or send help, so, having lost hope, they decided not to stay in the area. And never mind obedience or deliberation or orders from the Lieutenant, they made their departure a fact, and boarded ship intending to head out to sea, but they could not because the channel had again silted up. Nor were they able to send a boat or anyone out who could inform the Admiral of what occurred because of the undertow and the powerful waves from the sea breaking just at the river mouth. And the Admiral was in no small danger where he lay anchored with his ships, that whole coast was rough, and he had no boat, and the men he had were fewer, by the number the Indians killed in the boat. So everyone—those ashore, those on ship—was in a terrible state of anxiety, fear of danger, uncertainty, panic! What added to the fear, the damage suffered by those ashore, was the sight of the men drifting down river in a boat, dead from a thousand wounds, and over them, a great number of crows, or rather obscene, disgusting birds we call vultures, who feed only on things that are putrid, putrifying, they came circling down croaking and ate the corpses in a frenzy. Everything about those birds was a torture to the men ashore, and for sure, there was someone who took each bird as an omen and had the premonition that his life was going to have a disastrous end. Which looked more likely as they saw in the hours that passed that the Indians, with their victory, gained greater strength and greater confidence that they could finish off the Spaniards, they did not let them relax the length of a credo because the settlement was so badly located, the place worked against the Spaniards. The Indians would have finished them off if they didn't take the step of crossing to a wide open beach on the east side of the river where they threw up a barricade made of crates and barrels of supplies, then set up their guns at spaces apart and thus defended themselves, because the Indians did not dare come off the hill, they feared the damage the shot could do fired from the cannonry.

It was with great anxiety, suspicion, worry that the Admiral grew aware that it was ten days since he had sent the boat, and that he knew not a thing about either it or the men in the settlement, and he feared danger to himself also, given the totally unprotected place where he and the other ships had anchored, but [worried] especially because he lacked a boat, which is a dangerous thing, maybe the most dangerous. He was waiting for the sea to calm down so he could send in another to find out the reason for the first one's delay, and learn the condition of the men who stayed, hoping nothing negative had happened to them.

Then another grief came which increased the troubles he already had, the sons and relatives of King Quibia who were prisoners aboard one of the ships for transport to Castile, made an escape that was remarkable. The tactic they used to get free was the following: they were kept below decks during the night and the hatch was fastened—the hatch is about eight feet square, has a cover, and over that they put a chain with lock and key, it is as if they put people in a well or hole and sealed them in with a kind of door that has its latch topside. Aboard that ship, aboard the big ones generally, the hatch cover is beyond a man's height from below, sometimes two men's, and since the Indians could not reach up to it, they very quietly piled a lot of stones from the ship's ballast right under the hatch cover, making a small mound of them, enough to make them able to reach it. Now some mariners were sleeping on the hatch cover, and they had not chained it because if they did, the chain would hurt them. One night all the Indians, putting their shoulders against the hatch cover, gave a huge heave which threw it and the mariners sleeping on top of it to one side of the boat, and leaping out quickly, their head men dove overboard. But the ship's crew caught the noise, thus many other Indians were unable to escape, the mariners shut the hatch immediately, chained it, and the rest of the poor wretches remained below. And they now saw how desperate their situation was, and that they had no further way of escaping the hands of the Spaniards, and they would never again see their wives and children, never know liberty again, so, in the morning, the mariners found them all hanged from cords they had fashioned, most of them with their feet and knees on the planks, the lowest planks of the ship, or on the ballast which sits on those planks, because there was not enough height to hang themselves straight, so this was the way they did it. And thus, no prisoner was left on that ship, they had fled or died. Don Hernando narrates all this, and from what he says it seems there must have been other captives held on the other ships.

Don Hernando goes on: "Although the incident of the escape or death of the Indians did not damage the ships much, yet, in addition to adding to the bad luck, it could affect on those ashore, because maybe the cacique or lord Quibia would have been happy to make peace with the Christians in order to regain his sons, but now that he saw he had no hostages to worry about, he would make war on them more boldly."[29]   These remarks show how unconcerned Don Hernando was about the crimes that had been committed there, the unjust seizing of people, causing some of them to hang themselves, the poor beings, and [unconcerned] about the scandal left behind all over the region, and how it blighted the name

---

[29] *Vida*, cap. 99.

Christian. We should not proceed on without doing some reflecting on the attitude the missionaries of the gospel found who went later to evangelize the area, what reputation Christians had, and if the Indians would be culpable if they killed them all, refusing out of abhorrence to hear told the story or words of Jesus Christ because he was the God of the Christians. And we should entertain the possibility that Quibia, King of that area, had the right to make the just war he did on the settlement and its leader, the Lieutenant. And should recognise it was no wonder that bad luck occurred, as Don Hernando puts it, to the Admiral and his whole company, that all the elements in heaven and on earth should oppose them, since he and his whole company had done to those innocent peoples, who had done them no damage or injury ever, such irreparable harm, such detestable injuries and injustices.

Let me pick up the thread of Don Hernando's narrative: how the Admiral and those with him were harried by the many things going against them and by fears [of more], and how they were at the mercy of their anchor ropes—and that is most dangerous, people say—and knew nothing about the boat or the people left on shore, and there was someone who came forward to say that if those Indians were brave enough to jump into the sea just to save their lives, and it was a league to shore, the men aboard ship, in order to save themselves and as many [on the beach], should be brave enough also to swim it, if the one boat remaining could carry them in short of the breakers. The Admiral recognized the generosity, the bravery of these mariners, he was very glad of it, and accepted their proposal. He ordered the boat to take them to within gunshot range of the beach, because it could not bring them closer without great danger due to the huge waves that broke onto it. From there, Pedro de Ledesma, the navigator from Seville—I mentioned him earlier—was the one with the courage to jump in and swim, with a bold spirit, sometimes over, sometimes under the crests of the breakers which went rolling in, and he made it to the beach where he learned the full situation of the men and how there was general agreement that no one should stay there, exposed, in mortal danger, defenseless the way they were. For that reason they were asking the Admiral not to leave without picking them up, to leave them behind would be to condemn them to a certain death. They talked of doing only one thing, getting ready, so when the weather calmed they could climb into some canoes they took from the Indians and go out to the ships, because they could not do this with the one boat that had been left them. And they asserted that if the Admiral did not do this, they would board the ship they had and head out to sea and run whatever risks the venture held for them, and there were already some mutinous incidents, some disobediences to the Lieutenant and the other leaders.

With this information, and the response, the attitude of the men ashore, Pedro de Ledesma, the navigator, returned the way he came, swimming out to the boat awaiting him. They took him back and he went and gave a complete report to the Admiral of all that had happened. The Admiral now knew of the defeat and death of those who were lost on the boat, knew the rage of the Indians against them, a rage not easily calmed, knew how wounded and harried the Spaniards were, their attitude, their purpose not to remain there—and the latter affected him more than any of the setbacks—so he decided to bring them out, though it would be dangerous, very, to hold the ships off a stormy coast with no place to shelter, no hope of safety for the people in the ships or on shore if the weather grew fiercer. Thanks be to God, the weather calmed after they were eight days there at the mercy of their anchor ropes, and the men on shore could begin the transfer out of their effects, using the boat and two large canoes lashed together so they would not capsize, each man looking lively not to miss that embarkation. And so, in a matter of two days, not a thing of theirs was left ashore except the shell of a ship, which could not be sailed because it was all holed by worms.

j. Moon Trick

After the mutineers left and went on their headstrong way, the Admiral tried to heal the sick who stayed with him, and console them as much as he could.[30] He also tried to maintain peace and friendship with the Indians, because that way, and through barter, the Spaniards could all be provided with food, for the Indians were unfailing about providing it.[31]

So the sick got well, and the Indians persevered for some days in their custom of providing, but they never have, or work for, greater sustenance than what they need, and consider doing more a hardship, whereas Spaniards consume, even waste, more in a day than Indians eat in ten or fifteen, and Don Hernando says that the task of sustaining Spaniards for seventeen days, and with the first generosity, was no mean feat, so the food was supply was cut and the men had less.

It came down to this: the Indians saw that a sizeable number of Spaniards had mutinied against the Admiral, and the mutineers themselves had urged them to kill the Admiral because he did not purpose to settle there, but rather to kill natives. They began to have a low regard for the Admiral and those with him, and for these several reasons, they cut back each day on the provisions they brought. The result being that the Admiral saw himself

---

[30] *History*, bk. 2, cap. 33.

[31] Parallel treatment of episode in *Vida*, cap. 103.

in tougher and tougher straits, because to provision himself by force would require everyone to set out under arms to make war and leave the Admiral alone behind [he was gout-stricken and unable to move], but leaving him behind at his own wish would run them a great risk, and they might not remedy the situation even with a huge ransom.

It pleased God to provide for them in a new way, through a ruse of the Admiral's, so what they needed would not be lacking. Don Hernando tells it this way: The Admiral knew there was to be an eclipse of the moon in three days time, so he sent a message to the chiefs, the lords, the notables of the region, by means of an Indian he kept from Hispaniola—a ladino in our language—saying he wished to tell them something.[32] When they came the day before the eclipse, he told them that he and his men were Christians and servants and subjects of God who dwelt in heaven, and He was the Lord and Creator of all things. He treated good people well and punished bad people. And God, seeing that some Christians had mutinied, did not want to help them make their way across the island, as those the Admiral had sent had made their way, instead, the mutineers had suffered great harm, a waste of goods and effort.

By the same token, God was angry at the people of the island, because they had been neglectful in bringing the provisions necessary for exchange, and because of this anger He had against them, God determined to punish them, sending a great famine on them and doing them other damage. And should they perhaps not believe His words, God wanted them to see a certain sign of His punishment in the sky and so that they would see it that night, they should be on watch at the rising of the moon. They would see it appear very angry and the color of blood, signifying the evil God wanted to send down on them. After he spoke, they all left, some afraid, but some maybe laughing. At moonrise, however, the eclipse began, and the higher the moon got, the more it darkened, and the Indians began to be afraid, and they came with great cries of grief and loaded down with food to the ships, begging the Admiral to ask his God not to be angry with them, nor do them any harm, for they, from then on, would bring God's Christians all the food they needed.

The Admiral answered that he must have a little time to speak to God. He enclosed himself in his cabin. Meantime the eclipse increased, and the Indians kept crying aloud for him to help them. When the Admiral knew that the eclipse was full and that it would soon fade, he came forth and said he had asked God not to do the evil God had purposed to do, for the Admiral

---

[32] Nota Bene: A likely Indian informant for Las Casas, the way the "Diego Colón" was about the destruction of the men at Navidad. A ladino is a Spanish speaking Indian.

had promised God in the Indians' name that they would be good from then on, they would treat the Christians well, would supply them, and that God had pardoned them already. As a sign of this, they would see the anger of the moon begin to cease, losing the fiery color it had displayed.

The Indians, when they saw the eclipse cease, and the moon shine free at the end, gave the Admiral great thanks, and in amazement and in praise of the works of the God of the Christians, they all went back, filled with joy, to their homes, and once there, they were diligent and did not forget the good thing they believed the Admiral had accomplished for them, because they took great care to provide the Christians everything they needed and in abundance, and they were in constant praise of God, they believed that He could punish them for their sins, they believed that other eclipses they had seen in the past must have been threats of punishment God sent them for their sins.[33]

k. The Last Struggle

So the Admiral rested in Seville a few days, to recover from this succession of setbacks, then he set out for court in May, 1505.[34] It was in Segovia. When he arrived there, along with his brother the Lieutenant, to pay his respects to the King, the King received him with some semblance of pleasure, but not that due a man after long voyages, great dangers, enormous struggles and strains. The Admiral reported on the voyage he had made, and the lands he had discovered, on the richness of the province of Veragua, about his being beached and marooned on Jamaica for an entire year, on the disobedience and mutiny of the Porras brothers and their followers, and finally, on all the particulars of the voyage, incidents, dangers, struggles.

Some days later, when he sensed the time was right, he made a request in the following words:

"Supreme King: God Our Lord miraculously sent me to serve you. I say miraculously because I had landed in Portugal, where the king was more intent on exploration than anyone elsewhere. God blocked his sight, his hearing, his every sense, so that for fourteen years I was not able to make him understand what I said. I say miraculously also because I had letters of request from three princes, the Queen read them, may God keep her, and so did Doctor Villalón. Your Highness, after you knew what

---

[33] This, for Las Casas, is a parable of Spain, and the deceit whereby it destroyed ultimately the deeply spiritual Indian soul.

[34] *History*, Bk. 2, cap. 37-8.

I was talking about, granted me titles of honor. Now my
discovery is beginning to unfold, and reveals that it is, it
will continue to be, what I kept saying. Your Highness is
most Christian. I, and all those who have any knowledge
in Spain or abroad of what I have done, would think that
your Highness, who had honored me at the time when you
had nothing from me but my words, now that you see my
deeds, would renew the grants you had made me, and then
some, and renew them as you promised orally and in
writing over your signature. And if you do this, be certain
I will serve you for the few more days Our Lord will give
me of life, and I hope in the Lord—according to what I
feel, and what seems certain to me—that I will do such
signal service that the future will overmatch the past by a
hundred to one, etc."

The King replied that he well understood that Columbus had given
him the Indies and had earned the rewards the King had given him. And in
order to work matters out, it would be good to designate someone for the
task. The Admiral answered: "Let it be someone your Highness designates."
Then added: "Who is better able to do it than the Archbishop of Seville, for
he, along with your Chamberlain, has been the cause of your possession of
the Indies." He said this because it was that Archbishop of Seville, Don
Diego de Deza, a friar of St. Dominic, tutor to Prince Don Juan, who had
urged the Queen to accept the project, and the chamberlain Juan Cabrero, an
Aragonese, had done the very same—he was very much in the King's
confidence. The King then told the Admiral to inform the Archbishop in his
name. The Archbishop then said that in matters concerning the estate and
income of the Admiral, lawyers should be designated, but not designated as
managers. So far as I can tell, he meant lawyers not because the case had to
be argued, but because things were clearly owed the Admiral.

Since the King still caused delays, the Admiral again asked his
Highness to remember his services, his struggles, his unjust arrest, and with
what humiliation of his person and reputation he had been despoiled, without
any fault on his part, of the status their Highnesses had raised him to because
of his deeds on their behalf. Therefore the King should please show himself
to be a just and grateful one by ordering that the Admiral's privileges be
respected fully, the ones his Highness and the Queen had granted, restoring
him in his son [as heir], in the grants and possession of offices, dignity,
status, as they had given them to him originally, all of these things he had
been deprived of without a trial, or a defense, or a verdict, or a sentence
being passed, and thus contrary to all law. But above all, the King should

recall the promises his Highness and the Queen had made most recently in a royal letter when he was on the point of leaving on his last voyage, i.e., that he should consider it certain that his privileges would be protected totally, and they would keep to the grants contained in those privileges, and they would add new ones, because they were firmly resolved to honor and favor him further, as is evident in the letter they ordered sent from Valencia de la Torre. . .

In another session with the King, he said quite deliberately that he did not want to get into a lawsuit, he just wanted the King to accept his privileges, his documents, and whatever, because of them, pertained to him, and give him what he had already ordered, for he was exhausted, and wanted to go find any old corner he could get where he could rest. The King, recognizing that the Admiral had given him the Indies, told him not to leave, for he had it in mind to give him not only what pertained to him through his privileges, but wanted to give him gifts that came from his own royal treasury. The Archbishop of Toledo was also very favorable to him, Don Fray Francisco Jiménez, a friar of St. Francis, and other important people at court as well. They referred his case to the Council concerned with fulfilling the conscience obligations of the Queen, now dead, and of the King as well. They held two sessions, but nothing came of them. The Admiral thought that since his case was of such great importance, the King did not want to decide it without his daughter, the Queen, whom they were expecting to come at any moment, along with the King Don Philip, and the Admiral took some little hope in that thought, but kept up his petitions to the King. I have one before me, from among the many, and it goes this way. "Most serene and noble Majesty: In my plea is written what my documents require. I have expressed them already, and said that their fulfilment or denial rests entirely in Your Majesty's hands, and that everything would come out well. The position of governor I once held, and proprietorship, are the sources of my honor. I was unjustly deprived of that governorship. It has been a very long time since God, Our Lord, performed a miracle so openly—the man who deprived me, God put down, along with everyone of those who helped him. Aboard the best of the ships of the thirty-four in the fleet, and right in the middle of them, and just out of port, God sank him, and no one, of all those around, saw the when or the how of it. I most humbly beg your Highness to order my son appointed in my place to the honor and position of the governorship I once had, this touches my honor very deeply. As to the other, proprietorship, let your Highness do what is in your best interest, I will accept it as a complete gift. I think it is grief over the delay on settlement that has laid me up the most." He was flat in bed with gout. When he referred to the sinking of a ship and of the people who perished with it, he meant Commandant

Bobadilla who had sent him back in chains, and Francisco Roldán and his crowd who had persecuted him.

He wrote a certain memorial in which he attributes the losses he suffered in rents, and the shrinking of income on him, to not protecting and respecting his privileges, the interest on those privileges was great. And he says this among a lot of things: "The Indians of the island of Hispaniola were and are the riches of it, for they do the digging, they grow the cassava and the other foods for the Christians, they extract the gold from the mines and do all the other jobs and labors of men and beasts of burden." He says he has been told that after he left the island, six out of seven Indians died due to the mistreatment, the inhumanity meted out to them—some were butchered, some died from beatings and brutality, some from starvation and the wretched life forced upon them, most died up in the mountains and gulches where they had fled because unable to put up with hard labor. The loss of Indians meant a huge loss in income. He further says that even if he sent many Indians back to Castile and they were sold, he did so on the understanding that after they had been instructed in our faith and our way of life, our arts, our skills, they would be bought back and returned to the island to instruct the others. This is what the Admiral says, and what a charming naiveté was his, if it was naiveté and not greed. I am as certain as can be that greed was the cause of the troubles that landed on him, and of what he now suffered and suffered in these matters under negotiation. But as for what else he said, he was right, that was the way the Indians, the natives of the island died and died out, yet what he was sorry about was the tenth of gold the Indians would have extracted if they had not died, and sorry about the other things of this world he lost for the same reason . . .

The more petitions he and his sent to the King, the more the King replied with words and delay. In one delay, the King asked if they couldn't come to a mutual agreement—the Admiral would renounce the privileges the Kings had granted him, and they would make him compensation through Castile, and I think they began to hint they would give him Carrión de las Condes, and in addition a certain estate. The Admiral was very unhappy with this, and saw signs that the King intended not to keep to what he and the Queen had generously promised so often, orally and in writing, and so often renewed, over and above what his privileges required. He had this interpretation in mind when he wrote a letter from his bed, where he was now quite ill, complaining to the Archbishop of Seville. "It now seems that the King does not intend to keep to what he promised, orally and in writing, along with the Queen—may she be in glory. For me to fight for the opposite, ploughman that I am, would be to work the wind, and it would be well, since I have done all I could, to let God Our Lord now do something, I have found

Him always present and ready in my direst needs, etc." He appeals here, as someone does who is out of all other remedies, to divine judgment, and I think God will have supplied him with justice [by now].

So the King was delaying and delaying with the Admiral, and the Admiral was in a state of great anxiety about it, also his sickness from gout grew greater and more painful for him every day. The King, who had just come to Valladolid, left for Laredo, there to wait for King Don Philip, his son-in-law, and Queen Doña Juana, our Lady, his daughter. The two rulers arrived from Flanders a few days later, and the Admiral was made very happy by the news, because his hopes were renewed for getting justice, hopes he considered lost with Don Ferdinand. Yet he was sore at heart and very sad that he could not go see them, because he was stopped by the illness he had, nor could he send his son Don Diego. He sent the Lieutenant, his brother, to pay the respects of himself and his son to the Kings and to explain his inability.

He sent along this letter: "To their most serene Highnesses, princes most powerful, the King and Queen, our Lords. I think you will understand that no other time in my life did I want personal health as much as I do now, once I have learned that you were to arrive here by sea, because I want to come and serve you so you see the knowledge I gained on my voyaging. But this is the way Our Lord willed it. Therefore, I most humbly beg Your Highnesses that you count me as one of your royal subjects, servants, and hold it as something certain that even though this illness now torments me without pity, I am still able to supply Your Majesties with a service the like of which has never before been seen. These contrary times, these other difficulties which have been forced on me, against all reason, have brought me to the brink, so I was unable to come to Your Majesties, nor was my son. Quite humbly, I ask you to accept my intention, my wish, as from someone who hopes to be returned to his former honor and status, just as my documents promise. May the Holy Trinity guard and prosper the royal and lofty position of Your Highnesses." I am positive that if the Admiral had lived, if King Philip had not died, the Admiral would have gotten justice, would have had his status restored.

Right after he had sent the Lieutenant to pay his respects to the Kings, the Admiral's sickness from gout worsened by the hour, because of the winter which was harsh, but more because he saw himself abandoned, robbed, the services he had rendered consigned to oblivion, justice for himself in danger, and this even as the news grew and spread about the riches of the Indies, gold arriving in Castile from Hispaniola, with a promise

Indian Freedom

of more to follow every day.[35] He, recognising that he was failing, as the Christian he certainly was, received the last sacraments with much devotion, and when the time came for his passage from this life to the next, they say his last words were: "Into Your hands, O Lord, I commend my spirit." He died in Vallodolid, on Ascension day, which fell, that year of 1506, on 20 May. They brought his remains to Las Cuevas in Seville, the monastery of the Carthusians. From there they took them on to the city of Sancto Domingo and they are interred in the main chapel of the Cathedral church. . .

So he left this life a troubled, bitter, poor man, who had, as he said, no roof of his own to stand under, out of the rain, or to rest under, in this world, and he had discovered a world through his own efforts, a blessed world greater than any we ever knew.

---

[35] *History*, bk. 2. cap. 38.

- 3 -

The Columbus Letters

Prenote

Here are three Columbus letters Las Casas uses in his History of the Indies, *three of many. Their inclusion is for the purpose of showing Las Casas' use of sources, his judgment on events or writings, his openness to being judged himself by his reader because he includes, and fully, the relevant material or narratives. Recall Las Casas' conviction, when he was arguing the cause of the Indians from the mid-1530's onwards, that Columbus and Spain had no right to take possession of the Indies and Indians under any conditions. But Columbus and Spain presumed their right was absolute. So they violated, according to Las Casas, every divine and natural law that protected innocent peoples and lands, and they did so out of blindness to the facts, or out of greed for power and wealth. The letters of Columbus do reveal why Las Casas judged him to be a person of great genius and courage, but a person who was blinded by goals he thought were good, never mind what he had to do to accomplish these goals—unjust war, enslavement, etc. And Columbus was narcissistic enough to believe that God fostered him in what he was about. But he could have known and acted differently, Las Casas maintains, he had the humanity to do so, and he experienced Indian humanity towards himself. Recall also that Las Casas had full access to all the Columbus papers when he was writing this part of the History.*[36]

Letter from Second Voyage.

Ignorance got the Admiral into this error, this blindness—I think I said as much earlier—but inexcusable ignorance.[37] Perhaps he made the judgment that we had more of a right to peoples in the New World—merely

---

[36] See *The Only Way,* Introduction, pp. 48-9, esp. note 74.

[37] *History*, Bk. 1, cap. 122.

because they were infidels—than we did to the people of Barbary, though it
would be a mighty, mighty offense against God if we made war on, made
slaves of the Berbers if they lived in peace with us the way the peoples in the
New World do. It was because the men the Kings employed as a light to
their eyes ignored, in a dark and wicked way, the injustice that went on, that
the Admiral ignored it also. That he was not schooled in conscience is
surely no surprise. No matter. He knew, no one better, by experience, the
goodness, the kindness, the humility, the simplicity, the virtuousness of the
Indian peoples. Nor did anyone but himself make this known to the Kings,
to the Pope, to the world. His judgment was based on his native intelligence,
working as it should, concerning the good things done for him by them from
the start, and the good things he in turn did for them, before any other
Spaniard. He himself convicts himself of great guilt. The Admiral's
intention was good, if one looks simply at intention. And does not measure
it by deed. And allows for mistake and ignorance of the law. I truly believe
this—I think I have also mentioned this before. It is a bizarre thing, a
laughable thing—if the subject were not cause for tears—that he wrote to his
brother to load the ships with slaves, then said the following concerning the
number that should be the Kings': "*In this, in everything, keep a very
accurate count. Take none that are the Kings' or any other person's. Look
to your conscience obligation throughout. There is no other good than the
service of God. For whom all the goods in this world are as nothing. It is
the next world that is forever.*"

These are the very words he addressed to the Lieutenant and sent on
the two ships I spoke about. *I saw the letter itself and his signature on it.*
No recognition, no sense that it was an offense against God, a taking from
another person, to make slaves of so many innocent people. No recognition
that to send off ships filled with slaves, and have that be the primary source
of profit, he would have to make continual war on those wretched Indians,
or would have to seize them unsuspecting in their own villages—and this
happened later in many places—in order to fill the ships.

Letter from Third Voyage.

It was the Admiral, before he left for Castile in March of 1496, or
it was the Lieutenant after the Admiral left, who imposed on certain rulers
and lords the task of working the fields attached to the villages of Spanish
Christians.[38] This was in addition to what the kings and their peoples

---

[38] *History*, Bk. 1, cap. 150.

already paid. Or maybe it was the primary tribute, I have not been able to ascertain which. The Indians were to serve the Spaniards, using every man, woman, child, for their maintenance and for other personal services. From that originated the plague of *repartimiento* and *encomienda*—assigning, controlling Indians—a plague which has devastated, consumed the Indians entirely. I will detail this, please God, in the books that follow. If the kings and their peoples ever stopped providing these services, they were considered rebels in revolt. And they stopped either because they could not bear this, or did not wish to provide it, because they saw their liberty taken and themselves placed in durance vile, in addition to the thousand other routine harassments and cruel impositions and brutal, random treatment they got from the Christians minute to minute. As rebels, war was made against them. Those the Spaniards killed were killed with incredible inhumanity. Those they took alive, they made slaves. Slaves were the primary source of income for the Admiral. With that income, he intended, he expected to repay the money the Kings were spending in support of Spaniards on the island. Then provide profit and income to the Kings. Then make it attractive to merchants to come with merchandise, and to people to come and live. Without asking the Kings to pay the salary, or asking anyone else to pay it.

As to the secondary source of income, he says it is the brasil wood found in the province of Jaquima, which is on the south coast, eighty leagues westward, maybe fewer, from Sancto Domingo. He described both incomes to the Kings—now that he has five ships, which he sent off later, as I will relate—i.e., from four thousand slaves and four thousand quintiles of brasil wood, he assured the Kings they could gain forty millions, even to gain twenty would be big. And in that letter, he says the following:

> "From here, in the name of the Holy Trinity, can be sent all the slaves you could sell, and brasil wood. If the information I have is correct, I am told that four thousand slaves can be sold. At their lowest price, they are worth twenty millions. And four thousand sections of brasil wood, worth another twenty millions. The cost here would be six million. So, at first estimate, if this comes out as expected, there would be a good forty millions. And indeed, the reason given for this seems sound. People buy slaves a lot in Castile and Portugal and Aragon and Italy and Sicily, and the islands owned by Portugal and Aragon, and the Canaries. And I think not many slaves come from Guinea any more. Of those who come, one brings the price of three. I passed some time on the Cape Verde

islands. The people of the island do a large traffic in slaves, and send ships constantly to acquire them. I saw them ask eight thousand maravedis for the worst specimen. . . . Concerning brasil wood, they say they pay a great price in Castile and Aragon and Genoa and Venice, and in France and Flanders, and in England. So, from these two things, according to estimate, forty millions can be gained. Unless there is a lack of ships to come get them. But that will not happen, with the help of Our Lord, once people whet their appetites on a voyage."

A little further on, he says: "So, the slaves are here, the brasil wood, which almost seems alive, and even gold, if it please the Almighty who gave them, and will give them, when He sees it is suitable." Then further on, he says:

"Here there is no obstacle to having the income I described above. Just let a lot of ships come and take the things I spoke of. And I think the sea merchants will soon be addicted to it. Right now, both masters and mariners [He must be speaking of the five ships. LC] leave all rich, and with the intent to return immediately and take the slaves at fifteen hundred maravedis apiece, feed them, and the payment for them comes from the first moneys earned on them. And though they die easily now, it will not always be so. So did the Blacks and Canary islanders at first. There is even an advantage to the Indians [He means the Indians have an advantage over Blacks. LC], i.e. one who survives, his owner would not sell for whatever money they give him."

The Admiral's own words—awkward words in the ways of our Castilian, which he did not understand well, but more than that, callous words.

It is a strange thing, and I have said this before, that a man whom I have to say had a good nature and meant well, should be so blind in such a clear matter. One could indeed tell me it was not at all strange for him to be blind, for many learned men, whom the Kings kept close to them, were blind themselves. For they did not enlighten the Admiral, did not condemn the blindness he had. He based the whole income and temporal gain of the Kings, of his own people, of the Spaniards, the whole success of the enterprise of the Indies he had discovered on traffic in innocent Indi-

ans—better say their blood—made slaves in wicked, abhorrent ways, as if
Indians were pieces, he calls them that, or goats by the head, like the wild
ones they have on the Cape Verde islands. And on flooding Castile and
Portugal and Aragon and Italy and Sicily and the Portugese and Aragonese
islands, and the Canaries where, the story was, they bought lots of slaves.
I mean flooding scores of countries and provinces with Indians enslaved in
the holy and just ways I described, with no scruple about some of them dying
in the process—it is certain that not ten out of a hundred survive at the end
of a year—because, as he says, Blacks and Canary islanders also die. Is there
a greater or grosser callousness, blindness than this? And the good part of
it comes when he says that in the name of the Most Holy Trinity he can send
all the slaves they can sell in all those countries. I have often thought the
Admiral picked up this blindness and corruption, got it into himself, from
what the Portugese did, still do, in their dealings in Guinea—or rather, their
damnable tyranny.

Letter From Third Voyage.

It was in early October, 1500, that the two caravels left Sancto
Domingo with the Admiral and his brothers aboard in chains.[39] Our Lord
was pleased not to stretch the voyage, but to shorten the imprisonment,
because they reached Cadiz on 20 or 25 November. The Admiral and his
brothers were well treated en route by Alonso de Vallejo and the other
master. I said earlier he was named Andrés Martín de la Gorda, and his
caravel bore the same name. I think he was also charged with watching over
the prisoners. The masters wanted to remove the shackles. The Admiral did
not want it so, until the Kings should order them removed. I heard it said
back then that Master Andrés Martín, upon arrival at Cadiz, allowed a
servant of the Admiral to slip secretly ashore with letters to the Kings and
other people, before he handed over the data from the investigation. The
master thought the Kings would be moved by the letters, would read them
before the ones from the Commandant, then do what ought to be done for the
Admiral . . .
I have not found an original nor a summary of the letters the
Admiral would have written from Cadiz to the Kings. Maybe he decided not
to write them. But wanted them to know through others, because he felt so
humiliated by their power, and thought maybe it was their decision that
caused his arrest. He did, however, write a lengthy letter to the governess

---

[39] *History*, Bk. 1, cap. 181.

of Prince Don Juan, may he be with God. She was very fond of the Admiral and recommended him to the Queen as much as she could. The contents of the letter follow. The openness of the Admiral is apparent at the very start of it, and the little use he had for bloated titles, then in use in Spain.

"Most Kind Lady: If my complaint about the world is modern, the world's habit of bad treatment is ancient. It has fought me a thousand fights. I won them all up to now. Now arms and advice are no help to me. I am beaten down and cruelly. Only hope in the One who creates us all sustains me. His help always came swiftly. Once, not long ago, I was beaten, but He raised me up with His right hand, saying, 'O man of little faith, arise, I am here, be not afraid.'

"I came here with a deep desire to serve these Princes. And I served them in a way never heard of, never seen before. That new heaven, new earth Our Lord spoke of through St. John in the Apocalypse, the ones first announced through the mouth of Isaiah, God made me a herald of, and revealed that region. There was disbelief in everyone. The Queen, Our Lady, brought to the project a spirit of understanding, a forcefulness, and made of it a personal preoccupation, as if it were a dearly beloved daughter. I was to take possession of everything in her royal name. And those who were ignorant wanted to supply for their ignorance by shifting what little they knew into talk about difficulties and costs. But her Highness approved the project, against the talk, and supported it as much as she could.

"Seven years passed in talk, back then, and nine in doing things that were great and worthy of memory. People have no idea. I have returned. I am in such a state that the worst low-lifer thinks he can revile me. It is considered a virtue in the world for anyone able to resist doing it. If I stole the Indies, a land which is now being Christianized—that's the story at the moment—and handed it over to the Moors, Spain would not be more inimical to me than it is now. Who would believe that of a place with such nobility in it?

"I would very much like to be quit of this business, if it would be honest towards the Queen to do so. But the impetus of Our Lord and of Her Highness required me to keep on. To get some relief from the straits I was in due to the death [the Admiral refers here to the death at that time of the Prince Don Juan (4 October, 1497 in Salamanca)] I undertook a new voyage to a new region of the earth that until that date lay hidden. And if the new discovery is not held here in high esteem—just as the others were not—that is no wonder, because it seems to derive from my efforts.

"I thought this voyage to Paria would satisfy people because of the pearls, and the discovery of gold on Hispaniola. I ordered the Indians of Paria to unite and fish for pearls. We agreed that I would return for them, a half a bushel, as I understood it. But the same thing happened to me as had in so many other things. I would not have lost those pearls nor my honor if I had sought my own good and let Hispaniola be lost, or if my privileges and agreements were respected. And I say as much of the gold I had managed to build up to a goodly pile by the grace of God, despite the deaths and difficulties. When I arrived by way of Paria, I found almost half the men on Hispaniola in rebellion. They made war on me as if I were a Moor, right up to now, and on the Indians in the other direction, severely. [And why did you make war on them, oppress them unjustly? The Indians I mean. LC] Right then, Hojeda arrived and tried to finish things off. He said their Highnesses had sent him and his group on the promise of gifts and privileges and pay. He collected a large gang, freebooter types, none with wife or child, almost the only kind of man on Hispaniola. Hojeda harmed me badly. He had to go. He left word that he would be back with more ships, more men, and that when he sailed from Spain the Queen, Our Lady, was on the point of death. Then Vicente Yañez arrived with four caravels. There was confusion, suspicion, but no harm. The Indians later reported six other caravels brought by the magistrate's brother, but that was malicious, and after the other things when the hope was quite dashed that their Highnesses would ever send a ship out to the Indies, and the word around was that her Highness was dead.

"Then a certain Adrián rebelled once again, as he had before. But Our Lord did not permit his bad purpose to succeed. I made up my mind not to touch a hair of anyone's head, but with regard to him, his ingratitude, it was not possible to keep to what I intended, sad to say. And if what he wanted was to kill me and take over the power my King and Queen had put in my charge, he would do no less to my brother.

"For six months, I was anxious to come to their Highnesses with the good news about the gold, and quit governing dissolute men who feared not God nor King nor Queen, men filled with deceit and malice. But as a condition for leaving, I asked their Highnesses often, often, to send someone, at my expense, to be in charge of justice. And after I found the magistrate in rebellion, I asked again for a man, or some men, or some official with credentials. My reputation was such that if I built churches and hospitals, they would be called dens of thieves thereafter. Finally, the Kings came through. With someone quite the opposite of what the situation demanded. Good luck to him, because I had served two years in his office without being able to gain a single authoritative decree for myself or anyone else who was there. And this man arrived with a trunkful. God only knows if everything will work for him. Already, for starters, there are exemptions for twenty years—the working life of a man—in the matter of gold. A man can get five marks of gold in four hours. I will expand on this later.

"I wish Their Majesties would dispel a myth about what is hardest for people who suffer. My greatest suffering came from people's malediction of me, not from things failing me—lengthy service, possessions, authority. It would be a charity towards me, the restoration of my good name. People could talk about it everywhere, because the venture overseas is of such kind that it must be talked about every day, and highly prized.

"So comes Commandant Bobadilla to Sancto Domingo. I was in Vega, the Lieutenant in Xaragua where Adrián had his headquarters. The land is flat and rich and everyone was at peace. On the second day after he arrived, he made himself governor, he named officials, did executions, proclaimed exemptions for gold, for tithes, for practically everything else, for twenty years, the working life of a man. He came to pay everyone, though they had not at that point completed their service. And he proclaimed that he must send me back in chains, my brothers also. Which is what he did. So I should never return there, nor any of my descendants. He said of me a thousand false, uncalled for things. That was on the second day after he arrived, as I said. And I was absent, a long way off, and knew nothing of him nor of his arrival. He filled out some letters of Their Majesties that were left blank but signed, he had a number of them, then sent them to Roldán and his crowd, granting them privileges and grants of Indians. He sent me never a letter or message. He has not to this day. I thought what could he be thinking of, the one who took my place, raising up and favoring someone who had undertaken to rob Their Highnesses, who had done so much evil, damage, had dragged down someone who had sustained things through so much danger? [The Admiral was more than right about this. LC] When I knew the situation, I thought it must be like the Hojeda caper, or some other. It calmed me when I learned from the friars that Their Highnesses had indeed sent him out.[40] I wrote him a welcome on his arrival, and said I was in a hurry to sail for court and had sold what I held, but about the exemptions, he should not go so fast, and that I would hand the governorship over with open palms. Thus I wrote to the religious.

"Neither he nor they answered me. Instead, he struck a belligerent pose and required that everyone who came should swear an oath to him as governor, for twenty years, people told me. As soon as I heard about the exemptions, I thought to correct such a great error. And said that he should be moderate, he gave the exemptions without need, without reason, on an excessive scale, to drifters, but excessive even to those with a wife and children. I made it known, orally and in writing, that he was not to use his authorizations because mine were stronger, and I showed him the authorizations Juan Aguado occasioned. All that I did was to delay so Their Highnesses could find out the condition of the territory, so they would have a chance to reissue commands as to what would serve them best. The publication of tax exemptions in the Indies was halted. There was no need to proclaim exemptions in the Indies. The settlers who took land there profited right away. They were given the best land for their four years stay, worth nearly 200,000 maravedis, without their even putting a spade to it. I could not say if the settlers were married or not, but there were maybe six out of them all who did not purpose to pile up what they could and then leave right after. [This was the reason the ruin of the Indies sped up. Spaniards were there only long enough to grab what they wanted. LC]

"It is good to go out from Castile. And good to know who does and why. And settle [Hispaniola] with respectable people. I had an agreement with those settlers, they would hand in a third of the gold, pay the tithes, and this at their request. They accepted the conditions with great thanks to Their Highnesses. I criticized them when I heard they complained and expected the Commandant to do much of the same. But he did something further. He aroused their anger against me saying I wanted to take from them what Their Highnesses had given. And tried to lay the blame on me. And succeeded. And they should write the Kings not to have me in charge anymore. And I appealed this, for myself, for my possessions, because I have no other nation. He set up with them a criminal investigation

---

[40] Varela [p. 266] identifies them as Juan de Leudelle, Juan de Robles and Juan Trasier, "who wrote letters to Cisneros against Columbus."

concerning me. Hell has not known the like of it. Long ago, Our Lord rescued Daniel—and the three young men—just through what wits and strength Daniel had. With the same equipment, if it were the good pleasure of God, I could have rescued the whole situation, and the situation just described which happened after I was out in the Indies, by just allowing myself to look out for my own good. If it were honest of me to do so. But the business of justice and of expanding Their Majesties' realm had a deep grip on me. Today, since so much gold has been found, there is a dispute over what gains it most, robbery or mining. They get now one hundred castellanos for a woman, same as for a field, and this is done a lot, there are already many merchants who search out girls—the nine to ten year olds are at a premium, but all ages are thought useful.

"The bad-mouthing by the malcontents has brought me a greater loss than all my services brought me gain, a bad precedent for the present and future. I swear that a bunch of men have gone out to the Indies who did not deserve a goodbye from God or man. And they are now going back there. Bobadilla made them enemies of me. And it seems there was an understanding between them—judging from what happened and the ways it did—or, as the story goes, he spent a lot to get that understanding. I know no more than hearsay. I never heard of an official investigator who got the rebels together and used them against their chief, nor called other types not worth anyone's trust. If Their Highnesses will order a general investigation out there, they will see, I tell you, that it is a miracle the island does not founder. I think your grace will remember that when the storm drove me, without sail, into Lisbon, I was accused falsely of having gone there in order to hand the Indies over to the King. Their Highnesses later learned the opposite, that the accusation was made out of malice. I do not know very much, but I know no one who thinks me so stupid as not to realize that if indeed the Indies were mine, I could not last without the help of some prince. That being so, where could I get or keep a better, firmer support than in the King and Queen, our Lords? They have made me something of high worth out of nothing. They are the most noble princes, on land and sea, in this world. They judged that I served them, they preserved my grants and privileges. And if anyone threatened them, Their Highnesses increased them further, as is evident in the Juan Aguado incident. They ordered that I be honored. And, as I said, Their Majesties have been served by me already, and my sons are their servants. I could

not have reached this level with any other princes because where
there is no affection, all else halts.

"I was just talking about slander, made with malice, a
maligning of what I intended. Something I would not want to recall
even in dreams. Because Commandant Bobadilla decided in all this
to steep whatever he did in malice. I could show you it best if I wrote
with my left hand—it was his ignorance coupled with his gross greed
that made him act like this. I told you how I wrote him and the friars,
then set out, alone, as I said, because all the men were with the
Lieutenant. Alone also to lift any suspicion he had.

"But he, when he found out, imprisoned Don Diego, in a
caravel, loaded him with shackles. And did the same to me as soon
as I arrived. And the same to the Lieutenant when he came. We had
no conversation after that. Nor did he allow anyone else to talk to
me, to this day. And I swear to you, I do not know why I was made
prisoner. The first thing he did was seize the gold, which had not
been measured and weighed. In my absence. He said he wanted to
pay the men with it. And from what I heard, he took the first bit for
himself, then sent men out to scour up some new stuff. I had set aside
certain specimens of that gold, nuggets, large as eggs, some goose
size, some chicken, some pullet, and of many another shape. They
had been gathered by various people in a short space of time. They
were to please Their Highnesses and give them a greater understanding of the venture. And for that reason too, there were a number of
rocks shot through with gold. That was the first thing he did out of
malice, so Their Highnesses would not consider the venture worth
much until he could feather his own nest, which he was quick about
doing. The gold which was to be smelted shrank in the fire. A chain
which would weigh almost twenty marks was not seen again. I have
been very grieved over this matter of the gold, more than over the
pearls I could not present to Their Highnesses. Wherever the
Commandant thought he could do me damage, he did so immediately.
He could have paid everyone with 600,000 maravedis, no need to
steal from anyone to do it. There were more than 400,000 in tithes
and fees. No need to touch the gold. His largess was ridiculous,
though I think he began it with himself first. Their Highnesses will
know all about it when they order an accounting made, especially if
I am in on it. He says only that a great sum is owed, it is the sum I
mentioned, it is not so great.

"And I was deeply grieved when an investigator was sent in
on me. Who understood that if the investigation he conducted turned

up something serious, he was to remain in control. Would to God Their Highnesses had sent him or someone two years before. I know I would now be free of scandal and infamy, and my honor would not have been taken from me, I would not have lost it. God is just, and it must be that God knows the how and the why of things. They think of me here as if I were a governor who went to Sicily or to a city or village already under law, where the laws can be kept in their entirety, without fear of total breakdown. And this was grievous to me. I ought to be judged as a military man who left Spain to go conquer, out in the Indies, a bellicose and numerous people, whose customs and belief were quite opposed to ours. [The Admiral did not call them bellicose when Guacaganarí saved him, his person, his goods, when his ship was lost. The amnesia of the Admiral about the rescue is remarkable. LC] There, by the will of God [God permitted it, God did not want it. LC], I placed a whole other world under the rule of the King and Queen, our Lords. And from this, Spain, once called poor, is the world's richest. [Because these riches were acquired immorally, Spain ended up being the poorest nation in the world. LC]

"I ought to be judged as a military man who has had his weapons strapped on from a long time back, up to the present, without taking them off for an hour, a leader of knights of conquest, of veterans, not men out of literature, be they Greeks or Romans or others more modern—of which there are so many and such noble examples in Spain—nor any similar. I am blamed because there is no civilization in the Indies. The door is opened onto gold and pearls and quantities of everything else, precious stones, spices. And one can firmly expect a thousand other things.

"I said I would give some news about gold. This: on Christmas day, when I was under great pressure, warred on by bad Christians and by Indians, I was on the point of leaving everything, if I could, of escaping life. But Our Lord consoled me, miraculously, and said, "Be strong, and not afraid. I will provide in everything. The seven years for finding gold are not over. During those years and about gold, I will give you a sign." That day I learned there were eighty leagues of land, there were mines throughout. It is still true today, from the looks of things. Some men have gotten 120 castellanos in a day, other 90, as much as 250 have been gotten, or 50 to 70, many another man 20 to 50. That is a good take for a day, and many still achieve it. The average is 6 to 12. Whoever gets less is unhappy. It seems that those mines are like all the others and do not produce the same every day. The mines are new, as are the miners. The common opinion is that if everyone in Castile should go out there, he would not get less than one or two castellanos no matter how lazy he was, and the opinion is still fresh today. It's true that the miners have an Indian [It is not an Indian they hold, but many, who sweat and die at the mining. LC], but the mining depends on the Christian [The mine depending on the Christian means the latter holds the Indians by force, he beats and beats them, has no pity on them. LC].

"Think about how prudent it was for Bobadilla to give all this for nothing, and 400,000 in tithes, without cause, without their asking! Without first notifying Their Majesties! And that is not the only damage done. I know that my mistakes were not made for a bad motive. I think Their Highnesses understand it is so, as I explain it. And I know, I know they act mercifully towards those who serve them badly. So I believe, I am sure, they will have a much greater compassion on me. I am in this situation innocently and by force, as you will realize completely later. I am their creature. They will see my services and they will know day by day they are made richer by them. Let them put everything on a scale, just as Holy Scripture tells us good with evil will be on the Day of Judgment. If they still require that someone else be my judge, and I hope not, and that it be through an investigation of the Indies, I humbly beg that they send out two people of conscience who are respected. At my expense. They will find out quickly that one can get five marks of gold in four hours. Whether they do or not, they must settle this matter. The Commandant, when he came to Sancto Domingo, settled himself in my house. Whatever he found, he took for himself. Good luck to him, maybe he will need it. A pirate never treated a merchant as badly. My biggest complaint is over my papers. Which he has taken on me. I will never get a sheet back. And those of mine that most acquit me, he has kept most out of sight. Behold how just and honest the investigator! A hint of what else he has done, they say he has gone beyond the bounds of justice, absolutely. God, Our Lord, is present with power, as usual, and punishes all at the end, especially harm done by ingratitude."[41]

---

[41] See Varela, doc. XLI, Christopher Columbus to Doña Juana de Torres, Governess of Prince Don Juan. Varela prefers Las Casas' copy to all other copies of this famous letter.

- 4 -

Rogues' Gallery

Prenote

In 1496, Bartholomew Columbus was instructed by his brother, the Admiral, to subdue Hispaniola and force the kings on the island to pay tribute. The Admiral needed to show a quick profit to the Catholic Kings so they would continue to back his discoveries. Tribute exaction and slave taking would provide that profit. Both illegal and immoral. Bartholomew, called the Lieutenant, initiated a policy of terror during the time the Admiral was back in Spain, 1496-1498, in order to acquire tribute and slaves. Las Casas will later describe this policy of terror as it affected the whole of the Indies.[42] In this selection, he shows it at its early stages. But more than that, Las Casas shows the fidelity practiced by one Indian leader, Guarionex, as over against the treachery practiced by one Spanish leader, Bartholomew. The contrast symbolises the Indian-Spanish relationship later everywhere. Las Casas judges that Guarionex had justice totally on his side. And judges that Spaniards never felt bound to keep their word. So innocent Indian sovereignty was violated, and Indian conscience as well. The genius of Las Casas' narrative lies in the fact that he uses the same human reference points for both Indian and Spaniard, thereby revealing the fidelity of the one and the treachery of the other. Las Casas knew the Lieutenant some ten years after this event, and he knew the Columbus family for years thereafter.[43]

---

[42] *Bartolomé de las Casas' Pro-Indian Tracts*, Vol. 1, *New Laws to Halt Decimation*, trans. by Francis Patrick Sullivan, Introduction by Helen Rand Parish (Kansas City: Sheed & Ward, 1994—in preparation). See Introduction, p. 13.

[43] *Las Casas' Life of Columbus*, trans. by Francis Patrick Sullivan, Introduction by Helen Rand Parish (Berkeley: University of California Press, 1994—in preparation). See Introduction, "Columbus' Papal Appointment," and "Summation of New Insights."

a. Guarionex Doomed

Rebellions, quarrels between traitor and non-traitor, caused great suffering, terrible hardship among the Indians.[44] Wherever traitor or non-traitor went, both ate up their food, coerced them into carrying packs on their backs of up to a hundred pounds, did brutal and violent things to their persons, their children, their wives. Especially Roldán's men. His disgraceful behavior got more damnable and diabolic with everything he did. Both traitor and non-traitor ended up killing these innocent peoples—no fear of God, no cause from the Indians—killing them by means that were fiendish, inventive. Not every now and then, but every day and often, for recreation they shot a crossbow at an Indian to see if the arrow could go right through. They made an Indian run by, to cut him in half with a sword. By he went, the lamb for the slaughter, they took a back stroke at him, and if one slice did not cut him in two, they made another run by, another, another. They slaughtered as many as they pleased, and roaring laughing. And if the Indians lugging the hundred pound packs got tired, they hamstrung them, and piled their packs on those already loaded down, on women as well. The woman who was unable to bear up, they ran a spear through, added her pack to some other woman, who collapsed under the weight she carried, then they killed her too. And there were other damnable cruelties committed, one cannot imagine . . .

Guarionex and many of his people decided to flee and seek asylum in the realm of another king, king of mountainous territory whose rivers flowed north to the sea, across the breadth of the Vega. Where rivers flowed south, that was the realm of Guarionex. The northern king was Mayobanex, otherwise known to the Spaniards as Billygoat. I don't know why, mockery maybe. . . He was lord of a lot of people who lived spread throughout the mountains. They were called *ciguayos* . . . because they never cut a hair off their heads, they wore it hung down to the waist, even lower . . . The ciguayos were a forceful people, but hen-like in comparison to ours—they carried no weapons and went around naked.

When Guarionex reached the place of Mayobanex, he told, with tears and heavy heart, the tale of calamities he and his people suffered from the Christians. He begged Mayobanex to take him under his protection. He wanted safety only for his person, his wife, his children, relatives. He left his people unprotected, he could not defend them, could not hold out against the Christians. The word among our people was that some Spaniard had seized and raped his wife. Mayobanex received him with great kindness, was happy to, and listened closely to the story of his troubles, of the cruel,

---

[44] *History*, Bk. 1, caps. 120-1.

cruel oppression and persecution he and his people were undergoing. Mayobanex knew of the behavior of the Christians through reports that reached him daily. He grieved for Guarionex, he promised to protect him, to do everything he could to keep him free.

... The Christians noticed Guarionex was missing, noticed a lot of people were gone from the villages, and more going every day. They wrote from the fort at Concepción to the Lieutenant at Santo Domingo that King Guarionex was in rebellion. Guarionex was a principal ruler, his people were all near the mines, from them was gotten the most tribute. If he failed to come through with it, there was little from elsewhere. So the Lieutenant quickly marshaled ninety soldiers, the healthiest in Santo Domingo, and some cavalrymen, and set out for the Vega and the fort at Concepción. He began to interrogate every Indian he ran across, or could scare up—where had Guarionex gone? They didn't know. He pressured them with threats, he tortured them—and I have no doubt of it. That's what was done at every stage out in the Indies, and still is. The Spaniards thus learned that he was in the land of the ciguayos with King Mayobanex. The Lieutenant went right there, climbed into the mountains with his men, came down into a valley through which ran a swollen river, flushed two Indian lookouts—one got away, the other he caught. He wanted to torture the truth out of him, but the man told without torture. This: that a little beyond the river, there was a large party of men, ciguayos, up on the mountain side, waiting to attack the Christians.

They did indeed, with a war cry, and a fearsome sound it was. They shot off a volley of a thousand arrows, a squall of them, but they shot from far off—they did not dare come much closer, on this island at least, they knew how swords cut and the speed of horses. They exhausted their supply, had little effect. The Christians attacked, especially the cavalry, killed some, but the Indians had the hills near to hide in. They vanished during the night. The Christians camped in the mountains. Next day, they recommenced their pursuit of the Indians. They reached a village which they found abandoned. They caught an Indian who told that three or four leagues ahead was the village of Mayobanex, and he was there with a huge party of ciguayos ready to wage war. So the Christians went after them. From the hills where they hid, many shot arrows at the Christians, and wounded some. But the Christians did not give them time to form for battle, they attacked, they killed many, shot many with their crossbows, gutted many with their swords, chopped off arms and legs to a fare-thee-well, took lots of slaves.

The Lieutenant sent one captive to Mayobanex to say he hadn't come to make war on him or his people. But instead wanted his friendship and would be faithful to it as long as Mayobanex desired. The Lieutenant was in search of Guarionex, and knew Mayobanex had him hidden, and was making war on the Christians at his persuasion. The Indian was to ask, to demand that Guarionex be given over to the Lieutenant. Who would then be Mayobanex's good friend forever, and be favorable forever to whatever concerned his realm or his subjects. If he did not hand Guarionex over, he should know that the Lieutenant would go after him with fire and slaughter to his utter destruction.

It is crucial to note the reply Mayobanex made: "Tell the Christians that Guarionex is a good and honorable man. He has done evil to no one—that is a public, a known fact. For that reason, he is worthy of a heartfelt help in his humiliation and flight, worthy of support and protection. But the Spaniards are evil men, tyrants. They come for one reason, to seize land not theirs. They know only how to spill the blood of people who never provoked them. Therefore, say to them, I do not want their favor, nor to see them, nor hear them. Instead I intend to try, with all the power I have, my people have, to smash and drive out the Christians from this land. I take the side of Guarionex." And so no one will think I made up this reply out of my own head, whoever wants can consult chapter 6 of the first "Década" of Pedro Mártir where mention is made of the same.[45] . . .

This would not be a surprise among peoples advanced politically, refined intellectually in the arts and sciences. But off in regions remote from here and hidden from us? Among peoples who go naked, are unlettered, unlearned, primitive, with minimum social structure? To find such refuge and support, such protection and compassion, at the height of one's peril, is a surprise! And it leads us to judge they are as rational and human as any, any other human being. A judgment they merit.

When the Lieutenant learned the decision of King Mayobanex, he ordered a scorched earth policy—the Spaniards torched the villages in the area. Then they advanced. The Lieutenant tried again, sent messengers to Mayobanex telling him to send some of his closest advisors to arrange for peace, because the Spaniards did not want to destroy him or his people or his land. Mayobanex sent someone of high rank, plus two others as aides. The Lieutenant spoke at length with him. Told him to explain to his Lord Mayobanex that it was madness to be willing to lose himself, his people, his land, for Guarionex. The Lieutenant required only one thing of him, to hand over Guarionex, for due punishment—he had not paid the tribute he owed to the Kings of Castile, as set by the Admiral. And further, had fled and hidden out. If the King handed Guarionex over, he and the Lieutenant would be fast friends forever. If the King did not, the Lieutenant would destroy him, be

---

[45] Pedro Mártir, dec. 1, cap. 6.

sure of it. A neat claim the Lieutenant urged! And monstrous crimes had Guarionex committed against the Kings of Castile! The King had not paid them their tribute, the violently, tyrannically imposed tribute! He had fled, had hidden, unable to put up with such horrid injustice. The King had the right to wage a just war against the Lieutenant! Against those who trooped after him! And against the Kings of Castile, if the Admiral had done the imposing on their authority, on their consent. For my part, I am sure that if the Kings caught on to the imposition, and knew what blood was spilled to get the tribute, what scandal to the faith, what mockery of basic justice, what mindlessness, they would never have consented to it, wanted it, nor put their stamp of approval on it.

Once Mayobanex heard the statement of the messenger, he called together his people. He made them aware of the message and threat of the Lieutenant and the Christians. His people all said as one that he should hand Guarionex over since he was the reason why the Christians attacked and destroyed them. Mayobanex replied it was not a reason for handing him over to his enemies. Guarionex was a good man, had never done anyone harm. What was more, Guarionex had always been his friend, he was indebted to him. The man had taught him and his queen to do the regional dances of Magua—dances of the Vega, the region of Guarionex. And they were not to be held in poor esteem. But most of all, Guarionex had come to his aid, and that of his own realm. He in turn promised to protect and defend Guarionex. Therefore, Mayobanex could not abandon him, no matter what risk, what harm he underwent.

He summoned Guarionex and the two began to commiserate with each other. Mayobanex lifted his counterpart's spirit, urged him not to fear the Christians. Mayobanex would defend him, even at the cost of kingdom and life. He ordered lookouts posted, and men at the ready all along the routes the Christians could come. They were to kill any messenger, Christian or Indian.

Right then, the Lieutenant sent two messengers, Indians; one a captive taken in war, a ciguayan by birth, a subject of Mayobanex; the other, a relative, from the Vega, a subject of Guarionex. The Lieutenant crept along behind them somewhat, with ten soldiers on foot and four men on horse. A short way out, he found the two messengers dead on the road. The Lieutenant was furious about this; his anger against Mayobanex mounted; he determined to destroy him. He called forward his whole crew, went to the main village where Mayobanex was with a mass of his people ready for war—war with their little-or-no weapons, bare-naked and brave looking. The fury of the Christians hit them, they deserted their King. They knew from experience they stood no chance of winning against crossbows, swords—less than none against horses—they would all die. Mayobanex found himself alone, except for the few who stayed—relatives, close associates—so he decided to get lost in the mountains. The ciguayan people were enraged at Guarionex, he was the reason for their rout, their wretchedness. They decided to kill him and hand him over to the Christians so their own suffering would cease. But Guarionex took the only way of escape, up into the hills, eating plants raw and roots the Indians call guayaros, all the while bitter about his suffering which was so unmerited and mindless.

On the hunt, the Christians care nothing about delicate eats, they just want to have lots of cassava. They put up with terrible hunger, terrible hardship. And though they wear down the Indians pursuing them from place to place, though they seem to triumph over those naked wretches, God, the Just Judge, pummels and punishes them in the very things they do. They suffer severely from hunger and thirst up among the mountain peaks—the hideouts of the harried and hunted Indians. The Christians undergo unbelievable hardships—so great, so harsh, so extreme they beggar description. These men would really be the equal of true martyrs if what they suffered, in order to gain money and with money an earthly paradise—but end up on the road to hell stripped of every cent—they suffered for the sake of gaining the good that gave them the only right they had to enter these lands, i.e., to win these peoples to Christ, only that. But eventually those involved in this manhunt, manslaughter, were tired after three months, famished and worn out, so they asked the Lieutenant, now that the Indians were beaten, to give them leave to go to the Vega—the men who had places there—so they could get some home rest. He allowed this, but stayed himself, and thirty men. With them he went village by village, mountain by mountain, in search of the two lords, Mayobanex and Guarionex. So long as he did not find them, he killed or captured everyone he came across. The Lieutenant took enough Indians along to carry his packs and hunt up food, and trap for rodents. The other Christians took what Indians they could, wherever they went, for their use or for their pleasure. If they had a Castilian dog, they sent it hunting food, while they kept hunting men.

Then two hunters flushed and captured two scouts, or if not scouts, two men Mayobanex had sent for food supplies to some one of his peoples' villages. The hunters hauled them to the Lieutenant. He threatened to torture them, or maybe he did. Torture was in constant use in the Indies. Because Indians are ordinarily very faithful to their leaders. They keep their leaders' instructions secret so their whereabouts may not be found. The Indians sustain terrible torture before they reveal anything they were told to conceal. And many let themselves be cut to pieces rather than talk. But ultimately, under torture, or threat of it, the two said they knew where their lord Mayobanex was.

Twelve of the Christians volunteered to take him captive. They stripped to their skins. They rubbed themselves with a dark stain, reddish in part, from the fruit of a tree called bixa, exactly the way the Indians do when at war or when fleeing. They chose their guides very carefully. They reached where Mayobanex was, with just his wife, children, some relatives, and he was off guard. The Christians pulled their swords. They had brought them concealed in palm leaves—leaves called yaguas—borne across their shoulders as if bearing packs, the way Indians bear them. Mayobanex let himself be taken, terrified lest he and his wife and children would be hacked to pieces. The Lieutenant led them all off on a rope, king, queen, children. He was exultant beyond words at the capture.

He took the captives to Concepción, and put the king in shackles and chains for having given aid and comfort and protection to a fellow king—something Mayobanex was obligated to do by natural law, and by the respect and devotion he owed to his native land—when that fellow king had been put in a desperate and deadly situation, brutally, irrationally, unjustly. So he was treated dreadfully, stripped with shameless cruelty of kingdom, power, freedom, for something Moors would have to praise, and Jews, and Gentiles, and barbarians, and most Christians.

There was a cousin or sister of Mayobanex who was with him and his wife and children during the flight, during the terrors of the chase. Mayobanex had given her as wife to a neighboring chief from somewhere in that province of ciguayos. She was said to be the most beautiful woman ever seen on that island, though it had many outstanding for their beauty. She was captured along with Mayobanex and his family. Her husband lived as a fugitive in the mountains. His nights and days were filled with grief because he found no solution to his predicament, nothing to console him. He made the choice to go to the Vega and surrender to the Lieutenant. There he begged, begged in tears and dejection, that the Lieutenant return his wife to him, and if so, he, his household, all his people, would serve the Lieutenant like slaves. The Lieutenant readily returned his wife to him, and some of his principal people who had also been captured. The Indian was subservient from that time on. Of his own accord, he brought in four to five thousand men, unarmed, with just their staves, which are fire-hardened pointed poles they use for digging. He asked if he could prepare a cassava field for the Lieutenant, anywhere the Lieutenant chose. The place was indicated. He tilled a huge field. In the fifteen or twenty days he was there, his people were able to prepare a cassava field of such size that it was later worth thirty thousand castellanos.

It got known throughout the territory of the ciguayos that the woman, the wife of that lord, had been returned to him—she was that well known, that well admired, everywhere around. So the principal people throughout the region thought they might also win freedom for their king and lord Mayobanex. A large number of them agreed to try. They brought their small gifts of bread and meat and fish, already prepared. They have no other riches. The Indians never come with empty hands to see the Christians, especially to petition something. When they arrived, they begged every way they could that their king Mayobanex be freed from his chains. Then they would be obedient forever, and subservient to the Lieutenant and the Christians. The Lieutenant freed the queen, freed the captive members of her family, children, relatives, servants. But tears and supplications could in no way bring the Lieutenant to release their king from chains.

Some days after this, King Guarionex came out in the open to find food. He lived up in the crags and caves of the region, and could no longer sustain the wretched existence he had to lead, especially the hunger. He could not go unnoticed. Ciguayos people came every day to visit their lord Mayobanex at the fort on the Vega, Concepción, and bring him food. Someone was bound to tip off the Lieutenant that Guarionex was in such and such a place. The Lieutenant despatched a squad of Spaniards, plus some Indians, to go catch him. The found him easily and brought him back captive and under strict guard. They imprisoned him in the fort at Concepción, separate from Mayobanex. He was shackled in irons and weighted down with suffering, the man who was ruler over the better part of the whole island. For no fault of his own, for no reason. Right in the middle of his own jurisdiction. In addition to the thousand, the ten thousand hurts and harms and harassments he had sustained from the time the Christians landed on the island. They held him in that narrow prison, that bitter existence, for three years, until 1502, when they sent him to Castile in chains. They were the reason he perished at sea, dead by drowning. I will describe this in the next volume, please God.

As for the other good King, the faithful Mayobanex, I did not think to ask how he died when I had the chance, when we were discussing the two. I think he died in prison. When I came to the island, it would have been two years since his capture and suffering had taken place.

b. Ovando the Terrible

Prenote

The text that follows derives from Las Casas' experience of the Indies from 1501 onward. It is from Twenty Reasons Against Encomienda, *written in 1542, as part of a presentation to a reform commission set up by Charles V to fashion new laws for the Indies.[46] The laws were to forbid encomienda—a system of apportionment of natives to Spaniards for whatever use the Spaniards wished to make of them—because it was destructive of native life, and forbid wars of conquest, tribute exaction, enslavement, brutalizing labor, etc. Las Casas succeeded in having new laws written, they were all the product of his work.[47] He had to present the history of encomienda, its lawlessness, its lethal effects, in order to make his case convincing. So he had to hark back in time to the period when Ovando governed, 1501-1510, a period he witnessed for the most part, and he had to detail the growth of the terrible abuse of Indian life. In this text, he places the events against the backdrop of instructions sent out by Queen Isabella to her governor concerning the treatment of native peoples. It was misinformation about the Indians that provoked the writing of the letter, and there was a certain blindness on the part of the Queen concerning the right of Spain to be in the Indies in the first place. Las Casas does not, by including the Queen's letter, imply that what went on was just an abuse of a good system. It was a bad system, no matter how it was organized, because Spain had no right to Indian life or territory. Whatever the case, Las Casas really wants his hearers to know what was done to subjugate Indian life after the departure of Christopher Columbus in chains, how utterly inhuman, unchristian it was, and how the situation, still the same after 42 years, begged for a human, a Christian solution. The description of how encomienda came to be is the important element in the following text. After the wars of conquest and enslavement, it is the next step in the destructive pattern set going by Spain in the New World.*

---

[46] Bartolomé de las Casas, *Tratados* (Mexico City: Fondo de Cultura Económica, 1965), vol. 2, pp. 767-803 [hereafter *Tratados*]. For the history of the manuscript, see Wagner-Parish, Catalogue #19, pp. 268-9.

[47] Bartolomé de las Casas, *Conclusiones sumarias sobre el remedio de las Indias* (Madrid: Biblioteca Nacional, 1992). In this publication, Helen Rand Parish, in her article "Las Casas Ante La Congregación De Carlos V Sobre Las Indias Y Los Indios," says that the document "shows definitively the paternity or influence of Las Casas vis-a-vis the New Laws."

Eleventh Reason

Encomienda Unjust, Unlawful

The eleventh reason is this: The granting of the Indians in encomienda to the Spaniards has always lacked authorization by the Kings.[48] The person who first devised it—dividing up the Indians of Haiti wholesale among the Spaniards as if dividing herds of cattle, a division that resulted in decimating the population of the whole island—never had authority to do so. He went well beyond the limits, the bounds set for his office. Consequently, the encomienda he started was null and void always. That man was the Grand Commander of Alcántara.[49] Our gracious Catholic sovereigns Don Ferdinand and Doña Isabella sent him from the city of Granada in 1502, he was Grand Commander of Lares at the time, to govern Hispaniola. They were only three hundred, the Spanish Christians on the island then, not a one anywhere else in the New World. In the orders this governor carried overseas from Their Highnesses, he was instructed clearly, he was charged to govern and rule the Indians as free peoples, to govern caringly, benignly, with justice and charity. He was to put the Indians under no bondage, to permit no one to do them any injury, so that they would not be repelled from receiving our holy faith, so that they would not be revolted by Christian behavior. The Indians had their own villages, own homes, own work to do, their own peace, that was their way, and they lived in paganism as they did before we came. They respected and worked for some Spaniards of their own accord, the three hundred Spaniards who were married to the Indian women or the women of the Indian chiefs, though this latter kind of marriage was not lawfully blessed but had to be accepted as a practice later. Three thousand Spaniards arrived in Hispaniola with the Grand Commander of Lares. He kept them around him in the city of Santo Domingo where they had come ashore. He had not the wits to spread them out among the Indians on the island so they could find something to eat. Thus, they began to starve.[50]

The Commander concocted what seemed to be a solution. But it violated the instructions he bore to rule the Indians as free people. So he wrote the most gracious Queen some very damning things about the Indians, utter falsehoods!—those of us who were there at the time know the opposite was true—to influence Her Highness to give him a license to parcel out the

---

[48] *Tratados*, vol. 2, pp. 767-803.

[49] Nicolas de Ovando.

[50] For Ovando's mistake, see Las Casas' *History*, bk. 2, chap. 11. Columbus made the same mistake of concentrating the settlers of the first big colonizing expedition of 1493, cf. *History*, bk. 1, chap. 192.

Indians just as he had plotted. Among his other lies he wrote that the
Spaniards could not catch the Indians [long enough] to preach the Faith to
them, to catechize them in it. Because of the wide liberty they had, they
avoided, they fled from communication with the Christians, to the extent that
even when asked to work for wages they did not want to. Rather they wanted
just to loaf around. Therefore it would be better if they *had* to deal with the
Spaniards. That Commander had no more care, then or afterwards, to
provide what would help save the Indians' souls than he would for dogs or
cats. It was as if the Indians were obliged to guess that there was a law of
Christ to be preached to them, and guess that they should come naked and
penniless, abandoning land and home and wife and child, should risk death
along the roads, a hundred, a hundred and fifty leagues, to ask at the port if
preachers had come with a law they never heard of, preachers about whom
no one had ever said a word. It was also as if they were obliged to leave
their own homes in the way I just said, to feed the Spaniards.[51]

Her Highness considered the eager desire she always had in her
heart that every Indian should receive the knowledge of and faith in Jesus
Christ, God and Man, should become Christian and thus be saved. Then she
answered in the following way, saying among other things: "Because we
want the Indians to be converted to our Holy Catholic Faith, to be indoctri-
nated in its truths; and because that will be better done by requiring the
Indians to communicate with the Christians who have settled on the island,
mingling with them, dealing with them, each helping the other, etc." And
further on: "I have ordered that this letter be issued to that effect. In it I
command you, our governor, from the day you read our letter onward,
should compel, should press the Indians effectively to deal with, to
communicate with the Christian settlers on the island, to build the Christians' homes, to mine gold and other precious metals for them, to work the
fields, to maintain the Christians who are settlers living on the same island.
You should have each Indian paid, the day he works, a living wage which
you think he should have according to the quality of the farmland, of the
person served, of the job required. And you should order each local chief
to take charge of a certain number of Indians so that he could send them to
work where they were needed, and so that on feasts and on chosen days the
Indians could be gathered in designated places to listen to explanations of
the doctrines of our Faith. Thus each chief should report, with the number
of Indians you assign to him, to the Christian or Christians you name—in
order that the Indians should work at what these Christians command them,
paying them the day's wage you have set. The Indians shall go and do this

[51] Ovando's false information is told in more detail in the *History*, Bk. 2, chap. 11.

work as the free people they are, not as slaves, and you shall see to it that the Indians are well treated, the newly converted better than the others. You should not allow anyone to do them any evil, any harm, any offense at all. Let neither party to the relationship disobey this letter, under penalty . . . etc."[52]

These are her official words. In them Her Highness seems clearly to dictate *eight policies*. *The first*: She ordered sought the main goal she was obliged to seek: the conversion of the Indian peoples. That is why she says right off: ". . . because we desire that the Indians be converted to our holy catholic faith and be taught its truths . . ." She then adds, "and since this can best be done by communication, etc." This statement makes it so that every further order or direction she wanted carried out had to be fitting, conducive to fulfilling the primary goal. Therefore, every order or direction that had to be given by the Kings throughout the Indies, every command that had to be given and carried out by envoys to the New World, had to be ordained and directed towards the conversion of the Indians, whether the matters concerned were secular or sacred.

The second: She wished that each local chief be ordered to select a certain number of Indians to hire themselves out for a daily wage to the Spaniards. This group should be made up of some Indians, not all, and of those who were able-bodied workmen, not women or children, not the elderly, not the leaders who were chiefs among them, and some natives should be off while others were on the job, and there should be alternate shifts. That this is what Her Highness wanted is clear, because the Catholic King [Ferdinand] commanded exactly this later in the instruction he gave Pedrarias when he sent him to Tierra Firme, as I will present later.

The third: That respect should be had for the needs of the Indians, for the wives and children they had to support, and for those who lived in close proximity to the Christian settlements, so that they could return home each evening to rest, or at least on Saturdays—though to go home only on Saturdays was unjust, a greater cross than any law allows—and for other circumstances which prudence and discretion would make evident, as they must in everything we do.

The fourth: That the time for work should be limited, not unlimited. This is clear from the following excerpt, "and you should have each one paid

---

[52] Isabella's Letter of Dec. 20, 1503, to Ovando, is quoted in *History*, Bk. 2, at start of chap. 12; the entire letter is printed in *DII: Colección de documentos inéditos, relativos al descubrimiento, conquista y organización de las antíguas possessiones españolas de América y Oceanía, sacados de los archivos del reino, y muy especialmente del de Indias* [Documentos inéditos de Indias] (Madrid: Impr. de Manuel B. de Quirós, vol. 1, 1864), 31:209-12.

the day he works," etc. And the Indians should be attracted humanely to work so that they do it freely. Even though Her Highness said, "compel, press the Indians." She meant as free men are usually compelled. Any other way would contradict Her Highness' meaning since she commanded that they should work as free men.

The fifth: That the labor must be moderate, what the Indians could bear, and on workdays, not on Sundays and holidays. Although Her Highness ordered the Indians be hired to go to work, her purpose was not, ought not, could not have been that if the labor became so hard it was harmful or killing, the workers must perish nonetheless.

The sixth: That the wage they should be paid ought to be in proportion to the nature of the work, so that the laborers could gain something from spending their sweat and strength. Thus they could be compensated and be able to provide for themselves and for their wives and children, making up by the daily wage what they lost by their absences from home and from having to leave their own lands and crops untended, by which ordinarily they maintain themselves and their families.

The seventh: That the Indians were free. They should work as the free persons they always were, not as slaves they never were. They should be treated well. No one should be allowed to do them any harm. They should hire themselves out for definite periods as free men do. They should have the liberty to supply for their own needs. Whenever they got exhausted or became ill, they should be able to take time off to convalesce, because otherwise what liberty would they have? How could they be called free?

Those words should have been enough for the Grand Commander to make him understand that not only was the method he used wrong—it was not suitable at all for free peoples, not even for slaves, but only suitable for turning mortal enemies into corpses in a short time, without doing them even a fraction of the countless hurts and injuries the Indians underwent. How much more should reason and natural law, without any royal charge or command from Her Highness, have made him understand that the Indian peoples owed no one anything! They were human! They should be governed as humans! They should not be divided up, destroyed as so many heads or herds of cattle destined for the slaughterhouse.

The eighth: That if the work program Her Highness ordered pursued—a program based solely on a false report the Commander made to her—if it proved impossible, proved so harmful that it could not continue or be borne without the total destruction of the Indian population, then no one had to bear it, no one had to consent that the Indians be put under captivity and oppression for one single day just to get gold for the Spaniards. The Queen never intended that. This is most clear from her very words in the decree, from the instruction carried overseas by the aforementioned governor, and from the clause Her Highness put in her will which we cited above in the fifth reason. She was thoroughly Christian. She could not do otherwise and still save her soul. The Queen organized everything, above all, toward the well-being and salvation of the Indians as she was obliged to do. She never gave the governor power to do anything that would damn her and her subjects together in hell. It was not her royal prerogative to destroy subjects. If Her Highness had known the temperate land, the fragility, the poverty, the meekness, the goodness of the Indians, if she knew the brutal severity of the labor, the hardship of mining gold, the pitiful desperate life consequent on it, in sum the impossibility for every laborer of keeping alive, of not perishing—they did perish, without faith or sacraments—if she had known, she would never have given him the order, never commissioned him to any such thing! And if Her Highness had become aware that the work program she had set was so harmful to the Indians, who would doubt that she would abominate it and cancel it? Soon after she sent that decree, a few months later, she died. But Her Highness sent him that order (if it was one) thinking it a proper order only because of what he wrote about the new situation. She trusted him much more than she should, since the situation at that time was very new and obscure, and he did not know if up to then she had the full scope of the matter laid before her.[53]

In the early days on Haiti, the first Admiral of the Indies, the discoverer of the New World, thinking that he followed the royal will, made the Indians of the island liable for tribute. He obliged each one of those who lived in the vicinity of the mines to fill a hawkbell with gold. From those who did no mining he required a certain amount of cotton. From others, the things they could provide. After this, certain brutes among the Spaniards he had brought along, rebelled against him, broke with obedience, which then caused him to undergo severe hardship; and these rebels, in a district of that island called Jaraguá, a rich, populous place, assumed power over the Indians and began to make personal use of them, in total violation of orders. They made a deal, and the Admiral permitted them to hold [power] over some tribes, to have them work on holdings and farms. But once the breach of order that had occurred was known by Their Highnesses, they said in the instructions to the Grand Commander of Lares that the Indians should serve no one. Rather, they should be ruled and governed as the free people they were. That was the right order and policy of governance overseas; it was to be installed then. It is what we have now.

---

[53] Las Casas' analysis of the Queen's eight requirements parallels his longer one in the *History*, bk. 2, remainder of chap. 12.

Instead, Your Majesty, look at what that governor did to that land, did with those Indians, and after he received the letter from her Gracious Highness, the Queen!

Concerning what Her Highness decreed should be the principal, primary goal in the New World, i.e., the conversion and salvation of the Indians, Your Majesty can be very sure—I tell you this in all conscience—that for the entire time he governed, the nine years, the Governor took no more care of teaching and saving Indians, he did not lift a finger, did not bother his head, did not waste a thought, no more than if they were sticks or stones or, as I said earlier, cats or dogs.

Concerning the second goal, that a certain number of Indians be assigned to each local chief, etc., he destroyed the large villages that existed; he gave one Spaniard a hundred Indians, another fifty, a third some more, a fourth some less, according to the influence each Spaniard had with him, and as it pleased him. He handed out young and old, pregnant women, nursing women, chiefs and tribesmen. He gave out the local rulers of villages and areas, in one of the allotments he made to the Spaniards he wanted to honor and reward the most, stating the following in the writ of encomienda: "To you, so-and-so, are granted in encomienda from chief so-and-so this many Indians. You may use them in your mines, or on your farm, including the person of the chief, etc." The result was that everyone great or small, young or old, whoever had their legs under them, men and women, pregnant and nursing, worked and worked until they gave up the ghost.

Concerning the third goal, that respect should be had for the vital necessities of the wives and children, that the men should be with them each evening, at least every Saturday—though that little was unjust, as I said—the Governor allowed them to take the husbands to mine gold, ten, twenty, thirty, forty eight leagues away, some farther than that. The wives stayed behind on what are called cassava plots doing backbreaking work. They had to make earth mounds in order to grow the 'bread' they eat there; that is, they had to raise the earth they dug four hands high and twelves paces square. It is giants' work, especially digging the hard soil with sticks, not spades. Also, wives worked in separate places spinning cotton. They did a wide variety of other jobs, those they found to be the most apt to bring them in some money in earnings. The result was that husband and wife were split. They did not see each other for eight to ten months, for even a year. At the end of their separation they met one another. They arrived so tired out by hunger and so worn, so drained of energy, that they had little desire for intercourse. This way procreation stopped among them. The infants who were born died. Their mothers, drained by hunger and hard labor, had no milk to feed them. For that cause alone, on the island of Cuba, there died in the span of three months—I was there at the time—seven thousand children, starved! Some women smothered their children to death out of desperation. Some, aware that they were pregnant, used herbs to induce stillbirths. The result was that the men died in the mines, the women died in the fields. And so, once procreation stopped, everyone vanished in a short time, the land became empty of people. Think about it! This way the whole world could be emptied!

Concerning the fourth goal, that work for hire should be for specified times, not continual, that the laborers should be solicited gently, respectfully, etc., the Governor granted them for endless labor with no provision for rest. He agreed to more than hard labor for the Indians. He ordered them allotted brutally, sternly, cruelly, heartlessly, because the Spaniards, to whom he gave the Indians in encomienda, put executioners in charge of them: one in the mines, called the mine boss; one on the ranches, called the foreman. Soulless, pitiless men, who clubbed the Indians, hit them, whipped them with tipped lashes, called them constantly dogs—you never see in the bosses any sign of kindness, only extremes of unbending brutality. Indeed it would be cruelty to drive heartless Moors who had done great violence to Christians the way that these overseers drove the Indians. And the Indians are gentle, humble, tractable people, more than any other on earth. On account of the massive cruelties of the wretched foremen and mine bosses, and of the crushing labors they, the Indians, bore, they were absolutely sure they would be killed. So some Indians fled for the hills. Because of this, the owners designated certain men as sheriffs-at-large who were to track the runaways down. And in the towns, the places where the Spaniards live, the Governor had certain men, top men, whom he named temporary judges. To these he gave as salary for the job, beyond their regular allotment of Indians, one hundred more to be at their beck and call. These judges were the worst killers of the people. The cruelest of all. Every runaway the sheriffs caught was hailed before them. Before them, the plaintiff stood, the one who held the Indians in encomienda. He charged them, saying these or those Indians were dogs who did not want to serve him. Every day some took to the bush to loaf and skulk around. Let them be punished! Then the judge tied the runaways to a post. In his own hands he took a tarred rope they call *anguilla* in the galleys. It is hard as an iron rod. He lashed them with it so fiercely, so cruelly, they spurted blood in many spots where he struck. He left them like the dead. I have been an eyewitness often of such barbaric scenes. God is my witness, such things were done to that innocent flock. However much I tell Your Majesty, I think I cannot tell or report one/one thousandth of the incidents. Surely none of them can be exaggerated.

Concerning the fifth goal, that the work load should be moderate, etc. The Indians had to mine gold. They had to be men of iron to do it. They had to invert mountains, bottom up, top down, a thousand times, digging and crushing rocks. In order to pan the gold in the rivers, they had to remain immersed in water where the rocks were crushed by brute force. When the mines flooded, they had the hardest work, to empty them pail in hand. Finally, to understand what a job it is to mine gold and silver, let Your Majesty recall that pagan emperors gave no greater torture or condemnation to martyrs, excepting death, than sending them to mine metals. At one time, owners kept their workers at the mine for the whole year. Later they changed policy. They saw so many die! They agreed that the workers should spend five months mining gold. The gold would be smelted then for forty days. For those forty days the miners could rest. The rest was to work the fields they got their food from, which meant digging the earth and making the cassava mounds I described earlier. A far harder job than cultivating vineyards here or ploughing fields. During a year, what they knew of a holiday was a day when they were allowed to work less rather than more.

To do the work, the workers were given meager rations of cassava, the 'bread' of the land. It was made from roots which had little nourishment to them. No meat or fish to complement the diet. They were given local peppers, garlic, and roots like turnips, baked or boiled. Some owners who thought of themselves as generous in feeding the Indians had a pig a week killed for each fifty workers. The mine boss ate half of it or more. The other half went to the Indians, bit by bit, day by day. The way one gives blessed bread Sundays at church. Some misers, who felt no need to feed their workers, sent them scrounging the fields and bush for whatever fruit they could find in the trees, for two or three days, then forced them to work the next two or three days with what they had in their bellies, not a morsel more. This way one owner built a holding worth five hundred, six hundred castellanos. One of those who did likewise told me so with his own mouth. For the love of God, Your Majesty should consider what substance, what strength could be left in those bodies by nature so fragile and so starved to the bone, so exhausted from overwork—and how long they could sustain such a sad and straitened life, such a punishing workload, without a bite to eat!

Concerning the sixth goal, that the daily wage should match the work done, etc. Let Your Majesty order this to be made note of here. It is an important point to consider. The governor in question ordered as a wage rate for the lives, the hard work, the service the Indians gave the Spaniards, three coppers for two days! And that is the truth, to wit, half a castellano, worth two hundred and twenty five maravedis for a year's work. The money that would be given them is enough to buy in Castilian goods what the natives call *cacona*, which means 'trifles.' With two hundred and twenty five maravedis one could buy as much as a comb, a mirror, a small necklace of green and blue beads! And there were many years they received not even that much. Such was the suffering, the starvation of the Indians that there was little cure for it. They had no other thought than how they could either eat their fill or could die to escape their desperate situation.

This is the trifling wage, my most noble Lord, that the Governor set and commanded the Indians to be paid, to the perdition of their bodies and souls. They were damned both ways in the service of the Spaniards, three coppers for two days work.

Concerning the seventh goal, Her Highness' insistence that in all this the Indians should act as the free people they are, that no injury, no harm should be allowed to be done to them, that they should have the freedom to build their own households, to rest, to recuperate, etc. The Grand Commander took away their freedom entirely. He allowed them to be put into the harshest servitude, harshest captivity, which no one could understand at all unless he saw it. They were not free for one human thing. Even cattle usually have some time free to graze when they are turned loose in the fields. But the Spaniards I describe did not even give the miserable Indians time to graze, time to do anything else. Their state is clear from all I said earlier, and from the fact that the Governor switched the hiring authorized by Her Highness into a forced, unwilling, lifelong servitude. He gave them into slavery, absolutely. They did what the vicious greed and tyranny of the Spaniards wanted them to do, not like ordinary captives, but like beasts of burden whose masters lead them by a rope to do what they want. The few times they allowed the Indians to go to their home places to rest, the Indians found neither wife, nor child, nor farm to nourish them. Since they had not been allowed to make a life—they were not given the time to do it—they had no other recourse but to die. They got sick doing their constant, crushing work. It could happen easily, they are as I said of a very fragile constitution. They were put suddenly to heavy jobs they were not used to. They were kicked mercilessly and clubbed. They were told they got sick so as not to work, the lazy sneaks! When the bosses saw they grew sicker and nothing more could be gotten from them, they told them to go home, thirty, forty, eighty leagues away. They gave them for the road half a dozen roots, like turnips, and a little cassava. The sick men went as far as the first gulch, where they died in desperation. Some struggled on further, two or three leagues, ten or twenty, yearning for home, yearning to escape the hellish existence they bore, until they dropped down dead. I often came on bunched corpses or on men rattling with death, or others in their last throes croaking out with what voice they had left, 'Food! Food!' Does your Majesty think that the Governor in question fulfilled the will of her Highness which was that the Indians should be treated as free people? That he should not permit them to suffer any damage, any harm?

Concerning the eighth goal, it is clear that the Governor in question should have understood the Queen. She wished that if the policy she gave him to carry out toward the Indians—to make them communicate with the Christians in order to have them catechized—was difficult or impossible, or if it was lethal, a destruction of native life, she did not give him the power to impose it. Her Highness did not have the power to destroy these peoples either. Further, we must think that if Her Highness were told of conditions, she would not permit them. On the contrary, she would detest them, forbid them. It is a stunning fact about that man, the Governor, a huge number of miners died during each stint in the mines, eight months at a time, or year to year from the smelting of the gold, but he did not realize the work program he imposed was lethal, that it was like a rampant plague wiping every miner out of existence. He never changed, never reversed it. Yet he could not ignore how bad it was, all he had done, how unpardonable he was before God and before his sovereign. Before God, because what he did was of itself evil, against the law of God and nature, condemning to monumental servitude and ruination free, rational creatures. It was more a violation when he saw directly that the devastation of the Indians came from what he did. Before his Sovereigns, because he broke completely with his orders, he went overboard, doing exactly the opposite of what the blessed Queen commanded him. The one adjustment he made was when he saw that each of the brutal Spanish masters had killed a half or two-thirds of the Indians granted him in encomienda. The Governor put the Indians back into the selection pool and made a new set of allotments. For those he liked, he brought the number of Indians back up again to the number he granted formerly, the number they had destroyed once already. The Spaniards he did not like, he left without a share of Indians because he could not fill every demand. Thus it happened that every year or two there was a new allotment because [so many Indians died].[54]

Then the most Christian Queen died, Our Sovereign, knowing nothing of the tyranny overseas. Then the illustrious Lord, King Don Philip, succeeded to the throne. It pleased God to take him also. The kingdom went without a sovereign for two years. Then the Catholic King [Ferdinand]

---

[54] Ovando's conduct in contradiction of Isabella's eight points is told in greater detail: *History*, Bk. 2, chaps. 13-14.

succeeded, from whom the extent of the destruction in the New World was kept; no one told him the truth. There were seven years the King governed these kingdoms here, from the beginning of the year 1504, plus the years that passed before he began to govern solely, that makes it nine years that the Governor ruled the island of Haiti. In this time span, he destroyed nine-tenths of the population. And because succeeding governors followed the same practice, they destroyed the rest. In the years 1509 and 1510, those who went to colonize the islands of Puerto Rico and Cuba and Jamaica introduced that lethal policy. With it they devastated them all. There was one official of your Majesty on the island of Cuba, to whom three hundred Indians were granted. In three months time, and I was there—I was in on the exploration of that island from the start—he killed two hundred and seventy of them. So that there was a tenth of them left. I could tell you specific things I saw that would grieve your royal soul beyond endurance.

c. Greed
Prenote

How could human beings do such things to human beings? They were blinded by greed, greed for more than mortal wealth, for immortal wealth and the absolute independence such wealth seems to bring from mortality and conscience. Gold becomes god. Las Casas has to explain to the Reform Commission in 1542, as part of his Twenty Reasons Against Encomienda, what motivated Spanish behavior from the earliest days of the Conquest up to the time he was speaking. Otherwise, the Commission would conclude that things had just happened, no one was really responsible for consequences, there was no need to take steps to block greed, practical steps like abolishing encomienda, never giving power over people to poor men, guaranteeing Indian sovereignty over their own territory and subjects, etc. But Las Casas has also to explain to himself why Christians behaved so brutally—friends of his, co-religionists—why they could not see what they were doing. They were possessed, and thought that everything they did was justified by what possessed them, the way narcissistic people think that the ecstasy they receive from what they do justifies the doing. The doctrine on greed contained in the following excerpt is a very ancient one, derived from classical as well as Christian sources.[55] It is evil, it causes evil. The doctrine fits what Las Casas saw. It may not be enough for the modern reader who lives in a century that has "supped full with horrors" not explainable by greed. But blindness, whatever its cause, may be the apt metaphor for both periods of time, a chosen blindness.

---

[55] *Tratados*, vol. 2, pp. 703-733.

Seventh Reason
Colonists Corrupted by Greed

The seventh reason is this: According to any reasonable and just laws, or any learned philosophers who write on moral principles, one should never give power to poor men, to greedy men who want desperately as their one goal to escape their poverty, much less to men who are gasping, choking with the desire to be rich. Such natures never work and struggle for nothing. The hunger, the greed of the greedy always wants single-mindedly to obtain riches and to fatten its purse. While the purse is not fattened, there is no resting, greed cannot stay frustrated or unsatisfied. Nature abhors being frustrated or unsatisfied. . . as it abhors, it flees, a vacuum, a void. Nature cannot bear it. So the greedy must torment themselves night and day, must use every plot and ploy they can possibly invent to fill the bottomless pit of their purses, or they will never be satisfied or live at peace. For this reason it is very dangerous, according to Aristotle, to grant poor or greedy men authority and jurisdiction to govern people. History tells us the story of two men who were chosen by the Roman Consuls to be sent as governors to Spain. One was a poor man. The other was avaricious. When the debate about them was underway in the Senate, Scipio Africanus said that neither of the two was fit to be governor. He indicated that both of them would wreck the public welfare and the governmental system. They would suck the city dry as leeches suck a human body. Their main intent was to swallow whole the wealth of the entire people. By sheer necessity, once given power, they are driven to satisfy fully their raw appetite to get what they want, even if they risk the life of every subject over whom they have jurisdiction or power. Especially if they know they can get rich through their subjects and no way else. It is a fact that the bottomless hunger of men greedy to be rich cannot ever be satisfied in this life. Greed for riches never has limits. To quote Ecclesiastes 5:9: "Wealth never satisfies the miser."

This illness is more than dangerous. It is beyond human cure, as I will prove later. So in no way will the money-hungry man who has a power-hold over other people leave off stripping them, despoiling them of their wealth, squeezing it out of their blood even—not for any limit or law or punishment imposed on him, not for any reform measures that might be devised, not for any threat aimed against him. If the power-hold over people is not taken away from greedy men, they are never able, once they are conquered by their own greed, to satisfy finally the career of their greed in this life, their limitless greed.

I intend to explore in three separate arguments how this sickness which infects the greedy man is incurable by any human means, and how no human therapy suffices to stop a money-hungry man, in authority over peoples, from afflicting them or from leeching off the body politic.

First argument: Avarice is an insatiable void. It would be enough to cite again the authority of Sacred Scripture: "Wealth never satisfies the miser!" [Ecclesiastes 5:9] In addition to Scripture, I can prove it by natural reason. The more something shares the qualities of perfect happiness, the more desirable it is to the appetite—and therefore the more it prods and whets desire, even to the pitch of violence, to possess it. The desire to be rich in someone poor and avaricious is kindred to the desire in someone for total happiness. As happiness promises to be absolute, without fail for the one who gets it, so riches promise the same self-sufficiency, according to Boethius in Book II of *The Consolations of Philosophy.* The reason it is so, says the Philosopher in the fifth book of the *Ethics,* is that we trust money will gain us possession of everything. Scripture says the same, in Ecclesiastes 10:19, "Everything can be had for money." It is a fact that by money men get what they need, what they want in this world: honors, noble rank, status, family, luxury, elegant clothes, choice foods, delicious vices, revenge on enemies, an exalted personal reputation. The lovers of this world want just such things for their beatitude. They search for them. They risk life here and hereafter in mighty pursuit of them. They readily commit any crime, any sin at all for these goods. That is why St. Paul says in I Timothy 6:10, "Avarice is the root of all evil." Also Ecclesiastes [Ecclesiasticus] 10:10, "The greedy think little of their souls." Thus, says St. Thomas, they risk losing them, they put their souls in constant danger.[56]

Having wealth, having gold, is a close likeness to having heavenly bliss, sufficient in itself. So it is like a final cause, an ultimate goal one could want and want forever. Therefore the hunger, the desire of someone greedy is infinite, fiercely so. Therefore also such a bottomless desire can never be filled in this present life. And thus, since money is only the facsimile of happiness, not the full reality, the soul cannot find there its true self, cannot stop wanting what it is missing. Since the avaricious, the greedy, make wealth their be-all and have a taste for nothing else, they are at it all the time, they work for infinite wealth. The Philosopher describes this in his *Politics,* Book I: "The range of avarice is infinite." St. Ambrose says it too: "There is no way ever to satisfy avarice finally." The more one piles up wealth, the more one wants to pile it up. That spurs one to make

---

[56] [Classical writers and Church Fathers, plus scripture texts, stud the Seventh Reason on the psychology of greed. In this paragraph he cites: Boethius, *Consolations,* Bk. 3, Prose 5; Aristotle, *Ethics* 5, cap. 5 (*The Basic Works of Aristotle,* trans. by Richard McKeon, New York, 1941, 1133b; hereafter McKeon); Thomas Aquinas, *Summa theologiae,* $2^a 2^{ae}$, q. 118, art. 7.]

more. Because the more wealth one has, the closer one thinks to come to the perfect image of bliss one wants. The Philosopher explains in the sixth book of the *Physics* that all natural motion increases in speed and intensity the closer it gets to its goal. Since the ultimate goal of the avaricious is to possess everything money can buy, the more money they have, the more they think to get closer to the goal, and as a result, the more the desire to get there grows—that is the motion Aristotle means. The lines from Juvenal are borne out: "As money grows, lust for it grows."[57]

The second argument follows from the first. This way: If greed for riches in the greedy is insatiable because it is bottomlesss, for the natural causes and reasons just given, it follows that nothing human can cure this evil. Without divine grace, all human effort is little able to overcome a natural drive. Above all, in those who have allowed themselves to be controlled by such a vice as greed for riches. The vice of avariciousness is more difficult to treat, and so it is almost an incurable disease. Lust is easier to cure. Other vices are not comparable to these two. This is so for a couple of reasons.

One: Concupiscence, which comes from the venereal in a forceful nature, is a most powerful, deep-rooted inner drive. Yet lust for the things money buys is objectively, incomparably, a more powerful appetite than lust for the things love promises. The reason is that the scope of money is more universal, as I said earlier. It is like an absolute guarantee that one can buy everything. So it has the power to satisfy lust, but lust alone has not the power to satisfy it.

Two: Lust, longing for money and wealth, lasts all day every day. It is ceaseless. Lust for love is not. Even if lust for love is intense and deep and burning and reaches a pitch of violence when its passion is highest, it is short-lived. By contrast, lust for money gains in virulence and scope as the defects of human nature multiply. See what happens to the old: the older they get, the greedier; they lose their own physical and mental powers; more and more they feel they must have help and support from outside things.

For these reasons it is evident that lust for money is harder to cure than lust for love, than any other vice. Therefore it is the most dangerous vice, as St. Thomas says. We thus have some clarity on *the third argument*: that is, should a money-hungry man have any jurisdiction or power at all over people, he must automatically afflict and oppress them, sap them dry

---

[57] ["The Philosopher" is Las Casas' term for Aristotle following the standard usage of his time. In these two pars. he cites Aristotle (*Politics*, Bk. 1, cap. 9 [McKeon, 1258a]); St. Ambrose (Jacques-Paul Migne, *Patrologiae Cursus Completus, Series Latina, 221 vols. Paris, 1844-55*, 14:733 [hereafter *PL*]); Aristotle again (*Physics*, bk. 6 [McKeon, 231a-241b]); and a verse by Juvenal, from Satire XIV, line 139.]

to swallow what riches they have. It will do no good at all to try and check him with limits or laws or punishments or any other reforms if his power, his chance to rob is not taken away from him. He is completely incurable, he cannot be cured by human means. And even though this one proof is enough, still I want to give three further ones to back it up.

One. All crimes, all vices, all the lethal ways of being there are—if we are to believe the saints—flow from, stem from lust for money as from a fountain or a root of all evil. List them: betrayal, fraud, deception, lying, provocation, perjury, battery, robbery, plunder, inhumanity, a heart closed to mercy. Lust for money is blind, or it blinds or it fogs the mind so the mind cannot see its own just and true purpose nor the mortal dangers awaiting it. Greed looks at gold with more delight than at the sun shining. It is the stuff of every crime. It is the mother of backbiting. The greedy man gets his money from damage to others. Venerable Bede says greed abandons faith, breaks harmony, ruins charity, spawns countless evils. As St. Paul writes: "Greed is the root of all evil." [1 Timothy 6:10] Greed is not moved to mercy, it owns no father, it owns no mother. It is faithless, friendless, heartless to its neighbors, it rejects those nearest it as it would foreigners. Thus Bede. I would add here that the greedy man is unforgiving even to himself. He leads a life he does not own. His life is a constant gamble, as I said earlier.[58]

Two. As St. Ambrose says, the mental powers of the greedy are tied up in the cords of their greed. The mind is not free to judge. The judgment is warped. This means that the greedy man is unable to do anything rational. He has to follow wherever the drive for riches will take him. This is obvious because the type constantly focuses on gold, or silver, or profit; he thinks how and where to make it, he even prays to God! He begs God to give him gold—a sure sign of a hobbled mind, an unfree man. St. Jerome also says the same thing. The money-hungry man is a slave to wealth. Whoever loves money cannot act freely, but is at the beck and call of it, just like a slave. As the saying goes: "You will be the slaves of wealth if the love of wealth gets hold of you."[59]

And so we state, if a greedy man's lust for money is boundless, if the more the money, the gold, the silver, he has, the more the lust for them increases, then it is insatiable, then it is incurable. Furthermore, such a type, to get rich, is ready to betray, defraud, lie, slander, commit perjury,

---

[58] [St. Ambrose is the main source of the preceding material on greed (Migne, *PL* 17:758; his entire "De Nabuthe Jezraelita" deals with the topic—14:731-756) See also Migne, *PL* 218:1229, cap. 111 for complete patristic references on the qualities of greed, headed by a descriptive list uncannily like that of Las Casas in these pages.]

[59] [For St. Ambrose, see previous note; for St. Jerome, see Migne *PL* 22:89.]

violence, theft, plunder, brutality, and on and on. Such a type is blind to his eternal salvation, blind to the torments of hell his crimes warrant. Such a type is hardhearted, merciless, does not have faith, does not love peace, lacks charity, feels no pity, owns no father, no mother, trusts no one, relative or friend, has no compassion. He hates everyone and thus thinks to make money from their troubles. He is his own worst enemy, enemy of his life on earth, utterly neglectful of his soul. Finally, he is captive, a slave of money, forced to obey money as a master, to take pains obsessively, sleeplessly, because he must find it, must please it—he hopes to get from it his total consolation, his welfare, the consummation of all his desires, his final bliss. Above all, such a type is like someone out of his mind and gone crazy. His mind is not his own, it is enveloped in clouds, dimmed by fog, he cannot act as a free being acts; he has to follow where the thrust, the force of the lust for money drives him. The general corruption and weakness and viciousness and proneness to evil in human nature gives a push, a shove to all of the behavior described above, like a blast, a spur.

This type of man, if he ever gets power, or gets the chance, the possibility, whatever way it comes, to fulfill his desires and start to stuff his hungry, hollow purse—what use will it be to impose on him limits or laws or punishments or any other reform than the one of taking away his power, his authority over those he can fleece, afflict, oppress and tyrannize? Other than taking away every chance he has where he can behave that way? Once such a man has begun to do what he wants, will there be any deception, fraud, lie, perjury, that he will not use? If he stole a hundred thousand, would he not bribe with thirty or forty thousand if necessary the one who might indict him, and then keep the rest for himself? And he would steal it in such way that the victims of his lethal behavior—the fleeced, the oppressed, the grief-stricken, the dead—would never receive compensation in law, or liberation, or justice, relief, or redress. Rather, they would perish in despair like victims of tragedy. So controls are not enough, nor are laws, threats of punishment, nor any other reforms, to stop him from tormenting, fleecing, tyrannizing the native peoples. The only solution is to remove or never give authority, power, the right of access to human beings to poor and greedy men who lust for wealth.

Now to apply all I have said above to the main argument because it concerns Your Majesty so much. If it please you, I beg Your Majesty to pay close attention to the conclusions I am going to draw here. They are these. All who go to the Indies, go because they are paupers and want to be rich. They are impelled to go abroad by greed alone. Not only do they want out of their poverty, they want to be rich, not just rich, but filthy rich, with riches beyond what anyone ever hoped or dreamed existed in the world. They have given in and turned themselves willfully into slaves, slaves of greed; that is clear from what they have done overseas in each country and province, from the evidence presented in the fifteenth of the general reforms, from the facts of nature I have just described. The greed of these men is huge, it has no bounds, no moderation, no measure, there was never anything like it anywhere in the whole world. It is inconceivable to the human mind, the greed, the deranged hunger of these men to get their hands on and hold inexhaustible wealth, and with wealth to achieve a social status well above what they merit, especially wealth that is easy to get. At least they are certain it is there. Each hopes to discover a mine or two they can empty endlessly of gold and silver. I have seen and known every day for years how many men, once poor and mean, the dregs of society, have come back here from overseas bringing mounds of wealth they got there. And they have corrupted, infected with the same itch for riches the whole of Spain. Just look at it clearly through Christian eyes. It is truly a furnace aflame with desire for wealth. God is less adored than money, less valued, less esteemed. They must know, they must, all of them living there or here at home—they cannot get rich, or hold riches the way they want. I mean by lounging lazily around, paying nothing, doing not a lick of work of their own. They get rich by a violent appropriation of what the Indians have in their houses from the past, though this is usually a pittance, or by sweating riches out of the hard labor imposed on the Indians. This way lasts longer, it is more desirable to the Spaniards. It is the one way that brings utter ruin and death on the Indians. Given such greedy men in charge, what can one expect if the Indians are left to the Spaniards, if they are again granted to and put under the power of the Spaniards in encomienda, or as hereditary serfs, or as an inheritance, or as wards, or as anything else by which someone could have legal control or rule over them or any access to them? What will they do to these innocent, humble, gentle, timid Indians who dare not complain, who have no one to hear them or defend them and help them—they are kept out in the fields, in the hills, down mines, along roads, out in badlands, in places where all the means are found that anyone could ever want in order to mistreat them without its being known? What will the Spaniards do to them if not what they have done and are doing today? They suck riches out of Indians' flesh and blood, the only riches left in their huts. They shed blood; they expose them to every danger; they give them all sorts of unbearable jobs; they beat them with sticks, with whips; they abuse them with unspeakable tortures. And finally, and pitilessly, they corrupt and destroy life itself in the Indians a thousand different ways.

If it is true that everyone who is money-mad, whose goal is wealth, is never moved by pity, is stone-hearted, cuts off both father and mother, feels nothing for relatives and friends, is so hostile, so cruel to himself that his life is up for constant sale and every step he takes is a gamble for money's sake alone, then what pity do you think he will show for someone else's life, especially for life he thinks less of, values less than that of animals or dung in the streets? It will be very easy for him to make a misery of Indian life to get his riches—for him Indians are but usable tools in the process of enrichment. Aristotle gives the reason (*I Politics*): "The goal of each of the arts [of wealth-getting] is infinite, that is what they most want to reach. But the means used to reach their goal are not infinite."[60] Thus we use the tools as means to an end we want only insofar as they can help us reach it. The Spaniards use the Indians as no more than mere tools to acquire the gold, the wealth which they desire to have as their goal.

Christ never acted that way, He did not come into the world to die for gold. What He suffered for humankind was for the salvation of humankind. Your Majesty had no intention either of perverting, of twisting the purpose ordained by God, that things were made for people, not people for things. The mistake of substituting things for people has ruined the Indies for Your Majesty. And no wonder. The purpose of anything is its most perfect, most precious quality, Aristotle says. And according to the adage, a mistake about purpose is absolutely the worst mistake of all. Once there is a mistake about purpose, a perversion, one cannot do anything good or get anything right. Therefore what is it when one does the follow-ing—hands over meek, simple, humble and good people into the power of someone so blinded by error that he then uses them as lifeless tools, as if gold were alive and the purpose of life itself, overturning the natural order so clearly fashioned by God in his whole visible creation, making the rational beings God so much loves worth less than dung, the filthy dung of the earth? Gives Indians to someone whose mind is in prison and whose judgment is warped, to someone who is crazed and cannot act freely, who is corrupt in nature and behavior, who is famished for money, dying for money, sweating for money, gasping for money? Such people set no limits, no bounds, no restraints whatever! They understand money [alone], they count on it madly as their bliss. No matter the quality or quantity of laws and punishments made to control them! What else is it but placing a dagger in the hands of a maniac and offering him the throat of a beloved child to cut? What else is it but to put a man into the hands of his enraged, mortal enemy who has wanted for a long time to kill him? Then what else but to give the enemy plenty of room, plenty of time, after he has worked his [murderous] will and his victim winds up dead, to make a perjured denial that he killed

---

[60] [Aristotle, *Politics*, Bk. 1, cap. 8 (McKeon, 1256b).]

him? And this even if, right from the onset, some fierce laws and punishments were invoked to [deter] him? And more. Suppose a certain judge should know of a certain young man that he had a burning desire for a certain beautiful young woman, and suppose the judge put her in the young man's house, under his power, all the while menacing the young man with dire punishments, threats, warnings, of what he would do to him if he touched her. And suppose the same young man should swear, swear to behave as commanded. Suppose also that he should beg the judge to give her to him on whatever conditions of punishment the judge desires to set. What would you expect to happen in this case? No doubt, the [moral] death of the man and the judge, and the ruin of the woman. The sure perdition of all, exactly as would follow if they were all put in a bull ring in reach of the horns of enraged bulls or into a den full of starved lions.

Even if by some miracle the evils just described should not follow, nonetheless the one who puts another in such [mortal] danger as this, and does not have to, would certainly commit a grave mortal sin. Undoubtedly. Because no one has the right to put another in danger of physical death, much less the death of the soul which is brought on by mortal sin. And no one has the right to put himself in danger, even though the [lethal] effect should not ultimately follow, without being in violation of divine law. The reason is that once a cause is placed which necessarily or most probably produces an effect, to stop the effect is not within human power, only within divine. God reserved that power to Himself and forbids it to creatures. Exactly as I said above, to put the Indians in the power of the Spaniards is like baring the necks of one's own children to maniacs with knives in their hands, like exposing people to the smoking rage of their mortal enemies who have long been burning to get their hands on them. I am not saying that the Spaniards want to kill the Indians directly because they hate them. I say rather that the Spaniards want to be rich, stacked with gold, that is their goal, but rich through the sweat and blood of tortured and tormented Indians, using them as means, as lifeless tools. That is what causes the Indians all to die inevitably. It is exactly the case of putting some beautiful young woman into the power of a young man who is blinded by his own passionate desire. It is inevitable, if no miracle happens, that she will be raped and ruined, and he will sin mortally.

The death of the wretched Indians is more certain, more inevitable, by far, than the violation described in the example just given. The blind passion called greed is more brutal, it is more drawn out, it is repeated over and over, it is far more compulsive than the rotten passion called lust. I showed that already. So it amounts to tossing the Indians onto the horns of raging bulls, or pitching them to wolves, to lions, to tigers who have starved for weeks. I am convinced of it and say so: laws, penalties, threats would have the same effect on famished wild beasts—'thou shalt not take one bite'—as they would imposed on Spaniards—'thou shalt not get thy gold through the deaths of Indians'—as long as they have power over or access to Indians one way or another. I have a long-standing, long certain, broad experience of what happened. Because of it, I swear to You, I assure Your Majesty, that even if you order a gallows erected outside each door of each Spaniard's house, and proclaim to them on oath by the authority of your crown that for the first Indian they lose or let die they will be hanged on that gallows, even so they will not stop the killing! Not if Your Majesty lets them keep, or grants them any kind of power or direct authority. The reason is they have gotten off scot-free and will again. They are so shrewd at getting off and will remain so, that laws, punishments, the noose, have little effect on them.

d. Hojeda the Furious

Prenote

There were monsters of cruelty among the early Spaniards on the islands and mainland. Las Casas knew them personally, or knew people on their expeditions, so he saw the part they played in furthering the destructive pattern of behavior begun by Columbus. They were warriors, gold hunters, slavers, who wrapped themselves in legal fictions—licenses from the crown—then proceeded to a lawless behavior towards Indians that was hard to believe even by those who witnessed it. They looked heroic, and have been, at times, treated as heroes by later history. But Las Casas knew that not one of their actions was justified. The peoples of the New World had never attacked Spain, never knew it existed. So they were not on formerly Christian territory, they were not opponents or suppressors of Christianity, they were civilized, all evidence shows it, they were rational, political, fully capable of social existence, and were peaceful. It took Las Casas time to know this, he was part of the system that provided the legal cloak for the monsters, though he tried to behave well within the system imposed on the Indians. That part of the story will be described a little further on.

Alonso de Hojeda, the subject of the following excerpt, was an example, for Las Casas, of the terrible turning of potential virtue into actual vice—Hojeda was a man of courage, adventuresomeness, enormous energy, skill, even piety towards the Mother of God, plus obedience towards legitimate authority. But he made himself and his desires the god he served. He fell in love with the self he saw in the mirror of his own violence and greed, and violence and greed became his ultimate satisfaction. The time described in the excerpt is 1509-10. Hojeda had been involved with the Indies since the Admiral's second voyage, 1493.[61]

After four or five days at sea, [Alonso de] Hojeda made port and dropped anchor at Cartagena. The Indians in the area were volatile, ready at any minute to resist the Spaniards because of the harm they had suffered from the ones who came by, as traders supposedly, some years back. The Indians had, for the harm they suffered, attacked and killed some of our people. They had a poisonous, dangerous herb. Reports went back to the King that the natives of the area were hostile to Christians, in fact killed them. The report said nothing about the grievances, the violences, the evils done against the Indians. And there was no one at court to plead their side ... So the King granted a licence for our people to go to that land and make bloody, fiery war against those Indians, make slaves of them ... Alonso de Hojeda had such a license, and he was determined to use it.

He went ashore and launched a surprise attack on a village named Calamar so he could capture some Indians right away and send them back to Hispaniola for sale as slaves and he could pay off some of the many debts he had there. But Juan de la Cosa, a superb navigator, and along as captain general, remembered what they had learned about these Indians when he was with Hojeda there at an earlier time. These Indians were brave, they had a deadly herb, highly poisonous. So, in a prudent way, Cosa said to Hojeda, "Sir, I think it would be better to go set up a camp on the Gulf of Urabá first. The Indians there are not so fierce and they do not have a poisonous herb. Once we have gained that place, we could come back and gain this with ease." But Hojeda was super-confident in himself. Not once, in the thousand fights and perils he had been in, had anyone cost him a drop of his own blood, in Castile or the Indies. He paid no heed to the advice, but just before dawn, with a band of men, he attacked the village roaring "Santiago," slashing and killing and capturing whoever was in the village and had not escaped by fleeing. Eight Indians, who were not quick enough about running, holed up in one of those straw huts, and from there kept off their attackers with the many poisoned arrows they let fly. No Spaniard dared go near the hut. Hojeda, at the top of his voice, raged at them, "What a shameful crew, you this, you that, you the other, afraid to attack eight naked Indians who make fools of you!" One man, who was overexcited by the action, got his head confused by Hojeda's words and hurled himself through the rain of arrows to the door of the hut, but right at the door he took an

---

[61] *History*, Bk. 2, cap. 67. For other stories of Hojeda, see Bk. 1, caps. 82, 93, 102, 168.

arrow square in the chest and it dropped him dead. Hojeda was even more enraged because of this. He ordered fire set to both ends of the house. The eight Indians were burned alive in no time. He took 60 people captive and sent them back to the ships for holding.

He then decided, on the strength of his victory, to go after the Indians who had fled, hot on their heels to a village four leagues away, Turbaco by name. The villagers were alerted by the news brought by those fleeing. They took off with their wives, children, valuables, and hid in the hills for safety. When the Spaniards arrived in the morning, they found no one to kill or capture. The Spaniards were careless, they had no idea the Indians were intelligent beings and that violence taught them lessons, as did human nature. So, with utter disregard and blinded by their own greed and sinfulness, the Spaniards scattered each on his own through the hills looking for someone to rob. Once the Indians, through their scouts, recognized that the Spaniards had broken up, they came out of the hills and attacked with a shout that split the sky and with a volley of poisoned arrows that seemed to darken the day. And the Spaniards, caught in their carelessness—no one would ever dare attack them!—and in such a sudden charge, were fear stricken, they were like game encircled, they didn't know where to hide, where to run, they were stunned. If they ran one way, there were Indians ready for them; if they ran another, they were finished—those same poisoned arrows the Indians killed some of them with, they yanked from the dead bodies and used again to wound and kill other Spaniards who were still on their feet.

Juan de la Cosa, with a few men he collected around him, barricaded the entrance to an enclosure where Hojeda and another few were making a stand. Hojeda was up and down on his knees behind his shield to block the arrows. He was short and with his lightness, quickness, he kept from getting struck. But the second he saw all of his people down dead, and Juan de la Cosa and the group with him nearly finished, he took off at high speed, trusting the great quickness he had—and it was amazing!—right through the Indians, fleeing so fast he seemed to be flying. He got up into the thickest hills he could find and headed towards the sea, as best he could judge direction, and towards his ships.

Juan de la Cosa holed up in a hut stripped of its covering—or he stripped it as best he could, he and some of his men. The Indians couldn't burn them to death with just the frame. He fought until the last of his companions was down and dead. He felt the poison from the many arrows that had nicked him begin to work, so he sank in despair. But he saw one of his own men still left near him, fighting manfully away, the Indians hadn't touched him. He said to the man, "God has spared you till now, brother, so run for it, save yourself, tell Hojeda you left me dead." This man was the only one to escape, I think, plus Hojeda. There must have been a hundred men in the raiding party. Other people have said seventy died in that place.

The crew aboard ship suspected some disaster had occurred. They sensed they had lost track of Hojeda, their governor, and his party. They spotted no one, there was no one to ask. So they went up and down along the shore in the ships' boats to see if they could find someone who came from inland and could give them news good or bad. It was an anxious search. They reached a place where mangroves grow next to the water—they are a tree that does not rot, they sprout and grow and stand in sea water on great roots all thick and tangled together. They found Hojeda holed up there, his sword in hand, his shield on his back and on that shield three hundred arrow marks. He was so exhausted and hungry he could not speak. The men made a fire, they cleaned him up, gave him what they had to eat. Thus he got his wind back, his strength. And while they were there in that pitiful state, listening to him tell his sorry story and suffering, they saw Nicuesa's fleet heave into view. That caused Hojeda more grief, more anguish. He feared Nicuesa would want to get even with him for several quarrels that had taken place between them, and not many days ago, in fact not many hours, in Santo Domingo. So Hojeda told the rest to go back to the ships and leave him there alone, say not a word about him while Nicuesa was in port.

The ships' boats from Hojeda's fleet went out to welcome Nicuesa who was entering port at Cartagena with his own fleet.[62] Hojeda's men told Nicuesa the gloomy story of how, some days back, Hojeda and Juan de la Cosa went ashore with a party and destroyed the village of Calamar, took a number of slaves, then went further inland in pursuit and all disappeared. The men had the strong suspicion things had gone badly for them, for everyone they had along. The decision was to go look for them, bring them back if they found any, but on condition that he, Nicuesa, as a gentleman, not focus in this crisis on what lay between himself and Hojeda. Diego de Nicuesa was a gentleman, it angered him to hear this palaver. He told them to go right away and look for Hojeda, and if they found him alive, to bring him back. Nicuesa had no intention of harming Hojeda, but promised them instead that he was the man to help Hojeda in any crisis as if he were a brother. So they went and got Hojeda . . . who was very consoled and thanked Nicuesa greatly . . .

They then joined forces, a total of four hundred men, had them all swear a public oath that under pain of death they would take no Indian alive. They set out by night for the village of Turbaco. When they were near it,

---

[62] *History*, Bk. 2, cap. 68.

they broke into two groups. There are huge parrots in that region, red ones, called guacamayas. They screech a lot, they make a huge racket. When they sensed the presence of the Spaniards, they began their screeching. The Indians heard them. They had relaxed their guard because they thought the Spaniards all dead. But their great fear brought them suddenly out of their huts on the run, some with weapons, some without, every which way. They ran right into one group of attacking Spaniards who slashed them open. They fled from those and ran smack into another group who hacked them to pieces. They ran back to hide in the huts. To which the Spaniards set fire to burn them alive. Horror stricken and burned by the fire, the women with their babies in their arms, ran from the houses, but the instant they saw the horses—they had never seen such before—they turned back to the burning huts preferring the living flames to being eaten by those animals.

The Spaniards worked an incredible slaughter on that village, they spared no one, women, children, babies or not. Then they robbed. The story is that Nicuesa, or the whole group, took 7000 castellanos worth. As they went around the area looking for things to rob, they ran across the body of Juan de la Cosa tied to a tree, looking like a hedgehog for the arrows in him. He must have been loaded with poison and grotesque and gruesome looking as a fright. Such a fear struck the Spaniards that not a one of them dared stay in the area that night. Hojeda and Nicuesa went back to port confederates. There Hojeda said goodbye to Nicuesa, and ordered sail made for the Gulf of Urabá. That was the ultimate goal of his expedition. There he intended to get rich on his neighbor's goods. . .

. . . but because of contrary winds, he stopped 35 leagues down the coast at a small island called Isla Fuerte.[63] To make amends for the horrible thing he had done back at Cartagena, and to gain God's help for the future, he captured on the island what people he could, those unable to escape. He robbed the gold they had and anything else that proved profitable. He went on from there to the Gulf of Urabá, and inside it looked for the river of Darién. It was well known by the Indians as a place full of gold and fierce people. He found no river. So he picked a place and landed his party. Then, on top of a hill, he set up camp and called it Sant Sebastian, making the saint out to be a patron against poisoned arrows, the kind shot often in those parts. But God and His saints help no one commit injustices or evils, the kind Hojeda and crew were about. Sant Sebastian was not interested in protecting them, not even Hojeda, as we will soon see. Hojeda then scouted around for a site on which to build a town. As he did, a huge crocodile—it is an error to call it a lizard—came up out of a river and seized in its jaws the leg of a

---

[63] *Historia*, Bk. 2, cap. 59.

mare standing near, dragged it back into the river, drowned it there and made a good meal of it. Hojeda recognized he had too few people to sustain this deadly camp, Sant Sebastian. And he feared the people he was going to stir up and rob and capture. So he sent one of his ships back to Hispaniola with the gold he had seized, with the captive Indians who were to be sold as slaves. The sale would bring him people who were hungry to steal, and weapons, and other necessaries. This all happened around the beginning of 1510.

The houses, the huts at Sant Sebastian, were all made out of vegetation. So Hojeda built a strong fort out of thick logs . . . he then learned from certain Indians he had captured that there was a king in that region, a lord over many people, named Tirufi, and he had gold aplenty. He decided to go right there and not lose such a good chance. He left sufficient force behind him to protect the camp and fort, took the rest with him. The reputation of the Spaniards, their bad deeds, had spread throughout the entire area, for many leagues around. Otherwise innocent people who lived quietly in their homes, when they knew the Spaniards were coming, unleashed on them a rain of poisoned arrows, wounding many of Hojeda's men who died raving on the spot. There was no damage to the Indians. The Spaniards made a quick decision to retreat. Hojeda quickest of all, so they ran, they fled back to the safety of the fortress.

Within a short time, the food Juan de la Cosa had brought from Castile began to run out, and also the cassava brought from Hispaniola. Hojeda did not want to wait until it all went, so he decided to make some forays in the region to find and bring back food, taking it by force from the Indians. If they found some gold along the way, they were not to scorn it. They came to a certain village or group of villages. Right away the Indians came out after them and with their usual arrows wounded and killed some Spaniards. Hojeda, to avoid having them all killed, and his own person put in mortal danger, turned them around and they ran for the fortress, the Indians in pursuit right to the gate. Back inside the camp, the fortress, the survivors were hard pressed about how to bury the dead and heal those not too badly hurt, but few of those wounded by poison managed to live.

In a short time more, all provisions were gone. No one dared set foot outside the fortress to go look for food in the Indian villages. The poisoned arrows had taught them their lesson. They were so without nourishment that they ate grass and roots, not caring whether they were good or bad and lethal. Such stuff for food threw their systems off, they became terribly sick, many of them died. A man was on watch one night, he expired watching. Men just lay down on the ground and died, their only illness hunger. They thought death brought the least pain and sorrow, in death there was relief.

They were more dead than alive leading this miserable existence, but God chose not to abandon them, rather made the evil of others work them some good. It happened this way: there was someone named Bernardino de Talavera, here on Hispaniola, who lived down west. He had huge debts as did many another on the island. To stay out of jail, he decided to flee the place, but had nowhere to run except to one of the two regions we have been talking about. Maybe he had a previous agreement with Hojeda. Maybe he heard the news Hojeda had sent back with the ship that was to get provisions, i.e., that Hojeda was in the process of settling a very rich land. Talavera cooked up a plan to steal a ship. In on it were other crooks, debt-jumpers—a lot of these—and others who were on the run for crimes they had committed. The ship was anchored at Point Tiburón, two leagues away from the settlement of Salvatierra de la Cabana on the western end of Hispaniola. It belonged to some Genoese, and was a cargo ship for cassava and ham loaded on this island and brought to other areas. Talavera, with the help of 70 men, stole the ship. They showed up one day at the place where Hojeda and his crowd were starving to death. The relief, the exhilaration these latter felt, right to the soul, was beyond words, beyond appreciation. They were raised from death to life. They unloaded the provisions the ship held—bread, meat—for which Hojeda paid in gold and slaves, to the person on board who had had to come along, the person in charge of it. True to his reputation for being stingy—the story was he said he had been afraid for many years that he would die of hunger—he made a stingy handout to his men, considering the hunger they all suffered. Those who got meager shares began to mutter against him and plotted to leave that land and head off in the brigantines or in the ship that had just come. But Hojeda smoothed them, holding out to them the hope that Anciso would come, any day now.

During this period, the Indians did not relax their assaults, they attacked every day. They recognized the quickness of Hojeda, that he was the first one out against them, he beat them back, an arrow never touched him. They decided to set up an ambush so as to wound and kill him. Four bowmen went and hid behind thick reeds, their arrows well poisoned. They told the others to let loose a shout and launch an attack from just opposite them. They set things going according to plan. A shout went up opposite the ambush. Out of the fort came Hojeda, first and flying. When he reached where the ambush was set, the four bowmen shot their arrows and one hit Hojeda in the thigh, went right through.

Hojeda returned profoundly shaken, he knew he had to die raving in a few hours' time. No man had ever drawn blood on him to that point, for the thousand ruckuses he had been in, as he himself said, back in Castile and here in these parts. He thought this wound was going to finish him off. Impelled by this fear, he ordered some iron spikes heated white hot in a fire, and when they were, he ordered a surgeon to plunge both into the wounded thigh. The surgeon refused saying he'd kill him with that heat. Hojeda threatened him, swearing a solemn oath to God that if he didn't plunge them in, Hojeda would order him hung. Hojeda was doing this because it was true, the poison in the arrows worked because there was an excess of cold. The surgeon, to keep from being hung, plunged in the white hot spikes, one in the front, one in the back of the wound, using tongs. The heat penetrated not only the thigh and the leg, overcoming the poison and driving it out, but penetrated Hojeda's entire body, to such an extent that it was necessary to use up a whole barrel of vinegar wetting cloths and wrapping his whole frame in them. And that way the heat that invaded him was tempered. Hojeda suffered this voluntarily, he did not have himself bound or held, a proof of his fierce spirit and remarkable strength. He was cured this way, consuming the cold of the poisonous herb with living heat.

The food brought aboard the ship Bernardino de Talavera had stolen was eaten up, and the men began to grow famished, to feel the pressure of hunger and misery they had been in before—men were dying again of starvation every day.[64] And Anciso had not shown up with the help they hoped for. They began to shout at Hojeda, get them out of there, they were all going to die. There was talk among themselves, they were going to steal the brigantines, go to Hispaniola. They said and did other things depressed and desperate men do. Hojeda recognized their unrest and misery, so he decided to speak to them and set something going. Since Anciso was not coming, he was going to go to Hispaniola on the ship brought by Talavera, he would bring back provisions and whatever else. He was not going to take more than fifty days at the outside to return to them or send them help, but if he didn't come or send help in that time period, he gave them permission to strike the settlement and make for Hispaniola in the brigantines, or do whatever pleased them. His decision to head for Hispaniola pleased them because that meant they could hope for quicker relief. Hojeda designated Francisco Pizarro to be captain in his stead until Anciso should come, the man he had already chosen as his chief magistrate. Pizarro was later a Marquis in Peru. The seventy men who had come with Talavera, or most of them anyway, saw the wretched and dangerous life Hojeda's men led, they refused to remain ashore, they wanted to return to

[64] *History*, Bk. 2, cap. 50.

Hispaniola, choosing as the lesser evil what would happen to them on the island than the evil they knew awaited them ashore if they stayed.

So Hojeda set sail with Talavera and the others in the stolen ship. But they could not make it to Hispaniola, so they landed in Cuba, I think in the province and port of Xagua, though Spaniards had not yet settled there. They went ashore, abandoning the ship, and headed east overland to get close to Hispaniola. But something had happened, either aboard ship en route, or before they had boarded, or after they went ashore on Cuba. It was about who was captain or some other reasons I did not take the trouble to find out when I could have. Hojeda and Talavera turned on each other. Or maybe some of Hojeda's own people who were on the ship wanted to avenge themselves on him for some injury they thought they had received from him. At any rate, they all joined around Talavera, they made a prisoner of Hojeda, and kept him prisoner as they went their way through Cuba. But he went loose, because they had many a brush, many a skirmish with Indians, and Hojeda was worth more in a fight than half the rest. And because he was so bold and strong and quick, he mocked them all as his captors, he defied them saying, "Tough guys! Turncoats! Split up in twos here and I'll kill you two by two!" No one dared answer him or go after him.

The Indians took them on outside the villages to keep them from entering, even tried to kill them, because many of the Indians on the island of Cuba were really natives of Hispaniola, from which they had fled because of the destruction and death wrought by the Spaniards there on the people. They were very experienced in what Spaniards did—e.g., the killing, the cleaning out of innocent natives on the Lucayan islands. When those on Cuba saw Spaniards banded together, they judged, they feared the band had come to do the same to them. But the weapons the Indians used in war were few and nearly useless, some simple basics, and they were peaceful people, too timid to quarrel with anyone. Even if they joined forces and were a lot in number, they could do little damage, and they did little. But the Spaniards were exhausted and struggling so they dodged the Indian villages to avoid a fight, they stayed close to the shore line.

After they had gone over a hundred leagues, they ran into a marsh that met the sea, one that was knee deep or somewhat more. They thought it would give out shortly, so they kept going along their line. They were two or three days into the marsh and it was getting deeper, but they hoped it couldn't be much longer and didn't want to go back over the distance they had covered, it had been such a struggle, so they went on ahead. And the marsh grew deeper and they got further into it. They went on this way eight or ten days, hoping the marsh would give out, afraid to retrace their route because they had suffered incredible hardship and hunger back along it, up to their waists in mud and water, day and night. To sleep, they climbed up on the mangrove trees where they could catch some, though it was troubled sleep, bitter, sad. Their food was cassava bread, a mouthful of cheese if anyone brought some, axi, a native pepper, some roots—garlic or sweet potato, carrot-like or truffle-like, and raw. It was food each one carried in a bag or sack over his shoulder. They drank brackish water. So they kept on, kept hoping the marsh would give out, but the thing got deeper the further it stretched. They often came to spots where the mud and foul water reached their armpits, other spots up to their necks, others deeper, and men who couldn't swim drowned. The food got soaked in the sacks as the men swam. Wet cassava is gone, nothing one can do to restore it, like wafers tossed into a pond.

Hojeda had in his bag, along with food, a portrait of Our Lady, a pious picture, marvelously painted, Flemish, one given him by Bishop Don Juan de Fonseca, who was very favorable to him. Hojeda had great devotion to this image. He had always been a devout servant of the Mother of God. The men came on some roots of mangrove trees that grow up out of the water. They climbed up on them to rest a bit, those that were in that group, because the men were not all together, some were behind—those who either had little strength or little spirit or were disabled—and some were ahead. Hojeda took the image out of his bag, put it in a tree and knelt to it, urging the others to kneel to it, then begged Our Lady would she please help them. They did this every day and often, whenever they had the chance. It was now impossible to turn back. They could not retrace their route, coming it was so bitter and bruising. They did not even think of that, just about death, from drowning or hunger or thirst, as many had already done. They had only the hope the marsh would give out. It lasted 30 leagues, they were in it 30 days, struggling, miserable, as described. They had been 70. Half of them, I think, died either of hunger or thirst or drowning. (The struggles the Spaniards were willing to undergo in the Indies to find gold were the harshest, the hardest any man has known ever in this world, but those Hojeda underwent, and the others in that marsh, had to be the worst.)

Some finally reached the edge, God willing, the toughest of them, the most agile, those who could sustain best that awful situation. They found a travelled path and headed along it. Within a league they reached an Indian village named Cueba . . . and once there dropped down near dead from exhaustion. The Indians were stunned at what they saw. The men told them there were others still behind in a desperate struggle. They told them through sign language, or some of the men knew a few words of the language of Hispaniola, the language of the two islands is the same. The acceptance, the hospitality they received among the Indians—no one of them would have gotten a better in their parents' home. The Indians gave the survivors food in abundance right away, all they had, and it was considerable because Cuba was an island plentifully supplied with food, as I will describe later, please God. They washed the men, cleaned them up, put life back in them.

The chief of the village immediately sent a party of his people with food for the others still stuck in their wretched struggle. Orders were to help them free of the marsh, revive them, give them relief. The men who could not make it to the village on their own were to be carried. Orders were also to go into the marsh and find those who had faltered. The Indians did their job well, better than they were ordered to, they always do the same unless Spaniards have beforehand harrassed and maltreated them. After the survivors were all out and in the village, they were tended for a long time, fed, restored, consoled. It was as if the Indians thought they were angels . . .

. . . after they were restored . . . they went on to a province, a village named Macaca.[65] The Indians there received them very well . . . The Spaniards knew they were cut off from Hispaniola, had no way of crossing from Cuba. But they remembered there were Spaniards on Jamaica, it was only 20 leagues away from where they now were . . . Pedro de Ordas . . . offered to go in a canoe . . . They asked the chief to supply a craft and crew of Indians to make the crossing to Jamaica. He did so willingly . . . They crossed, made the island, and notified Juan de Esquivel . . . Right away he provided a caravel provisioned with what the survivors needed . . . and sent Pánfilo de Narváez as captain . . . He brought them to the island of Jamaica . . . After a time, Hojeda, recovered from the trouble-ridden life he had led since his departure from Hispaniola, returned to it . . . The others who had gone from Cuba to Jamaica with him remained there, they did not dare come to Hispaniola for fear of being brought to justice, for stealing a ship, for the abuse Hojeda had gotten at their hands. But the Admiral's justice officials knew they were in Jamaica, so sent for them, especially for Bernardino de Talavera. He came back a prisoner, others as well, the guilty ones, or at least the more guilty ones. They were convicted by due process, and the judges sentenced Talavera to be hanged, which sentence was carried out . . .

Hojeda remained in Santo Domingo for a long time after, more than a year I think, I saw him. Some men waited to kill him one night when he had been out passing the time in conversation with good friends. The would-be killers were men who had been with him most, or on the last voyage. But he frustated even them in the attempt. I think he raced down a street a step ahead of their strokes, just as he had always done in similar fixes.

---

[65] *History*, Bk. 2, cap. 61.

The end came not long after this, as God would have it, the end of his days. He died sick and poor, poor, he didn't have a cent to bury him, I think, for all the pearls, the gold he had gotten or stolen from the Indians, for all the slaves he had made of them the times he hit the mainland. He willed himself to be buried right at the door of the church and monastery of St. Francis, under the sill. They are not correct who say the Admiral wanted to arrest him, so he sought sanctuary at St. Francis, and died there of the wound he had received at Urabá. I saw him, as I said, alive, free and well walking about the city. After I left, I heard he had died.

That was it for Alonso de Hojeda, the man who so often on this island shocked and brutalized the Indians. He was the first one to violate justice on Hispaniola, using a power of jurisdiction he did not have, cutting the ears off a very important chief, a chief who, with much more certain right, could have hung him or those with him, cut them to shreds, a right given that chief by the natural law. And could also have done in the Admiral who sent them, as unjust and violent thugs who invaded the chief's and neighboring kingdoms and realms. Hojeda was also the one who, through a clever trick, a lawless maneuver, seized King Caonabo and dragged him captive to Isabella. Caonabo drowned, in chains, aboard a ship that was to take him to Castile—in violation of all justice and reason. And Hojeda was a plague on the mainland, and on other islands as well, places that never gave him cause, and he took from them many an Indian to be sold in Castile as a slave . . . May God have granted him to know, before he died, that the evils he inflicted on the Indians were sins.

e. Pedrarias and the Ultimatum
Prenote
Spain needed holy reasons for its unholy behavior, with them it could act without sin. Clearly it knew it was inflicting violence, but violence was excusable in a just cause, so the reasoning went. Spain, therefore, had to concoct just causes. All of them are summarized in the following documents, which are from 1512, and were given to Pedrarias de Avila when he went out to Darién as governor in 1514, replacing Vasco Nuñez de Balboa. Las Casas sees the documents as either mockery or madness, particularly the second one, called the ULTIMATUM [Requerimiento]. In the first, the King explains what right behavior towards Indians ought to be. But implicit in it is the right to use force. And force is in fact being used in the very area Pedrarias is to govern. Vasco Nuñez has already plundered it. In the ULTIMATUM, Christianity has been reduced to a distortion, and Las Casas names it as such, and expresses a true sense of Christianity as a corrective. But the ULTIMATUM had a life of its own, a version was given to Cortés in the 1520's for Mexico, and to Pizarro in the 1530's for Peru.

Vasco Nuñez decided to send his startling news on to the King—he had discovered the Sea of the South [Pacific] and pearls, fresh discoveries both . . .[66] He sent a close friend, someone from Arbolancha, a Basque who had been with him every step of the way. He gave him the choicest pearls to present to the King in his and his men's name . . . [Back in Spain] Bishop Fonseca and Secretary Conchillos brought Arbolancha to see the King who received him graciously and was delighted at the good news he brought, and the pearls, asking how they were gotten and where. Arbolancha answered all the King's questions. He gave a complete account of how things had gone on the expedition, detailing the tough struggle they had to put up, the crucial victories they had won over the Indians, and everything else they did to achieve the goal they set for themselves. But he said nothing of the awful scandal given, the violences done the Indians all through that region, the deaths, the robberies, the unjust taking of prisoners among the inhabitants. Nor did the King ask about this. Nor did the Bishop, nor did Conchillos, both of whom were more obligated to ask. But they all spoke their questions and answers as if they were discussing victories and aftermaths in Africa or Turkey.

. . . The King knew about the loss of Alonso de Hojeda and Juan de la Cosa and Diego de Nicuesa, along with their parties, knew about the strife, the splits between Spaniards still in Darién, knew that Vasco Núñez, by force or fraud, was at the source of it all.[67] So the King set in motion the process of sending out from Castile someone highly qualified to take over governing the region in the King's name. . . The person considered was Pedrarias de Avila. . . The King decided he should be sent as governor . . .

So he ordered Bishop Fonseca of Burgos to consult and agree on the instructions Pedrarias would have to take along so he would know how to manage, and the governance would not go awry as it had on Hispaniola.[68] Here are some excerpts:

> "You must bring it about by your good behavior that the Indians get along with the Christians in peace and in love—bring it about in every way you think or feel would help towards this goal, or in whatever form or fashion that might hold out a hope that this could happen. This is the way to act correctly towards the Indians. The main thing to do to achieve this goal is not to allow any promise made to them to be broken. Instead, before a promise is made, it should be looked into carefully to see if it can

---

[66] *History*, Bk. 3, cap. 52.

[67] *History*, Bk. 3, cap. 53.

[68] *History*, Bk. 3, cap. 54.

be kept, and if it cannot, it should not be made. If it can, it should
be kept strictly so they place great confidence in your word. You
must not allow any evil, any harm done to them, so they do not
riot or rebel out of fear. You are, in fact, to punish those who do
them evil or harm in disobedience to your orders. Under this
policy, they will prefer to convert and come to the knowledge of
God and of our holy Catholic faith. It is worth more to us to gain
a hundred this way than a hundred thousand the opposite way.

"But in case they do not choose to come under our sovereignty in
this fashion, and if it is necessary to make war on them, you must
be sure no war is made if they are not the aggressors, if they have
done us no evil, no harm to our people, nor made an attempt to do
so. And even if they have done violence, before hostilities, you
should present them with the ULTIMATUM requiring them to
submit to our sovereignty—once, twice, thrice, even more times,
as many as you think are in conformity with the instructions you
carry. And since you will have there, or along with you, Christians who will know the Indian tongues, you will let the Indians
know through them, and right away, what good will come to them
if they submit to our sovereignty, and what evil and destruction
and death and slaughter will come to them from war. And those
who will be taken alive will be made slaves of the Christians.
They must be made to understand what it means to be a slave.
They should recognize this, they may not pretend ignorance later.
There is a firm basis in what has just been said for them to be
made slaves, and for the Christians to own them in good conscience.

"But you must be especially awake to one possibility. Since
Christians come into possession of Indians, they want it to be by
war, not by peace. They are always talking up war. There is no
excuse for not meeting with the Indians, be well aware of this.
They must be given certain standing through this process. The
best advice on the matter, overseas, will be that of the Reverend
Father Fray Juan Cabedo, Bishop of Darién, and that of the clerics
who are less prey to passion, and less eager to profit from the
Indians.

"In case you have to give our people Indians to control or have as
household servants, you must see to it that you stick to the
instructions you carry—they are the result of careful inquiry. That
way the Indians will be better preserved, better treated, better

trained in our holy Catholic faith. For that reason you are to obey the least instruction. But if you should notice anything that ought to be done for the Indians, beyond what your instructions contain, done for their well-being, their conversion, you would be right to do it so they can receive better treatment and can live more at ease in Christian company. The sum and substance of this is that everything here said, and in the preceding chapter, is so the Indians can be drawn by love and openness and friendliness and good treatment to our holy Catholic faith. Force and harsh treatment of them are excluded whenever possible. That way Our Lord will be well served and I will consider it a great service to me.

"You must do things this way there, and not as on the island of Hispaniola. Indians are less inclined to work, they are used to loafing. We learned on Hispaniola that they ran for the hills to escape work. We must conclude they will do a better job of running where you are because they have continuous land. They did not on Hispaniola. All they lose in Darién are their houses. Thus it seems doubtful, a difficult thing to entrust Indians to Christians they way they are entrusted on Hispaniola . . ."

Do you see [in this latter paragraph] the slander those who killed, who keep killing Indians, sent back to the Kings and those on the Council?[69] To justify a little the Indian deaths they caused and the round of work they put them to! Oh what a judgment in eternity they must have suffered who made up those monstrous lies so as to be able then to consume those innocent peoples—defamed, harrassed peoples, hounded, beaten, demeaned, abandoned and forgotten peoples, by everyone who could help them, demoralized, defenseless peoples! They did not flee work! They fled the torments of hell they underwent in the mines and in other jobs of ours! They fled starvation, beatings, constant lashings, they fled injury and insult, hearing themselves called dogs constantly, they fled cruel and unusual treatment done them, without recourse, night and day. They fled certain death!

What follows is the formal demand Pedrarias was to use when requiring the Indians to submit and become subjects of the Kings of Castile.[70] It was later provided for the rest of the Indies.

[69] *History*, Bk. 3, cap. 56.
[70] *History*, Bk. 3, cap. 57.

Ultimatum

"We speak for the King, Don Hernando, and the Queen, Doña Juana, of Castile and León, both conquerors of barbaric peoples. We are their agents. We inform you, as best we can get across to you, that our God, our living and eternal Lord created heaven and earth, a man and a woman. And from them, you and we and people in the world derive, we are their descendants, their offspring. So are all who come after us. Next, due to the mounting number of offspring derived from them, over five thousand years, in that region where the world was first created, it was necessary that people depart, some to one place, some to another, and so split up into varied kingdoms and provinces. For they were unable to live or survive all in the one place. Over all those peoples, God Our Lord put one man in charge. That was St. Peter. He was to be the lord and master whom everyone should obey. He was to be head of the human race wherever people were to be found, whatever their law, their group, their belief. And God gave him the world as his realm to rule. And though God told him to set up his throne in Rome as the most apt place from which to govern the world, God also granted him the power to locate this throne anywhere whatever and rule and govern anyone, whether they be Christian or Moor or Jew or Gentile, whatever be their group or their belief. This man is called Pope, which name means august, great father, ruler of humankind. All who lived at the time of St. Peter obeyed him, accepted him as lord and master in charge of all there is. All who lived subsequently thought the same of those who were chosen pontiff in succession to St. Peter. The pontificate continues up to the present day, and will continue until the world ends. One of the recent pontiffs who succeeded to St. Peter's dignity and throne, as I just described them, acting as lord of the world, granted these islands and mainland of the Ocean Sea to the King and Queen named above, and to their successors our Lords in the realm. And granted everything on those islands and mainland. And did so in certain documents they issued on the matter—so the process is described—which documents you may see if you wish. As a result, their Majesties are lords and masters of these islands and mainland due to the aforesaid grant. So you are under obligation to do what others have done, to accept as lords and masters Their Highnesses, just as nearly all the islands have, who have been given this notice—have accepted them, served them, continue to serve them as subjects are required. Then freely and with no resistence, no delay they acccepted to submit to religious men—once they were told to—men Their Highnesses sent to preach and teach our holy faith. And all those peoples became Christian of their own free and favorable will, for no reward, for no favor. They are Christian now. And Their Highnesses have accepted them happily and graciously, have ordered them treated as their own subjects and vassals.

"Therefore, as best we can, we insist, we demand that you grasp this well, what we say to you. That you take it on yourselves to examine and understand it over a reasonable period of time, then recognize the Church as Lady and Mistress of the world entire, recognize the supreme Pontiff, called the Pope, then, in his name, recognize the King and the Queen Doña Juana, our rulers, as being his viceregents, recognize them as rulers, lords, kings over the islands and main, by virtue of the donation described above. And you must consent to allow that religious order priests should preach and make known to you the aforesaid faith.

"If you listen to the faith and submit yourselves to Their Majesties, you will do well. We will accept you in their name with full love and charity. We will leave you your wives and children and homes, free, no enslavement. Thus you can do freely with them whatever you wish and think best. And we will not force you to become Christian. But you can, if you wish, convert to our holy Catholic faith after learning its truth. This is what almost all the inhabitants of the other islands have done. What is more, Their Highnesses will grant you many privileges, many exemptions, many favors.

"But if you refuse to comply, if you delay your decision out of ill-will, we assure you that with the help of God, we will go after you with force of arms, we will war on you everywhere, every way we can, we will force you under the yoke of obedience to the Church and Their Highnesses, we will capture your persons, your wives, your children, we will make slaves of you, we will sell you, dispose of you as slaves as Their Highnesses will command. We will do to every one of you all the damage we can, treating you as subjects who refuse obedience, are unwilling to accept their superior, who resist, who reject him. And we declare that the damage and death effected by all this will be your own, not Their Highnesses' fault, not ours, not that of these soldiers along with us. And we ask the notary here present that he provide a signed statement that we made this ultimatum. And we ask those present to be witnesses of the same."

Ask, if you have any sense—and even if the Indians understood our language, its vocabulary, or what our language, our vocabulary intended—what new knowledge did we bring them?[71] What did they learn hearing us say there was one God for the world, creator of heaven and earth, creator of humankind, all of humankind? They thought the sun was God. There were other gods whom they believed had created humankind and all else. What reasons, witnesses, what miracles were to prove to them that the God of the Spaniards was more of a god than their own? Who was more the creator of the world and human beings, more than the gods they believed in? If Moors and Turks came and gave them the same ULTIMATUM, insisting that Mohammed was God, creator of the world and humankind, would they be required to believe it? Even if the Spaniards provided better testimony and more convincing proofs in their ultimatum about their God being the creator of the world and humankind, better than what the Moors would provide about Mohammed?

Next. How, with what compelling reasons, miracles, did the Spaniards prove that their God had greater power than the Indians' gods? So the Spaniards' God could constitute a man named St. Peter the lord and master of all human beings in this world, a man all were obliged to obey? Even though the Indians had their own kings, their own native lords, and thought they had no others in this world. So what attitude would they have, what love, what reverence would be sparked in their hearts—in the hearts especially of kings and princes—towards the God of the Spaniards at hearing that, by order of that God, St. Peter or his successor gave their lands to the Spaniards? The Indians considered their kings rightful ones, free, in possession of their powers from a long time past and from their predecessors. And they were asked—sovereign and subject alike—to accept as overlord someone they had never seen, never heard of, with no knowledge of whether he was good or bad, or what he intended with them—govern them, rob them, destroy them? And the bearers of the ultimatum were fierce, bearded men, well armed with lots of weapons. What could, what should an Indian, in his right mind, expect from such a bunch?

And what about this? Were they required to obey a foreign king without having a treaty or contract or agreement made between them about a good and just way the king was to govern, or the services they had to provide him as their part of the bargain? That kind of treaty work is usually done at the start when people elect or accept a new king or a successor king. It has to be done and sworn to. Reason tells us and natural law. . .

---

[71] *History*, Bk. 3, cap. 58.

I would like to ask the Council who decided that this ULTIMATUM should be made on those peoples who lived in peace under their own lords and native rulers, lived in their own homes without offense—no harm to anyone—what credence were the Indians obliged to give to that document or to the donation? And what trust, what credence to the Bulls issued under the papal seal that were presented to them there? For not submitting to these, did the Indians merit excommunication, or merit to have some other spiritual or material evil inflicted on them? Did they commit some sin by refusal? Shouldn't all of this have seemed to them like raving, like madness, wrong-headed every which way, a babble? Especially when Spaniards told them they had to submit to the Church? Look at it! Doesn't an understanding of what the Church is, and what obligation anyone has to submit to it depend on knowing what it is, on believing all that our Christian faith teaches us? Do we not believe there is a Church, do we not respect its visible head, do we not submit to it, obey it, because we accept and hold a true faith in the most Holy Trinity, Father, Son, and Holy Spirit? And because we accept and profess the fourteen other articles of faith pertaining to the Divinity and the Humanity of God? . . .

The King's Council was ignorant, that is clear . . . Please God they will be forgiven for it. And for how unjust, fruitless, scandalous, crazy, absurd, their ULTIMATUM was . . . You have to laugh, or better weep, that a Council of the King would believe these people more obligated to accept the King as their Lord than Christ, Creator and God! They cannot be forced under threat of punishment to accept the faith. But the Council, to get them to submit to the King, ordered them forced!

Pedrarias and his fleet reached the port of Darién, it's a half league from the town, I believe.[72] Right away, before someone else landed, he sent an aide to let Vasco Nuñez know of his arrival. At that time Vasco Nuñez had four hundred and fifty men, maybe less, but they were toughened by trials, so amounted to many more than the twelve to fifteen hundred Pedrarias brought. When the aide reached town, he asked for Vasco Nuñez. People answered, "Right there!" Vasco Nuñez was overseeing, helping his slaves build or cover a straw hut. He was in a shirt that was cotton broad-cloth worn over another of linen. He had rope sandals on his feet and baggy breeches for his legs. The aide was shocked that this was Vasco Nuñez whose exploits and riches were legend already in Castile. The aide thought he would find him seated on some throne of majesty. So he approached Vasco Nuñez and said, "My Lord, Pedrarias has just arrived at port with his fleet. He comes as governor of this region." Vasco Nuñez told the aide to

---

[72] *History*, Bk. 3, cap. 60.

tell Pedrarias that he was welcome, Nuñez was happy at his arrival (God knows if that was true!), and he, plus all in town, as servants of the King, were ready to accept and obey Pedrarias.

When the whole town had the news of the arrival of fleet and forces down at the port, there was a hubbub, people jabbering in groups everywhere ... The talk was about the best way to meet Pedrarias, walk down armed as when encountering Indians, or unarmed, as townspeople. Opinions differed. Vasco Nuñez took the safest tack, one that would cause the least unease. So they all went the half league and unarmed, in civilian dress. Pedrarias, an alert man, wise in the ways of violence, had his men at the ready, not quite sure that Vasco Nuñez would accept him in good grace, nor the men behind him. When Vasco Nuñez reached the place where Pedrarias and his wife, Doña Isabel de Bobadilla, were waiting side by side, he and his company bowed to them most respectfully. Then Vasco Nuñez, with gracious words, promised, in his own name and that of all the rest, obedience and service to Pedrarias, the King's governor, from then on ...

The day after they all arrived and settled in, Pedrarias started to inquire of the Spaniards who were there before he came if reports were true, the fabulous descriptions Vasco Nuñez wrote the King about the Sea of the South and pearls on the islands thereof, about the rich gold mines and other wealth. He found out things were exactly as Vasco Nuñez had described them—except for hauling the gold in with nets, like fish. That description was not from Vasco Nuñez. It was the silly fantasy either Colmenares or some others had broadcast, and the stupid greed of Castile had believed. . . Pedrarias saw it was not so. But the new arrivals kept up their asking where and how gold could be hauled in with nets, like fish. Right then, I think, they began to lose heart, they saw no nets nor gear for fishing gold, nor were people discussing it every instant. Then this happened: they heard about the struggles men there had undergone, heard the gold they had was not hauled in with nets, but robbed from the Indians. Yes, there were many mines, rich mines, in the region, but gold was gotten from them only with fierce labor. So the newcomers began to wake up to the truth, to find out they had been badly fooled.

Pedrarias ordered next a criminal investigation into Vasco Nuñez. The lawyer Espinosa conducted it, he was head magistrate. Espinosa ordered Nuñez taken and fined some thousands of castellanos for the injuries done to the jurist Anciso and others. But ultimately, out of respect for Nuñez' exploits, which he saw as a great service to the King, Espinosa freed him concerning the death of the hapless Nicuesa and from the pile of other charges laid against him. There is no mention, in the records of the investigation, of the robberies, the killings, the enslavements, the scandals

Vasco Nuñez had committed against the many chiefs, leaders, individual Indians. There was no one, not even the agent of the King, to accuse him. Because to kill or rob Indians in the Indies was not considered criminal . . .

Even as Pedrarias was making arrangements for sending his people out to set up towns, the food and supplies brought aboard ship from Castile began to run out.[73] There were a lot of people eating. Rations ordered by the King got slimmer. There was not enough to fill their bellies. The people Pedrarias brought began to sicken and die, some from hunger, some because the places where they were put were unhealthy—near swamps, hollows, in jungles—or because the air of the region was lighter, clearer, healthier than almost all of the climate of Spain. And Spain was so far away. He himself was not spared serious illness, though he had better supplies. On the advice of the doctor or doctors he brought, he left Darién, he and the rest, and went to the river Corobarí nearby. It was thought to be a healthier place.

The illness of Pedrarias delayed the outfitting and dispatching of settlers, it did not delay the deaths of many men. They died daily of hunger and disease. But many more from hunger, from lack of food, than from disease. The King's rations were totally spent. The hunger got so bad that many a gentleman died moaning, "I want bread!" These were men who pawned their inheritances back in Castile, men who swapped a smock of embroidered silk or other rich clothing to get a pound of corn bread or Castilian biscuit or cassava. One man, a notable Pedrarias had brought, one day walked down the street crying out he was dying of hunger, then right in front of the whole town dropped on the ground and gave up the ghost. The scene was unbelievable, people dressed in rich and silken robes fringed with brocade worth small fortunes, falling down dead one after the other from sheer hunger. But some did leave town for the fields where they foraged for and ate the tenderest grasses and roots they could find. They were like beasts. And some who were stronger gave up dignity and hauled in from the hills bundles of firewood to swap for whatever food anyone would give them. So many died each day they were buried in a single pit that was dug. Often, if a single grave was opened, the diggers were unwilling to close it because, sure enough, in no more than a few hours others would die and be company for the one. Corpses went for days without burial. The people who were still healthy and had a bit to eat did not have the strength to bury the dead. There was little care to provide funeral rites, or prepare the corpses for burial. They all saw with stark clarity how gold was netted in like fish.

The situation was disastrous, and for Pedrarias too, plus his entourage. So he allowed some important notables to return to Spain. A

---

[73] *History*, Bk. 3, cap. 61.

boatload of them was forced to stop at Cuba where we killed their hunger. We were in a land of great abundance. The opposite of the starved place the boatload had just left. Not that the land there was sterile. It is extremely fertile. It overflowed with food before we came. But the Spaniards wiped out the people, some through killing upon killing, some through living capture, through export of them to these islands to be sold as slaves, the rest through being forced to flee the territory. So the region was depopulated. But it is sure that if the Spaniards had behaved as true Christians towards the caciques, the chiefs, the native peoples, they would have been provided for, sustained, and many more than their number, even made rich the way they wanted. But they did not deserve it. They did not have in mind what God had in mind when God invited Spain. The belief that gold could be hauled in like fish, and the burning desire to do just that, netted them death.

. . . Las Casas proved [in the Council] that in the 6 year span since Pedrarias began his tyrannical undertaking, the King had lost money. For Pedrarias' departure, it cost 52-54,000 ducats.[74] After he reached Darién, in 1514, and on until 1519, he robbed over a million ducats in gold—and I think I give a low estimate—he drove into hell over 500,000 souls, deprived of faith and sacraments. During the whole of this time, he had not sent the King a single castellano—unless the 3,000 castellanos Juan Cabedo brought are counted, he was bishop of the mainland during this time. More about him and his business later. Now this was the practice of Pedrarias and the King's officials: from all the gold they acquired by robbery through their forays and attacks on Indians in the various regions where they went marauding, they set aside a fifth for the King. Then from that fifth, they paid themselves a salary. If any gold was left over, they kept it in order to pay next year's salaries—if their robbing failed, their salaries would not. Using this tactic, they sent not a peso's worth of gold back to the King.

---

[74] *History*, Bk. 3, 141.

Part II.
The Rise of Conscience

- 1 -

Pedro de Córdoba, O.P.

Prenote

The first voices Las Casas heard protesting the destructive behavior of Spaniards towards Indians on Hispaniola came from the Dominicans who landed on the island in 1510. Their superior was Pedro de Córdoba, a man of nearly the same age as Las Casas. He is the parent of Las Casas' awakening and subsequent career as a protector of the Indians. De Córdoba was not to live long, until 1521, but his influence on Las Casas is recognizable throughout the latter's long career. The small portrait of De Córdoba drawn by Las Casas reveals the spiritual kinship between the two men.

Córdoba's spiritual leadership

Fray Pedro de Córdoba [was] a man mature in virtue.[75] God, Our Lord, gave him many gifts, vested him with graciousness in body and soul. He was a native of Córdoba, born of nobility and Christian. Physically tall, physically handsome. His judgment was superior, prudent, instinctively discrete, much at peace with itself. He was quite young when he entered the Order of St. Dominic. He was a student at Salamanca. It was there at St. Stephen's that he took the habit. He matured rapidly in the arts, philosophy, theology, and would have been *summa cum laude* if he had not gotten

---

[75] *History*, Bk. 2, most of cap. 54, captions added. Reprinted with permission from *The Only Way*, pp. 197-200.

intense, prolonged headaches from severe practices of penance. The headaches caused him to cut back very much on his studies, to be satisfied with a modest command of the sacred sciences. Though he tempered his studies, he intensified the rigor of his penitential practices throughout the course of his life, every time the state of his health permitted it. He was a preacher, a devout and skilled one, that was among the many talents God gave him. He gave a remarkable, praiseworthy example to everyone, so inspiring were his practices of piety in the way of virtue on the quest for God. It seems certain that he departed from this life as clean of sin as on the day he was born. He was transferred from Salamanca, with other mature religious, to St. Thomas of Avila where fervor was flourishing at the time.

. . . Fray Domingo de Mendoza . . . sent the said Fray Pedro de Córdoba—28 years old then—as vicar in charge of two other friars, though they were older. He assigned also a lay brother to the group. These four members brought the Order of Preachers to Hispaniola. The lay brother later returned to Castile. That left three, three whose lives began to permeate the place with their belief and their holiness. They were welcomed in by a good Christian who lived near town, Pedro de Lumbreras by name. He gave them a hut to live in at the edge of his place. There were no houses in those days, just small huts made of thatch. He gave them cassava root to eat, a kind of bread poor in nourishment if eaten alone, not with meat or fish. They got but few eggs, and some fish, on rare occasions, if there was a catch. And cooked cabbage, without oil often, simply with *axi*, a pepper the natives use. There was an utter lack of Castilian products on that island. It was hard to get wheat bread or wine, even for mass. They slept on beds made of interlaced branches on notched poles covered with dry straw for a mattress. They dressed in a habit of coarse cloth and a cloak of untreated wool. Given this comfortable life and marvelous menu, they fasted seven months in a year with no break, as the Order required of them and still requires. They preached, they heard confessions with God-like strength. They had to have it.

Every Spaniard on that island had perverted the Christian practices, especially the fasts and abstinences required by the Church. The Spaniards ate meat on the Sabbath, even on Fridays, even for the whole of Lent. Their slaughterhouses were going all the time, unashamedly, even religiously, as they are for Easter time. The Friars through their preaching, and more through their severe penance and abstinence, brought the Spaniards to an awareness of their behavior, to give up their gluttony during the seasons and days established by the Church. There was a kindred grand corruption in money matters and usury. Yet the Friars stopped it, made many give back the money. Other notable effects worthy of Christianity and the Order of St. Dominic followed their providential arrival.

Córdoba's missionary leadership

At the time they came ashore in the port city of Santo Domingo, the Admiral [Diego] Columbus had gone, along with his wife Doña Maria de Toledo, to visit the town of Concepción de la Vega. They were staying on there. So Fray Pedro de Córdoba, the holy man, went to tell the two of his arrival, on foot, without pomp, eating roots for bread, taking for drink cold water from the many arroyos. He slept on the ground in the open fields and in the hills with a cloak for his bedding. Thirty leagues hard journey. The Admiral, and Doña Maria his wife, received him with great kindness and favor. They bowed to him as anyone would on seeing him for the first time. His appearance, for all his 28 years, was venerable and saintly and peaceful and ascetic.

He came on Saturday, I think. On the Sunday which fell in the Octave of All Saints, he preached a sermon on the glories in paradise God prepared for his elect, preached with intensity and eagerness a sermon that was lofty, heavenly. I heard it and thought myself lucky to do so. He urged his audience, all of them, that at the end of their served meals they should send off to church the Indians they kept to do the household work. So the congregation sent them, men, women, great and small. Córdoba, seated on a stool with a crucifix in his hand, using some interpreters, preached. He began with the creation of the world, narrating its history up to the point where Christ was put on the cross. It was a sermon eminently worth hearing, and remembering, very fruitful for the Indians—they had never to that point heard someone like him or such doctrine. He was the first ever to preach to them or to other island natives in the many years since the Spaniards came. Most Indians died without hearing the faith preached. The Spaniards as well could draw much profit from that sermon. If what he said was preached in any quantity to the Indians, there would have been a much greater harvest of native souls than there was. God would have been better known, better loved, much less offended. Finally, having paid his due respects to the Admiral, having completed his business in a few days' time, he returned to Santo Domingo. He left behind with all those who heard or saw him vivid impressions of his love and his piety.

Then, if I remember rightly, the force behind this first mission, Fray Domingo de Mendoza, came in one of the newly arrived ships bringing a solid group of sturdy Friars. They were all outstanding religious. They had offered to come knowingly and willingly. They knew for certain they would bear great burdens on the island. They would eat no bread, drink no wine, have no meat, they would not travel on horseback, not dress in linen or wool, not sleep on sheepskin mattresses. They would have to put up with the menu and discipline of the Order. And even that much would often be lacking. And this was the prospect that moved them to suffer for the sake of God. Eagerly and joyfully. As a result only stalwart religious came out.

Once there, in that town, among that people, Fray Domingo de Mendoza and his brethren were impressed beyond words by Fray Pedro de Córdoba and by those with him. Since they were all now in number over 12 or 15 as I recall, they agreed unanimously, and with a will to do good, to add certain rules and regulations to the established constitutions of the Order—and whoever keeps the existing ones does a good deal already—so as to live a greater austerity. They had in mind that when they kept the new rules they surely kept the old constitution, the one put in place by the saintly founders of the Order, kept it inviolably alive and effective. I recall that they decided on one policy among others: they would not beg for bread, nor wine, nor oil, while they were healthy. If such food was sent unasked, they would eat it and thank God. For the sick, one could beg from door to door. So it fell out that on Easter day they had nothing to eat except some boiled cabbage, no oil, garnished only with *axi* and salt. They kept to this life of austerity for many years, at least for the whole time the saintly priest Fray Pedro de Córdoba lived. They did great works of penance. The religious spirit waxed mightily in their practice of obedience and poverty. The pristine period of St. Dominic was brought to life again there. Fray Pedro de Córdoba's reputation for holiness grew so much that the king of Portugal wrote asking the king of Spain or the officials of the Order to send him Dominican friars from the Indies, either to reform Portugal or to fill out the ranks of the Order in India or anywhere else.

There was a command that each Sunday and feast day of obligation a friar should preach to the Indians after dinnertime, just as the Servant of God Pedro de Córdoba had begun it in the church at Concepción de la Vega. I, who am writing this, took on that task at one time.

* * * *

The Vicar [of the Dominicans], Padre Fray Pedro de Córdoba, reached Spain and went to court. . . .[76] He spoke at length to the King, giving him a full account of the facts and the reasons, and what had moved them to preach [against Spaniards holding Indians in encomienda] . . . The King gave him a most respectful hearing. Fray Pedro was, in his person, a very impressive man. There was an aura of holiness about him, so anyone at all who saw him or spoke with him or heard him speak knew God lived in

[76] *History*, Bk. 3, cap. 17, near the beginning.

him. He had the inward grace and outward manner of sanctity. The King conceived a great esteem for him and treated him as one does a holy man. And the King was right to do.

- 2 -

Antón Montesino, O.P.: The Sermons

Prenote

The "other" Spain now speaks out against the mistreatment of Indian peoples on the island of Hispaniola, and Las Casas records the event, the principles that inspired the Dominicans to protest, and the consequences of that protest. The Dominicans knew what charity was required of Christians, but they also knew the laws that should govern civilized peoples, and knew the dignity natural law provided every human being, a dignity that could only be violated for just cause, i.e., capital crime. They learned quickly about the mistreatment of the Indians, saw no just cause for it, and proceeded, through their best preacher, Antón Montesino, to call the mistreatment mortal sin. The sermons caused a critical review of policy back in Spain.[77] But, as Wagner-Parish states: "That was the sum of the first protest against the encomienda: Montesino had preached, a junta had deliberated, the Laws of Burgos had been promulgated [December 27, 1512], and the lot of the natives was no better than before."[78] For Spanish authority opted to see the Indians as deficient human beings needing guardianship. The sermons that follow are remarkable documents for their religious compassion and their grounding in lawful behavior.

Sermons

That time [1511], the Dominicans were growingly aware of the pitiful life led by the native peoples of that island [Hispaniola], the terrible

---

[77] Las Casas describes it in his *History*, Bk. 3, caps. 13-16.
[78] Wagner-Parish, p. 11.

enslavement.[79] They were being eaten up. And the Spaniards who owned them took no more heed of them than if they were useless beasts. When Indians died, the Spaniards were only sorry for it because they lost them for work in the gold mines or at other jobs. But it never meant they treated the Indians they had left with more compassion or leniency—still the same hardness, harshness they had used in the past to oppress and exhaust and destroy those peoples. There were gradations among the Spaniards. Some were absolutely brutal, pitiless, merciless, with one goal in mind, to get rich whatever it cost in Indian blood. Others were less cruel. Still others, one has to hope, were affected by the Indian misery and suffering. But they all, the one and the other, placed first their own self-interest, specific, this-worldly interest, tacitly or expressly, not the well-being, the life, the salvation of those poor creatures. I know only one man who was kind to the Indians he used, a man named Pedro de Rentería. I will have something more to say of him later, God willing.

So the Dominicans were for some time watching, and wondering at, and thinking about what the Spaniards were doing to the Indians. There was the total lack of concern on the Spaniards' part for the spiritual or corporal life of the Indians. There was the innocence of the latter, the priceless patience, the gentleness. So the Dominicans began to measure deed by law, as do those who are spiritual people and friends of God. They began to discuss among themselves the ugliness, the enormity of the injustice, unbelievable! They were asking themselves, "Are these Indians not human? Are we not bound to keep the rules of charity, the rules of justice towards them? Are they not on their own lands with their own lords, their own authority? Have they harmed us in some way? As to the law of Christ, are we not bound to preach it and work every way we can to win them over to it? And the story is that there were crowds and crowds of people on the island. How come they have perished so cruelly in the space of fifteen, sixteen years?"

What occurred next is this. A Spaniard who had been in on the killings, the cruel massacres committed against the native peoples, beat his wife to death. He suspected she was guilty of adultery. And she was one of the native rulers in the Vega, a ruler of many subjects. He fled into the mountains for three or four years, afraid of the law. This was before the Dominicans came. He found out about their arrival and about the holiness of life they breathed, so he came one night to the straw hut that had been given them to live in, and he told his whole story. Then pleaded and pleaded with them to give him the habit of a lay brother. It was his purpose, with God's help, to serve for the rest of his life. This they granted him out of charity because they saw in him signs of conversion—a detestation of his past, a desire to do penance. And he did do

---

[79] *History*, Bk. 3, cap. 3.

great penance thereafter. We are sure he died a martyr's death at the end. God often reveals the mightiness of His mercy in great sinners, working miracles through them. I will write about his martyrdom later, if it please God that I am still alive when I come to that part, it will be near the end of the third book. This man, Juan Garcés, Fray Juan Garcés, was fairly well known to me. He it was who revealed to the friars in detail the frightful cruelties he and all the others had inflicted on those innocent native peoples, during the wars, during the peace, if peace it can in any way be called. He was the eyewitness.

The religious were deeply saddened at hearing about deeds so completely foreign to humanity, to Christian ideals. They felt a deeper desire to attack root and branch this hideous, this strange kind of tyrannical injustice. They felt a burning desire for the honor of God. They felt a deep sorrow over the injuries done to the law, the commandments of God, over the horrible reputation given the faith among those peoples by the atrocities just described. And it struck them to the heart, the loss of such a great number of souls who were without anyone to grieve for them, or tell about them, how they died, how they were still dying. So they prayed and prayed and prayed to God, they fasted, they kept vigils, so God would enlighten them and they would make no mistake in such a crucial matter—they were aware of what a shock, what a scandal it would be, waking up people from the abyss of a dream they dreamt unawares.

After mature and repeated deliberation, they decided to preach openly from the pulpit and make clear the state of soul our sinful people were in who held and oppressed the Indians. If the Spaniards died in this state, they would reap in the hereafter the reward of their inhumanity and greed. At the command of their Vicar, that most prudent servant of God, Pedro de Córdoba, the most learned among them together composed the first sermon which was to be preached, then all signed their names so it would be clear the sermon represented the view, the deliberate, agreed upon view of them all, not just that of the one who preached. The task of giving the sermon was assigned, under holy obedience, by the father Vicar, to the best speaker among them, next to the Vicar himself. His name was Fray Antón Montesino, the second man of the three who brought the Dominican Order to the island. This priest, Fray Antón Montesino, had the gift, he was fierce in his attack on vice, and was very effective in his passionate choice of words and phrases. He got great results from his sermons, or so people thought. The friars assigned the first presentation to him, he had the power. The subject had never been raised for the Spaniards on the island, a new thing, none other than the flat statement that to kill an Indian was more of a sin than the killing of a bug.

The season was Advent. So the friars agreed on the fourth Sunday for the sermon. That day, there was a passage from the Gospel of John to be sung:

"The Pharisees sent someone to ask St. John the Baptist who he was, and he replied, 'I am the voice of one crying out in the desert.'" And to have the whole city of Santo Domingo come to the sermon, every single one, at least of the leading figures, they invited the Second Admiral, governor of the island at the time. They invited the King's officials and all the lawyer types there. They went to individual houses telling people a sermon of theirs would be preached in the main church, they wanted people to know of something that affected them all and deeply. The friars asked all to come hear them. Everyone was quite willing, some out of the great esteem and reverence they had for the friars, their virtue, their strictness of life, their religious discipline, and some out of desire to hear what the friars said was affecting everyone's life so deeply. If they knew beforehand what it was, the subject would never be preached, they would not want to hear it, would not allow it.

Came the Sunday and the time to preach.[80] Padre Fray Antón Montesino mounted the pulpit. He took as the basic text of his sermon, "I am the voice of one crying out in the desert." The sermon was written out and signed by all the friars. He gave his introduction, said something which related to the Advent season, then began to describe the barren desert of conscience in the Spaniards of the island and the blindness with which they lived. They were running a real risk of damnation. They had no sense of the mortal sin they were immersed in so constantly, so unawares, and they would die in it. He then picked up the precise theme and said it this way: "I have gotten up here to make you aware. I am the voice of Christ in the desert of this island. Therefore, it would be wise of you to pay attention, more than that, to listen with your whole heart, listen with every pore. That voice will be one you have never heard before, the harshest, hardest, most fearful, menacing you ever thought to hear." Montesino described that voice for a good stretch, using words that were aggressive and fierce, the kind that made their flesh crawl and made them think they were already at the last judgment. Then, in full thunder and filled with his theme, he declared to them what that desert voice held within itself. "You are all in mortal sin," he said, "you live in it, you die in it, because of the cruel tyranny you work on these innocent peoples. Tell me, by what right, with what justice, do you hold these Indians in such cruel and horrible servitude? By what authority have you made such hideous wars on these peoples? They were living on their own lands in peace and quiet. By what right have you wasted them, so many, many of them, with unspeakable death and destruction? By what right do you keep them so oppressed and exhausted? You give them no food, you give them no medicine for the illnesses they incur from the excessive work you put them to every day. And they die on you. Or, to put it better, you kill them. Just to get

---

[80] *History*, Bk. 3, cap. 4.

at gold, to acquire gold, day after day. And what steps do you take to have someone teach them? So they know their God and creator, so they are baptized, so they hear mass, so they keep feast days and Sundays? The Indians, are they not human beings? Do they not have rational souls? Are you not required to love them as you love yourselves? Do you not know this? Not understand this? How can you be so asleep, so deep in such a torpid dream? Take this for certain, in the state you are in, you can no more save your souls than Moors or Turks who neither have the Christian faith nor want it!" The way he unfolded the voice he had earlier described so fully was such that he left them stunned. Many were numb, many turned stony, some felt bad, but, from what I heard later, not a one changed heart.

When he finished his sermon, he came down from the pulpit with his head erect—he was not a man who wanted to show fear. He acted unafraid for having roughed up his hearers by doing and saying what seemed right according to God. With his companion, he returned to the thatched hut and, as it happened, nothing to eat but some cabbage soup without oil. They were occasionally short of rations. After he left, the church was filled with muttering, I think they almost didn't allow the mass to finish. One might well conclude there was no reading from "The Contempt Of This World" that day at masses for the rest of the folk.

As the friars were finishing eating what could not have been a very tasty meal, the whole town was gathering at the Admiral's house, Don Diego Columbus, the second to hold that dignity and royal office, son of the First Admiral who had discovered the Indies. Foremost were the officials of the King—treasurer, accountant, King's collector, inspector general. They were of one mind to rebuke and chasten the preacher and the other friars, if not punish him as a man who gave scandal, who spread new, strange teachings, condemning everyone. He had spoken against the King and the sovereignty the King held over the Indies, had said they could not hold Indians, though the King had granted them. These were grievous sayings, unforgiveable ones.

They came calling at the friars' door and the porter opened. They told him call the Vicar and that friar who had preached such wayward stuff. The Vicar came out, alone, the venerable Padre Fray Pedro de Córdoba. They told him brusquely, no politeness about it, to summon the one who had preached. Córdoba, who was a very shrewd man, said there was no need. If his lordship and their graces wanted something, he was the authority over the religious and he was the one to deal with. They insisted with him for some time that he have that preacher summoned. Córdoba kept deflecting them, with great prudence but firmly, in quiet but serious words—his habitual way of speaking. He was a man gifted by Divine Providence. He had virtues that were natural and acquired. And in his person, he was so gracious, so religious, that his whole bearing won him absolute respect.

When the Admiral and the others realized that official language and official reasons had no effect on the Vicar, they began to soften their tone, to be a little more civilized, and they asked him to summon the preacher. They wanted him present so as to talk to him, to ask him on what basis and why there was a decision to preach such a bizarre, offensive doctrine, in disservice to the King and detriment to all those living in that city and on the rest of that island. The holy man, once he sensed they had changed mood and were getting control of the passions they had come with, summoned Padre Fray Antón Montesino, and for Montesino, the fear be damned with which he came. When they were seated, the Admiral, speaking for himself and the others, laid out their complaint. How had this priest dared to preach things of such disservice to the Kings and such damage to the whole island, stating that they could not hold Indians—the King himself had given them. He was sovereign over all the Indies. He had given them especially because the Spaniards had gained those islands through great struggle, had subjugated the pagans who held them. And since the sermon had been so scandalous, such a disservice to the King, such an insult to all those who lived on the island, they had decided that the padre should reverse himself on everything he had said. If he did not, they intended to provide an apt remedy.

The Vicar answered this by saying that what the padre had preached had been the judgment of all the friars, at their will and consent. And this after much examination, much consultation and mature deliberation among themselves. And after this consultation and mature deliberation, they had decided the sermon had to be preached, it was a gospel imperative, something necessary for the salvation of all the Spaniards and all the Indians of that island. Indians whom they saw dying every day, with no one taking more notice of their deaths than if they were beasts of the field. And the friars were obliged to do this by God's command derived from the promises they had made in baptism. So first as Christians, then as Friars Preachers of the truth. In doing what they did, they intended no disservice to the King. The King had sent them there to preach what they thought necessary for people's souls. They intended, in fact, to serve the King in full fidelity, and they were sure that from the moment the King was fully informed about what was really happening here, and about what they had preached concerning it, he would consider himself well-served, and he would thank them.

This reasoning, this speech the holy man gave in defense of the sermon had little effect in answering or calming the reaction provoked in the men at hearing that they could not hold Indians the way they did, under tyrannical control—what other way were they to satisfy their greed! Take the Indians from them, and they would be cheated out of all their desires, their wishes. So each one of them there, especially the authorities, said flat out what was uppermost in their minds. They were agreed that the priest take back what he had preached, and on the following Sunday. They got to the point of such blindness that they said if you don't reverse your preaching, pack your things for down to the ships and back to Spain. "It will take no work at all to do that," the Vicar replied. And that was so. For things, they had just habits of coarse cloth repeatedly stitched. They had some capes of the same stuff, used for cover at night. Their beds were poles laid across forked sticks on top of which were straw mats. As for mass supplies and some little books, they could all fit in two trunks.

The men saw how little fear the friars had in the face of threat, so they shifted to a softer tone. They played the game of asking the friars to review the matter, and after a good review, reverse their preaching, to the satisfaction of the whole populace which had been and still was so greatly scandalized. And they kept insisting that what was preached in the first sermon should be moderated to the satisfaction of the populace. So finally, the friars, just to get rid of them and their empty-headed demands, told them go along home, this same Padre Fray Antón Montesino would preach again the following Sunday, he would deal with the same subject after having thought it over, and he would try to satisfy them and address himself to all they had said. Agreed. So the men left buoyed with that hope.

Right off, the men, or some of them anyway, spread the word that they had it agreed with the Vicar and the friars—the preacher, on the following Sunday, was going to reverse everything he had said.[81] There was no need to cajole anyone into coming to hear that second sermon. Everyone in that city was going to be in that church, one person telling another they should go listen to the friar who had preached the previous Sunday, he was going to reverse himself completely. Sermon time came, Montesino in the pulpit. The theme announced for his retraction, his reversal, was the passage from holy Job, chapter 36, starting with the words, "I will repeat what I know, and from the beginning . . . I will show my words were without deception." [But this way,] "I will repeat, from the beginning what I know is the truth, what I preached on Sunday last, and I will show that my words, which angered you so much, were true."

Once the smarter men heard this theme, they saw at once what would result, and they were hard put to let him continue. He began to develop his theme, and present again everything he had preached in the previous sermon, and to support with further arguments, further citations, his affirmation that they

---

[81] *History*, Bk. 3, cap. 5.

held these oppressed, exhausted Indians unjustly, tyrannically. And he repeated his certainty—they could be sure they were damned if they stayed in their sinful state. So, in order that they could cure themselves in this world, he let them know the friars would not absolve a one of them, especially those who went on slave raids. And they could tell anyone they wanted about this, they could write anyone they wanted in Castile. The friars were convinced they were serving God by saying this, and were doing the King no small favor. He finished the sermon. He went back to the house. Everyone else stayed in church infuriated, muttering, worse-minded towards the friars than ever, finding themselves cheated out of the empty and wicked hope they had of hearing a retraction, as if, should the friars retract, the law of God changed, the law against which the men acted when they oppressed and wiped out the Indians. . .

The men left church in a rage, went off to eat, found no delight in food, instead a bitter taste, I would think. They had no more use for friars, they understood you could talk to them and it did you no good. So they decided to tell the King with the first ship how these friars, who had just come to the island, had scandalized everyone by spreading a new doctrine and condemning them all to hell because they controlled Indians and used them in the mines and at other labor. This went against what His Majesty had ordered. Their preaching was nothing else but an abolition of his sovereignty and of the income he got from this part of the world.

When the letters reached court, there was an uproar. The King wrote summoning the Dominican Provincial of Castile, he was the superior of the Dominicans on the island, the island was not then a province itself. The King complained of the friars the Provincial had sent out. They had done him a great disservice by preaching things against his sovereignty, disturbing and shocking mightily the whole region. The Provincial was to remedy this. If he did not, the King would order a remedy.

- 3 -

The Caonao Massacre

Prenote

More and more, the basic humanity of Las Casas was being called to the side of the Indian. The description of the Caonao massacre on the island of Cuba in 1513 comes from Las Casas' recollection of the event years afterwards, but as he writes, the massacre seems to be happening again right before his eyes. He experienced it first as a horrifying aberration, but when he records it, he has known for a long time it represented a policy of terror at work to break the Indian spirit, on Cuba and elsewhere, as the conquest broadened.

One time, the Indians came out to greet us with food and gifts, came ten leagues from their large village.[82] Then, when we got there, they gave us fish in abundance, bread, food, to the limit of their larder. All of a sudden the devil got into the Christians. Right before my eyes, they put to the sword without provocation or cause more than three thousand souls who sat in front of us, men, women, children. I saw there cruelty on a scale no living being has ever seen or expects to see.

Another time, a few days later, I sent messengers to all the chieftains in the province of Havana telling them not to be afraid. They knew through the grapevine that I was trustworthy. I told them not to run away but come out to meet us, no one would harm them. The whole country lived in fear due to the recent massacres. I did this with the Captain's assurance.[83] When we came to an area, twenty-one caciques, chiefs, came out to greet us. On the spot, the Captain seized them in violation of the safe-conduct I had guaranteed. He wanted to burn them alive the next day, arguing that it was smart to do so, some of those leaders were bound to harm

---

[82] *History*, Lib. 3, caps. 29-30.

[83] [Pánfilo de Narváez. The names to follow are taken from Alonso De Santa Cruz's description of Las Casas presentation before the Council of the Indies, in which Las Casas gave the names. See Alonso de Santa Cruz, *Cronica del emperador Carlos V*. Madrid: 1920-1925. 5 vols. *Crónica*, Part 6, cap. 42, pp. 216-22.]

us some time. I found myself in a fierce struggle to save the chiefs from the stake. Meantime they escaped.

It was after the Indians of that island were put in the same calamitous slavery as those on Hispaniola, after they saw themselves dying, all of them, perishing without recourse, that some began to take to the hills, others hung themselves out of desperation, husbands and wives, and they hung their children along with themselves. More than two hundred Indians committed suicide this way due to the viciousness of a tyrannical Spaniard I know by name. A massive number of people died in that manner.[84]

There was an official on the island who received an allotment of three hundred Indians. At the end of three months' time, he had worked to death in the mines two hundred and seventy of them. Thirty survived, a mere tenth. They gave him another three hundred and more, and he killed them, more, and he killed them, until he died and the devil took his soul. In three or four months, during my stay there, seven thousand children died of hunger because their parents had been hauled off to work the mines. I saw other things as fearsome.[85]

Then the Christians decided to hunt out the Indians who were in the hills. They did terrifying massacres there. That way they wiped out the population of the whole island. We see few left today. It is an awful pity to see it, a wasteland, a man-made desolation.

---

[84] *History*, Lib. 3, cap. 82.
[85] *History*, Lib. 3, caps. 78 & 84.

- 4 -

The Odious Choice

Prenote

The following excerpt is placed here to reveal the intense humanity of the Indians under pressure from the lawlessness of the conquistadors. The story takes place on Cuba during the time it was being "pacified," in the period 1512-14. Las Casas was on the island, as chaplain to the "pacifying" party, with the mission of inducing the Indians to a peaceful submission, a task he was mainly successful at because the Indians had learned to respect him. But incident after incident of violence—see the prior entry—removed his blindness and turned him from an accomplice in a bad system to a mortal foe of that system.

Of the Island of Cuba

In the year 1511 Spaniards landed on the island of Cuba.[86] As I said, it is as long as the distance from Valladolid to Rome. It has areas of large population. The Spaniards started out again doing what I said they did, but much, much more viciously this time. Some stark things happened. There was a cacique, an important chieftain, who had the name Hatuey. He had come to Cuba from Hispaniola with many people to escape the disasters, the brutal deeds inflicted by the Christians. He had settled on the island of Cuba. He got the news from some Indians that the Christians had landed. So he gathered most or all of his people and said to them: "You know already there is talk that the Christians are headed this way. You know from experience what happened to chief so-and-so, so-and-so, so-and-so. Those who did it on Haiti (the same as Hispaniola) are coming here to do likewise.

---

[86] From "Brevissima relación," *Tratados* vol. 1, pp. 43-5. For a history of the tract, see Wagner-Parish, Catalogue # 18, pp. 267-8. For the incident as described in the *History*, see Lib. 3, caps. 20 & 25, esp. 25.

Can anyone guess why they do it?" The people answered: "No, unless they are by nature cruel and wicked." The chief answered: "It is not for that reason alone. It is also because they have a god they adore and love much. They take from us the wherewithal to adore that god, they try to conquer and kill us for that." He picked up a small basket near him filled with gold in jewelry form and said: "Look here at the god of the Christians. If you agree, let us do careitos' [rhythms and dances] before it. Perhaps we will please it and it will order the Christians not to do us harm." They all shouted back: "Do it! Do it!" They danced before that god until they were all exhausted. Then the chief Hatuey said: "Look, whatever the truth is, if we keep this god, they will kill us anyway to get it from us. Let us throw it in the river." Everyone agreed it was what to do. So they threw it in a large river nearby.

The important chief kept dodging the Christians from the moment they came to that island of Cuba.[87] He knew what they were like. He fought them when they crossed. They caught him finally. And because he fled such a wicked, cruel people, because he defended himself against someone who wanted to kill him or hound him to death, and all the people of his tribe, they had to burn him alive. After he was bound to the stake, a religious of St. Francis, a holy man who was on the scene, said some things to him about God and our faith, things the chief had never heard before, essential things, because of the short time the executioners allowed. If he would just believe what the religious said, he would go to heaven where he would have glory and eternal rest. If not, he must go to hell and there suffer eternal torment and pain. After a short reflection, the chief asked the religious if Christians went to heaven. The religious told him yes, those who were good went there. The chief then answered without another thought that he did not want heaven, but hell, so he would not be where there were Christians, so he would not have to behold such a cruel race. Such is the repute, the respect, our God and faith have gained due to the Christians who went out to the Indies.

---

[87] *History*, Lib. 3, cap. 21.

- 5 -

Las Casas' Awakening

Prenote

Las Casas was a major figure in the sixteenth century, that is now clear from recent biographical work. When Las Casas speaks of himself in the History, *he speaks as someone implicated personally in the problem of Spanish presence to the New World, and as the one who worked out the basic solutions. He is like a Churchill writing the history of World War II. Spanish conscience becomes visible in Las Casas, he moves along lines Spain should have adopted. His awakening truly forms a part of the history of the time, and part of modern history as well, because his interpretations of the causes of things back then are being validated by more and more evidence, even beyond that which he himself provided. The narrative is sometimes in the first person, sometimes in the third, but in both instances a reader can recognize that the man's personal consciousness was broad and embracing, he could see himself and others as if they were in the same space, engaged in the same issues, with the same risks to their souls, concerning the same Indian peoples.*

What comes from this awakening is eventually the Church doctrine of Indian liberty enshrined in the papal Bull, Sublimis Deus *[1537], and Spain's New Laws for the protection of Indian peoples [1542].*

Las Casas' Account of His Awakening

. . . We told how Diego Velásquez, in charge of Cuba for the Admiral, marked out five places for settlement where all the Spaniards on the island were to live in groups.[88] There was one already populated,

---

[88] *History*, Bk. 3, cap. 78 end, & cap. 79; chapter breaks omitted, captions added. Reprinted with permission from *The Only Way*, pp. 186-91.

Baracoa. The Indians who lived near each settlement were divided up and given to the Spaniards. Each Spaniard had an itch for gold and a narrow conscience. They had no thought that those natives were made of flesh and blood. They put them to work in mines and at other projects the Indians could accomplish as slave labor, put them to work so promptly, so pitilessly that in a few days' time many native deaths showed the brutality of Spanish treatment. The loss of people on Cuba was quicker, fiercer, during the early period than it was elsewhere. The explanation: the Spaniards roamed the island *pacifying* it. They took many Indians from the villages as servants for themselves. The Spaniards reaped but did not sow. As to the villagers, some fled, some, nervous and fearful, cared only to escape being killed as many another was killed. The fields were picked clean of food and abandoned.

Since greed fed the Spaniards, as I said, they cared nothing for sowing and reaping food, they cared only for reaping gold they had not sown, however they could, eating whatever scraps of food they managed to scrounge up. And they set men and women to work without food enough to live on, never mind work on, in the mines. It is a true story, one I told elsewhere, what a Spaniard recounted in my presence and that of several others, as if he were telling a fine way of doing things. He had his allotted Indians raise so many thousand mound rows. (That is how they grow [the root] cassava bread is made from.) He sent them every third day, or two on, two off, to the fields to eat whatever growth they found. With what they then had in their bellies he made them work another two or three days in the mines. He gave them not another bite to eat. Farm work means digging the whole day, a far harder job than tilling our vineyards and food gardens home in Spain. It means raising into mounds the earth they dig, three to four feet square, three to four hands high. And not with spades or hoes that are provided, but with pole-length, fire-hardened sticks.

Hunger, having nothing to eat, being put to hard labor, caused death among these peoples more quickly, more violently, than in any other place. The Spaniards took healthy men and women to do mine and other work. They left behind in the villages only the sick and the old, left no one to help them, care for them. So the sick and old died from anguish and age as well as from mortal hunger. I sometimes heard, back then when I traveled the island, as I would enter a village, voices calling from inside the huts. When I went in to find out what they wanted, they answered, *Food! Food!* There was not a man or a woman able to stand on two legs that they did not drag off to the mines. As for the new mothers with their small boy and girl children, their breasts dried: they had so little to eat, so much work, they had no milk left, the babies died. That was the cause of the deaths of 7000 baby boys and girls in the space of three months. The event was described in a report to the Catholic King by a creditable person who had investigated it. Another event also occurred back then. An official of the king got 300 Indians as his allotment. He was in such a hurry putting them to work in the mines and at the rest of his jobs that at the end of three months only a tenth of those Indians remained alive.

The crushing of Indians took this route and grew in ferocity each day. As greed grew and grew, so did the number of Indian dead. [While this was going on] Padre Bartolomé de las Casas (mentioned briefly above) was very busy looking after his own holdings. As the others did, he sent his allotted Indians to the mines to dig gold, to the fields to plant crops, profiting from his Indians as much as he could, though he was always careful to maintain them well in every way possible, and treat them kindly, and alleviate their hardships. But he took no more care than the others to recall that these were pagan peoples and that he had an obligation to teach them Christian doctrine and gather them into the bosom of the Church.

Hearing the call in Cuba

Diego Velásquez and the group of Spaniards with him left the port of Xagua to go and found a settlement of Spaniards in the province, where they established the town called Sancti Espíritus. Apart from Bartolomé de las Casas, there was not a single cleric or friar on the whole island, except for one in the town of Baracoa. The feast of Pentecost was coming up. So he agreed to leave his home on the Arimao river (accent on the penult) a league from Xagua where his holdings were and go say Mass and preach for them on that Feast. Las Casas looked over the previous sermons he had preached to them on that Feast and his other sermons for that season. He began to meditate on some passages of Sacred Scripture. If my memory serves me, the first and most important was from *Ecclesiasticus* 34:18 ff: "Unclean is the offering sacrificed by an oppressor. [Such] mockeries of the unjust are not pleasing [to God]. The Lord is pleased only by those who keep to the way of truth and justice. The Most High does not accept the gifts of unjust people, He does not look well upon their offerings. Their sins will not be expiated by repeat sacrifices. *The one whose sacrifice comes from the goods of the poor is like one who kills his neighbor. The one who sheds blood and the one who defrauds the laborer are kin and kind.*"

He began to reflect on the misery, the forced labor the Indians had to undergo. He was helped in this by what he had heard and experienced on the island of Hispaniola, by what the Dominicans preached continually—no one could, in good conscience, hold the Indians in encomienda, and those friars would not confess and absolve any who so held them—a preaching Las Casas had refused to accept. One time he wanted to confess to a religious of St. Dominic who happened to be in the vicinity. Las Casas held Indians on that island of Hispaniola, as indifferent and blind about it as he was on the island of Cuba. The religious refused him confession. Las Casas asked him why. He gave the reason. Las Casas objected with frivolous arguments and empty explanations, seemingly sound, provoking the religious to respond, "Padre, I think the truth has many enemies and the lie has many friends." Then Las Casas offered him the respect due his dignity and reputation because the religious was a revered and learned man, much more so than the Padre, but he took no heed of the confessor's counsel to let his Indians go. Yet it helped him greatly to recall his quarrel later, and also the confession he made to the religious, so as to think more about the road of ignorance and danger he was on, holding Indians as others did, confessing without scruple those who held or wanted to hold Indians, though he did not do so for long. But he had heard many confessions on that island of Hispaniola, from people who were in the same mortal sin.

He spent some days thinking about the situation, each day getting surer and surer from what he read concerning what was legal and what was actual, measuring the one by the other, until he came to the same truth by himself. Everything in these Indies that was done to the Indians was tyrannical and unjust. Everything he read to firm up his judgment he found favorable, and he used to say strongly that from the very moment he began to dispel the darkness of that ignorance, he never read a book in Latin or Spanish—a countless number over the span of 42 years—where he didn't find some argument or authority to prove or support the justice of those Indian peoples, and to condemn the injustices done to them, the evils, the injuries.

Responding in Cuba

He then made a decision to preach his conclusion. But since his holding Indians meant holding a contradiction of his own preaching, he determined to give them up so as to be free to condemn allotments, the whole system of forced labor, as unjust and tyrannical, and to hand his Indians back to Governor Diego Velázquez. They were better off under the Padre's control, to be sure. He had treated them with greater respect, would be even more respectful in the future. He knew that giving them up meant they would be handed over to someone who would brutalize them, work them to death, as someone did ultimately. Granted, he would give them a treatment as good as a father would give his children. Yet, since he would preach that no one could in good conscience hold Indians, he could never escape people mocking back at him, "You hold Indians nonetheless. Why not release them? You say holding them is tyranny!" So he decided to give them up completely.

To get a better understanding of all that happened, it would be right here to recall the close friendship the Padre had with a certain Pedro de la Rentería, a prudent, deeply Christian man. [I spoke of him earlier somewhat saying that he was the only encomendero I remember who cared for the Indian soul.] They were not just friends, but partners also in the estate. They received together their allotments of natives. They had decided together that Pedro de la Rentería should go to the island of Jamaica where Pedro had a brother. The purpose: to bring back pigs to fatten and corn to plant, plus other things not found in Cuba since it was cleaned out, a fact already established. For the voyage they chartered a government ship for 2000 castellanos. So, since Pedro de la Rentería was away, and since the Padre had decided to give up his Indians and go preach what he felt obliged to preach and thus enlighten those who were deep in the darkness of ignorance, he went on a day to Governor Diego Velázquez. He told him what he thought about his own situation, the situation of the Governor, and of the rest of the Spaniards. He stated that no one in that situation could be saved, and he stated that he intended to preach this to escape the danger, and to do what his priesthood required. Thus he was determined to give back his Indians to the Governor, to keep charge of them no longer. Therefore the Governor should consider them available and should dispose of them as he wished. But the Padre asked the favor that the business be kept secret, that the Governor give the Indians to no one else until Rentería returned from the island of Jamaica where he was at the moment. The reason: the estate and the Indians they held in common might suffer harm if, before Rentería returned, the person to whom the Governor gave the Indians might move in on them and the estate prematurely.

The governor was shocked at hearing such an unusual story. For one thing, that a cleric who was free to own things in the world should be of the opinion of the Dominican friars—they had first dared to think it and dared to make it known. For another, that the cleric had such a righteous scorn for temporal possessions that, having such a great aptitude for getting rich quickly, he should give it up. Especially since he had a growing reputation for being industrious: people saw him most zealous about his property and his mines, saw other acquisitive qualities in him. But the governor was mainly stunned, and answered him more out of consideration for what touched the Padre in the temporal realm than for the danger in which the Governor himself lived as top man in the tyranny perpetrated against the Indians on that island. "Padre, think of what you are doing. No need for scruples! It is God who wants to see you rich and prosperous. For that reason I do not allow the surrender you make of your Indians. I give you fifteen days to think it over so you can come to a better decision. After a fortnight you can come back and tell me what you will do."

The Padre replied, "My Lord, I am most grateful that you want me to prosper, most grateful for all the other kindnesses your grace has done for me. But act, my Lord, as though the fortnight were over. Please God, if I ever repent of the decision I broached to you, if I ever want to hold Indians again—and if you, for the love you have of me, should ever want to leave them with me or give them to me anew—if you accept my plea to have them, even if I wept blood, may God be the one to punish you severely, may God never forgive this sin. I ask your grace one favor, that this whole business be kept secret and that you do not allot the natives to anyone until Rentería returns, so his estate suffers no harm."

The Governor promised. He kept his promise. From then on he had a far greater respect for the Padre. And concerning his governance, he did many good things that touched on native matters and his own personal conduct, all due to the effect of the Padre (as if he had seen him do miracles). The rest of the Spaniards on the island began to change their view of the Padre from before, once they knew he had given up his natives. Such an action was considered then and always the consummate proof that could demonstrate sanctity. Such was and is the blindness of those who came out to the New World.

The Padre made the secret public the following way. He was preaching on the feast day of the Assumption of Our Lady in that place where he was—[the town of Sancti Espíritus] mentioned earlier. He was explaining the contemplative and the active life, the theme of the gospel reading for the day, talking about the spiritual and corporal works of mercy. He had to make clear to his hearers their obligation to perform these works towards the native peoples they made use of so cruelly; he had to blame the merciless, negligent, mindless way they lived off those natives. For which it struck him as the right moment to reveal the secret agreement he had set up with the Governor. And he said, "My Lord, I give you freedom to reveal to everyone whatever you wish concerning what we agreed on in secret—I take that freedom myself in order to reveal it to those here present." This said, he began to expose to them their own blindness, the injustices, the tyrannies, the cruelties they committed against such innocent, such gentle people. They could not save their souls, neither those who held Indians by allotment, nor the one who handed them out. They were bound by the obligation to make restitution. He himself, once he knew the danger of damnation in which he lived, had given up his Indians, had given up many other things connected with holding Indians. The congregation was stupefied, even fearful of what he said to them. Some felt compunction, others thought it a bad dream, hearing bizarre statements such as: No one could hold Indians in servitude without sinning. As if to say they could not make use of beasts of the field! Unbelievable!

- 6 -

Freedom

Prenote

Las Casas' efforts, after his awakening, were at first to adjust the life of the Indian and the life of the Spaniards to each other by creating community schemes which would allow fruitful cooperation. In fact, his earliest memorial on remedies for the Indies, written in late 1515, or early 1516, may well be responsible for parts of Thomas More's Utopia.[89] *But cooperation could only occur after the abuse of Indian life was halted.[90] Everything depended on Indian freedom within the adjusted system. That is the burden of the excerpt which follows. It was written many years after Las Casas' efforts began, so what he meant by freedom, or understood by it in the 1516-1519 period was not exactly the same as what he meant or understood in the 1550's when he wrote the* History. *In the later years, he saw no adjustment possible without the complete and free consent of Indian peoples all over the New World. And what Cisneros says in the excerpt and what he means are contradictory realities, though Las Casas did not realize it. However Las Casas developed, as time went by, he sought constantly to free the Indian from Spanish injustice. So freedom becomes a leitmotif of Las Casas in the long struggle that lay ahead.*

This is the right moment to tell the following.[91] The cleric [Las Casas] saw what deep roots tyranny had set down on the islands and on that part of the mainland where there were Spaniards, which meant Darién and surrounding areas. And tyranny was causing the natives there to perish. But he was not bold enough to bring up the phrase Indian freedom, nor touch on the topic in conversation or argument. It was as if he avoided an absurdity

---

[89] See Baptiste, *Utopia*, p. 9.

[90] For the best summary of this period in Las Casas' life, see Helen Rand Parish's Introduction to *The Only Way*, pp. 23-4.

[91] *History*, Bk. 3, cap. 88.

or a blasphemy. Until one day. He was talking to the Cardinal about the oppression, the servitude suffered by the Indians, and the point was with what justice could they be made to suffer such oppression and servitude. The Cardinal suddenly burst in, "No justice! What is this? Are they not free? Who has any doubt they are not free beings?" From that moment on, the cleric [Las Casas] was bold enough, the word rushed out of his mouth everywhere he argued, the Indians are free, everything done against them was done in violation of their basic freedom. And every argument mounted against the tyranny of the Spaniards and on behalf of the Indians was based on this principle. The incident shows that the Cardinal had indeed understood the radical, the basic justice that had to be extended to the Indians because of the servitude they were forced to endure—freedom, over and over in the preamble to his instructions, the Cardinal calls the Indians free, he insists they are free.

- 7 -

Black African Slavery

Prenote

An issue about Las Casas arises almost immediately and should be faced here. He has been accused of starting the Black African slave trade. Helen Rand Parish sums up the material—the falseness of the accusation—in the following way: "Early on [c. 1516], Las Casas did repeat a suggestion made by friars, laymen, and officials, to bring over a few Christianized Black slaves from Spain, duty free. But the suggestion was not followed. Independently, an exclusive license was 'bought' by a courtier and resold to Genoese merchants at an exorbitant price, to ship four thousand Blacks from Africa. And this monopoly deliberately blocked all but a trickle of slaves for a decade and more, until the gold was gone and most of the Indians wiped out on the islands and coasts of the Caribbean. Then high prices for Blacks yielded a ten-fold profit! It was the sugar industry, the new bonanza, that brought large shipments of African slaves to the deserted West Indies. And it was Bartolomé de las Casas who discovered in 1552 that the Portuguese (with Papal blessing) had used Europe's defensive war against Islam to cloak a lucrative trade in innocent Blacks captured on the Guinea coast. Far from promoting the traffic, Las Casas was the only person in his century to denounce Black African slavery."[92]

Las Casas' Early Involvement

... some Spaniards on the island contacted the cleric Las Casas.[93] They saw his purpose, saw that the religious of St. Dominic would not

---

[92] *The Only Way*, Addendum III, pp. 201-2.

[93] *History*, Bk. 3, caps. 102, 129; captions added. Reprinted with permission from *The Only Way*, pp. 202-08.

absolve those who held Indians unless they gave them up. If he could get them a license from the King so they could import from Castile a dozen Blacks, they would free their Indians. The cleric agreed and requested in his reports that the favor should be done the Spanish settlers on the islands, and they each should be given a license to bring in from Spain about a dozen Black slaves. The settlers could thus continue to work the land, consequently they would free their Indians. When the cleric Las Casas first gave that advice—to grant the license to bring Black slaves to the islands—he was not aware of the unjust ways in which the Portuguese captured and made slaves of Blacks. But after he found out, he would not have proposed it for all the world, because Blacks were enslaved unjustly, tyrannically, right from the start, exactly as the Indians had been.

Las Casas' Judgment on Himself and on the Spaniards

. . . Before sugar mills were invented, some settlers, who had some wealth they had gotten from the sweat and blood of the Indians, wanted a license to buy Black slaves back in Castile. The settlers saw they were killing off the Indians. But they still had some. So they promised the cleric Bartolomé de las Casas that if he succeeded in getting them the license to import a dozen Blacks to the island, they would allow the Indians they held to be set free. With this promise in mind, the cleric Las Casas got the king to allow the Spaniards of the islands to bring in some Black slaves from Castile so the Indians could then be set free. As we said earlier, Las Casas was in favor with the King who had recently come to power, and watch over the new territories had been put in Las Casas' hands. The Council, with the accord of the authorities in Seville, decided that a license should be given to import 4000 Black slaves, for starters, to the four islands, Hispaniola, San Juan, Cuba, Jamaica. Sure enough a Spaniard from the Indies who was then at Court found out about the decision, and slipped the information to the Governor of Bresa—a Flemish gentleman who had come with the King and was of his inner circle—so he could request the franchise. He requested it, he got it, he sold it to the Genoese for 25,000 ducats. The Genoese were shrewd and set a thousand conditions. One was that for eight years no further license be given out to bring Black slaves to the Indies. The Genoese then sold individual licenses for individual Blacks at eight ducats apiece minimum. Thus, the permission the cleric Las Casas had gotten so the Spaniards could have help in working the land, so as to free their Indians, was turned into a profit-making scheme. It proved to be a great setback to the well-being and liberation of the Indians. The cleric, many years later, regretted the advice he gave the King on this matter—he judged himself culpable through inadvertence—when he saw proven that the enslavement of Blacks was every bit as unjust as that of the Indians. It was not, in any case, a good solution he had proposed, that Blacks be brought in so Indians could be freed. And this even though he thought that the Blacks had been justly enslaved. He was not certain that his ignorance and his good intentions would excuse him before the judgment of God.

There were at that time only ten or twelve Blacks on the island; they belonged to the King, they had been brought in to construct a fortress which overlooked the river mouth. But once the license was given and implemented, others followed and frequently, so eventually 30,000 Blacks were brought to the island [Hispaniola], and I reckon 100,000 to the Indies as a whole. But the traffic did not help or free the Indians. And the cleric Las Casas could not exert further influence—the King was away, the Council got new members every day, and were ignorant of law, law they were obliged to know, I have said this often throughout my History. As the sugar mills increased daily in number, the need to put Blacks to work in them also increased; the water-powered ones needed at least 80, the mechanical ones 30 to 40, so the profit to the King increased. Something else followed from this situation. The Portuguese had made a career in much of the past of raiding Guinea and enslaving Blacks, absolutely unjustly. When they saw we had such a need of Blacks and they sold for high prices, the Portuguese speeded up their slave raiding—they are still in a hurry. They took slaves in every evil and wicked way they could. And Blacks, when they see the Portuguese so eager on the hunt for slaves, they themselves use unjust wars and other lawless means to steal and sell to the Portuguese. And we are the cause of all the sins the one and the other commit, in addition to what we commit in buying them.

Las Casas' Condemnation of the African Slave Trade

I want to cite here one stark story from among the many offenses, grave evils, gruesome injustices, the shocking damages done by the Portuguese in their discoveries during that period of time, done against the natives of those lands—Moor or Indian or Black or Arab—innocent of anything against the Portuguese.[94] The year was 1444. The story is from Juan de Barros, lib. 1, cap. 8, 1st decade, and from Gómez Eanes de Zurara, lib. 1, caps. 18-24. Gómez gives the fuller version.

---

[94] *History*, Bk. 1, cap. 24; captions added.

Some rich and important people of the city of Lagos in Portugal pressed the Infante to give them a license to go to the discovered territory, and they would give him in return a certain share of the profits they made. The Infante complied. So they armed six caravels. The Infante appointed as Captain of the fleet a man named Lanzarote who had been in his service. They left Portugal, they reached an island we now call Las Garzas, on the Eve of Corpus Christi, where they killed many natives who were at their evening rest. From Las Garzas they went on to attack an island called Nar, it was nearby and well populated. On Corpus Christi Day (good day, good deeds!), at sunup, they attacked the natives who were still in bed and off guard. The war cry was, "Santiago, St. George, Portugal, Portugal!" The natives were terror stricken by the attack, so large, so sudden, so wicked. Parents abandoned children, husbands abandoned wives; some mothers hid their offspring out in the grasses, the thickets. Everyone ran aghast, out of their heads.

A Portuguese chronicler says this: "Finally, Our Lord God, who rewards every good deed, saw to it that those who took this risk for His service should win the victory over their enemies and receive profit and praise for their labors and costs. They captured and held 155 natives. They killed many another who put up a fight. Many another drowned escaping." Can there be a more senseless description than this one? To serve God, the chronicler says, they killed, they sent to hell so many infidels, they left that whole island in shock and hatred of the name Christian and filled with grief and bitterness.

There were only thirty Portuguese, and not enough shackles to hold all those peaceful people. So the Portuguese left some men with part of the captives, took another part back to the ships. They were jubilant on arrival, then returned in their boats to pick up those left. You see how peaceful, how unwarlike the natives were, if thirty Portuguese from far away can capture 150 of them abed and asleep in their huts.

The ships went to another nearby island, called Tider, to make another haul, but they were spotted first; the Portuguese found it empty, the natives had fled to the mainland, a matter of 8 leagues distance. The Portuguese tortured a Moor, or whatever they were, so as to find out where more people could be located. They kept on from island to island for two days, then in raids they made on the mainland they took into captivity a further 45 natives. On their return trip to Portugal, they took en route 15 fishermen and one woman. In all they captured on their slave raids 216 human beings, people who had never harmed them, who owed them nothing, people who were weaponless, who lived at peace in their own places. When the ships returned to Portugal, Lanzarote was received by the Infante with great ceremony. He personally named Lanzarote a knight and heaped honors on him.

The next day, Captain Lanzarote spoke to the Infante: "Lord, Your Highness well knows you are due a fifth of these captives we brought back, a fifth of all else we got from our foray in that land where you sent us in the service of God and in your own. Due to the length of the voyage and the time it took to sail it, the men are exhausted, and more so due to the fret and fear they themselves had to live with, so far from home, making captives, not knowing how things would come out. And many are sick and quite worn down. Given all this, I suggest it would be a good idea for you to order that the ships be unloaded tomorrow and the haul be brought to a field outside of town where a five-way split can be made of the slaves. And Your Highness can come and choose what will please and satisfy you most." The Infante answered that it was a good idea.

The next day morning, Captain Lanzarote ordered the masters of the caravels to empty them and bring the captives to the field. But before they divided them, they chose out a Moor, the best of the lot, as an offering to the Church of the place, the city of Lagos, where the raiders all lived, and where they made port. The Infante was in residence there at the time. They chose out another Moor to send to San Vicente del Cabo where, the story goes, the slave lived later very religiously. The raiders wanted to give God his share after the bloodshed, the unjust and wicked enslavement of those innocent people, as if God were some wicked, malevolent tyrant they could please and He would approve the viciousness of those who made the offering. Those awful men did not know the scripture passage: "God does not approve those who harm their neighbors sinfully, then offer God a sacrifice from their ill-gotten goods. Such sacrifice is instead like honoring and serving a father by hacking his son to pieces as he looks on." (*Ecclesiasticus* 34) The fact that the Moor they gave to San Vicente del Cabo, or that many others, or all, grew holy later does not excuse those who seized them, nor do they gain remission of their sins by such a gift as they made. The holiness was not their doing, it was due entirely to the infinite generosity of God who chose to draw such a priceless good out of such damnable evils. It is a Gospel truth and Catholic law that one cannot commit even the smallest venial sin in order to draw the greatest good one can imagine from it. How much less commit the greatest of mortal sins.

Back to the theme. I want to include here, and word for word, no addition, no subtraction, what Gómez Eanes writes in his account—I mentioned him earlier—about the pack of people Lanzarote took captive. I think Gómez was there, an eyewitness. He says in exclamation, "Oh, heavenly Father, You rule the infinite host of Your holy city without effort,

Your divine excellence is so, and You keep in order the orbits of the higher globes in their nine circles, and You make the aeons short or long according as You please. I beg You that my tears should not count against me. Their being human has a hold on me, not their beliefs. So I weep from sorrow over their suffering. If brute beasts with their brute feelings can recognize the suffering of their own kind by the instinct of nature, what can you expect my human nature to do seeing before me that stricken group, as I remind myself they are all by generation children of Adam?

"Next day, it was 8 August, early because it was hot, the crews began to work their boats, unload their captives and take them ashore as ordered. The captives, when gathered in the field, were a strange sight to see. Some among them were nearly white, handsome, slim; others were darker, seemed like mulattos; others black, like Ethiopians, gross in face and body—it appeared to people that they saw a reverse image of the world. What heart, hard as it might be, would not feel pity stir at the sight of such a group? Some had their faces down, wet with tears; some looked at the others and were groaning with grief; some looked to high heaven, fixing their look on it, shouting aloud up to it, as if asking the Father of Nature for help; others beat their cheeks with their palms, or threw themselves flat on the ground; others made lamentation in a song-like manner after the custom of their homeland. And though the words of their language could not be understood by us, their sorrow was understood indeed. A sorrow that increased when those in charge of dividing them came and started to split them one from another to make even groups. To do this it became necessary to take children from parents, wives from husbands, brothers from sisters. For kin and kindred no rule was kept, each captive landed where luck would have it. Oh mighty Fortune, you wheel back and forth over the things of this world as you please! Would that someone could place before the eyes of those pitiful people some knowledge of the good to come in future centuries so they could have some consolation in the midst of their great suffering! And you, who work this partition, respect and pity such misery, see how they cling together, you can scarcely pry them apart. Who could make the separation without violence? Things were such that those who were put in one partition—children who saw their parents in another—got up and ran over to them; mothers gripped their other children in their arms and huddled with them on the ground, heedless of the lashes on their own flesh, so the children would not be torn from them. So the partition took a lot of trouble.

"It was difficult enough with just the captives, but the field was also full of people, from the city itself and from the surrounding areas. People had quit work that day, work they had to do for a living, just to see something new; and what with some deploring what they saw going on, and some approving, they made such a hubbub that they rattled the ones in charge of the partition. The Infante was there, mounted on a powerful horse, accompanied by his people, giving away his goods like a man who does not want to be rich himself. He gave away in a short time the 46 souls that fell to his fifth. His principal wealth was in good conscience, and the salvation of those souls pleased him mightily, they would otherwise be lost.

"His judgment was not an empty one, for, as we said already, as soon as the slaves learned the language, they readily became Christian. And I who write the history in this volume saw, in the city of Lagos, lads and lasses, the children, the grandchildren of those slaves, born here—and they such good and true Christians, it's as if they were Christians forever back, the offspring of those who were the first baptized. And though the grief of those being split up was indeed great at the moment—especially after the split had been made, and each owner had carried off his share, and some sold theirs, who were then taken to other parts of the country, so the story goes that a father remained in Lagos, a mother was taken to Lisbon, children elsewhere—though the grief was acute at the start, the damage was at the beginning. Later, after it all, everything would change to joy and happiness, for they received the Christian faith, they gave birth to Christian children, and many later got back their freedom."

This is the way, to the letter, the incident was put by the Portuguese historian Gómez Eanes. He seems little less foolish than the Infante, unable to see that neither the Infante's good intention, nor the good results that later followed, excused the sins of violence, the deaths, the damnation of those who perished without faith or sacrament, the enslavement of the survivors. Nor did intention or results make up for the monumental injustice. What love, affection, esteem, reverence, would they have, could they have for the faith, for Christian religion, so as to convert to it, those who wept as they did, who grieved, who raised their eyes, their hands to heaven, who saw themselves, against the law of nature, against all human reason, stripped of their liberty, of their wives and children, of their homeland, of their peace? Even the historian himself, and the people who stood around, wept with compassion over the sorry affair, especially when they saw the separation of children from parents, of mothers and fathers from children. It is obvious, the error, the self-deception of those people back then. Please God it did not last, it does not still last. It is from his exclamation, so I think, that the historian shows the event to be the horror that it is, though later he seems to soft-soap it, to blur it with the mercy and goodness of God. If anything good did come of it later, it all came from God. What came from the Infante and the raiders he sent out was brutality, theft, tyranny, nothing more.

- 8 -

The Just War of the Indians

Prenote

The Indians had the right to wage defensive war against the Spaniards, Las Casas insists on this throughout the History of the Indies. *But his narratives make a further point—the Indians are intelligent, resourceful beings, their full humanity is obvious, however much they are overpowered by superior weaponry, i.e., cavalry, swords, crossbows, firearms, attack dogs, etc. The excerpts that follow highlight the intelligence and humanity of the Indians, even while presenting again the theme of their right to wage defensive war. The style of writing Las Casas uses presents human beings on the two sides, lets us see we are dealing with human tragedy, for the soul of the Spaniard is revealed as much as that of the Indian.*

The year is 1516.[95] The Spaniards had not forgotten their responsibility to chew up the gentle islanders on Cuba, nor forgotten they had to go depopulate other places near and far, hauling back to Cuba the native dwellers thereof. Because the Spaniards saw that in their haste to mine gold, the Indians they forced to do it were dying on them. So they followed what was done on Hispaniola. When the Hispaniolans saw their native population dropping, they thought up the sending of flotillas to raid what were called the Lucayan islands. We have described this fully enough. So the Spaniards living on Cuba followed this tested method. Two or three of them made common cause, putting together what money they had squeezed from the blood of Indians they had killed or were killing. And they outfitted one, two, three caravels or ships. They then sent these off—and Diego Velázquez, governor of Cuba, gave them broad license to do this—to the Lucayan and

---

[95] *History*, Bk. 3, cap. 92.

other islands, there to seize and haul back cargoes of Indians, Indians who were living in lands and homes of their own, in peace and quiet.

There was one flotilla in particular, and the following occurred to it. A ship and a brigantine, with 70 or 80 Spaniards for complement, left port from Santiago de Cuba, it is on the south coast of the island. They sailed towards the mainland, practically reaching where the Yucatan bends the corner, though they did not sight mainland. They came on some small islands, ones the First Admiral had originally discovered in 1502 or 1503. [But these men thought they were the first to discover the same!] These islands were the Guanajes, there are two or three of them, I think.

The Spaniards came up on them, the islanders off guard and feeling safe. The Spaniards attacked one, and with their swords and lances killed all they could, captured all they could, then went to the next island and did likewise, filled the ship with captives, as many as it could hold, then headed back for Cuba, just the ship, with the intention of returning for the remaining natives on the islands. They left 25 Spaniards behind with the brigantine, to go hunt down and hold whoever was left, until the ship now taking the prisoners returned.

The ship reached Cuba and the port of Carenas, what we now call Havana. There, almost every Spaniard went ashore to get a rest. But eight or nine stayed aboard to watch the vessel and the Indians who were below decks under the hatch in the pitch dark. The Indians were well aware of how bad the situation was, they were wide awake and alert to everything, so they recognized that overhead there were fewer footsteps, much less noise. They recognized that most of the Spaniards had gone ashore and left the ship with no one or just a few aboard. So they worked to force the hatch, the square cover controlling access to the hold, and they either broke the thin chain used to fasten the cover, or worked it free without breaking it, but in such way that the eight or nine mariners who were there to guard the ship did not notice, they were either fast asleep or distracted.

Next, the Indians burst from below decks and killed the mariners, all of them. Then a remarkable thing, they raised the anchor, if you please, like mariners used to sailing their whole lives long, something no one ever saw such people do, naked, weaponless people, heretofore thought of as beast-like and barbaric and treated as such. They climbed the rigging almost as readily as seamen, they spread sail, they headed the ship in the direction of their islands some 250 leagues from that spot. The Spaniards on shore, the crew who were enjoying their recreation, when they saw the anchor raised with such vigor, the sails set, the ship steered as if they were all aboard doing it, they were fear-stricken, they began to leap up and down and shout, thinking it was their pals, the skeleton crew, who were doing this, shouting were they out of their minds! Then they noticed it was a lot of Indians who were moving agilely about, manning the ropes, the tackle, steering the ship back along the route they came. Then the crew on shore began to understand something bad had happened to their pals, the Indians had killed them, the Indians were headed home. The Spaniards stood there watching them until they disappeared. I do not know how long it took, but it is certain that the Indians made it home, as if they were very practiced mariners and steered by compass and chart.

When the Indians reached the island, they found the 25 Spaniards totally unprepared to see the ship in other than Christian hands. The Indians attacked them fiercely, using the lances, the truncheons, the rocks that were on board. The two groups locked in combat, many on both sides were wounded, but the Indians began to prevail against the 25 Spaniards. The latter, sensing the tight fix they were in, and that they couldn't hold out, decided to retreat to the brigantine they had left in order to fight, and with it to flee down the coast. And in order to leave a trail for when Spaniards came, they carved a cross into a tree that grew right next to an inlet. They removed the bark of the tree and bared the words, "Headed for Darién."

Now back the story up a bit. When Diego Velázquez found out that the Indians had killed 8 Spaniards and had run off with the ship, he decided immediately to outfit two more with enough Spaniards to go after the rebellious Indians and to help the 25 Spaniards left behind on the is-land—and they had named it Sancta Marina—left behind so they could then scout other islands from there, other lands, and from these reap further results for Our Lord and Their Majesties, attracting the Indians thereof to the knowledge of our holy Catholic faith. These are the very words Diego Velázquez used in a letter he wrote the Admiral, Don Diego Columbus. I have a copy of it. With such language, such pretense, Diego Velázquez—and the rest of the tyrants—baptized their loathesome tyrannies and ambitions and greeds, heedless of the Indian souls they thereby plunged into hell as a result of the murder, the atrocities they committed against those Indians, heedless of the bad repute they gave the Christian religion, the scandal, the chaos they sowed throughout that entire region with the violence they did to those simple people, gentle peaceful people, heedless of the injustice they worked plucking them from their own land and homes and carting them off to others far away, very different places from what they knew, carting them off as captives so that at the end of it they all perished, not a one survived. These were the services the Spaniards offered God and Their Majesties, this was the conversion of these peoples to the Catholic faith, offered out of great zeal, by Diego Velázquez, by the rest.

To resume, Diego Velázquez learned of the Indian takeover of the ship, so he outfitted two more and manned them with Spaniards. They reached the island, saw the cross and words carved into the tree, left immediately to search for the 25 Spaniards, island by island, until they reached one they had named Sancta Catalina, and near it found the caravel or ship the Indians had escaped in, it was up on the rocks, a reef, and burned. The Spaniards, out of devotion to Sancta Catalina, attacked the island they had named for her, fought a battle with the people living on it, killed all they could, captured all they could, then went on to another island named Utila and repeated their performance, so that in sum from both islands they captured almost 500 people, split them between the two ships, shoved them into the holds, then closed the hatch on them.

With this mighty deed accomplished, and quite satisfied with themselves, the Spaniards went back to the first little island, went ashore to recuperate so as then to set out for Cuba already quite rich men. The Indian captives stashed in one caravel sensed that very few Spaniards remained on board. They found a way, by heaving and heaving, to break or slew the hatch, then quickly started to pour out of the hold. The Spaniards caught on and came at them with weapons and clubs, ordering them to stay below while beating on them. The Indians heeded neither their force nor their advice, but with a lunge came up and attacked the Spaniards with the sticks and stones they brought from below decks. With a furious energy and abandon they fought so hard the Spaniards could not hold out. Half leaped overboard. The other half the Indians killed, and the ship was in Indian hands. Once they had it, they grabbed all the lances and shields, any other weapons that were there, and made ready to defend themselves. The Spaniards who were ashore resting, saw what happened on the vessel, so they returned immediately to the other one, then bore down on the first and began to combat the Indians. They in turn fought back fiercely, bravely, the women as much as the men, using bows, arrows, lances, shields, rocks, for two long hours, so much so that the Spaniards were awed by them, exhausted and cut up. But the Spaniards began to prevail over the Indians, who, when they saw themselves losing, many of their people dead, jumped into the sea, all the men, many of the women. The Spaniards hauled in the women they could with the ships' boats. Some of the men got away and swam ashore. It is likely the Spaniards killed a number of them. So the other ship was recovered. The two then, with more than 400 aboard—the women, the men the Spaniards were able to capture or retain from their raids, plus 20,000 pesos of low grade gold—sailed back and made port at Havana. Diego Velázquez is the one who relates all this, in the letter he wrote the Admiral about what happened, the one I mentioned above.

These battles should be enough to confound the malice and show up the falsity of those who defame the Indians as pitiful beasts. It is evident in both combats, the strategy they used to free themselves from such unjust capture, and the shrewdness and the calculation and the courage. If they ever had the weapons we have, naked though they are, we would have had to enter their kingdoms and lands in some other way than by killing and capturing and robbing, as we have constantly done till now in our sinful way. But because we have found them naked, with no weapons really that were worth anything against ours, we have destroyed them, wiped them out. There was nothing missing in their humanity. They were capable, rational, courageous.

Urraca

I said earlier that Pedrarias wrote the King that it would be best to transfer the population of Darién, the city and the cathedral seat, to Panama.[96] Because Darién was an unhealthy place, not the right one for Spaniards to colonize. His main motive was to make more of a profit in Panama, he thought the port of Nombre de Dios better suited to traffic with the Sea of the South. And that is true, except the place is as unhealthy as Darién, maybe twice it. The Spanish inhabitants of Darién were recalcitrant, they had already built house and home there. What happened was that the King read Pedrarias' letter and answered it by ordering that if Darién was not the suitable site, he should move to Panama, the site he had named, or some other he thought might be better for the location of a cathedral church. Once Pedrarias received the authorizing letter, he wrote immediately to Gonzalo Hernández de Oviedo whom he had left at Darién as his lieutenant. Oviedo was to pack up and move everything there was at Darién, by land or by sea, and move everyone, all to Panama. So every settler got his things together, moveable goods, animals, bound for Nombre de Dios, then they crossed to Panama, though with enormous difficulty and wrangling and delay after delay—plus grief for the Indians, and pain and hunger and hard labor and even some deaths, I would think, because Indians were the ones who bore the brunt, who bore the pain, who did the work until they dropped. There was one Indian leader named Urraca, one among other chiefs and leaders in the area Pedrarias and Espinosa with their lieutenants were raiding and constantly ruining. Urraca was an important, powerful chief, and his authority covered the province of Veragua, also extending to the

[96] *History*, Bk. 3, cap. 162.

mountainous region around it. He took a lot of punishment from the Spaniards against his subjects—attacks, humiliations. He was very angry very often at having to take it, having himself and his people treated like the other native groups, especially when the Spaniards got the idea he had a lot of gold. But he was brave and bold and smart and persistent in warfare, so he often gave the Spaniards grief when, in the exercise of their tyranny, without cause or reason, they attacked him the way they did the other groups. He never fought Spaniards without wounding a lot of them, some he killed, they were never able to nail him.

Espinosa, off on his usual tyrannical business, left Panama on the Sea of the South in two ships, with some men and two or three horses, to go west along the coast and subjugate the natives on the islands named Cebaca. There were thirty such, of all sizes, 70 leagues from Panama. He sent Francisco Pizarro overland, with a number of men he thought sufficient, and they were to subjugate natives also, killing, capturing, destroying all who would not surrender. In that process, the land group was often cut up, but the result was always the same, the misfortunate Indians with their naked skin and their weapons of wind ended up dead or captured and beaten. What with terror going on through the area, 50 leagues of it, the Indians who could not defend themselves, or hide or flee, surrendered themselves into Spanish hands. This was the Gospel preached or fostered by the Spaniards, our brethren, all across the mainland. And we can always be certain, from many previous examples, that whenever 50 Spaniards set out to make war or conquer—pacification, they also call it—they take with them 500 captive souls, men and women, to carry unbearable loads and be at their service. It is grievous, painful, pitiable, deplorable, to see what those Indians suffer, the labor, the fatigue, the hunger, the bitter life, the even more bitter death of the many who die along the way!

Espinosa reached the islands. Their inhabitants came out to meet him peacefully, they did not dare resist or fight. And since his basic Gospel text was first to ask if they had any gold, or any knowledge of where to find it, they answered by signalling that up in the high mountains, where Urraca was king and lord, there was gold in abundance . . . Once he heard that happy news, good Captain Espinosa left the ships with skeleton crews and landed the rest of his people on shore, something he was quite expert at, landed the horses also, and headed a straight route for the region of King Urraca. Urraca had sighted the approaching ships from the high perch of his mountain home. He knew they had not arrived for nothing, they might well have come looking for him, so he was already on the alert, and had placed the women and children, the elderly, those not engaged in the fighting, out of harm's way. Once his scouts notified him that the Spaniards were close, he went after them with fury and ferocity, it was like cats clawing at lions and tigers. They encountered first some Indians the Spaniards had along to do things, they were the advance party, out ahead either scouting or doing something else they were told. Urraca's people killed these first, then loosed darts and arrows against the cavalry, next wounded and killed as many of those on foot as they could. In a fierce fight with the Spaniards, they wounded many, they harassed them mightily since they were so numerous and came at them from all sides. They pressed the Spaniards so hard the latter were almost done for, were losing heart. But it seems that Francisco Pizarro, from the group he had, must have split off Hernando de Soto plus 30 men to go make a raid in the same region. They happened to be near this battle, heard the clamor of it, so came on, and the Indians, seeing help arrive in the nick of time for the Spaniards, drew off a bit. The roughness of the terrain was in the Indians' favor, the horses were not much of a threat, and when that is the case in the Indies, the Spaniards can do far less to the Indians, would not otherwise have wiped them out so quickly.

Espinosa sensed that for the time being he could make little headway against Urraca, so he decided to turn back and do it by night. But Urraca and his people were wide awake, they heard them going, they went after him, got to a dangerous pass and there waited. In that pass the Indians fought like raw lions to cut him off, but the Spaniards killed a lot, wounded a lot with their swords and crossbows, and made it through the pass to freedom. And they thought it no little help of divine grace to find themselves out of that danger and they returned to the ships feeling more than a modicum of fear.

Espinosa went further down the coast to another island, one they had named Sancto Matías. From there they made an attack straight on shore, the coastal territory of Boreca. A great many Indians came out to oppose his arrival—prompted by the news they had of what the Spaniards did—but as soon as they saw the horses they started to run for it, afraid the horses would eat them up. The Spaniards pursued them, entered their village, took the women and children and whatever else they could, after doing the killing and wounding and robbing and burning every which way. The head of the village, when he saw captured his women, his children, his people, chose then to surrender to the Spaniards, judging that the loss of them, absence from them, was a worse thing than the loss of his own liberty. So, in tears, he begged Espinosa to give him back his women and children. And Espinosa did so out of compassion.

He found out from this chief that another chief lived nearby and he had gold—remember, gold was the first thing the Spaniards asked about. So Espinosa sent Francisco Compañón to raid the place. He attacked the village just before dawn, but did not take the villagers by surprise, they counter-attacked so fiercely, with such courage, they forced the Spaniards to turn and retreat a good distance back along the route they had come. But the Spaniards felt put to shame, as they say it, and in danger they can rally themselves. They did an about-face with renewed courage and attacked again, wounding and killing whoever faced them until they reached the village where the Indians had built an enclosure out of wood, as a fortress. The Spaniards broke in and killed more inside. The Indians could not escape the enclosure, they tangled up in each other, which gave the Spaniards an excellent chance to use their weapons, their sword thrusts.

Espinosa then took his full force and went across country to attack the province of Acharibra and its people, ordering the ships to meet him there. But the Indians were aware of him coming, so they went out and attacked him, but no good, because once they saw the horses, they ran and kept running. Espinosa, after this, decided to return to Paraquita where he intended to settle, it was in the territory of Natá. So there you have the way the faith was preached in that area, how the Christian religion was made known, made attractive.

Paraquita, or Natá and the area around it, is very fertile, open, level and lovely, and near the mountains of Urraca or Veragua.[97] Right from the start it was reputed to have a lot of gold. That is why Espinosa wanted to settle it and concentrate there all the Indians of the region and surrounding areas, to work for the Spaniards, exactly what the Spaniards were always after. So he wrote Pedrarias asking permission to settle, giving him the reasons he thought convincing. Pedrarias answered yes, it ought to be done, but he himself wanted to do it, so Espinosa should return to Panama, but leave the number of men he thought sufficient for the task of settling. Espinosa left Francisco Compañón in charge. He was a first class killer who had been in with Espinosa on all the slaughters. Espinosa also left 50 men and 2 mares—as much damage was done using the mares as using the stallions—then with the remaining men he went back to where Pedrarias was waiting.

King Urraca was on the lookout every minute, so he knew of Espinosa's departure for Panama, and knew only a handful of Spaniards remained behind in Natá. He gathered a force and one night attacked the Spaniards. His scouts came on three in a hut outside their compound. They ran a lance through one, and he was dead; they seized the second, but the third ducked free, retrieved his weapons, made a great hullabaloo to bring other Spaniards running, then with force and fury he went after the Indians

---

[97] *History*, Bk. 3, cap. 163.

and killed five. In the resulting confusion, the Indians let the second man escape and started to fall back, and that allowed the two Spaniards then to regain the compound where their fellows were staying. The captain, Francisco Compañón, became aware of how many Indians Urraca had attacked them with, so he sent Hernando de Soto hell-bent to inform Pedrarias of the fix he and his men were in, then right after him Pero Miguel, two dependable men. Pedrarias was no slow-poke about such dangerous fixes, he immediately sent Hernán Ponce and 40 men aboard a ship, and they arrived just at the moment when Francisco Compañón and his men had decided to abandon the territory. Because Urraca had gathered together all the possible men in the area and had the Spaniards sourrounded, they were unable to go even a stone's throw from the compound to forage for roots they could eat. Once Urraca saw the ship, he judged that all the Spaniards of Panama had arrived, so he lifted the encirclement and withdrew to his mountains.

After he had sent the ship, Pedrarias decided to follow with 160 men, two horses, and some artillery pieces, with Francisco Pizarro as captain of the troop. Once he reached Paraquita, or Natá, and in it the place where Compañón and his men were located, he found out that Urraca and his men had withdrawn. So he ordered Hernán Ponce and 30 Spaniards to remain in the compound with Compañón, and next day, he, Pedrarias, left with the rest of the troop to find and capture Urraca. And Urraca was waiting to battle him, joining forces with another chief named Exquegua and a lot of men, at the entrance of the latter's village, a place strongly in his favor. Pedrarias would well have wished to duck this fight once he saw the place chosen did not allow a good use of his horses. But he saw himself attacked and pressed from several directions, so he charged the Indians with all his people, and the Indians stoutly resisted his attack, thus the two fought almost the whole day long, and many were wounded. I do not know the count of Indians killed. As for the Spaniards, they seldom are, the Indian weapons are such toys. But toys or not, they made it a bad day for the Spaniards, they fought them so fiercely that Pedrarias sensed he was in deep trouble and would have wished himself back in Panama and at ease. Then there was the weapon of last resort, artillery fire, the rounds scattered the Indians. But that did not mean Urraca lost heart completely. For four consecutive days, the Indians took to the field to fight. After that, Urraca saw they could not win against artillery fire and the horses, so he decided to break off, reinforce the men who were left, then fortify a place at a river named Atra, where men from both north and south coasts could meet and help him do battle.

Pedrarias decided to go after him, see if he couldn't capture him. He approached the place where Urraca was holed up with his forces. Urraca thought up a way to fool him. It was this: he sent out a few Indians, had them pretend they were unaware of Spanish presence, so the advance party would capture them, would demand from them where Urraca was, and they would answer he was up on a certain mountain, and he had with him a huge amount of gold. Urraca concocted this ruse of war because he knew the hunger and thirst for gold the Spaniards had, and how they would then pursue it helter-skelter, every man for himself, and then he, with the ambushes he had set up in certain passes, could smash them. So the Indians he sent for the trick were captured. And right away Pedrarias sent Diego Albítez with 40 men. On his way through the mountains he ran into the ambush, the Indians attacking so quickly not a one of the Spaniards remained without a wound or an injury, and the one choice they had was to run for their lives. Pedrarias sent the same Albítez back up the mountain in pursuit of the Indians, this time with 60 men, but he found no one. He came back along the flat of a river where he spotted them, and the Indians attacked him shouting at the top of their voices and fought to keep the Spaniards from crossing at a shallow place on the river. There were a lot wounded on both sides. The vanguard of the Spaniards began to lose courage, so Diego Albítez and some others hurried to reinforce them, but they fell into the river where they were thoroughly soaked and had a hard time emerging. The Spaniards finally prevailed after a lot of wounds and work. They pursued the Indians, slicing and slaughtering as many as they could catch.

Pedrarias then sent squads of Spaniards ranging through various parts of the region, robbing, burning, wrecking, capturing any and everybody they found. Then he ordered the same for the areas of Bulaba and Musa, two other chiefs who had aided Urraca. Thus the whole country was bruised and beaten down and depopulated, the people of it fleeing panic-stricken for the mountains, leaving behind many dead and many who fell into captivity.

Pedrarias decided to reward the Spaniards who had fought so hard in the campaign and he set up a village for them in the area. He thought it would be best placed in or near the Indian one of a cacique or chief named Natá, and decided to name it that. He then assigned a certain number of Indians to each Spaniard who wanted to settle there—it is what the Spaniards out in the Indies do, especially those who are the conquerors, they take little care to till the soil, then or now, but eat the fruits of their so noble conquests at the cost of the Indians, body and soul. And that process was and is called making allotments of villages and giving them out as encomiendas to the Spaniards who then draw their total livelihood from them. [The Indians he assigned] were from villages he had subdued throughout the region with his tactics of war and violence. Pacifying an area, the Spaniards call it. And the

Indians usually decide to stay with their villages for fear that elsewise they will be hacked to pieces. And they serve the Spaniards when the latter pass through or summon them to come. Though they never think that service will be so harsh, so constant, that it will finish them off the way it does. That region is now empty. It was before fruitful and full of people.

Once Pedrarias had set everything in order, allotted the Indians, imposed his tyranny, he named as his lieutenant and man in charge Diego Albítez, while he himself returned to Panama. As for the allotted Indians, they answered the summons, and came to work at building houses and planting fields for the Spaniards, they hunted, they fished, did all the other work required to sustain a village of 50 or 60 Spanish settlers, more work there than back in Castile to sustain a village of 2,000. Because the Spaniards demand that the Indians serve them as nobility are served, as royal dukes, and not just served but adored. The Indians experienced this strange burden as intolerable, so some showed up late, some not at all, some fled, and the Spaniards called fleeing rebellion. Diego Albítez sent parties after them. The Spaniards call this a round-up. The ones they catch, they either kill, or punish as a warning, or shackle. Thus Albítez forced them to come and serve their tyrant encomenderos.

Urraca, the chieftain, every time he saw a chance, was mindful to pay the Spaniards a visit with the people he could gather, and he gave the Spaniards many a good morning. The Spaniards he surprised off guard, he did not have to come visit twice to take vengeance on. Then the Spaniards sallied out and burned, ravaged across the land, the province of Urraca. They spent 9 years at this, but they could never tame him. The truth is he couldn't be tamed on their terms unless he submitted to captivity and enslavement and tyranny as did the rest, for that is what would eventually happen to him and his people. It is the reward, the satisfaction our people grant the Indians for the damages, the stupendous injustices we inflict on them, then and now. Urraca was an intelligent, courageous man, and he knew how right the war was that he fought against people who had done him so much harm, and kept on doing him harm, against all justice, no provocation, no reason for it, no cause for it, he lived in peace in his own land. He had no desire to yield.

The Spaniards tortured severely those of Urraca's Indians they caught, to make them reveal where the huge stash of gold was that Urraca and his people were reputed to have, and that infuriated Urraca more every time. After a period, Pedrarias sent Compañón to be in command of the town of Natá. The Spaniards there were mightily afraid of one very brave Indian in particular, a lieutenant of Urraca, because of the frequent attacks he had made on them. Compañón tried many maneuvers to get hold of him, and since he could not do it in battle, he tried treachery, to catch him under a flag of truce. So, assured by Indian messengers and assured by false promises, Urraca's man came to the Spaniard's settlement and right into their hands. Compañón seized him, breaking his word—a rotten device used often against the Indians in that area, whereas the Indians kept their promises, for the most part. Compañón put him in chains and sent him to Nombre de Dios, far from his own territory. But they did him a favor actually, they didn't burn him, as those who call themselves Christian often do. Urraca was deeply grieved by this event, so he put a lot of effort into gathering men together from the coasts of both seas, north and south, and when he had them, he made them a powerful speech. "There is no reason we should give these Christians any rest. Not only do they seize our lands, our authority, our women and children, our gold, whatever we have, and make slaves of us, but also they do not keep the faith they promise, nor the word, nor the peace. So let us fight against them and try if we ever can to kill them, and unburden ourselves of this intolerable weight, and do so while our forces last. It is better for us to die fighting a war than to live a life of exhaustion, bitterness and dread." The Macchabees, Judas and his brothers, spoke exactly this way in their own struggle. The Indians agreed, they all swore to die fighting, while they had life and strength left. So Indians allotted to Spaniards rebelled and killed five who lived off-guard in the villages where they had lorded it over their subjects. After killing these Spaniards, the Indians in great number came down on the hated village of Natá. The Spaniards responded, everyone fought fiercely, many dead, many wounded every which way, the Indians especially—it was the horses that did them great damage because the battleground was open and clear. This war lasted many years, a number of Spaniards died in it, a far greater number of Indians, no comparison. But these unfortunate people with their naked bodies and useless weapons saw themselves getting killed every day and no results from it, no remedy, no hope, and they were tramping through mountains and valleys, tired, broken, again and again on missions of war—there was sweat and hunger and the thousand other struggles that kind of life entailed, especially out in the Indies. So most of the villages decided to surrender to the Spaniards, become their servants, have done with the wretched life. Only Urraca, the king, and his people, the ones who had survived the slaughter, refused ever to submit, he retained his fierce abhorrence of Spaniards, it grieved him his whole life long that he could not get rid of them. The Spaniards left him alone in his territory, they stopped hunting him, they knew they never made war on him without many of them getting killed in the process or badly mauled. So Urraca died in his own land, in his own house, surrounded by his own people, died a pagan, with no more knowledge of God than he had before he first heard the name Christians. Who will have to answer for his loss? And who for the loss of so many souls, who had no blocks to receiving the faith if it was preached to them? It is clear who, to any real Christian!

- 9 -

Cumaná

Prenote

The basic problem Las Casas tried to solve early on was how to bring about peaceful co-existence, cooperation between Indian and Spanish life in the New World. It led him to set up a colonization project on the north coast of South America, at Cumaná, in 1521. Gaining the grant to do so was a long, torturous process involving the major players in Spain and the New World, and even after gaining the grant, events interfered with the project.[98] The project was to involve secular as well as sacred interests on Spain's side, and Indian interests on the other. A fiasco resulted, one best described by Las Casas in the following excerpt. The intensity of his struggle, the principles involved, and his own judgment on himself, all leap out of the narrative. The narrative itself is masterful and shows Las Casas' use of personal experience and investigative skills to present the truth of an incident in a way that revealed the larger issues.

This is the pact he signed with the officials on Hispaniola, a series of items.[99] That the cleric be given the fleet that had been sent to make war on the Indians, plus the brigantines and boats the fleet had, plus what was aboard the ships. As for complement on that fleet, the captain commanded 300 men. 120 were to be hired on salary, and the others discharged. The remaining ones were to serve under a captain, and the officials designated the former one, Gonzalo Ocampo, and he was to guarantee the peace so that the cleric Las Casas, with the missionaries he was to have along with him, would be free to preach to the Indians. This was the first item, but like those conjurations that begin with God and end with the devil. The next item was aimed at continuing the pearl traffic and the tyranny involved in that process,

---

[98] See Helen Rand Parish's Introduction to *The Only Way*, pp. 25-6 for an accurate sketch of the sequence of events.

[99] *History*, Bk. 3, cap. 157.

179

though the item did not say so expressly. It said, "according as the Indians agreed to it," but the Indians never agreed to it, unless a miracle of asking happened. Another item indicated that the said pact and fleet had this purpose, the said cleric Bartolomé de las Casas would verify what provinces and peoples ate human flesh, also those that did not want peace and commerce with the Spaniards, and those that did not want to accept the faith or the preachers thereof. He was then to say: "I declare this province to be one where human flesh is eaten, and these people unwilling to be friends of the Spaniards, and these people unwilling to accept the faith or the preachers thereof." Then the captain, with his 120 men, was to make war on them forthwith, and make slaves of every one taken alive. This really was the primary goal for the officials, the purpose controlling everything. They hoped and thought the cleric was going to fill with slaves their houses, their barns, their plantations. They were so blind they forgot that the cleric had gone around for five or six years, and everyone knew it, working himself to death, back and forth from Castile, so that they could not make slaves, so the ones they had made slaves would be set free, even if they were caribes, those who ate human flesh.

* * * *

The cleric was alone except for some staff and a few others he had hired to help . . .[100] Several religious of St. Francis had come to settle in Cumaná with the people [who had just gone back to Hispaniola]. Their superior was a friar named Juan Garceto, not a Spaniard, from Picardy, I think, he had come out to Hispaniola earlier with a certain Fray Remigio. Fray Juan was a very good religious, a prudent man, and he was eager to benefit the Indians with the faith. The Franciscans saw the cleric as having both the resources and protection required for converting the Indians, and that overjoyed them, they came out to greet him singing the *Te Deum*, "Blessed is he who comes in the name of the Lord." And he, the cleric, was grateful to God to find them there. Their monastery was made of wood and straw, had a good orchard in which orange trees grew, producing marvelous oranges, a section of vineyard, vegetable garden, wonderful melons plus other tasty things. . . The monastery and garden were within a crossbow shot of the sea, and right next to the bank of the river called Cumaná, from which the whole region takes its name.

The cleric ordered a warehouse built just off the edge of the friars' orchard, where he could store all the matériel he had brought. As soon as he was able, he let the Indians know through the Franciscans—and they through an Indian woman named Doña Maria who knew a little Spanish—that he, the

---

[100] *History*, Bk. 3, cap. 158.

cleric, had been sent by the King of the Christians, now newly on the throne in Spain, that they were no longer going to be harmed by Spaniards, but instead treated well, they were to live together in great peace and friendship, as they would see in time. He tried in this way to relax them and gain their good will. He gave them things he had brought, and the men with him were always respectful, they never gave the least cause for scandal.

I said earlier that the small island, Cubagua, where the pearls were gathered, had no drinking water, nothing fresh, just some holes with brackish stuff, so whatever people there drank they had to bring from the river at Cumaná, seven leagues away from the island. The settlers who lived in the area were supposed to build him a fort at the mouth of the river. He was afraid they would not do so. They were lovers of pearls. The fort might block them from fresh water if they did not act as they were supposed to act—in fact, the fort would have been a certain way of making sure no one along that whole coast would dare cause the Indians any harm or cause them any scandal. So the cleric hired a master mason to build one, and agreed to pay him the monthly salary of 8 pesos gold, or thereabouts. But the Spanish apostles on Cubagua caught on to the cleric's move and they found a way, through menace or money, to remove the master mason. So the cleric lacked a most important weapon, for even though building a fort was crucial for protecting those who settled there against the Indians, it was much more crucial for halting the raids, the shocking humiliations and chaos perpetrated by the Spaniards living on Cubagua . . . Not many months, even days, later, the pearl lovers came in their boats on the pretext of getting water from the river, and they caused trouble among the people in the nearby villages. Some vexed the Indians by living off them, dead weight, and the Indians especially resented the Spaniards' itch for their wives and daughters, they knew from experience what Spaniards did. Others asked the Indians constantly to give them gold or sell them other Indians for the price of bottles of wine. With wine, the most vicious Indians trick the young and the simple and sell them to the Spaniards. And wine was the money Indians loved the most, to get it they gave or would give whatever was asked of them. But the consequence was this, they did not know that wine should be cut with water. So they got drunk readily, and just as readily, once drunk, got into quarrels, grabbed weapons—bows, poisoned arrows—and thus wounded each other, killed or seriously damaged each other. What a nice preparation for hearing the Gospel and being drawn to the Christian religion!

From here on the cleric had to swallow bitter, bitter things, had to recognize the obstacles to his project, they were so effective as to wreck it completely. Whatever he had said to the Indians in the King's name was contradicted by what the Spaniards did. He reached such a pitch that he even stopped and wondered if there wasn't some way he could get out of this terribly troubling situation. He went across to the island of Cubagua and made stern demands on the one who was chief magistrate, but that had no effect. He knew his own life was in danger, the lives of the religious, and those of the rest with him. He laid the situation bare with the friars, especially with Fray Juan Garceto who was a very prudent man, as I said earlier. They went over the state the mission was in, they were in. And Fray Juan thought that the troubles were going to increase rather than diminish, unless the King or Council put a stop to them with the severest of penalties. For that to happen, the cleric himself, no one else, would have to go bring King or Council to do so. The cleric had to admit he thought much the same—there was no remedy without express new royal penalties and threats of punishment—but it seemed a mockery that he should have to go get action in person, it seemed not to make sense. One, by just being in place, the cleric prevented some evils from happening. Two, with him gone, the whole area would be so unprotected that no part of it would be free of pillage—robbery, slaving, etc, and that would cause an even greater hostility and hatred towards Spaniards than there was before. Thus the Indian chances, their willingness to hear and accept the faith would be shoved further off, made more remote than ever. And another reason, though this was the least and by far, there would be very little to protect the matériel he had there, worth 50,000 castellanos, part of which he owned.

Fray Juan made a reasonable response to all these points, but the reasons were not compelling, did not have the kind of clarity or evidence needed to satisfy the cleric. They talked and talked the matter over, until they reached the point where, at the insistence of Fray Juan, the cleric began to consider it might be a wise thing to return, though it didn't yet seem so to him—it wasn't the evidence so much, but God had something in mind for him. He made this decision: while the two ships were being loaded with salt for transport to Hispaniola, and until they were almost ready to leave—that would mean almost a month—he would each day say Mass and his required prayers as a petition to Our Lord to reveal to him what would be best to do. And after Mass each day, they would talk the matter over, then at the end of the period, it would be decided whether he should stay or go . . .

The day came when the ships were quite ready to leave. The friar and the cleric said their masses and presented their decision to God, then after, held their talk. The friar, staying with his first decision, said to the cleric, "You have to go, my lord, no way should you remain." The cleric judged that such was the will of God, so he said, "God knows how much this is against my judgment and therefore against my will. But I will do it because it seems right to your reverence . . ."

The decision made, he named Francisco de Soto captain or head of those he left behind. De Soto was a native of Olmeda, formerly a servant in the royal household. The cleric had brought him from Spain, a good person, sensible, but poor, and because of that brought a lot of evil on himself, on the mission, on everyone there. The cleric gave De Soto instructions he had drawn up. One of the items was that for no reason whatsoever should he let any of the vessels left behind leave port. There was a swift one named San Sebastián, the other a moorish type craft with a lot of oars, for which reason the Indians call it a centipede, they are quite afraid of it. De Soto should be constantly alert to the Indians for if they were restless, if they threatened, if he saw danger, then he should, with all discretion, board people and matériel and sail to Cubagua. If the danger was sudden, violent, and there was no time to save the matériel, then save the people no matter what. The cleric had De Soto sign a copy of the instructions. He put aboard ship, of all the things he owned, two trunks, one of clothing, one of books. So he left the friars, who were sad to see him go, and he no less than they.

After the cleric left, the first thing Francisco de Soto did, the man the cleric left in charge, was to send off the two ships, one up the coast, the other down, to bargain for gold and pearls, and people think slaves also, if the ships could get any.[101] The Indians of the region decided to kill the cleric's people and the friars and as many Spaniards as they could. And do so either because of the attacks made on them by the Spaniards before the cleric left, or done after he left, or because of their own badness which made them unworthy to live without suffering and impediments to reaching knowledge of God. They did the killing 15 days after the cleric left, but people think it was planned before that, and maybe even with him in mind, since none of the peace and love and justice he had promised them in the name of the new King of Castile had come true. The religious found out about the decision three days before the Indians did it. There was sufficient indication. They asked Doña Maria, the Indian woman I spoke of, and her words of reply were no, and they were for the sake of the Indians present, but she said yes with her eyes and facial movements. So the religious and the cleric's people were certain three days beforehand. At that precise moment a ship showed up, it was trading. The cleric's people asked if the ship would take them, I am not sure if the friars asked also, but the men on board refused, out of fear, or out of malice, deliberately leaving them there to get killed. They could have saved themselves if Francisco de Soto had obeyed the cleric's orders not to send the ships out of port. There is no doubt the whole group could have been saved, not a one lost, though they might not

---

[101] *History*, Bk. 3, cap. 159.

have saved the matériel. During the three days before, the religious and Francisco de Soto went anxiously from place to place, house to house, person to person, asking when the thing was planned for, and when they knew the attack on them would be the next morning, the cleric's people set up twelve or fourteen artillery pieces around the house. But when they tried the gunpowder, they found it so wet it wouldn't fire. First thing in the morning, when the sun rose, they put the powder out to dry, but at that very hour, the Indians attacked them with a fierce yell, killed two or three of the cleric's people, then set fire to the house or lodge, and it started to burn with them all inside it. They cut a passageway out of it, another into the orchard of the religious which was surrounded by a cane paling, and got into the orchard while the Indians were busy setting the fire. Just then Francisco de Soto was on his way back from one of the villages, which wasn't a crossbow shot from the house and monastery, right on the seashore, as I said, and the Indians hit him in the arm or on the hand with a poisoned arrow. He made a desperate effort to get into the orchard.

The religious had dug a canal a stone's throw long for water to come from the river right to the orchard. There was a canoe in it, or an Indian craft that held 50 people. The friars and the cleric's men ran to it and jumped aboard. But one lay brother, a devout man of very good life, when he heard the Indians yell, had fled and hidden himself in a stand of cane so no one saw him. The rest, friars and laymen, 15 or 20 people, in the canoe, made it down the canal and into the river. They were headed for the open sea, and for Punto de Araya where the salt beds are, and two ships loading salt, about two leagues of gulf away. The river was large, the current swift. The lay brother came out of the stand of cane and appeared on the riverbank. When they saw him, though they had gone well past where he came out, they made a huge effort to return and rescue him, but could not overcome the current. He saw their trouble, he waved them away and gone. A short time later the Indians killed him, made of him a martyr.

The Indians had been so occupied in setting fire to the house or structure, thinking the Spaniards were inside, that they did not hear the friars and laymen making their escape. When they did, they immediately got a pirogue, a canoe made in a special way and very light, put everyone it could hold aboard, weapons and all, bows, arrows, and went in pursuit of the Spaniards. The latter were a league out to sea already, their hands blistered and skinned from rowing. When they saw the Indians after them, they almost lost heart, but kept rowing as fast as they could. Then the craft of the friars and laymen and the pirogue of the Indians hit land at the same time, the one a horseshoe throw away from the other. But that shore was choked with thistles which had thick, fierce spines, so fierce that a man in full armor would not dare wriggle through them except very carefully. The Indians were naked head to foot, they were hard put to cover the short distance to where the friars and laymen were. In fact the thistles were so thick they couldn't make the distance at all to kill the Spaniards. Fray Juan Garceto told me afterwards that he saw an Indian right close to him, right over his shoulder, or several Indians bent on getting him, with a rock or a bludgeon. . . He fell on his knees, closed his eyes, raised his heart to God, hoped that they would hit him and have it over. But when they did not, he opened his eyes and saw no one. The reason, apart from the will of God, was that the friar was so entangled in thorns and the Indians so naked, they didn't dare go after him. This was the way the party escaped, and the Indians returned empty-handed from their pursuit. Garceto kept to his thorn fort for a long time, in fact went in deeper, but eventually came out all cut, with thorns in him and every inch of him in pain. They all reached where the ships were loading salt. They were taken aboard and everyone was down. Francisco de Soto didn't make it, I said he had been hit with an arrow. Someone said they saw him against a rock in the thorn grove. People went there in a boat, a league and a half, and found him still alive, three days after being wounded—he had been without food or drink—and they brought him back in the boat. The poisonous herb causes a great thirst, so he asked for water immediately to quench it. They gave it, and he began right then to rave, and a short time later died. So, in the action, the Indians killed a total of four of the cleric's men and one friar, and the number includes Francisco de Soto.

The cleric meantime was en route to the island of Hispaniola, ordinarily a voyage that can be accomplished in five or six days. But the pilots aboard the ships mistook the way, they did not know the landfalls, they thought the coast of Hispaniola was that of Sant Juan, so they actually anchored 80 leagues west of the port of Santo Domingo, at Yaquimo. Then they were two months forcing their back against the currents prevalent in that area, and they are mighty all the way to Santo Domingo. . . The cleric decided to sail the ships further west, go ashore, send the ships on their own to Santo Domingo . . . and he himself to go overland. . . Meantime, some ten or fifteen days after the Indian uprising and killings, the salt ships arrived, and on board the friars and the men who had escaped, and they gave out the news in Santo Domingo of what had occurred. A rumor began to spread that the pearl island Indians had killed the cleric Las Casas and every one of his people, good news for a lot, bad news for a few. Good news because a sure block to the fulfillment of their desires was gone, and they were now dead certain there would be war against those mainland Indians, and slaves made, and that is the pitch of their piety, yesterday, today.

The cleric was coming cross country from Yaguana to the city of Santo Domingo. There was a party with him. They were resting at a river, Las Casas sleeping under a tree, when some wayfarers came along. When they were asked what news they had of Santo Domingo or of Castile, they replied, "Nothing much really except the Indians of the Pearl Coast have killed the cleric Bartolomé de las Casas and his whole retinue." The cleric's group said, "We can tell you that's impossible." They were standing there arguing when the cleric woke up, like coming back from the dead, heard the news, and didn't know what to say or believe. But given the conditions he had left back on the Pearl Coast, and given the incidents that had already happened, he became afraid, he began to think all the effort he had put into the project was wasted. And when, later, he found out more about what happened, he concluded it had been a divine judgment, God's decision to inflict punishment on him for having made a pact with those he knew were not in it to help him for the sake of God and out of zeal to win souls who were perishing out in those provinces, but in it only out of greed, to make themselves rich.

He had offended God, it seemed, blotching the purity of that spiritual mission and goal he had set strictly for the sake of God. And that was to promote the religious, and himself, in an effort to bring light to those peoples by the preaching and teaching of Christian faith and doctrine. And he had blotched it by base and utterly worldly human means, in fact inhuman means, means absolutely out of harmony with those used by Jesus Christ. Even though God does admit the use of human means to achieve the highest purposes, God does not need machinations for the preaching of the Gospel. The cleric could evidently have waited a longer time to name the 50 he needed to help him, and not have allowed alongside the infected proposal the officials made to him. He could have named people who were really Christian. Even though they were also motivated by one day becoming Knights of the Golden Spur and gaining a twelfth of the King's revenue, plus other grants in their favor, human grants, it still seemed as if the plan was a safer one, and honestly based. For one, because he had to choose not just anyone, but those really Christian types. For another, the entire temporal success of those chosen depended on the peacefulness of the Indian peoples and their acceptance of the faith . . . It did not depend on war and killings and the capture of free peoples and the damnation of souls and the defamation of the faith and abhorrence of the name Christian. The people he actually entered the pact with made their success to depend on war, etc.

But the cleric's response to this was that if he was in such a hurry to accept the pact the Audiencia offered him, he did it to prevent the death and damage the fleet [given him] would otherwise have done. But a reply to that could be, evidently, he was not obliged to that extent, etc. Maybe, after it all, one can honestly believe that God saw his good intent, not what came out, that it was an error in God's service, and for that reason he escaped the judgment that will come on the others involved. But, with God's help, if he had been there, the ships would not have left that place, nor would he have been so passive about the great danger during the three days after they found out about the Indian decision and were sure of it.

So the cleric continued on his way toward Santo Domingo knowing the sad news, very disconsolate but very anxious to know from start to finish what had actually happened. There were some friends who came to the road to meet and console him and offer him four or five or more thousands of ducats to resume and carry forward the mission. If they were moved to this by God alone and by zeal for souls, or moved to this for temporal gain—and here, on this island, more want the gain than the souls—God alone is the one who knows, and is the one to judge, and will be the one to judge on the day of final reckoning.

- 10 -

Enriquillo

Prenote

From the incident that follows, Las Casas derived the major insights of his missionary career. The narrative describes an Indian cacique on Hispaniola in the 1520's, early 1530's, during the time Las Casas "seemed to sleep." He had joined the Dominican Order in 1522, in the aftermath of the Cumaná fiasco, out of discouragement with his own efforts on behalf of the Indians, discouragement with the conquest system of oppression and exploitation, and the Dominicans were the group that had, in part, prompted his awakening, then promoted him in his pro-Indian role. Enriquillo had been raised a Christian, his new wife had been violated by the Christian encomendero, he could find no justice, so he led his people into the hills where he baffled all attempts to capture him, proving himself to be a military genius at defensive war. Las Casas lays out the entire story, including the part he himself played in bringing Enriquillo back into a settled place and a peaceful relationship with Spaniards. Las Casas accomplished this without arms of any kind, with only the assistance of an unarmed lay brother. He learned that Enriquillo believed in Christianity, though not at all in the force that pretended to propagate it. He responded to peace, not to war. Christianity could only be offered through peace, to anyone on earth. Any hint of violence and true Christianity vanished. These ideas form the core of a major piece of writing by Las Casas, The Only Way, *a piece he had sketched out by 1534 when he left Hispaniola for work in Central America.*

Some awful things happened in those years on the island of Hispaniola.[102] Though the Indians there were dying off, the Spaniards, nonetheless, kept working them, driving them. One Spaniard named

---

[102] *History*, Bk. 3, cap. 125.

Valenzuela—he lived near Sant Juan de la Maguana, a lecherous young man
who had inherited from his father his wicked and tyrannical ownership of
Indians—he had an allotment whose cacique, chief, was named Enriquillo.
He had been brought up as a child in a Franciscan monastery. It was in a
Spanish town called Vera Paz, in the Province of Xaragua . . . where
Behechio was king, one of the five on the island and the most important. . .
The friars had taught Enriquillo to read and write, taught him Spanish ways
of behavior. He was an apt pupil and took it all in. He spoke our language
very well. He showed in all he did that he had profited from the friars. The
land he was cacique of was the area the Indians call Baoruco. It is mountainous, alongside the south sea of Hispaniola, thirty, forty, fifty, seventy
leagues from the port of Santo Domingo, contiguous to that south coast.
When this chief of the province of Baoruco finished his schooling with the
Franciscans upon reaching his manhood, he married an Indian woman who
came from a noble family who named her Doña Lucia, as Christians in the
bosom of Holy Mother Church.

Enrique was a tall, impressive man, finely proportioned, his face
neither handsome nor homely. It was the face of a serious and stern man.
With his Indians, he served young Valenzuela, but under duress, as they say,
patiently putting up with the slavery and the mistreatment he received every
day. He had a few meager possessions. One was a mare. The young tyrant
he served simply took it from him. Next, not satisfied with outright theft, he,
as owner, violated the cacique's marriage and raped his wife. And because
the cacique took this badly—he protested directly to Valenzuela himself,
asked him why he had done such a brute thing—Valenzuela gave him a
beating, so the story goes. Blaming the victim, it is called. Enriquillo went
with his complaint about the rape to the governor's agent living in town. He
was Pedro de Vadillo. Enriquillo got the protection from him the Indians
always get from justices in the Indies and from officials of the King—Vadillo
warned Enriquillo what he would do to him if he ever again came with complaints against Valenzuela. They say Vadillo tossed him in jail or put him
in stocks. In sad shape, and finding no help in that justice official, he
decided to come in to Santo Domingo, after his release, and complain to the
Audiencia about the harm, the humiliation he had undergone. He was
destitute, exhausted, starving, because he had no money nor way to acquire
some.

The Audiencia gave him a supporting letter, but sent him back to its
agent Vadillo with no further action. That is the same satisfaction the
Audiencias, and even the Council of the King, provided for victimized,
suffering Indians, i.e., to hand the victims back to their enemies. When
Enriquillo reached the village, he presented his papers, and the justice he

received from Vadillo was to be cursed out and threatened, it was worse than the first time, so they say. Then, once the owner Valenzuela found out, worse still was the bad treatment and humiliation—he was going to whip Enriquillo, kill him, hack him, beat him up. He would rather thrash him than feed him. I have no doubt he would. It revealed an old practice and how worthless the Indians were always thought to be, ruler and subject alike. Revealed also the license, the brutal right the Spaniards usurped over the Indians to mete out punishment—they feared neither God nor man.

Cacique Enriquillo put up with these new abuses, new brutalities. [He was called this diminutive by those who knew him when he was young and a pupil of the Franciscans. So the name stuck and everyone used it.] . . . And he kept his counsel. There were certain months of the year when replacement groups were brought in to serve. The cacique was the one who went back and forth, he brought them in. If there was one Indian short, the cacique received the punishment—was locked up and battered, beaten, bruised, and other violences to boot. Enriquillo had his master's leave to go change groups—the Indian could easily have been his master's master. The change time came. He decided not to return and serve his enemy, nor send any of his Indians either. He was sure this was the just thing, and confident in his territory—it was harsh, no horse could manage it—and he was confident in his strength, in the few Indians he had, he would defend himself on home ground. The Spaniards called this an uprising, they still do, and called Enrique a rebel, the same for the Indians, uprising, rebels. By its right name, it is flight, from cruel enemies, who were killing them, chewing them up. Flight, as a cow or bull flees a slaughterhouse.

When Enrique did not come back, did not bring Indians to serve at the fixed time, Valenzuela judged that he must be mad and gone reckless over the maltreatment he had received, must be, as the Spaniards say, in rebellion. So Valenzuela went with eleven men to haul him back by force and maltreat him some more. When Valenzuela reached the place, he found Enrique and his people waiting, in arms—spears fitted with points of iron or fish bone, bows and arrows, stones, and whatever else they could use for weapons. They came towards Valenzuela, Enrique out in front. He told Valenzuela to go home alone, neither he nor any of his Indians were going with him, not a one. But master Valenzuela considered Enrique a slave, and no more than dung on the street—the same way all the Spaniards considered these people, and do still, less than worthless. So he began to call Enrique a dog and bad mouth him with every rotten word in the book, then attacked him and his Indians. But they counterattacked, and so quickly they killed one or two of the Spaniards, mauled most of the others, so they all turned and ran for it. Enrique did not permit pursuit, he let them go, but shouted to

Valenzuela, "Be glad I didn't kill you, Valenzuela! Go! And the rest of you! And don't come back here again! And keep an eye out!" Valenzuela, with his men, returned to Sant Juan de la Maguana hotfoot, his pride pricked but not cured.

Right away, news spread throughout the island that Enriquillo was in rebellion. The Audiencia decided to send people and subdue him. Seventy or eighty Spaniards joined forces and set off on a search. They were nearly exhausted and nearly starved when they found him, on a mountain. He came at them, killed some, wounded others. Routed and humiliated, they chose to take their defeat and shame home. Enriquillo's victories and reputation spread throughout the island. Many Indians fled their servitude and oppression under the Spaniards and sought protection and safety in Enriquillo's band, as if in a mighty fortress made of rock. They flocked to him the way people did to David when he was fleeing the tyranny of Saul, i.e., those who led lives of pain, or oppression from debt, or bitterness of soul, just as described in the Book of Kings, chapter 22 [sic: 1 Samuel 22:2]: "And everyone who was in distress, and everyone who was in debt, and everyone who was discontented, gathered to him; and he became captain over them. And there were with him about forty [sic: four hundred] men." In pretty much the same way, nearly three hundred men from all over the island came to Enriquillo, put themselves under his leadership. His original group was not quite a hundred, from what I knew. He taught them how to fight defensively against the Spaniards whenever they showed. He never allowed any of those who joined him to attack and kill any Spaniard first. His purpose was entirely to defend himself and his people against Spaniards the many times they came to subjugate and punish him. The war Enriquillo and his people fought against the Spaniards was just. How much so, and how right it was for the Indians to join him and choose him as lord and king, can be shown by looking at the history of the Maccabees in Holy Writ, and at Spanish history which tells about the deeds of the Prince Royal, Don Pelayo. Both the Maccabees and Don Pelayo fought just wars of self-defense. And were able to go on and exact vengeance, punishment for the injuries, the destruction, the death, the loss of territories they had sustained. The same right was involved. So in terms of natural law and the law of nations—and I omit mentioning an argument drawn from our faith, which supplies, for Christians, an additional title to self-defense based on nature—Enriquillo had an extremely just title to go after the Spaniards, so did the small number of Indians who survived on that island the cruel hands, the horrible tyranny of the Spaniards, to go after and destroy and punish and clear out the Spaniards as their mortal, mortal enemies, the ruiners of the large societies that existed before the Spaniards came. All this the Indians were doing and permitted to do according to natural law and the law of nations. The proper name for it was self-defense, not war. Take it further. Enriquillo had an even greater right, the right of a prince. There was no other ruler or lord left on the island. He could thus proceed to pursue and punish, to execute justice on every Spaniard he would find. There is no contradicting this, the way some people do, who are ignorant of both fact and law, when they say the prince of the island was the King of Castile, it was to him that one went when seeking justice. That argument is specious and wrong-headed. For this reason: the lords, the chiefs of this island never recognized the King of Castile as their overlord. Instead, from the minute they were found until the present day, they were subjugated, in actual fact, with no legal justification. They were killed in wars, they were subjected constantly to the worst kind of servitude, to the point where they were snuffed out, as the first book of this *History* makes clear, and the remainder of it will. What is more, there was never justice ever on this island, nothing ever done to rectify things for the native dwellers of the place. And wherever justice is absent, the one aggrieved and oppressed can seek justice on his own authority. That is a maxim of jurists, it is a truth, a teaching of human reason.

What I just said is no derogation from the supreme and universal lordship of the Kings of Castile over the entire New World, that granted by the Apostolic See. Not if the Kings had gone in there and acted towards it as they should. Things have to be ordered, have to be conducted according to the rules of reason, not according to the selfish interests of anyone no matter who. The way all the works of God are ruled and guided, by reason. I have written lengthy treatises on this subject, in Spanish and in Latin.

Some men under him killed two or three Spaniards, but not on his orders.[103] The Spaniards came from the mainland and had fifteen or twenty thousand pesos worth of gold. The Indians were ones who had formed a group already before they joined up with Enriquillo, or they were a scouting party, under his command, on the lookout for Spaniards, and did some bad things, things he had not ordered. But he did not discipline them so they would not leave him defenseless. His standing orders were that when they came across Spaniards, they were to strip them of their weapons then let them go. That was one of his main objectives, to get hold of spears and swords. He and his men became, in a short, short time, so adept in the use of these weapons that they seemed like long time brigands who were out slashing every day. They stood toe to toe with the Spaniards when they met them, trading blows for a good part of the day, it was fearful to see. Often,

---

[103] *History*, Bk. 3, cap. 126.

armed parties were sent after him. He stripped them of their weapons, and thus acquired a lot. And the Indians who came to his cause tried to steal from their masters all the weapons they could. His vigilance was extraordinary, wherever the band went, the care he took, the concern he had to protect himself and his people. He was like someone who had spent a life leading campaigns in Italy. He had his lookouts, spies, in all the ports and places he knew the Spaniards could use as jumping off places after him. And once he knew from the agents he had out in the countryside that Spaniards were around, he took all the women, children, elderly, and sick, if there were any, all the non-combatants, plus fifty men-at-arms, took them all ten or twelve leagues off, to secret places he had up in the mountains. He had spots planted there, so there was food. He left someone in command, his nephew, not up to his elbow in height, but very forceful, plus his warriors. They were to wait for the Spaniards. And fight like lions against them when they came. Then Enrique would show up and with fifty men attack the Spaniards on their flank, thus turning them, wounding and killing them. And never, in the many times the many Spaniards came out against him, did he not rout them, he always won. In one incident, he defeated a large group, and seventy-one or two of them hid in caves in the rock, to escape the Indians who pursued them. But the Indians knew they were there, and wanted to bring wood, make a fire, and roast them. Enrique commanded: "I do not want them burned. Take their weapons away, leave them unharmed. Then send them home!" Which is what the Indians did. And that way captured a lot of swords, lances, crossbows, though they did not know how to use the latter. One of the seventy Spaniards became a friar in the monastery of Santo Domingo, in Santo Domingo. When he saw himself trapped and thought he would not survive, he vowed to do so if he did. I learned from him the incident I just described. And it is a clear argument for the goodness of Enrique. He could have killed all the Spaniards involved, but chose not to do so. His orders were that outside actual combat, no one should kill a soul!

If it happened that Enrique and his fifty men arrived, after they had left their womenfolk under cover, and the Spaniards had not yet shown up at the place where the Indians awaited them, Enrique was so on the alert himself that he was the first to spot them. And he kept to the following discipline: he slept at dusk, the length of time he needed, then got up, took two young men with him as aides, who had his spears at the ready, took his sword, two swords I think, because he kept two at the head of his hammock when he slept. He had his beads and said the rosary as he kept on the move throughout the whole of his territory. He was the first usually to see the Spaniards, or among the first, and to alert his people. To maintain security, he took other precautionary measures. He had fields planted in a variety of places up on the mountains. And straw huts, in a thirty or forty league area, which were ten and twelve leagues apart, huts where the women, the children, the elderly, were safe, for a time in one, for a time in another, as he judged it best, never just in one. He had a lot of dogs for hunting pigs—there are pigs aplenty in that region—and feeding his people, and he had ordered a lot of chickens raised. And in order to keep the barking of the dogs and the crowing of the cocks from revealing their whereabouts, he had a hideaway built for both dogs and fowl, with just two or three Indians and their wives, no more, to look after them, while he and his people always kept a good distance away. When he sent his Indians, a few, say two or three, out fishing or hunting or some other place, they were not to look for him back where he had left them, they never knew exactly where they would meet him again. He arranged this so if the Spaniards captured his Indians, no one of them could talk or under torture reveal his whereabouts and the Spaniards could catch him. He ran no risk when he sent large groups out, because the Spaniards could not easily nab all of them. He reckoned some would escape and warn him.

Reports of the victories, the energy, the courage, the shrewdness at war of Enrique and his people spread all over the island day after day. The Spaniards never went out against him that they did not return beaten, so the story went. The result being that the whole island was tense and troubled. Whenever a party was made up to go after him, no one went willingly, and no one went unless coerced into it by threat of punishment from the Audiencia. This went on for thirteen or fourteen years, and cost the King's Treasury eighty to one hundred thousand castellanos.

A religious of the Franciscan Order offered to go speak with Enrique. The religious, a servant of God, a foreigner, a man I described earlier, was the one who brought a small number of Franciscan friars to the island—learned and apostolic people—for the purpose of preaching the Gospel to the Indians. He was called Fray Remigio, and I think he was one of those who educated Enrique. He was to make peace with Enrique, since it was impossible to subdue him by war. They brought the friar by ship to a place they were somewhat sure Enrique or his people stayed. But also because once he saw a ship offshore he would think Spaniards were after him, and he would therefore be anxious to know where they came ashore, and would send a party to be sure. So a party of Indians did come to where Fray Remigio disembarked. The minute they met him, they asked if he came on orders from the Spaniards to spy on them. He said no, he had come to speak to Enrique and tell him he should make friends with the Spaniards, he would not be harmed henceforth, and would not have to live life on the run and hounded as he did now. The friar further said it was out of a desire to do them good that he undertook to come and go to the difficulties he did. They told him he must be lying because Spaniards were evil people who always lied, they never kept their word or told the truth. He really wanted to deceive them, just as the Spaniards did. The Indians were ready to kill him. The friar found himself in a tight situation. But they did not kill him because Enrique had ordered no killing any Spaniard except in combat against them. Instead, they stripped him of his habit, right down to his shorts, near naked, then split up his clothing among themselves. He kept asking them to let Enrique know that one of the priests of Saint Francis had come, and it would please him very much to see Enrique. He asked the Indians to take him to where Enrique was. They left him there and went to tell Enrique. As soon as he knew, he went to see the friar immediately, and showed through gesture and word how sorry he was over what the Indians had done. He asked forgiveness, even though what was done was against his orders, and asked the friar not to be angry. This is the customary way the Indians console those they see have been grieved by some occurrence. The padre asked him, urged him, to be friends with the Spaniards, he would be well treated henceforth. Enrique replied that he wanted nothing better, but he knew what Spaniards were like, they had killed his father and grandfather, all the chiefs and people in Xaragua, and depopulated the whole island. He referred to the beatings, the brutalities he had suffered under Valenzuela, and said he had fled his own land in order not to die at Spanish hands the way his forebears did. Neither he nor his people had done anyone any evil. They simply defended themselves against those who came to capture and kill them, or make them live the life they had lived until recently, one in which they knew they would have to die, all of them, as their forebears had. There was no need of further talk with a Spaniard. The Padre then asked for the return of his habit. Enrique told him his Indians had torn it up and divided the pieces up among themselves, and he was sad to his soul over this. The ship which had brought the friar stood offshore within view, so they signalled it, and it sent its boat in to land. Enrique kissed the padre's hand and said goodbye, almost in tears. The sailors took the padre aboard, put their capes around him, and returned him to Santo Domingo and his monastery where they had plenty of habits, not silk, but poorer stuff, as befitted their poverty.

    . . . Ciguayo and Tamayo were two others who, with other bands, rebelled and plagued the whole island, but not under Enrique, though everyone thought they were following Enrique's orders.[104] So the whole lot of Spanish settlers lived with a greater fear. When Enrique learned of what

---

[104] *History*, Bk. 3, cap. 127.

Ciguayo had done, and Tamayo was doing, he made a smart guess as to what people would think the truth, i.e., Spaniards would judge he had ordered what happened, and that worried him very much. And I know this for sure. I will write about it more at length in the next book, God willing. Enrique happened to have with him as part of his band an Indian named Romero, the nephew of Tamayo. He agreed to go and find Tamayo who was operating near the villages of Puerto Real and Lares de Guahaba, about a hundred leagues from where Enrique was. He was to ask Tamayo to come join Enrique, he would be safer, so what happened to Ciguayo would not happen to him, one day or another. The Spaniards were out to get him. Enrique would treat him well, would retain him as captain over some of his own people, and all together they would become stronger in their defense of themselves. The nephew finally persuaded Tamayo it was the wisest course, so he came, with lots of spears, swords, clothing, all captured, to join Enrique. Who thus halted the great damage Tamayo would have done all over the island. And that action reveals the great goodness of Enrique, also the discretion, the prudence he employed to keep someone so destructive to Spaniards from doing them any evil. He drew the man into his own group the way he described.

Every year an armed party was made up to go after Enrique. The King and the settlers spent many thousands of castellanos on it. There was one of about 150 Spaniards, maybe more, captained by a settler from a town they call Bonao. He was named Hernando de San Miguel. He was a veteran on the island, from the time of the first Admiral, had come to it when very young, had grown up in the harsh struggles and brutal, unjust wars fought against the island people, so he was able to go barefoot through the rock strewn mountains as though he was shod. In addition, he was a well-off man, nobility, a native of Ledesma or Salamanca. He looked a long time for Enrique, but was never able to catch him off guard, so never joined battle with him, if my memory serves me. One day, the two groups found themselves in close proximity to each other, but neither could get at the other, so they talked back and forth. This was possible because one group was on the edge of one cliff, the other on the edge of another, both lofty, both close, but a crevasse, a gorge separated them, it was about five hundred feet deep.

They both sensed the proximity, so both sought a truce, a halt so as to be able to talk. It was mutually agreed on, no one was to take a pot shot at anyone else. The captain of the Spaniards asked Enrique to appear and speak with him. Enrique did. And the Captain told him that the life he led and the one he forced the Spaniards to lead was a harsh one, not good. It would be better to live in peace and safety. Enrique answered he thought the same, it was something he desired, and had for a long time back. But it was not up to him. It was up to the Spaniards. The captain replied that he had authority and power from the Royal Audiencia, given in the city of Santo Domingo on behalf of the King, to make a treaty of peace with Enrique and his people. The treaty would allow them to live in liberty on one part of the island, for them to choose which they wanted, and Spaniards would leave them alone, would not harm any one of them, nor do anything out of the way. The Indians were to return all the gold they had taken from the Spaniards, who came from the mainland, when they killed them. And from across the abyss he showed Enrique the document he had from the Audiencia. Enrique said he agreed to make peace, to be friends with the Spaniards, all of them, to do harm to no one, to return all the gold he kept, and said he would keep his word. Then the two talked about how and when they would meet. They agreed there that on a specific day the captain would come with just eight men, Enrique with just eight, no more, to the sea coast, and they designated a specific spot. On this agreement, they parted.

Enrique then took steps to carry out his word. He sent men to construct at the site of the meeting a large shelter made of trees and leaves, and within it, a platform on which they placed all the pieces of gold. It looked like a royal pavilion. The captain set about keeping his word. In order to celebrate the peace with greater festiveness—though this was a dumb move—he ordered a ship which patrolled the area to come and stand in close to the agreed upon place. He himself approached along the beach with a small drum and his men, all lively and excited. Enrique was already there with his eight men and lots of food, waiting in the shelter. He saw the ship come in close, saw the captain coming with extra men, Spaniards to the beat of a drum, boom, boom. It looked to him as if they had broken their word. He was afraid they were up to some trick. So he decided to skip and get lost up in the mountain with his men, those he kept as his guard. And he ordered the eight Indians to tell the Spaniards when they reached the shelter that he was not able to meet with them because he was not feeling well. The eight were to give the Spaniards the food that was ready there, and all the gold. They were to be very hospitable and accommodating in every way. When the captain with his men arrived, he asked for Enrique. The eight replied as Enrique had told them to do. The captain was chagrined about his dumb move—or maybe not, maybe he didn't recognize it—and not finding Enrique there. Because he was sure, and he wasn't wrong, that right there the anxiety, the panic, the fear gripping the island, would be brought to a halt. In fact, though the threat didn't halt entirely, it was suspended until, at a later time, it was removed entirely, as I will narrate, please God, in a later book. So, the eight Indians fed the Spaniards, waited on them very graciously, this is the Indian way, then handed back all the gold, not a speck of it missing.

The captain thanked them. He told them to tell Enrique how sorry he was not to have seen him personally and embraced him. He was sorry for his mistake. And though Enrique had stayed away for a reason, they should nonetheless be friends, he should do no further harm, and none would be done to him from then on out. The Spaniards boarded the ship and returned to the city. And the Indians to where Enrique was staying. Starting that day, there was no further desire on the island to hunt down Enrique. And there was no further damage done right up to the time when peace was fully agreed upon, a period of about four or five years.

* * * *

. . . I was the one who went to Baoruco—with God's grace and with a Dominican brother the Order assigned me—and brought Don Enrique to peace, and back into service to our Lord, the Emperor, and I strengthened him in his resolve.[105] I stayed a month with him, confessed him, his wife, his officers. And I dispelled all of the well-founded fears he had. He did not want to leave the mountains, but I persuaded him to come out with me to the town of Azua where he met and made happy friends of the villagers. I got him to agree to go and reassure the other villages of Spaniards, to bring back under obedience to his Majesty several other rebel leaders and their men, but most of all, got him to settle his own people some seven leagues from Azua, and provide that whole area with bread and other foods. That whole process is now well on the way to completion.

* * * *

And those in charge should well remember that this was the most deadly way they had—splitting families for forced labor—for killing everyone off, the count of the dead is over a million souls.[106] I saw with my own eyes how large the population was. Only the Indians with Enrique survived, and only because he knew how to win by his own wits and a most just cause. I went to him to offer him peace, and I secured it with him, then brought him to the town of Azua on my own, and worked out an agreement with the folks there, then brought him to Santo Domingo, and there enlisted him on the side of his Majesty. And I know for sure that the gentlemen of the

---

[105] Bartolomé de Las Casas, "Carta al Consejo de Indias [30-4-1534]," *Opúsculos, cartas y memoriales.* Ed. by Juan Pérez de Tudela Bueso (Madrid: Ediciones Atlas, 1958), p. 57a [hereafter, *Opúsculos*]. (Biblioteca de Autores Españoles, vol. 110).

[106] Bartolomé de Las Casas, "Carta a un personaje de la corte [15-10-1535]," *Opúsculos*, p. 65b.

Audiencia did not care to record what happened, but rather denounced me to the Royal Council, which in turn issued a reproof against me. The divine judgment will judge the justice of that.

- 11 -

The Only Way

Prenote

The genesis of The Only Way, *through its three versions, has been established by Helen Rand Parish. There is the original version of 1534, written in the aftermath of the Enriquillo experience. It was to become the blueprint for the Mexican ecclesiastical conferences of 1535, 1536, both of which have recently been uncovered by Helen Rand Parish.[107] Las Casas was in attendance at both. Then there was the revised version done at Oaxaca in 1539, just before Las Casas returned to Europe to struggle for the New Laws. He revised it to include the papal documents on Indian freedom which* The Only Way *had caused to come into existence. The decrees of the conferences were carried to Rome in 1537 by a spokesman, Bernardino de Minaya, O.P., who succeeded in having Paul III issue the documents.[108] Lastly, there is the "stuffed" version in 1552, with Las Casas including mountains of proof texts for his points so the document could be used in the schools.*

The soul of the document is the portrait of the peaceful Jesus, of the way he brought people to his vision of life and relationship, a way he commanded his disciples to follow. The true followers of Jesus did as he commanded. So the ideal missionary has the traits of the master—he wants no power over people, no wealth from them, he is moved by respect for others, by charity towards them, and he preaches by example first and foremost. War, violence, are the utter opposites of the way just described, and are characteristic of the brutal missionary. Whoever has used war is bound to repair all the damages done to the other in the name of Christ. Crucial to this whole approach is Las Casas' conviction that the Indians are

---

[107] Helen Rand Parish and Harold Weidman, *Las Casas en México* (Mexico City: Fondo de Cultura Económica, 1993). [Hereafter, *Las Casas en México.*]

[108] *Las Casas en México*, pp. 15-38, esp. pp. 15-23.

fully capable human beings, in every way the Spaniards are, and therefore are to be treated in a fully human way.

The papal documents are powerful expressions of the rights of Indian peoples, "Sublimis Deus" particularly, but they seemed to have had little effect on Spanish behavior towards Indian peoples. In fact, "Pastorale Officium," which was to provide sanctions for obeying "Sublimis Deus," was revoked by Paul III in 1538 for reasons of European politics. But the documents do reveal that it was Las Casas who basically formed Church policy.

Prologue: Humanity of the Indians

It was due to the will and work of Christ, the head of the Church, that God's chosen should be called, should be culled from every race, every tribe, every language, every corner of the world. Thus, no race, no nation on this entire globe would be left totally untouched by the free gift of divine grace. Some among them, be they few or many, are to be taken into eternal life. We must hold this to be true also of our Indian nations. [They are as called as we.]. . .

The reason is, they are all human beings. Their minds are very quick, alive, capable, clear. This mind comes to them primarily from the will of God who wished to make them so. Then, secondarily, it comes from the fostering influence of the heavens, from the kind conditions of the places God gave them to live in, the fair and clement weather.[109] For most of the Indies has land that is dry, land that is open, spacious, level, pleasant, fertile, and in fine locations. The hills, valleys, mountains, plains are uncluttered, they are free of stagnant pools, they are blanketed with aromatic plants,

---

Nota Bene: *De único modo* (hereafter *DUM*) ms., par. 1. The first four chapters are missing from the only known manuscript of *De único modo*, probably cut off by Las Casas himself. They are reconstructed very briefly here from the fragmentary summary at the start of Chapter Five. Notes and reconstruction of this section are by Helen Rand Parish. For full text and notes, see *The Only Way*, pp. 63-7. This excerpt is reprinted from *The Only Way* with the permission of Paulist Press.

[109] Bartolomé de las Casas, *Apologética Historia Sumaria quanto a las cualidades, dispusición, descripción, cielo y suelo destas tierras, y condiciones naturales, policías, repúblicas, manera de vivir e costumbres de las gentes destas Indias Occidentales y Meridionales cuyo imperio soberano pertenece a los Reyes de Castilla [Defense of the Indian Civilizations]*, ed. by Edmundo O'Gorman, 2 vols (Mexico City: Universidad Nacional Autónoma de México, Instituto de Investigaciones Históricas, 1967), cap. 263, from first half of par. 1. Corresponds to *DUM* ms., beginning of par. 2 [hereafter, *Apologética*].

medicinal herbs of all kinds, and commonplace charmers spread everywhere so all the fields are smiling. Every morning they breathe a scent which lasts until noonday, a scent that delights and strengthens a traveler's soul. They are a consolation. Both mountains and trees are lofty throughout the region, at least between the two tropics, the stretch of 45 degrees to either side of the equator, to use nautical terms. They are huge, imposing. And it is a fact that often, for a man to be able to gauge their size, he has to throw his head back the way he must when he wants to look at the pitch of the sky. There is an experience which surely indicates the temperate nature of the region, its even, gentle, wholesome, delightful climate. When ships come from Spain and begin to raise the first islands or any of the coast of Tierra Firme, people aboard ship sense a marvelous fragrance, fresh smells coming offshore. It is as if rose flowers were right there present to them. . . [110]

Next, this condition of mind comes to them from the fine state of their bodies and sense organs, the inward, the outward, from sound and healthy nourishment, from the excellent sanitary conditions of the land, the habitations, the air of each place, from the people's temperance and moderation in food and drink, from the state of their sensual passions—calm, quiet, controlled—from the lack of upset and anxiety—their habitual state—about those worldly affairs which elicit the passions of the soul—pleasure, love, anger, grief—and even after being disturbed, for the things that passions do and the effects they cause. . .[111]

Then too there exist extraordinary kingdoms among our Indians who live in the regions west and south from us. There are large groupings of human beings who live according to a political and a social order. There are large cities, there are kings, judges, laws, all within civilizations where commerce occurs, buying and selling and lending and all the other dealings proper to the Law of Nations. That is to say, their republics are properly set up, they are seriously run according to a fine body of law, there is religion, there are institutions. And our Indians cultivate friendship and they live in lifegiving ways in large cities. They manage their affairs in them with goodness and equity, affairs of peace as well as war. They run their

---

[110] [*Apologética*, cap. 21, par. 6, except last sentence, joined to par. 10—corresponds to next fragment of *DUM* ms., par. 2. N.B. caps. 23, 24, & 29 of the *Apologética*, on the heavens and climate influencing Indian character and capacity answer Bernardo de Mesa's claim that Indians were servile by nature due to the climate and the islands. Cf. *History*, Bk. 3, beg. of cap. 9, Mesa's 2nd prop.; and beg. of cap. 11, Las Casas' indignant comment.]

[111] [*Apologética*, cap. 263, remainder of par. 1. Corresponds to *DUM* ms., remainder of par. 2.]

governments according to laws that are often superior to our own... [112] The quality of their minds is seen finally in superb artifacts, finely, beautifully fashioned, fashioned by hand. They are so skilled in the practical arts that their reputation should place them well ahead of the rest of the known world, and rightly so. The practical things these people make are striking for their art and elegance, utensils that are charmingly done, feather work, lace work. Mind does this. The practical arts result from a basic power of mind—a power we define as knowledge of how to do things the right way, a planning power that guides the various decisions the artisan makes so he acts in an ordered and economical fashion and does not err as he thinks his way along...

And in the liberal and allied arts, to date, these people offer no less an indication of sound intelligence. They make objects that are high art and with a genius that awes everyone. The genius of an artist shows in the art work. It is as the poet says: "The work applauds its maker." Prosper remarks in one of his *Epigrams*: "It must be so, that an author shows in the fine things he has written. They sing praise to their maker."

The Indians are highly skilled also in the arts we educate ourselves to, the Indians we have taught thus far: grammar, logic. And they charm the ear of an audience with every kind of music, remarkable beauty. Their handwriting is skillful and lovely, such that one cannot tell often if the letters are handwritten or printed... I have seen all this with my own eyes, touched it with my own hands, heard it with my own ears, over the long time I passed among those peoples.... [113]

Due to all these influences—the broad/celestial, the narrow/terrestrial, the essential/accidental—the Indians come to be endowed, first by force of nature, next by force of personal achievement and experience, with the three kinds of self-rule required: 1) personal, by which one knows how to rule oneself, 2) domestic, by which one knows how to rule a household, and 3) political, knowledge of how to set up and rule a city.

Their political rule presupposes fully developed personal and domestic elements, i.e., farmers, artisans, soldiery, wealthy people; religion, temples, priests, sacrifices; judges and agents of justice; governors; customs; and throughout, everything touched by qualities of mind and will... their society is the equal of that of many nations in the world renowned for being politically astute. They surpass many another. They are inferior to none.

[112] Bartolomé de las Casas, *Apologia [adversus Sepúlvedam]*. In Juan Ginés de Sepúlveda/Fray Bartolomé de las Casas, *Apologia*. Ed., introd. and Spanish trans. by Angel Losada (Madrid: Editora Nacional, 1975), ff. 22v-23, omitting Sepúlveda's contempt. A preliminary par., for all that follows.

[113] [Both pars. above open with sents. from *DUM* ms., par. 3. Rest is from *Apologia*, ff. 23v-24, minus Sepúlveda's contempt, & ff. 24-24v, minus bad historians.]

Those they equal are the Greeks and Romans. And in a good many customs they outdo, they surpass the Greeks and Romans. They surpass the English, the French, and some groups in our native Spain. In the possession of good customs, in the lack of bad ones, they are superior to so many other peoples that these latter do not merit comparison to our Indies.

All of this stands clearly proven and explained. Our comparisons show that in the entire world, in the old days of paganism, there were countless peoples who were much less rational in their use of mind than our Indians, peoples who had customs far more horrible, vices far more depraved. That conclusion is enough to confound those who have so rashly, perhaps unforgiveably, defamed our Indians, to make those defamers ashamed in and for themselves, to make them admit their error. . . . And all those who know of them should consider them false witnesses. The more so because, as we have seen through comparison and contrast, the Indians are and were ahead of others, many, many others, more ordered in their use of mind, more ordered in their use of will, with less of the taint of malice and malignancy.

Since all these Indian peoples, excepting none in the vast world of that hemisphere, universally have good and natural intelligence, have ready wills, they thus can be drawn to and taught a complete and sound morality, and more so to our Christian belief, even though some peoples in some places have not yet developed political maturity, an ordered body politic, the kind we said many possessed. And some have certain corrupt customs. But these are curable finally with human effort, and more so, better so, with the preaching of the Gospel.[114]

It is clear as clear can be that the nations of our Indies fall into [a special category of pagans]. They have and hold their realms, their lands, by natural law and by the law of nations. They owe allegiance to no one higher than themselves, outside themselves, neither *de jure* nor *de facto*. We find them in possession of their countries, with plenty of princes over plenty of principalities having great numbers of people, people who serve and obey their lords and masters, while the latter exercise full authority over their people without hindrance, exercise full power in large and in small, so no one would have the legitimate right to seize their power, or their realms, so distant from our own, so far from harming us or our Church or our Catholic faith or any member thereof. They are of the fourth kind of pagans, no one can doubt it.

---

[114] [*Apologética*, cap. 263, pars. 2, 3, and first half of 4. This is Las Casas' own later summary of Indian capacity; but note that the final part of par. 4 forcefully repeats the basic doctrine of *The Only Way*. See Appendix I.B, section 1, penult. par.]

Cajetan spoke of this fourth kind of pagan more clearly and distinctly than of the other three when commenting on Thomas Aquinas, *Summa Theologiae*, Secunda Secundae, q. 66, art. 8, especially when he said as follows: "There are some pagans who . . . have never been under Christian rule, who live in lands never reached by the name of Christ. Their rulers, though they are pagans, are legitimate authorities, whether they govern in a monarchy or a republic. They are not to be deprived of their authority because of their pagan belonging. Such authority is a matter of positive law. Divine law deals with pagan belief. Divine law does not invalidate positive law. I know of no law abrogating their temporal possessions. No king, no emperor, not the Roman Church itself, can make war on them for the purpose of occupying their territory or subjecting them to temporal rule. There is no just cause for such a war. The reason: Jesus Christ, the King of Kings (to whom all power is given in heaven and on earth) did not send armed soldiery to take possession of the earth but holy men, preachers, sent sheep among wolves." Further on [Cajetan] says: "So we would sin mortally if we sought to spread the faith of Christ by way of war. We would not be the legitimate rulers of the conquered, we would have committed a mighty theft, we would be held to restitution for being unjust aggressors in an unjust occupation."[115]

So let us turn now to explaining the way, the natural, overall, single and settled way of calling God's chosen, God's elect, to the faith of Christ, of inviting them into the Christian way of life.[116]

The Only Way: Winning the Mind and Will

One way, one way only, of teaching a living faith, to everyone, everywhere, always, was set by Divine Providence: the way that wins the mind with reasons, that wins the will with gentleness, with invitation. It has to fit all people on earth, no distinction made for sect, for error, even for evil.[117]

---

[115] [*Doce dudas*, Second Principle, 3rd par. from end, here followed by 4th par. from the end, but minus the repetitious sent. after Cajetan's Latin passage—*Opúsculos* [*BAE* 110]: 490ab, 490a. N.B. Although *Doce dudas* was put together in 1564, Las Casas wrote these Principles in 1539. See *Las Casas en México*, note 39, also last par. of note 58. Both contemporary summaries of *The Only Way* include the 4 kinds of infidels—see *The Only Way*, Introd. And note to Appendix II.]

[116] [*DUM* ms., par. 4, omitting scholastic announcement of proofs to come.]

[117] *The Only Way*, p. 68.

The Ideal Missionary

We can now select out five basic traits from all the material we have just presented, traits that reveal as a whole how the Gospel must be preached according to the mind and mandate of Christ.[118]

One. Those who hear the Gospel preached, non-Christians especially, must sense that the preachers want no power over them as a result of the preaching. Chrysostom's view. He said that when Paul preached, Paul did not use the language of seduction nor the language of deceit. The seducer wants power, the politician wants control. "No one can say we lied to gain control of people." It comes down to Paul's statement: "We are not after glory from human beings; not from you, not from anyone else." (1 Thessalonians 2:6) Paul's success had provoked suspicion. Chrysostom thinks he said what he said to get rid of that suspicion.

Two. Those who hear the Gospel preached, non-Christians especially, must sense that the preachers are not really itching after their wealth. So Paul says: "Preaching cannot be a cover for greed." (1 Thessalonians 2:5) Or, in Anselm's wording: We were not after what you had when we preached, it was not our wish; we kept to the Lord's instruction, the one which went to the root of all evil. He forbade the apostles to keep gold or silver or any coin. St. Jerome, reflecting on Matthew's Gospel, says that if the apostles made money, people would think they preached for lucre's sake, not for the sake of saving souls.[119] Whatever they then said would be laughed at as propaganda. Chrysostom says, about this second rule: 1) The precept of poverty frees the disciples from suspicion. 2) It frees them from worldly worry—their entire concern can be for the word of God.[120] Paul states the matter: "It was trust in God that let us preach the Gospel to you without stint." (1 Thessalonians 2:2) 3) He showed them that He, Christ, was their power. Christ's question later brought it home: "What else did you need that time you preached?" (Luke 22:35)

Three. Preachers should address audiences, especially non-Christian, with modesty and respect. They should create a climate of kindness and calm and graciousness so that their hearers would want to listen and would have a greater respect for the message. This is why Paul said:"I became like a child." Or a peaceful person, as I noted from Chrysostom: "I said nothing that smacked of arrogance." (Homily on 2 Thessalonians) And Chrysostom

---

[118] *The Only Way*, p. 103-112.

[119] [*Catena Aurea*—S. Thomas, *Opera*, Parma, 11:131a.]

[120] [*Catena Aurea*—S. Thomas, *Opera*, Parma, 11:131a.]

adds the words "in your midst," meaning "not wanting to lord it over any of you." He says the same in the next homily: "A teacher must never harm students with truths intended to help them. To take care of a flock of sheep, Blessed Jacob wearied himself night and day. The one who has charge of a flock of souls should do more, much more, whether the job is hard or easy, when the one goal is involved, the salvation of the souls he teaches, and the glory that he thereby gives to God."[121]

Athanasius comments also on [the Pauline phrase] 'I became like a child': "Paul means kind, innocuous, even weak, i.e., incapable of evil, and dead to pride. Those who are like children never think evil, never think pride."

Chrysostom comments on the comparison, "as a nurse cares for her charges [1 Thessalonians 2:7]. . . so must a teacher. . . . Does a nurse tell lies so the children praise her? Does a nurse squeeze money out of nurslings? Does she batter and bruise them? Are not nurses better with children than mothers?" He speaks of the way love works. Then he goes on [paraphrasing verse 8]: "So if we base our service on love and care for you, we take no pay for it. Just the opposite, we would give our lives for you and nothing would stop us."[122]

Athanasius comments on the same comparison, 'as a nurse, etc.': "Now Paul shows the scope of his altruism. A true teacher treats peaceably, patiently, even the stubbornest student he finds, the way a nurse treats a child, even a child that kicks and scratches her." And Primatius says about the further phrase: "He simplified himself, he became childlike in all he did so he could draw someone higher by his example. The nurse prattles also, she eats in little bites, she takes little steps so the child feels easy with her."

And Anselm comments: "She sits on the ground, takes the child in her lap and suckles it, she strokes it and makes sounds to teach it speech. We have sat on the ground for you. We took you to the bosom of belief like a loving mother long on patience. We breast fed you the faith. We stroked you with visions of the life to come. We told you about the human Jesus in infantile words, so we could lead you to adult speech about His divinity."[123]

So a preacher who draws people to the truth of Christ must treat them graciously, respectfully, especially those who are set against it, or not eager to hear it, or ready to laugh at it. This is what Paul taught Timothy:

---

[121] [Jacques-Paul Migne, *Patrologiae Cursus Completus*, Series Graeca, 161 vols. (Paris, 1857-1866), 62:399-406, 405 (hereafter, *PG*).]

[122] [*PG*, 62:403.]

[123] [Anselm's only treatment of 1 Thessalonians 2:7 is in his "Oratio ad sanctum Paulum." Cf. Franciscus Salesius Schmitt, *S. Anselmi Opera Omnia*, t. 2, 33-4 l. (Stuttgart, 1968, 2 tomes).]

"And the Lord's servant must not be quarrelsome but kindly to everyone, an apt teacher, forbearing, correcting opponents of his truth with gentleness. God may perhaps grant that they will repent and come to know the truth, and they may escape from the snare of the devil, after being captured by Him to do His will." (2 Timothy 2:24)

Chrysostom says, commenting on Psalm 119: "Do not tell me someone is savage and unbearable. The time to show oneself peaceable is exactly when one has to deal with savage and unbearable people, hardly human, hardly civilized. Then a teacher shows his worth, then his efforts and his results become clearly visible."[124] And Chrysostom says (Homily 58, *On Genesis,* ch. 32): "It takes a great soul in us to go beyond loving and serving wholeheartedly those who love us, and win the friendship of those who hate us by our unfailing charity. Gentleness is powerful. Throw water on a pyre and it controls the blaze. Say a gentle word and cool a soul that is hotter than a forge."[125]

Paul had that greatness of soul, gentleness. He used it without stint toward those to whom he preached, his persecutors included, "that he might gain everyone for Christ." Paul is like the father who loves beyond love a son who is taken with a fit. The more the son lashes at him, the more compassion he feels, the sorrier. Paul too, the more he sensed the passionate intensity, the anger of those who harrassed him, the more he offered a healing love. Just notice the control, the kindness with which he tells us about those who whipped him five times, who loaded him with irons, or bound him hand and foot, who thirsted for his blood, threatened to pull him to pieces every day. "I do this," he said, "to draw them to act like God, though it is not within their logic."

Four. There is a further trait to be drawn from the previous material about what is crucially needed in the way one presents the faith, if the preacher is to save himself as well. It is the love called charity. Paul sought to save the whole world with it. Gentleness and patience and kindness are kindred spirits to charity. "Love is patient, it is kind, it suffers all things, it bears all things . . ." (1 Corinthians 13:4, 7) If you want proof of how his heart was on fire with charity, listen to him say: "So being affectionately desirous of you, we were willing to have imparted to you, not the Gospel of God only, but also our own souls, because you were dear to us." (1 Thessalonians 2:8) "Greater love than this no one has than that he lay down his life for his friends." (John 15:13) And notice what he said to the Corinthians. It shows how kind, how respectful his preaching was even to his persecutors, even to

---

[124] [*PG,* 55:343]
[125] [*PG,* 54:512.]

those who refused the faith a hearing. "I am afraid that God will make it humiliating for me when I come to visit you. I will be a reproach to those many who used to sin but have done no penance since for their former impurity and fornication and lewdness." (2 Corinthians 12:21) And: "My little ones, I am in constant labor until Christ is born in you." (Galatians 4:19) There was a lustful man whose lust grieved him deeply. Paul grieved for the man more than the man for himself. He prayed for him: "Love this man even more."(2 Corinthians 2:8) And when Paul was absent from the community of the Church he lived a sad and lonely life : "For I wrote you out of much affliction and anguish of heart and with many tears, not to cause you pain but to let you know the abundant love that I have for you." (2 Corinthians 2:4) "To the Jews I became as a Jew, in order to win Jews; to those under the law I became as one under the law; to the weak, I became weak. I am made all things to all people so that I might save all." (1 Corinthians 9:20-22)

Chrysostom, from whose book *In Praise Of St. Paul,* Homily 3, the preceding [scriptural] citations were taken, says further: "Do you know you are watching someone overcome selfishness completely? He wanted to bring everyone to God. He brought all he could. The whole world was like a child of his. He worried, he traveled, he hurried people into the kingdom of God with his teaching, his visions, his meditations, one minute praying for them, the next cajoling them, then scaring them, routing the demon ruiners of their souls. With letters he wrote, with visits he made, with a word here, with a deed there, done by himself or by a disciple, he tried to firm up the weak, to strengthen the strong, to raise the hopeless, to heal the penitent, to quicken the sluggish with the smell of praise. He had a harsh voice for enemies and a harsh look. As a good soldier or good doctor adept at his trade, he watched out for his men, watched out for his patients, unreservedly, one man doing everyone's job everywhere.

"He was outstanding doing the corporal works of mercy, and as outstanding doing the spiritual. He left ample evidence of his practical concern. For one woman's sake he writes to a whole community. Listen to what he says: 'I am sending Phoebe, my sister in faith. She is from Cenchreae. Please receive her in the Lord as you would someone holy, and please help her whenever she needs you'. (Romans 16:1-2) This kind of love is a hallmark of holiness.

"He prayed repeatedly for those his preaching could not persuade, stubborn people, hard people. He wrote: 'I want deeply, I pray God for their salvation.' (Romans 10:1) Paul, the insatiable servant of God, a parent to Christ's people—I say Paul, keeper of the world—has saved us all through constant, tireless prayer, his words to us always being: 'For this reason, I bend my knee to the Father of Our Lord Jesus Christ, from whom all kinship, all paternity in heaven and on earth are named. That He might give you Christ to live in your inward self through faith, according to the riches of His glory and confirmed in strength by His Spirit.' (Ephesians 3:14-17)

"Do you see how forceful constant prayer is? It transforms us into temples of Christ. We can further know the power of prayer when we see Paul place no trust for saving humankind in his racing around everywhere like a bird, in being jailed, or whipped, or chained, or being in danger of life and limb; no more than in his casting out demons or reviving the dead or healing the diseased. He worked on the world with prayer; and after working miracles, after reviving the dead, he sought help in prayer, the way a winning athlete goes right back into training. Sometimes just prayer is enough to revive the dead, and to revive everything else.

"Paul nourished his soul by night with prayer. He could then bear easily whatever came, however harsh—he could bare his back to whipping as if he were made of stone. Though he was peerless in every virtue, his charity burned brighter than any other. The way steel put in a forge turns a total red, so Paul, fired up with love, turned into total love. He became like a first parent, he became like every parent in the love of all their children: his love, his loyalty transcended that of carnal and spiritual parentage both. He spent on them his money, his mind, his body, his soul. That is why he called selfless love the whole law, the keystone of holiness, the mother-lode of goodness, the first thing and the last. 'The goal is selfless love from a pure heart.' (1 Timothy 1:5) And further: 'Every law, i.e., not to commit adultery, not to murder, is based on the one law, love your neighbor as you love yourself.' (Romans 13:9) Since love is the first thing, love the last, and every good thing in between, we must try to be like Paul especially in this, because he became what he was through selfless love. Do not cite to me as more important the dead he often raised, nor the lepers he often cured with his miraculous power. God asks you to do none of these. But capture Paul's selfless love and you will capture heaven. Through it Paul reached the peak of perfection and nothing made him more worthy of God than did the virtue of perfect love, etc."[126]

Five. It is found expressed already in Paul's words cited above. "You witnessed, as did God, the way I related to you who came to believe, how respectfully, how carefully, how honestly, how blamelessly."(1 Thessalonians 2:10) Words added to the text say: "both before and after your conversion."

---

[126] [*PG., 50:483-7, at 485-6 passim.*]

"How respectfully," i.e., under God, as the gloss in the text notes, and St. Athanasius says also, doing all that has to be done with due reverence for God. And Anselm interprets it: "How respectfully . . . I related to you through the openness of all my dealings." "How carefully," is interpreted by the gloss on the text and Athanasius to mean, "doing right by my brethren, not wronging them, i.e., putting the squeeze on no one for their money." "How blamelessly," meaning a harm to no one.

Or, as Anselm reads it, "How carefully" keeping the balance of justice toward neighbors by doing right; and "How blamelessly, how straightforwardly and honestly I treated you, not to give you cause for complaint against me." Or, "How blameless I was toward you. I never criticised you when I had to live with your shortcomings. There was a reason to act this way toward you, to help you: something you all recognise, you know this, and something in addition, that it was with love I brought each of you around, etc."

Take 2 Thessalonians 3:7: "You yourselves know how you ought to imitate me." Take the words, "in order to give you in my conduct an example to imitate." Ambrose says in his commentary: "Watch how Paul is influential in what he does as much as in what he says. A good teacher practices what he preaches. Clearly what is taught is learned, but let the teacher neglect to practice it and the pupil profits little thereafter. You move an audience by what you do more than by what you say. Give those great credit, who profit from words their teachers fail to practice. Paul set the example, for the weak members of the flock, on how not to lose one's influence."[127]

And Anselm again: "I need not explain to you a tradition you know. We must set the example, so those who want to follow the right way should walk the path we do." Polycarp, disciple of John the Evangelist, says about Paul words to the Philippians: "'All of you, defer to one another in your dealings; be blameless among non-believers, so you gain their praise for your good deeds, and God is not mocked because of you. Woe to those who make God's name a mockery. Teach everyone the good behavior you yourselves practice."[128]

Clearly, the fifth element prescribed for the preaching of Christ's Gospel is living example: a life visibly virtuous, a life that harms no one, a life blameless from any quarter. A teacher must live his own words, must

---

[127] [*PL,* 17:459]

[128] [In these multiple brief commentaries on three words of St. Paul, Las Casas gives no lead to any standard compilation he is using. It may have been either a manuscript source not currently available, or Pedro de Córdoba's jottings on the ideal missionary from such a source.]

teach by practice more than by presentation. A teacher who talks, only talks, has a frigid effect, in fact is not a teacher but a faker and two-faced. So apostles teach first by deeds, second by words. No need for words when their deeds did the preaching. The evidence shows they led such holy lives that those who carped at them carped at their doctrine not their decency. As Chrysostom puts it: "They put up with being called seducers and quacks for the Gospel's sake, but no one could ever scoff at their lives." No one ever called an apostle guilty of lust or greed, the accusation "seducers" described only their doctrine.

[Chrysostom continues:] "You must respect someone whose moral life is a beacon, whose truth stops the critique even of enemies. It is not right to attack such people with curses and slander, the ones who live faultless lives—you can hear Christ saying as much: 'So let your light shine before people that, seeing what you do, they may give glory to God the Father who is in heaven.' (Matthew 5:16) No one but a blind man would call the sun black; what everyone else sees would shame his contention. The same concerning a man of great dignity, of great moral life, no one but a blind man would dare blame him. It's rather to attack the teachings that non-believers loose their barbs. They dare not loose them at the purity of his life. The life, they hold in awe and admiration, as does everyone."

Therefore Chrysostom says: "Live so the name of the Lord is not mocked: let us not accept people's adulation, but let us not lack their esteem, let us do what is good and right. Let us be honored for both princi-ples—'You will enlighten people of the world like lamps,' says Paul to the Philippians (2:15). God chose us to be such, like stars; to become like yeast as teachers of others; to be angelic with people on earth; to be men with a man-child; to be almost a soul for the soulless; so people profit greatly from our company; so we can be seminal; so we can produce a bountiful harvest. No need of a word if the life we lead is a beacon of holiness. No need of a teacher if we act out of integrity. There would be no non-Christian if we cared to be Christian as we ought, if we kept to the counsels of God, if we did not return blow for blow, if we blessed when we were cursed, if for evil given we gave back good. Only a wild beast would not come at once to believe the truth of salvation if he saw believers act as Christians ought.

"The proof is, there was but one Paul, yet he brought many to know God. If we were Pauls, what a world we could attract! There are more Christians than pagans. One teacher suffices for a hundred pupils in other schoolings. In this schooling, the teachers being so many, the pupils ought to be so many more, but not a one comes, not a one is attracted. Pupils watch the lives of teachers; if they see us itch for the same things as they, lust for the same, long for primacy and prestige, what esteem could they have for Christian doctrine? They see the sordid lives the Christians lead, base souls wallowing in mud, loving money as much as anyone, much more in fact, equally fearful of death, equally fearful of impoverishment, equally impatient of illness, equally avid for fame and power as anyone else, equally cutthroat of each other for lucre's sake. How can pagans acquire belief? By miracles maybe? We are past miracles. By seeing holiness of life? Holy life is plainly gone. Prompted by charity? There is not a trace of it visible. We will surely answer not just for our own sins but for others' failures also—we caused them!

"I beg that we come to our senses, we open our eyes, that we act on earth as if in heaven. And say with Paul: 'Our way of life is the way of heaven; let us sustain it in the struggle, the struggle on earth.' Maybe someone objects: 'We had our holy people once. A pagan could now come and say, why believe? You do not do what you say [your apostles] did, I can see it. If we are to believe just stories, we can bring in stories of philosophers to tell you, great people, of wonderful life, of moral probity. Show me another Paul, another John. You Christians today are ready to kill or be killed for a pittance, you sue and sue for a foot of ground, you are reduced to total chaos over the death of a child.'"[129]

Chrysostom again, on 1 Corinthians 1, (Homily 3): "This is the way we win them, this the way we struggle, by holiness of life we gain their souls, a far better way than with words. This is the struggle at its best, the argument at its surest, the deeds we do. It is no gain at all for us to talk much and often yet show no improvement in our lives. People watch what we do, not what we say, then respond: 'Take your own advice before you insist with others.' If you say heaven holds limitless goods and you seem to fixate on earthly goods as though there were no hereafter, your fixation will convince me, not your words. When I see you lifting others' goods, see you distraught over your losses, see you many times over a criminal, why should I believe your talk of resurrection?

"Pagans do not actually say this, but they think it, in their souls. It is this behavior that keeps the pagan from becoming Christian. Let us recall them by our living example. Many an unschooled man has moved a schooled mind this way, as if to show philosophy the reality itself; goodness of life has a voice clearer than a trumpet or schooling, more powerful than a tongue. So if I say be angry at no one, and then unload a thousand angers on the pagan I preach to, how can I pull him with good words when I pelt him with wicked deeds?

---

[129] Thus Chrysostom on 1 Timothy, ch. 3, in Homily 10. [*PG*, 62:551-2]2.]

"So let us draw pagans by the good life we lead, let us build the church through their conversion, let us grow rich this way. There is nothing to equal soul-worth, not the whole material world. You could shell out huge sums to the poor, you do more if you convert but one soul: 'If you draw worth from the worthless, you will be a messenger from me.' (Jeremiah 15:19) It is a high and holy thing to help the poor; higher, holier to fetch back a soul lost in error. Whoever does so is a Peter, a Paul. We can accept their counsel, not to endanger ouselves as they did, putting up with famine, disease and the rest—our time is a time of peace—but to intensify our apostolic desire. This way, even housebound, we can fish for souls. For a friend, a relative, a neighbor. Whoever does, acts as the disciple of Peter and Paul.

"Why do I remind you of them? The answer will be Christ's: 'If you draw worth from the worthless, you will be a messenger from me.' If today you win no one, you will tomorrow; if you win just one, yet your reward will be full. You will not win all, yet some from all. Not even the apostles won the world. But they broached the question universally, and they gained their reward for each one. For God rewards what we purpose to do, not the profit we gain from good works. Though you as teachers give a pittance, God will reward you as the widow was. Though you cannot save the globe, do not think less of small efforts, do not let global desires distract you from local ones. If you cannot carry a hundred, take care of ten; if not ten, then look to five; if five are too much of a demand, look to one; if you cannot care for one, keep hope, keep trying.

"You know, do you not, that merchants use silver as well as gold in their transactions? If we grasp the small we will grasp the large; if we ignore the small, the large will be hard to grasp. Those who grasp small and large come out enriched. It is the way we also must proceed, so that enriched by small and large we may enjoy the kingdom of heaven given by the grace and kindness of our Lord Jesus Christ." Thus Chrysostom.[130]

Papal Endorsement of Peaceful Conversion

"Paul, Bishop, Servant of God's servants, to all Christ's faithful who will read these words, health to you and my apostolic blessing.[131] God, though beyond us, so loved humankind that he made us able to share in reachable, visible goodness with the rest of creation—but further than that

---

[130] [*PG*, 61:29-30.]

[131] *The Only Way*, pp. 114-5.

to share in the highest goodness, unreachable, invisible, and see Him face to face. Sacred Scripture also testifies that we were created to attain eternal life and eternal bliss. And no one is able to reach life and bliss in eternity except through faith in Jesus Christ. So we have perforce to admit that we humans are of such nature and condition that we can receive the faith of Christ. Anyone who is a human being is capable of receiving that faith. No one but a fool would think he could attain a goal, and not use the means absolutely necessary to attain it. So Truth Incarnate, Who is never deceived or deceiving, said, as we know, when He sent preachers out to preach the faith: 'Go, and teach everyone.' All, He said, without exception, since all are capable of learning the faith. Satan saw and was jealous of humankind. He fights goodness always to destroy it. He concocted a novel way to prevent the word of God being preached to people for their salvation. He got certain of his lackeys, who wanted to satisfy their lust for riches, to affirm rashly that East and West Indians—and others like them who came into our ken recently, and therefore lacked a knowledge of our Catholic faith—were brute beasts, were to be subjected to our control wherever they were. These lackeys reduce them to slavery, they load them with afflictions they would never load on any beast of burden.

"We are the unworthy Viceregent on earth of the Lord. We try with all our might to lead into the flock of Christ committed to our care, those who are outside the sheepfold. We are aware through what we have been told that those Indians, as true human beings, have not only the capacity for Christian faith, but the willingness to flock to it. We wish to provide apt solutions for the situation. The Indians we speak of, and all other peoples who later come to the knowledge of Christians, outside the faith though they be, are not to be deprived of their liberty or the right to their property. They are to have, to hold, to enjoy both liberty and dominion, freely, lawfully. They must not be enslaved. Should anything different be done, it is void, invalid, of no force, no worth. And those Indians and other peoples are to be invited into the faith of Christ by the preaching of God's word and the example of a good life.

"The same credence is to be granted copies of this present decree as is granted to the original—copies notarized by a notary public or by the seal of any person empowered by ecclesiastical office. This we declare through the present decree, notwithstanding earlier ones or whatever else to the contrary. Given at Rome, St. Peter's, in the year of the Lord's birth 1537, the 2nd of June, the year 3 of our pontificate."[132]

---

[132] [For a critical edition of "Sublimis Deus," see *Las Casas en México*, Apendice 14, which details the copyist's error in the original Bull and the errors in most printed copies.]

What is pertinent to our purpose in the document is the following: 1) The Indians and others are to be invited to the faith of Christ, 2) by the preaching of God's word and by the example of a good life. In these two principles everything we argued earlier is included: People are to be drawn to Christ through a way that wins the mind with reasons and wins the will with motives. An amply proven argument.

The Brutal Missionary

The religious, then, who work to catechize the Indians of the New World, while working also to reform them by bodily torture—whips, chains, chastisements done with their own stroke or at their command—are guilty of grave wrong.[133] And of graver wrong if they try to punish those Indians for any sin whatever they committed before or after conversion, even if the religious are authorized to do so by the bishops.

Proof of this corrollary. We speak of sins after conversion, bad as they may be, because we cannot consider the sins that were or are committed prior to the reception of baptism. The reason: The natives had then no civil or ecclesiastical judge outside their own.

There are many proofs for the present corollary. Briefly, the first: As we have already demonstrated, whoever wants to teach others, to win them over to some value, especially a gospel value, must win the souls of his hearers right at the start. An audience in a state of good will opens to a preacher. The preacher produces good will by the warmth of his voice, the joy on his face, the gentleness of his bearing, etc.

But if the preacher of the word of God treats his neophytes to bodily torture—whips, chains, chastisements, done with his own stroke or at his command, for sins the neophytes committed after conversion—if he punishes them, pounds them, they will have to hate him for it. As a result, they will not want to hear a word, nor believe a word said to them further. They will not want to retain what they heard and believed in the past. "No choice of a thing, no say in it, no love of it. No love of a thing, easy scorn of it. No good not chosen. The Lord commanded: Take no staff for the road, you could do someone violence with it. It is wiser to enkindle contempt for the world and love of God and heaven with prayerful, persuasive preaching than by unleashing violence on people, etc.[134]

---

[133] *The Only Way*, pp. 151-56.

[134] Gratian, causa 20, q. 3, cap. 4 [*Corpus Iuris Canonici*. Ed. by Emil Friedberg. 2 vols. Leipzig, 1879-81, 1:849-50 (hereafter, Friedberg)].

Even children can turn angry under punishment and be insolent and rebellious towards their parents. That is why Paul warns parents not to provoke their children. He says: "Parents, do not provoke your children to impotent rage, you will make cowards of them." (Colossians 3:21) He could have said, make mean and mocking spirits of them. The standard gloss on the passage is: "He required parents to be restrained with their children. Or the children treated strictly would react against them and offend God. Anger is heedless. Often the angry person harms himself." [135] The newer people are in the faith, the truer the cautions of St. Paul. So the religious, the missioners who try by violence, etc.

The second proof. We also concluded in Part One that intellect and will must be free in those who hear the faith proposed to them. The intellect free of disturbance by the four dominant passions of the soul, free of any interference. The will free of whatever goes counter to it. Neither of these powers should be impeded in their activities, because the truths of the faith are accepted only in freedom. The two powers need peace and tranquility. If the preacher of the Gospel terrorizes his hearers, hearers who have newly entered the precincts of the Church, if he tortures them with harsh beatings, imprisonments, with such like afflictions, if he punishes them for any sin whatever, they will of necessity be filled with anger toward the missioner, their tormentor, their punisher, and be filled with grief, sorrow, fear, hatred, as well as anger.

The human mind is panicked by terror, by strife, by fear, by violent language. It is panicked most by wounds inflicted on the body. The mind is saddened, hurt, angry. The outer senses close off hearing and seeing. The inner, the imagination and its products, are shattered, so mind and its reasoning go blank. It is not possible for these powers, battered and hobbled as they are, to make judgments on experience. The will shrinks from such effects, they repel it so much. So what is left for it to do but refute, repel, hate the truth of faith it hears, it has to hear, and with it, its missioners. So the religious, the missioners, are guilty of grave wrong who do such things, etc.

The third proof. Again through the teaching of St. Paul in 2 Timothy 2:24, where he says: "The servant of God should not be quarrelsome. He should be peaceable towards everyone, ready to teach, patient, able to correct gently those who resist the truth." If he must not be quarrelsome, much, much less can he strike, can he punish backsliding converts in his audience

---

[135] [Nicholas of Lyra, *Bibliorum Sacrorum cum Glossa Ordinaria*, Lyons, 1545, 137rb.]

with whips and painful punitions. Athanasius says: "It is right for a teacher to be kind and gentle even to those he finds recalcitrant, the way a nurse behaves toward the child she minds, even if it scratches and kicks her." As we said before, you will not find Paul, or any of the saints, inflicting punishment on anyone, by their own hand or on their own orders, however gravely the person may have sinned.

That St. Paul punished someone who turned to vice, giving him over to Satan to trouble him in body for a time, was an exception to the rule, and needed for an exceptional circumstance. (1 Corinthians 5:24) If missioners had such power these days, they would do well to use it. The evil results would not ensue which follow from the missioners own punitive action or punitive orders. In fact evil results would cease. Great fruit of souls would follow. Maybe the "giving over to Satan" meant excommunication, as St. Thomas says about this Pauline passage. If so, it was a spiritual punishment, one vastly different from material, corporal punishment. That is self-evident. It is not what we are speaking of here. If he has the power and authorization from Pope or Bishop, a missioner can judge it meet and just to excommunicate some of the newly converted who lapse back into sin, without doing any physical damage. And only if the newly converted understand the meaning of excommunication, and it is likely they will not think it worthless.

The fourth proof. The corollary is proven by the severe complaint St. Denis wrote to the monk Demophilus. The reason: Demophilus treated with unbending anger a certain convert who fell back into sin. Demophilus cut him off completely. It is a famous case and the letter is both beautiful and devout. It is a fulsome confirmation of our corollary. Please look at the whole of it. Denis says, among other things: "Better to teach the ignorant than torment them. We do not lash the blind, but lead them by the hand." A little further on, he says: "It is a thing of utter horror that you should damn, disclaim, drive out someone the all-good Christ sought among the mountains, found fleeing, and, fresh from the find, brought back on his sacred shoulders." Chrysostom uses the same theme of leading the blind: "Therefore, just to do our duty, we offer him an arm and we speak to him warmly." Therefore missionaries do a grave wrong if they want to punish physically, by their own hand or someone else's, the newly converted natives who sin again.

The fifth proof. The same conclusion is proven through much that the saints have written—we cited them often above, especially the writing of St. Gregory: "The preaching that produces faith by the cudgel is willful and bizarre." And: "Whoever with sincere attention . . . wants to bring those who are strangers to Christianity into the true faith, should try with gentle means, not with severity, etc."[136]

The sixth proof. The wrong we spoke of can be shown amply through the teaching of Blessed Prosper [*sic:* Julianus Pomerius]: "I say that if you recall what the dispute about holy priests was, you have a sufficient response. As I said, the teachers in the Church must have the power to judge so they can be involved, they must have patience so they can bear with those who are unwilling to reform. Thus they fulfill the Pauline instruction given to Timothy in these words: 'Convince your peers, your elders, correct your juniors.' (2 Timothy 4:2) Then Paul quickly added: 'in true patience and teaching.'

"Someone who is corrected gently shows respect for his corrector; someone subjected to harsh and hyper-correction takes no correction, no message of salvation.

"Paul says somewhere else: 'Let the stronger among you bear the failings of the weaker.' (Romans 15:1) They can bear easily with them as weak, not with them as incorrigible, etc."

And further on: "For if the weak are cut off from communion with the Church, those whom castigation could not cure, they will sink under the excessive weight of sadness. They will avoid meeting the holy people through whom God could restore them. Or else, if driven to it, they will leap at every chance to sin, shamelessly, and the evil they did in secret they will do openly. Thus, in despair of regaining grace, they fall into such a craziness that they switch the words of those who warn them into wicked puns with a 'who cares' attitude. And the reproaches made against them, for boasting of their badness, feed their terrible lives with wicked delights. To avoid these consequences, therefore, the weak are to be borne with calm faith—they cannot be castigated for their weakness.

"The truth is, that if you induce a healthy shame in a sinner because of the shame you feel for his sin, if you infuse in him the disgrace you take on for his sin in the soul of your compassion, you will suppress in him easily all desire to sin, you will remove the whole rebel urge which is at the bottom of badness. Then a sense of shame, the watchdog of morality, hangdog shame will clothe his actions. What disgusted him earlier, when he was disgusting, will attract him now. What attracted him earlier, when all that was good disgusted him, will disgust him now. He will copy holy people willingly. In becoming like them, he will slowly transform his prior ways. After the hard work of reaching the heights of virtue, it would be equally as hard for him to return to the vices he was so happy to leave behind. As

---

[136] As quoted in Gratian, dist. 45: cap. 1 & cap. 3 [Friedberg, 1:160].

virtue weighs on vice, so the pleasure of vice tastes bitter to the lover of virtue. The person who has in mind only the salvation of the sinner, who wants to help him, treats all sinners, confronts all sinners peaceably."[137] These are the principles of Prosper [sic: Julianus Pomerius].

I beg my brothers to meditate on these principles often, often, and not let themselves become torturers of the children they begot for Christ in the Church, children they must beget again and again until the time Christ is formed in them. Let my brothers become weak with the weak, let them bear everything, with warnings, with beseechings, with tears openly, as Paul did, in order to save others.

Let them lead a holy and pure life. Let them be exemplary in their speech, in their relationships, in their charity, in their faith, in their chastity, so no one may demean their person. Let them be as Paul described to Timothy (1:4): as angels who deal with humankind, as men who raise their young, as spiritual kind who deal with material kind. So that the material kind feel uneasy in their presence, and are filled with shame and confusion if they do not follow them, do not believe in them—the way we just described it, the way Chrysostom did earlier. No need for the missioner then to inflict physical punishment, wielding the switches, whips, with his own hand or having another do it.

And yet they may put the fear of God into the fractious if they think it will help—i.e., decribe the frightful judgement to come, the torment the fractious will suffer forever. If they think their efforts are useless, nonetheless they did not labor in vain, the damnation is due to others, not to themselves, their own reward is reserved in a safe place. That should be no small consolation.

Papal Condemnation of Armed Oppression

Finally, we recall the Papal Encyclical "God Who is beyond us," which insists on peaceful conversion.[138] The High Priest and Vicar of Christ Himself gave teeth to that decree ["Sublimis Deus"] when he made the Archbishop of Toledo the judge and executor of it. The Archbishop was in Toledo at the time. The Pope gave him complete power to force the tyrants not to injure, not to oppress the Indians as they had done against every law. And power to give relief directly to the Indians concerning their freedom and ownership of their own goods. His commission to the Archbishop says this:

"To our beloved son, health and apostolic benediction. We have a pastoral duty to perform with all zeal towards the flock confided to us by God. We are made sad by the loss of them, made happy by the gain of them. We do praise the goodness of their works, but we make suggestions derived from the wider scope of our apostolic responsibility. It comes to our attention that our

---

[137] [*PL*, 59:449-50.]

[138] *The Only Way*, pp. 156-7.

beloved son Charles, ever august Emperor of the Romans, King of Castile and León, to check those who seethe with greed and take a brutal stance toward humankind, forbade all his subjects, by public edict, to make slaves of the Indians, East or West, or to dare deprive them of their personal goods. So we are mindful also of those Indians, though they are outside the flock of Christ. They are not for that reason deprived or to be deprived of their liberty nor the ownership of their possessions. They are human beings, therefore capable of faith and salvation. They are not to die in slavery. They are to be invited, through preaching and by example, to live. So we also condemn the outlaw acts of such wicked men. We want to prevent it happening that the Indians find it harder to embrace the Christian faith because they are demoralized by pain and loss. To you, then, in whose character we have a special confidence in the Lord—for your probity, your providence, your piety, your experience of these Indians and other peoples—to you, through this document, we make the following commission and command: 1) That you become a bulwark of defense for the aforesaid Indians in the aforesaid circumstances, yourself, or through another, or others. 2) That you strictly forbid anyone to make a slave in any way of the aforesaid Indians, or rob them of their goods under any pretext—anyone at all, whatever their dignity, their status, their condition, their grade, their nobility—forbid on penalty of excommunication, a judgement already made and incurred *ipso facto* if they act against this. They cannot be absolved from this penalty unless by Us or by a reigning Pontiff, except at the moment of death and after previous repentance. 3) And against the disobedient, you are to proceed to publish this threat of excommunication; and proceed further, to other measures apt for the circumstances, measures necessary and in any way suitable as you may determine, ordain, dispose, which will seem to you consonant with your prudence, your probity, your piety. By this commission, we give you full, free control in these matters against those who do the opposite. Given at Rome, etc."[139]

The last way of proving our proposition is now laid out, through the decrees of the Church, its succession of saintly Popes.

Therefore the Guilty must Make Restoration

On peril of losing their souls, all who start wars of conversion, all who will in the future, all who assist in any way we just said, all are bound to restore to the devastated pagan peoples whatever they took in war, permanent or perishable, and make up for whatever they destroyed. Make up totally.[140]

---

[139] [See the definitive text of "Pastorale Officium" in *Las Casas en México*, Appendix 12.]

[140] *The Only Way*, p. 171.

Part III.

Creating
Pro-Indian Law

- 1 -

The Atrocities of the Conquest

Prenote

People associate Las Casas with horror stories about the Indies, they associate thinking about solutions with others, e.g., Vitoria. But it is clear, at this point, that Las Casas is at the origin of Church policy. This excerpt, and the next, will make clear that he is at the origin of state policy as well, i.e., the New Laws of 1542.

But take the horror stories for a moment—the few we translate below—and realize that every one presented to the reform commission of 1542 had stacks of investigative reports to back them. And the purpose of the recounting was to prepare the heart and mind of the King and commissioners to act and stop the atrocities. The purpose was not to blacken Spain's name. That only happened when people later ignored the context of the presentation, ignored the effect of the presentation—the creation of New Laws by Spain itself—and simply used the material in a damning rather than a reforming way.

New Spain

New Spain was discovered in 1517. [141] The discovery was a very bad experience for the Indians. And it cost the discoverers some lives. In 1518, so-called Christians returned there to rob and kill, though they said they went there to colonize. From that year to this, 1542, all the injustice, all the violence and tyranny the Christians have ever done in the Indies reached their greatest pitch of intensity. The Spaniards have lost all fear of

---

[141] (See *Historia,* Lib. 3, cap. 96-98. Refers to Francisco Hernández de Córdoba.)

God, all fear of the King, and have forgotten their humanity. The horrors, the cruelties, the massacres, the raiding, the slaughter of peoples, the looting, the violence, the tyranny, were all indeed numerous and great across the broad and rich territories and kingdoms of the Mainland. What we have described of them is pitifully small in comparison to what was done. But even if we could describe it all, and what we have not is endless, nothing compares in number or in kind to what was done, what was perpetrated from 1518 to this day, this year, 1542, or what is done, is perpetrated on this September day, sinful, sickening things. The norm we set down earlier is true: Things got worse from the start, more lawless, more hellish as time went on.

The massacres lasted from the date of entry into New Spain, the eighteenth of April, 1518, until the year 1530. For twelve unbroken years, the devastations the blood-drenched hands and swords of the Spaniards worked without halt in the four hundred and fifty leagues that comprised the city of Mexico and its environs. Within that space were four or five realms as grand as Spain and far more fertile. They were areas much more populated, much more, than Toledo, Seville, Valladolid, and Zaragoza with Barcelona included. God never put so many people in the past or present in those Spanish cities, however great their population was, as there, within those leagues of land. One has to travel eighteen hundred just to do the perimeter. The Spaniards massacred more than four million souls in the space of twelve years within the four hundred and fifty leagues, sliced them to death, speared them, burned them alive, women, children, young, old, while the wars they called conquests—again, their word—lasted, but they were really cruel tyrants carrying on violent invasions, condemned not only by the law of God but by all human law as well, like the violence the Turk does to the Christian Church to destroy it, but much worse. The count does not include the number they killed and are killing each day by the awful servitude I described, the day-in-day-out wearing down by abuse.

Frankly, words are not enough, the human power to know does not suffice to describe the hideous things that were done in the various places—at one time in one place, successively in other places—by those open enemies, those mortal enemies of the human race, all done within the region I described. And some things were so aggravated by circumstance and kind that in truth they could not be adequately told no matter what the effort or what the time or what the writing. Yet I will describe something of what happened in some areas. But I swear under oath I know I can describe only one incident in a thousand.

One of the massacres they performed was in a large city called Cholula. It had more than thirty thousand people. The chiefs of the place and the region around came out to welcome the Christians and, at the head of the procession, all the priests with the chief priest, all respectful, all reverential. They led the Spaniards to the center of the city to lodge them. The lodgings were in the homes of the ruler or the nobles. The Spaniards decided to perform a massacre—a chastisement, as they called it—to make themselves feared and fearsome in every nook and cranny of that country. That was the fixed policy at all times wherever the Spaniards went in those lands, i.e., pull off a cruel, notable massacre so those flocks of sheep-like people would fear them. So with this foremost in mind, they sent a summons to all the chiefs and nobles of the city and of the places subject to the city, the primary prince included. When they came within to speak to the captain of the Spaniards, they were all seized without anyone being alerted who could give out a warning. The Spaniards demanded five or six thousand Indians as baggage bearers. They arrived, and the Spaniards put them in the courtyard of the palace. Just to see the Indians when they prepare themselves to carry packs for the Spaniards is to have great compassion on them, to pity them. They came naked, stark naked, in loin cloths only, and with a small sack over the shoulder to hold some meager rations. The Spaniards had them squat on the ground as meek as lambs. When they were all gathered together in the courtyard along with some others who happened to be there, armed Spaniards were deputed to block the exits. The other Spaniards drew their weapons and sliced and stabbed all those sheep in the courtyard. Not a one of them could escape the smoking slaughter. Two or three days later, a fair number of Indians came out alive covered with blood. They had managed to hide under the pile of dead, so many dead. They came pleading to the Spaniards, pleading for mercy, not to be killed. But the Spaniards were merciless, pitiless, and hacked them to pieces instead, as they came out. As for the chiefs, all of them, more than a hundred who were tied up, the Captain ordered them torched and spitted alive on poles stuck in the ground. One chief did untie himself, perhaps the principal one, the king of the region. He got himself, along with twenty, thirty, forty men, to the main temple they had there, it was like a fortress, they call it Cuu, where he holed up safely for a good part of the day. But no one fights the Spaniards off, especially poorly armed people like the Indians. The Spaniards set fire to the temple, they burned alive those inside. Who kept shouting: "You monsters! How did we ever harm you? Why do you murder us? Leave! Go to Mexico! Montezuma will revenge us! The sovereign of us all! On you!" The story goes that a captain of the Spaniards was singing while the five or six thousand were being hacked to death in the courtyard, singing this: "Nero watched from the Tarpeian rock, while Rome burned; young and old were screaming. He felt nothing."

They did another massacre at Tepeaca, a much larger city than Cholula, with many more people living in it. The slaughter was huge, the cruelties enormous.

They went from Cholula to Mexico City. The mighty king Montezuma sent thousands of presents to greet them, lords and nobles, festival groups along the road. He sent his own brother to meet them at the head of the causeway into Mexico—two leagues long—his brother along with many nobles and many gifts of gold, of silver, of clothing. At the entry to the city, he himself came to meet them borne on a golden sedan chair and surrounded by his entire court. He conducted them to the palaces where he had ordered them lodged. On that very day, as I have been told by some who were there, they took the great king Montezuma prisoner, by a ruse, he thought he was safe, and they set an eighty man guard on him, and later put him in irons. There are many things more to tell, important things, about this time, but I leave them untold. I want only to relate what one of those tyrants pulled off, it stands out. The captain of the Spaniards had gone back down to the port of entry to subdue another captain who had come to replace him. A certain subaltern was left in charge, with little more than a hundred men to guard king Montezuma. That group of Spaniards plotted to commit another horrible crime to intensify people's fear of them everywhere in the region. It was a policy they used often, as I said. The ordinary Indian people and the nobles of the entire city and court of Motezuma had one task in life, to please their imprisoned lord. They held festivals for him. One was to have dances in the afternoon in the plazas of every section of the city, traditional dances they call "mitotes," similar to the "areitos" on the islands, in which they wear their finery, their jewels, and everyone is involved, it is the main kind of festival, of entertainment. Nobles, knights, those of royal blood, held their festival dance nearest the palaces where their king was held prisoner. In the square nearest the palace, there were more than two thousand young nobles, the flower drawn from the nobility of the entire kingdom of Montezuma. The leader of the Spaniards joined them with a platoon of men. He sent other platoons to each of the other sections of the city where the festival was also held. The Spaniards faked an interest in watching them. The leader gave an order that at a set time they should attack the people, who were drunk and unsuspecting as they danced. He signaled, his men shouted: "Saint James and at them!" And they started with naked sword to cut open naked, defenseless bodies and spill that noble blood. They left no one alive. The Spaniards did the same to the people in other plazas. It was a massacre that convulsed the region and all its peoples, it sickened and saddened them, filled them with bitterness, grief. They will never stop lamenting it from now until the world ends, or they all cease to be, never stop singing about that disaster in their ritual dances, as we do here in ballads as we call them, that loss of the whole future of a nobility they prized so much in years past.

The Indians saw the injustice, the horror, on a scale beyond belief, inflicted on completely innocent people. They had endured with some patience the capture of their highest leader, no less unjust a thing, because that leader ordered them not to attack, not to make war on the Christians. But after this the whole city rose in arms and went after them, and many a wounded Spaniard barely escaped with his life. The Spaniards put a knife to the chest of the captive Motezuma, had him go out on a gallery and order the Indians not to attack the palace, or the Spaniards would fix him for good. But the Indians had no desire to obey Motezuma further in anything. Instead, they agree to elect another lord, a chief who could lead them in battle. But just then, the Captain who had gone down to the port of entry came back successful, and brought many more Christians with him, and when he approached, the Indians ceased combat for a matter of three or four days until he got inside the city. Once he was inside, the Indians joined forces, warriors from all over the region, and waged war as one, so fiercely, for such a length of time, that the Spaniards feared they would all be killed. So one night they decided to flee the city. The Indians detected the flight and killed many Christians on the bridges over the lake. In a war that was perfectly just, perfectly moral, as I have said. Any just or reasonable man, whoever he is, would say it was so. What happened later, after the fight inside the city, was that the Christians regrouped. They then proceeded to slaughter the Indians in ways that were shocking and monstrous. They massacred hordes of people. And they burned many a noble lord.

After the great and sickening barbarities they wrought in the City of Mexico and in the cities, the region, for ten, fifteen, twenty leagues out from Mexico where a huge number were slaughtered, the brutal Spanish plague went further, it spread, it infected, killed off the whole province of Panuco. One time there was a marvelous number of people there, but a wholesale slaughter took place. The Spaniards went on to destroy the province of Tututepeque in the same fashion. Then the province of Ipilcingo, then that of Colima, each one a territory larger than either the kingdom of Castile or that of León. It would be a diffficult, an impossible task, beyond any doubt, to recount the brutalities, murders, cruelties, the Spaniards perpetrated in each region, impossible to tell, unbearable to hear.

Let it be noted here that the title by which they entered that land, by which they began to destroy all those innocent peoples, to reduce the population in those areas which should have caused so much joy, delight, to those who were true Christians, precisely because of their large numbers of people, the title was the ULTIMATUM that the Indians come and agree to obey the King of Spain, and if they did not, the Spaniards would kill them or make them slaves. And those who did not come immediately to fulfill these crazy, stupid declarations and put themselves in the hands of wicked, cruel, beastly men, were named rebels and traitors to the service of His Majesty. That was the report they sent back to his lordship, our King. The blindness of those who ruled the Indies made them unaware, ignorant of what was expressly stated in the King's laws, stated more clearly than any other of his primary principles, i.e., no one is a rebel, nor can be called one, who is not first a subject. Christians should think about this, as anyone should who knows anything about God or good sense, anything about human laws, the effect of the sudden ULTIMATUM made by the Spaniards on the natives—how it would affect the feelings of any people whatsoever living peacefully in their own lands, unaware they owed anyone anything, ruled over by their own native king—an ULTIMATUM which says: "Surrender your obedience to a foreign king whom you have never seen nor heard of, and if you do not, know that we will then cut you to pieces." And the Indians knew from experience that was exactly what the Spaniards would then do. But there is something even more frightful: the Indians who do submit, the Spaniards reduce to a hideous servitude in which, under the terrible workload, under extended torture—a stretched out version of what they suffer who are put to the sword because the Spaniards fear them—they perish inexorably, husbands, wives, children, future generations. And though the Indians or any other peoples in the world might come to obey, to recognize a foreign ruler as king due to their terror tactics, the Spaniards, these corrupt, chaotic men, who are blinded and impassioned by ambition and diabolical greed, do not see they gain not an ounce of legal authority this way. It is truly fear, fear, which according to law, natural, human, divine, has the value of air when it comes to legal worth. But it has the value of guilt that sticks to them and begs for hellfire, as do the offenses, the harm they cause the Kings of Castile, ruining their realms, annihilating any right the Kings have throughout the Indies, insofar as these men have the power to do so. These and none others are the services the Spaniards have provided the Kings of Castile in those lands overseas. They provide the same today.

With this so-called just, so-called valid title, the captain in question sent two subalterns, both more cruel, more savage than he, both more cynical and merciless than he, into regions that were large and fertile and flourishing, as full as can be of people, the region of Guatemala, which is on the southern sea, and the region of Naco and Honduras or Guaimura, which is on the northern sea. They have a common frontier which divides the two of them into separate confines, three hundred leagues from Mexico. The captain in question sent one subaltern overland, the other on shipboard by sea, and with each, many horses and foot soldiery. [142]

What they did, the two, in terms of evil, and I tell you the truth, especially the one who went to the region of Guatemala, because the other soon died an evil death, I could collect, I could recite, so many incidents of evil, ruin, murder, depopulation, of brutal injustice, they would put fear in the present century and those to come, I could fill a huge book with them. For this man surpassed all the past and present raiders in the number of abominable things he did, of people he killed and lands he devastated—they were countless.

The one who went by sea, aboard ship, robbed, ravaged, pulverized on a grand scale the coastal peoples, even as they came to meet him with gifts, in the region of Yucatan which was on the way to the region they were headed for, Naco and Guaimura. Once they reached the area, the leader sent further subalterns and full complements ashore all along it to rob, kill, ruin whatever villages and people were there. One especially mutinied with three hundred men and drove inland toward Guatemala. He sacked and burned whatever villages he found, robbing and killing the people in them. He did this in deliberate fashion for more than a hundred and twenty leagues. If anyone followed his tracks they would find the land devastated, depopulated, and the Indians alive would kill them in revenge for the damage and destruction he left in his wake. A short while later, the Indians did kill the principal captain who had sent the subaltern, the one who had mutinied. Afterwards, there was a succession of others, many others, cruel monsters who laid waste to the region, the provinces of Naco and Honduras, by massacres and fearful cruelties, by making slaves of people and selling them to the ships that brought wine and clothing and other goods, then by the tyranny of ordinary servitude from the year 1524 to the year 1535. And these provinces were an earthly paradise to behold, they were heavily populated, more than the most crowded human place there could be in this world. We travel them today and as we do we see them so thinned out, so ravaged that they would move anyone to pity, hard as he or she might be. More than two million people perished in that eleven years' time. There were not two thousand people left in two hundred or more square leagues, and they perish day by day in the servitude of which I spoke.

Now to swing back and speak of the main monster, the captain who went to the region of Guatemala. He was worse than any in the old days there and the equal of any in the present from the provinces adjacent to

---

[142] (Pedro de Alvarado by land; Cristóbal de Olid by sea.)

Mexico City. It is four hundred leagues distant from Guatemala by the route he took, as he himself noted in a letter he wrote to the man who had sent him out. He left a trail of murder and robbery, he burned, looted, sacked the whole land where he went, using the legitimization I mentioned—by demanding that the people surrender to men who were brutal, unjust, cruel, in the name of the King of Spain, someone unknown to them, someone they never heard of, someone they thought must be even more cruel and unjust than his followers. But the Spaniards, right after they read the ULTIMA-TUM, without even giving the Indians time to think, began to murder and torch them.

The New Kingdom of Granada

In the year 1539, and in search of Peru, many monsters got together from Venezuela, from Santa Marta, from Cartagena. [143] And others from Peru itself came down to explore the interior of the region. And they discovered below Santa Marta and Cartagena a three hundred league stretch of land there, prosperous, wonderful regions filled with huge numbers of good and gentle people, like the others out there, and extremely wealthy in gold and precious stones, the kind called emeralds. The Spaniards gave the region the name, the New Kingdom of Granada. The reason: The monster who arrived in the region first was a native of the kingdom here called Granada. Many of the men who came from every direction were wicked and cruel, they were well known butchers and spillers of human blood. They were savvy and seasoned in the great sins we spoke of in other parts of the Indies. Therefore their fiendish deeds, and the conditions which made them worse, the qualities that made them more serious, were on such a large scale that they surpassed by far all that any of them or anyone else had done, had perpetrated in the other provinces.

They have done a massive amount of evil in the past three years. They continue to do it today. I will state, but briefly, how much. A governor held an investigation of the principal thug because he, the governor, did not want to allow in the robber and killer of the New Kingdom of Granada so he could continue his own robbing and killing. There were many witnesses, about the destructions, the outrages, the massacres he did and is still doing. The investigation was read by the Council of the Indies, and they have it on file.

The witnesses in the investigation report the following: The whole realm was peaceful and in service to the Spaniards. The Indians gave them

---

[143] [Jiménez de Quesada, Federmann, Sebastián de Benalcázar.]

the fruit of their labor constantly; they worked field and farm for them and supplied them with much gold and precious stones, emeralds, as much as the Indians had in their possession to give. The villages, the chiefs, the people were partitioned among the Spaniards, which is really what the Spaniards want, the means to gain their ultimate end which is gold. And the people were subjected, all of them, to the usual lawlessness and servitude. Given all this, the captain, the principal monster who ruled the region, seized the lord and king of the entire area and kept hold of him, for six or seven months, demanding gold and emeralds from him. There was no justification for this, no reason. The king I spoke of was called Bogotá. They made him so afraid that he said he would give them the house made of gold they demanded of him, hoping thus to free himself from the clutches of those who were holding him for that reason. He sent Indians to bring him gold. Several times they brought large quantities of gold and gems. But since he did not produce the house of gold, the Spaniards said they would kill him because he had not kept to what he had promised. The monster told the Spaniards they should petition justice in his presence. So they petitioned him for redress, lodging an accusation against the king of the region. The monster made the ruling condemning the king to torture if he did not hand over the house of gold. They tortured him on a rack. They threw hot fat on his belly. On each foot, they put a horseshoe nailed to a post. He was attached by the neck to another post. Two men held his hands. Others held fire to his feet. From time to time the monster entered and told him he was going to kill him this way, little by little if he did not give them the gold. That finished the king, he died under the torture. While they were working on him, God showed His detestation of those cruelties by burning down the whole village where the crime was committed.

The rest of the Spaniards, in imitation of their good captain, and because they knew nothing else than to cut those peoples to pieces, did likewise. They tortured, each one of them, in various and ferocious ways, the chief of the village or villages which they, the Spaniards, had in their charge. And the chiefs were at their service along with all their people. And they were handing over as much gold, as many gems in their possession as they could. The single reason for torturing them was so they would surrender more gold and gems than before. Acting this way, Spaniards burned and butchered all the chiefs of the realm.

Terrified by the raw cruelties effected by one particular monster against the Indians, an important lord by the name of Daitama fled with large numbers of his people to the mountains to escape such absolute brutality. They thought of the flight as a safety measure, as an escape—if it worked for them. The Spaniards called it mutiny, rebellion. The captain, the head monster, found out. He sent some people to help the lesser thug, the cruel one just referred to, the one the Indians fled from, to the mountains, because of his ferocity, peaceful Indians who suffered under his gross tyranny and evildoing. He went after them. One could not hide from him even in the bowels of the earth. He found great numbers of Indians. He cut to pieces and killed more than five hundred souls, men, women, children. No mercy for anyone. Even though, as the witnesses say, that same lord Daitama, before they murdered his people, had sought out that cruel man and handed over four or five thousand castellanos. In spite of this, the thug did the horror described.

Another incident. A large number of people offered their services to the Spaniards. They were serving them with their usual humility and simplicity. They were unsuspecting. One night a captain came to the town where the Indians were in service. He ordered every one of them put to the sword. While they were either still asleep, or still eating and resting from the day's work. He gave the order because he thought it a good thing to do, the massacre, to put the fear of him deep in everyone in the entire land.

Another incident. The Captain ordered all the Spaniards to swear to the number of chiefs, notables, and common people each one had in service in each household. Then he ordered the Indians brought to the plaza. There he had all their heads cut off. Four to five hundred people were then killed. The witnesses say that he thought to keep the land under control that way.

The witnesses say of one monster in particular that he perpetrated outrageous cruelties, murdering, slicing off hands and noses from many men and women, destroying huge numbers of people.

Another incident. The Captain sent the vicious man I described above, along with a group of Spaniards, to the province of Bogotá to find out who the ruler was who succeeded to power after the previous ruler died under torture. He searched over many leagues of territory, taking as many Indians as he could manage. And they would not tell him who the ruler was who had succeeded to power. So he cut the hands off some, he had others thrown to savage dogs who ripped them to pieces, men and women both. That way he killed off many Indians of both sexes. One day, just before dawn, he attacked some chiefs or leaders and their large group of Indians. They were at peace with the Spaniards and unsuspecting. He had assured them, given them his word that they would not be treated badly, not harmed. Under that truce, they had come down from the mountains where they had hidden out, to settle on the plain. Their village was there. Thus their guard was down, they trusted the word that the Spaniard had given them. He seized a large group of people, men and women. He ordered them to stretch their hands out along the ground. Then he himself, with a cutlass, chopped a hand off each one, and he told them he inflicted this punishment on them because they refused to tell him who the new ruler was who had succeeded to power.

Another incident. The Indians did not give a chest full of gold to the cruel Captain as he had demanded. So he sent a troop to make war on them. The troop killed huge numbers, they cut hands and noses off men and women, no one can say how many. They threw others to savage dogs who tore them and ate them.

Another incident. The Indians of one province in the region knew that the Spaniards had burned to death three or four important chiefs. So they fled out of fear to a rugged cliff to protect themselves from an enemy so utterly bereft of human feeling. As the witnesses testify, there would have been four to five thousand Indians on that cliff. The captain I spoke of sent an important, well known monster—who surpassed many in taking on the task of decimating that territory—with a crew of Spaniards to punish the Indians on the pretext that the Indians were rebels for fleeing such a plague, such a massacre, as if they had done something unjust, as if it were the Spaniards' role to punish them, to take vengeance on them! It was the Spaniards who deserved, and without pity, the worst of tortures—they are so pitiless, so merciless with the innocent Indians. The Spaniards went to the cliff stronghold. They attacked it in force. The Indians were naked and weaponless. The Spaniards shouted up to the Indians to be peaceful. They assured them they would do them no harm, the Indians should not resist. So the Indians surrendered. The vicious, vicious leader ordered the Spaniards to take all the strong points of the cliff, and once taken, to attack the Indians. Those lions and tigers attacked the gentle sheep, they slashed and disemboweled so many they had to stop to rest, there were that many they cut to pieces. After they rested a bit, the captain ordered them to kill and pitch over the cliff—there was a long drop—everyone who remained alive. So they pitched everyone off it. The witnesses say they saw a rain of Indians, seven hundred, plunge down off the cliff and smash to pieces where they hit.

And to bring the horrible outrage to completion, the Spaniards made a sweep of all the Indians who had hidden in the bushes. The captain ordered them all run through. So the Spaniards killed them and threw them down from the cliff. Even the horrible things just described were not enough for him. He wanted to outdo himself, to intensify the hideousness of his sins. So he ordered all the Indian men and women taken alive by individual Spaniards—because in those slaughters individuals Spaniards usually cull out a few men, women, children, for their own use—ordered them put in a straw hut—he had selected and spared those huts he thought would be most useful—then ordered the Spaniards to set fire to it. So they burned the Indians alive, a matter of forty or fifty of them. Some others he ordered thrown to vicious dogs who bit them to pieces and ate them.

Another incident. The very same monster went to a certain village called Cota. He seized many Indians and had the dogs tear apart fifteen or twenty of their principal people. He cut the hands off a great number of men and women, tied the severed hands to a rope, wrapped the rope around a length of pole so the rest of the Indians could see what he had done to the captured ones. There were seventy pair of hands. And he cut the noses off many women and children.

No one could possibly express the savage cruelties worked by this man, this enemy of God. They are too many to tell, the things he did in that territory, unheard of, unimaginable, things he also did in Guatemala, or wherever else he had been. Because he has roamed the region for many years committing these crimes, ravaging, ruining the land and the people.

And the witnesses say even more in that deposition: that between the cruelties and killings, massive in number and kind, which were inflicted in the past—and still are in the present—in the New Kingdom of Granada by his henchmen, the individual captains, and [the cruelties and killings] he permitted those monsters and smashers of the human race in his own entourage to inflict, they had the region stripped to a wasteland. And [the witnesses say] that if Your Majesty does not order halted quickly the massacre of Indians just to extort from them the gold they no longer have—because they have already handed it over—it will come about in a very short time that there will be no Indians left to work the earth, which will then become desolate and empty of all people.

What should be noted here is the cruel, plague-like brutality of those hell-bound monsters, a brutality that was vicious, unrestrained, demonic. In the two or three years since that kingdom was discovered—it was once, according to all who have been there and according to the witnesses cited in the investigation, one of the most populous places of any in the world—the conquerors killed it, decimated it, pitilessly, with no fear of God or King. And the word is that if His Majesty does not shortly halt these diabolical deeds, no human being there will remain alive. And I think the same, because I have seen with my own eyes vast segments of territory overseas destroyed in a very short time and left without a soul.

There are other large regions which border on parts of the New Kingdom of Granada, they are called Popayan and Cali, plus another three or four, comprising more than five hundred leagues. Monsters ravaged and ruined them the same way they did the previous ones, robbing, killing, plus doing the tortures, the outrages already described, and the people were huge in number. Because the land is blessed. And those who have recently returned from overseas say what a great and grievous shame it was, as they passed through, to see so many large-sized villages burned to nothing. Where a village had two to three thousand inhabitants, they found no more than fifty left, and some were totally emptied, totally ruined. And in some areas they found a hundred to two hundred, three hundred leagues entirely empty of people, large towns burned, destroyed. To cap it all, some mighty and vicious monsters came from the kingdoms of Peru, from out of the province of Quito, and entered the New Kingdom of Granada and Popayan and Cali, moving in the direction of Cartagena and Uraba. From Cartagena, other wretched monsters set out on a journey toward Quito. Next, others from the direction of Rio San Juan, which is on the south coast. Eventually they joined forces. Together they ripped up and decimated more than six hundred leagues of land, driving to perdition huge numbers of souls. They do the same this very day to the tragic peoples, innocent peoples who survive.

How true the rule is, the one I stated at the beginning of this account: time increased the tyranny, the violence, the injustice of the Spaniards toward those peoples, those gentle flocks, things got more brutish, more beastly, more evil. And that which is done now in the New Kingdom of Granada is worthy of the full fire and torture of hell, along with other things worthy of the same. And the following will bear out the rule.

Consequent to the murders and maiming of the wars, the conquistadors put the people into a horrible servitude, a fact I described earlier. They parceled the Indians out to fiends, some got two hundred, some got three. There is a story about a fiend of an owner who had a hundred Indians summoned before him. So they came, meek as lambs. When they were all there, he had thirty or forty decapitated, then said to the others: "I intend to do the same to you if you do not serve me well, or if you leave without my consent."

And those who read this should weigh well, before God, what sort of deed it was, if it does not go beyond any conceivable cruelty and injustice, and if it is not in accord with the facts to name those Christians fiends, and if it would not be better to hand those Indians over to the devils in hell than to hand them over to Christians in the Indies.

There is another story to tell. I do not know what could be more vicious or more diabolical, more like the savagery of wild beasts, it, or the one I just told. The report is that the Spaniards in the Indies had trained to obedience dogs that were absolutely vicious, for the purpose of tearing the Indians to death. And anyone who is a true Christian, even anyone who is not, should try to think if anything worse than the wicked deed to be described has ever been heard of in this world. To keep the dogs in food, the Spaniards, on their trips, drive Indians chained together, who come along like a herd of swine. The Spaniards kill some, then hold an open meat market of human flesh. And one Spaniard says to another: "Give me a hunk of one of those brutes to feed my dogs until I kill one later." It is as if they swapped hunks of pork or mutton. There are others who go hunting with their dogs in the morning. When they come back for their meal and are asked how it went, they answer: "Went well, I killed fifteen, maybe twenty of the brutes with my dogs." We have proof of all these diabolical things, and of others as well, proof from the lawsuits the monsters brought against one another. Could anything be more wicked, or savage, or inhuman?

Closing Statement

I want to stop with that story, until news may arrive of grosser evils, if there can be grosser ones than those I cited. Or until I go back there and see things once again. I have been an eyewitness without interruption for forty-two years. I testify before God and in all conscience, and I hold it for certain, that the ruination that has been visited on those peoples overseas, or those territories, the damage, the destruction, the depopulation, the massacres, the murders, the outrageous and hideous cruelties, the ugly refinements of those cruelties, the violences, the injustices, the looting, the bloodletting—all of which is going on right now throughout the Indies—that ruination I have not exaggerated. In all the things I stated and stated again, I have not exaggerated in number and kind more than one in ten thousand of what was done and is being done now.

So that Christians, any Christian, may feel a greater compassion for those innocent peoples, so that Christians may grieve over the decimation and damnation of the Indies, may blame and abhor and detest the greed, the ambition, the cruelty of the Spaniards, let them, all of them, hold the following truth as proven, along with the other truths I stated above: from the moment the Indies were discovered until the present day, the Indians never, anywhere, did evil to a single Christian unless evil had first been inflicted on them, or they had been robbed, or been betrayed. Rather, they thought of the Spaniards as gods come down from the heavens. They always welcomed them as such until their deeds showed who they really were and what they really wanted.

It may be well to add something further. Right from the start and up until now, the Spaniards took no care to have faith in Jesus Christ preached to those peoples, as if those peoples were dogs or some other dumb beasts.

Rather, they made it primary policy to forbid the religious to preach—by the many harassments and persecutions they laid on them. For the Spaniards saw that preaching would prevent them from amassing the gold, the riches their own desires dangled before them. There is no advance today throughout the whole of the Indies in the knowledge of God—God is a log, or the sky, or the earth—over what those people knew a hundred years ago. Except perhaps in New Spain, where religious did enter, a very tiny corner of the Indies. So all the Indians perished, and are perishing now, minus the faith, minus the sacraments.

I, Fray Bartolomé de las Casas, a friar of Saint Dominic, came to this Court of Spain, by the mercy of God, seeking to halt the hell of the Indies so that the massive number of souls there redeemed by the blood of Christ should not perish inexorably and forever, but rather should know their Creator and be saved. And I came out of compassion for my country, Castile, that God not destroy it for its monstrous sins committed against the faith and honor due to God, committed against its neighbor. And I was persuaded [to put this in writing] by some important people who reside in court, who are zealous for the honor of God and moved by the sorrows and tragedies of others. And though I had intended to do it without prompting, I had not carried the intention out because I could not spare the time from my endless tasks.

I finished it in Valencia, the eighth of December, 1542, when the violence was fiercest, when things were at their height, all the violence, the oppression, the tyranny, the massacres, the robbing and ravaging, the havoc, the decimation, depopulation, torture and tragedy we spoke of above, out there in the Indies everywhere Christians are found. Though things are more brutal and sickening in some places than in others. Mexico City and its environs are a little less bad off. Or at least no one dares do things publicly, because there and nowhere else may be found some justice, though it is little enough. Though there they destroy them also through diabolical taxation. I have the great hope that as the Emperor and King of Spain, our Lord Don Carlos, the fifth of that name, comes to understand the evils, the perfidy inflicted now and in the past on those peoples, against God's will and against his own—because the truth has been scrupulously hidden from him right up to the present—will bring a halt to such evil, will heal the New World God has given him charge of, because he is a lover of justice, a practitioner of it. And may Almighty God enrich for many years to come his glorious and fruitful life, his imperial reign, as a source of health for the universal church and of final salvation for his royal soul. Amen.

- 2 -

Twenty Reasons Against Encomienda

Prenote

Las Casas proposed remedies for the terrible situations he described. There were sixteen, but the eighth remedy, against encomienda, was the most extensive, the most important. The abolition of encomienda had to occur if other solutions were to have any meaning. For it really was a lawless state, granting to encomenderos unlimited rights over land and Indian labor, with no provisions made for the protection of Indian life or limb.

Excerpts from Twenty Reasons Against Encomienda were presented earlier because of their narrative and analytical importance, i.e., describing the origin of encomienda under Ovando, 1501-1509, and analyzing the motivation behind the conquest, greed. Here we meet Las Casas' doctrine on freedom, Indian freedom especially, and how encomienda violates that freedom. He will develop this doctrine to fuller and fuller proportions as time goes on, until, in the 1550's, he sees absolutely no just reason for Spain being in the New World at all except through the freely given consent of the governed.

He succeeds in causing New Laws. We know, from a newly discovered manuscript containing a list of all the points he presented to the commission, that each point resulted in a law, those reforming the Spanish system of governance, those spelling out the abolition of encomienda and

240

the ills associated with it. [144] *But abolition was to be gradual, and Las Casas saw that as a fatal flaw.*

Ninth Reason
Indians Are Free Beings

The ninth reason is that all people and their cities in the New World are free. [145] They do not lose that freedom by accepting and holding Your Majesty as their supreme ruler. Rather, if they have some defects in their governance, the rule of Your Majesty would clear up, would repair those defects, and they would thus enjoy a greater liberty. That was the mind of our Most Christian Queen Isabella. She showed that mind openly and continually in her royal decrees and letters, even going beyond that codicil of hers I cited earlier. I have a letter of Her Majesty which she sent a few days before she died, 20 December 1503. In it she ordered the Grand Commander of Alcántara who was the Governor of Haiti at that time—it was the only one of the Indies she dealt with—that the Indians be treated as the free peoples they were, as I will bring out in the eleventh reason. At Burgos, in a solemn consultation of certain learned men, theologians and jurists who belonged to the Council of the Catholic King, it was determined and decreed that the Indians were free peoples and should so be treated. [146] The same decision was made unanimously by the Royal Council [of Castile] at the previously mentioned meeting convoked by order of your Majesty [in 1529]. And you yourself decided, ordered and declared the same in conjunction with your Royal Council and learned men, theologians and jurists, and people of safe and sound judgement, in the year 1523. I will bring out the details in reason nineteen.

Take it as true, then, that the peoples and places of the New World are free. They are obligated to no one in any way for anything before they are discovered, during their discovery, today after their discovery—save only to Your Majesty, a service, an obedience, a specific kind, the kind free peoples and places owe their supreme king and Lord. Take it as true also, the special condition of these peoples which makes them even freer than

---

[144] Bartolomé de las Casas, *Conclusiones sumarias sobre el remedio de las Indias.* Portfolio containing three separate items: a complete facsimile of the newly acquired manuscript and commentaries by Isacio Pérez Fernández and Helen Rand Parish. Madrid: Biblioteca Nacional, 1992.

[145] *Tratados*, vol. 2, pp. 741-59.

[146] [Ferdinand's Laws of Burgos are printed in Roland D. Hussey, "Text of the Laws of Burgos," *HAHR*, 12:306-22; or Simpson, *The Laws of Burgos of 1512* (Ibero-Americana, no. 7, Berkeley, 1934).]

other peoples, i.e., that the Kings of Castile have no claim to these peoples. They are not an inheritance, not a purchase, not an exchange. They were not conquered in a just war motivated by the just cause of having harmed Spain, or the universal Church, or any member of it, or summoned to make restitution or satisfaction and been unwilling to do so. They were not squatters in bad faith on some territory. They did not harbor stolen goods, with no intention of giving them back. No such circumstances.

The fact is that these peoples will accept of their own free will the supreme Lordship of Your Majesty. If they have not accepted our Kings in the past, the reason has been that no one up to now has asked them to, nor given them a chance to be asked, nor considered them as worth more than the animals they beat the bush for. The Indians have seen no just or sound reason why they should accept Your Majesty. They have no knowledge of Your Majesty's grandeur, your justice, your liberality, your goodness, your power, nor that of your [predecessors] in Castile. Rather, they know widespread violence, insult, tyranny, injustice, cruelty, criminal acts done by Spaniards. That is why the Indians think so badly of Your Majesty and your predecessors, all the Kings of Castile. They have good reason, though you have not deserved what they think. They have a mortal hatred of Your Majesty, a horror toward your whole lineage. They think Their Highnesses, as Your Majesty, know and consent to, foster and urge that they be treated just as I described. Furthermore, note the title which Their Highnesses and Your Majesty hold, the apostolic mission granted by the Holy Apostolic See. It is the basis for your entire authority over the New World. It states the goal the Kings promised to seek voluntarily, the preaching of the faith in the Indies, the announcement of the Holy Gospel of Jesus Christ, in order to convert the natives to it. And that is a privilege for the Indians' sake primarily, as I said earlier, not so much for Your Majesty's. The privilege requires great prudence, great control and moderation, great gentleness and kindness, both in early dealings with those peoples, exploring their kingdoms peacefully, lovingly, on best behavior, and later in governing them and in dealing with local Indian populations for whom the place is their birthright where they live and are. The purpose is to have them receive our holy faith freely and without odium, so that they may be formed and fashioned and fitted to the Christian religion. The further reason is that no occasion great or small be given for them to curse the name of our God and thus thwart the attainment of salvation. They should love Your Majesty and the Kings of Castile. They should praise God with delight for having given them such a just, kind, king and lord of all, whose rule makes the condition they are in now a condition of greater freedom and power associated with free men. For anyone to accept our faith, he or she must have what faith calls for in a beginner, a clear liberty of choice. God has left it to the responsible free will of each person to accept or reject faith. And just as the final state which God promises in the whole process has to be based, is based on the free will choice of those people called, not on coercion or any violence one can inflict on them, so, without any doubt, most noble Lord, the means to that final state must not be against their will—if the means are to be kept orderly and just—but rather must accord with it, must have the approval and consent of the converted. To show that this is the way it must be done, there are rules and gospel and commandments and strictures which God imposed, the Lord of all creation whose authority everyone must obey.

It is clear that no power on earth has the right to reduce the liberties of innocent people without tossing away the key to justice. Liberty is the highest, the most precious of the temporal goods of the earth. It is cherished early by all creatures from the least to the most aware, above all by rational beings. It is an extremely protected right in any law, as even the laws of our own realm make clear. They oblige us to judge for liberty in doubtful cases, not against it. The same is true in the [canon] laws of the Church. [147] Free men will not accept any impairment of their freedom, unless it comes from their free choice and not from force. Anything that happens apart from choice is force—violent, unjust, perverse, null and void according to the natural law, since it means making free beings into slaves. There is no greater harm [to life] than this except for death itself. If you cannot take the goods of free and innocent people away from them justly against their wills, much less can you plunder them, rob them of their state of free human being, usurp their liberty. This is beyond comparison to any value or reputation. If a father cannot put a child up for adoption against the wishes of the child, even should the adoption be for the benefit of the child who might thus inherit all (or at least the statutory quarter) of the wealth of the adopting parent, then surely the king cannot transfer or donate his subjects to a lesser lord, stripping them of their relationship to the crown. The parental power a father has over a child is a more ancient one, a more fundamental one. It is of nature and absolutely necessary. It is not based on the consent of the child but on the structure and force of nature itself. The power of a king over his subjects, developed more recently and by the law of nations, is based on the free consent of subjects, and thus does not have the force of nature nor of absolute necessity. If the currency of the realm cannot be changed without the consent of cities and subjects who live therein because of a possible, serious damage which could come to both (as in the appropri-

---

[147] *Decretals*, lib. 2, tit. 27, cap. 26, *De sententia et re judicata*, last canon [Friedberg, 2:409]; and *De probationibus*, lib. 2, tit. 19, cap. 3 "Ex literis" [Friedberg, 2:307].

ate canon [148]), much less can the cities and subjects be given away, put under another lord and lordship with enormous damage, prejudicial to their liberty. Beyond this, if tenant farmers and serfs, according to Your Majesty's laws, cannot be transferred to the control of other masters, to make sure that their state in life is not worsened and their living made more bitter, much less should it be allowed to transfer totally free people to other masters who are not the king, from whom they could receive any threat great or small to their freedom, any harsh and terrible treatment. It is a huge threat to the liberty and life of peoples to be under many masters. They increase both workload and taxes, as I argued in the previous segment, even if such masters rule justly, something we cannot presume or expect from most of them.

Therefore, if it is in the best interest of princes not to lose their subjects, nor allow them to diminish in number, nor allow the shrinking of goods and services they get from them, then to a much greater degree, it is in the best interest of subjects not to be transferred to some other, lesser lord, not to be deprived of the direct, benevolent protection and control of the prince. For the difference is [well] known between the rule of kings and lesser authorities. It is the latter that people abhor and run from as from something that threatens serious harm. By contrast, it is always the former, the rule of kings, that they love and eagerly want. For this reason people usually think it a harsh and bitter servitude, a real damage, a cause for revolt, to be deprived of direct royal rule and jurisdiction, to be put under the control of lower authorities. Every law that is just, every learned legal opinion without exception, holds and asserts that such alienation is cruel and cannot happen. In the laws of the kingdom of Castile, it is set down firmly that the king cannot cede or alienate cities or towns or districts or fortresses or villages, boundaries or jurisdictions from the crown. The law sets down the following conditions, among others, for alienation: not unless representatives are summoned from six cities of the province where the transfer is to take place. Should the transfer be done any other way, it must be considered null; and neither sovereignty nor the subjects are transferred by virtue of that decree; and the said subjects can, without fear of reprisal, resist with force such a transfer. It does not matter what the royal charters say; the grants, the warrants are invalid on their face, though they contain primary and secondary authorization and all sorts of attached threats and punishments. The law is set up truly and justly. It presumes there are deceits, that those deceits are squarely opposed to the common good.

---

[148] *Decretals, De jurejurando*, lib. 2, tit. 24, cap. 18, the canon "Quanto" [Friedberg, 2:365].

Lastly, it is a general rule that a prince cannot do anything which would bring harm on his people unless his people consent. I see Your Majesty, out of a sense of justice and rightness, following the custom set by the Catholic Kings, your grandparents, and acting everyday to convoke a general assembly and summoning representatives to come to it. And so I am arguing that to grant the Indians to the Spaniards in encomienda, or as hereditary serfs, or as anything else, would be a servitude so harmful, so gross, so outlandish, so horrible, that it would ruin them, would debase them from their state of being free and human in teeming cities, to a state of decimated cities and abject enslaved beings—not only that, but to the condition of brute beasts. And it does not stop until the Indians are dissolved like salt in water and disappear totally in death, as I said earlier. It makes obvious sense to say this could not, cannot be done to them without their consent, without each and every one of them submitting to the servitude by their own free wills. In addition, not only is such subjection and alienation contrary to right reason, to natural law and justice, contrary to charity, it is also a despotic and cruel imposition, it is horrible. That is very clear from what I said earlier! Such treatment is equally against God and God's law. It is a shameful insult to God's holy faith, a choking of it, a harsh attack on it, because it keeps the faith stunted and not growing as it should grow among those peoples. It stifles the preaching of the law of the Gospel. The Son of God said the opposite: "Let this Gospel be preached in the whole world." (*Matthew* 24:14) He ordered it in the strictest, most binding sort of command, that the Gospel should be preached under pain of mortal sin and eternal damnation: "Go into the whole world, preach the Gospel to every creature." (Mark 16:15) "Go forth, teach all nations." (*Matthew* 28:19) What is more, such treatment leads to the total, absolute ruin of all those communities, to the complete depopulation of the New World. It is Your Majesty's duty to watch over it, shelter it carefully, defend it, preserve it. The care is called for by the divine law of charity and love of neighbor, as befits a Christian prince. The preservation is called for by the charge, the mission imposed on you by the Vicar of Christ's command. Therefore all the sufferings, all the deaths among the Indians result in damage to, in the loss of honor and revenue for both the royal crown and the royal coffers.

For these reasons, for the horrible results which derive from subjecting the Indians to the Spaniards, even if the Indians should want to submit freely and consent to such a radical debasement of their state in life and total loss of freedom, as they lose it now—even if they should, such a consent would be null and void, they could not agree to it! On the contrary, Your Majesty would be required by divine law to interdict the granting of the Indians to the Spaniards in encomienda. It truly entails bitter enslavement, tyrannical oppression. How much more, then, is the requirement on you to forbid it, to stop it, to root it out from every corner of those lands, like some lethal, contagious disease loose inside the whole area. Granting encomiendas is in such violent, hateful opposition to the will of those peoples, is such a wicked grievance to them, that it is to the point where countless Indians, men and women, have despaired and killed themselves. Many have ingested poisoned food or drink which then kills them. Many have fled to the forests where wild beasts destroy them. Many, from pure sorrow, seeing that their bitter and burdened lives will never know joy or relief, wither away, they shrivel and die. I have seen it happen right before my eyes. I know a man, a Spaniard, with a reputation for absolute contempt for the Indians, for absolute cruelty. Because of him, the story goes, more than two hundred Indians on the island of Haiti killed themselves in the ways I just said, by taking a liquid made from poisonous roots. A like number on the island of Cuba hanged themselves because of the same man.

Furthermore, to every people and place under authority in this world there belongs the universal right and privilege not to have their rulers transfer or surrender royal, hereditary power over them to some lesser power. That is a fundamental rule of basic justice and basic reason. Yet in spite of this, sometimes rulers, when they are under extreme pressure, do just the opposite, with or without benefit of law. They give up part of the realm. They cannot avoid doing so. And one could argue that if they could avoid doing so they would. Therefore, since maybe they incurred huge debts in defense of the state, they compensate or have compensated their subjects in other ways for the damages they have caused them because of the debts. But in no way can nations and peoples in the New World be recompensed for the unbearable, incalculable, calamitous, irreparable harm that comes from being parceled out wholesale in the encomienda or turned into hereditary serfs of the Spaniards. It is no less than their souls that they lose along with their lives, as everything I have treated in this discourse shows clearly. Rather, one hopes first to attain, from the rule exercised over them by Your Majesty, the light of faith, the conversion and salvation of all those Indian souls. This is why the matter must be discussed, must be judged, must be decided according to divine and natural law, not according to any human law. Unless it should be a law made in favor of the Indians that would be based on right reason, as jurists tell us.

What is more, given the special case mentioned earlier, it is the privilege, the right, of their free wills to accept Your Majesty's lordship. In such an acceptance, they are going to agree to and enter into, with Your Majesty, a most favorable contract, the most apt and helpful condition they can have for making their own civil life more secure, more worthwhile, stronger, more lasting. And Your Majesty has to swear a solemn oath to them, as princes usually swear an oath to free peoples and kingdoms when they accept some new ruler over them. And princes have always done so since humankind began to spread across the face of the earth. It is reasonable and just for them to do so. Holy Scripture speaks of it and approves it as good.

For that reason, for all the reasons and explanations given, beyond the common, the universal reason I just outlined, I now advise Your Majesty with reverence, with respect, with the humility due such a noble ruler of so many subjects, especially from me. Your Majesty cannot in any way dispense with the oath, that is, you cannot allow the Indian villages and peoples to be parceled out and granted to the Spaniards in the encomienda system, much less to be given as hereditary serfs. The reason: who can sentence a guiltless continent to such a cruel death—political, physical death—without a hearing, without a defense, without a verdict, in the absence of the condemned, whose death then unleashes a flood of evil and destruction? That would be to dispense with divine and natural law without a just and legitimate reason. In fact, it would breach both laws, breach the express command of Christ, to the great damage of our Faith, to the hurtful restriction of divine worship, to the total destruction and disappearance of a greater part of the human race. There is no ruler on earth, neither temporal nor spiritual who holds the absolute or statutory power to do this, wholly or in part, without mortally offending the Divine and Sovereign Majesty. No ruler has the almighty power from God, through whom all live and rule, to destroy people, to destroy God's church, and so offend Him. Rather rulers have power in order to build up a people, to foster them and the Church, and to serve God in it. Therefore, the Indians must not be granted to the Spaniards, in the encomienda system, nor as hereditary serfs, must not be cut off from the royal crown in any other way. They are free peoples by the power of nature itself.

- 3 -

Selections from the New Laws of 1542[149]

[Primary Policy]

The preservation, the fostering of the Indians, has always been the primary purpose of our policy, and that they receive instruction in matters concerning our Catholic faith, and that they be treated exactly as the free peoples they are, as our vassals. Therefore we impose the responsibility on our Counsel to pay close attention to, and to take special care concerning the preservation of the Indians, the right governance of them, the good treatment, and to be cognizant of how to carry out effectively what we have commanded or will command concerning the good government of our Indies, and the administration of justice in them. [The Council] is to see that [our commands] are kept, are carried out fully without any flagging, faultiness, or neglect.

Thus, since the major focus of the Audiencias [High Courts] in all the important matters they deal with in our service is to watch very carefully over the good treatment of the Indians and their preservation, we command them to inform themselves constantly concerning the violations, the bad treatments which, in the present, in the future, are inflicted on the [Indians]

---

[149]My translations are from the Spanish text of the New Laws as they occur in Alonso de Santa Cruz, *Crónica del Emperador Carlos V* (Madrid: Patronato de Huérfanos de Intendencia é Intervención Militares, 1923), Tomo IV, cap. XLIII, pp. 222-36. I have added the captions. The chapter in Santa Cruz follows immediately upon the one describing the intervention by Las Casas before the King and Reform Commission, so Santa Cruz, Charles' contemporary and chronicler, indicates the parentage of the New Laws by his alignment of materials.

by governors or private individuals, and the way the same people have observed the rules and regulations they were given concerning the good treatment of the Indians. And in cases where there is violation, present or future, the Audiencias will, from now on, correct the situation, punishing the culprits severely within the limits of the law. And they should not allow that, in cases between Indians or against them, ordinary procedures be followed or postponements be allowed, as usually happens due to the malice of some lawyers and prosecutors. Instead, the cases shall be determined forthwith in accord with Indian custom and usage provided these are not clearly unjust. And the Audiencias should see to it that lower court judges keep to this practice.

[Prohibition of the Enslavement of Indians]

Item: We ordain and command that from this day forward, no Indian may be enslaved for any reason whatsoever, war or anything else, even if the reason is rebellion, or commercial exchange or anything else. And we desire that Indians be treated as vassals of ours, of the Crown of Castile, since that is what they are.

No one may use Indians under any title—naboria, tapia, or any other—against their will.

Since we have put in place the command that no Indian, from this time on, can be enslaved for any reason, and we include those who, up to this time, have been enslaved contrary to reason and the law, and contrary to rules and regulations already provided, we order, we command that the Audiencias call the parties before them and just on the basis of the known truth, should set the Indians free then and there if the slave owners do not show legitimate title to their possession. And since we do not want Indians to remain unjustly enslaved due to a lack of advocacy on their behalf, we command that the Audiencias appoint people who will represent the Indians in this matter. These representatives are to be paid out of the Treasury's income from fines. They are to be trustworthy and diligent people.

[Prohibition of the Abuse of Indians]

Item: With regard to the use of Indians as packbearers, we order the Audiencias to take a special care that they be not so used. Or if such use of them in some places cannot be avoided, it should be such that no threat to life results from excessive weights, nor to the health and preservation of said Indians. In no case may they be used against their wills or without pay. The Audiencias shall punish severely anyone who contravenes this law. There are to be no exceptions made for people of rank.

We have been told that pearl fishing has been conducted without suitable controls so death has resulted for many Indians and Blacks. We therefore order, under penalty of death, that no free Indian be brought to the fisheries against his will. And the bishop and the judge assigned to Venezuela shall order what they consider will preserve the slaves, both Indian and Black, who go to the fisheries, and what will stop the deaths. And if they decide that the danger of death cannot be avoided for both Indian and Black, then pearl fishing should cease. We place a far higher value—it stands to reason—on the preservation of their lives than on any income we might derive from pearls.

[Prohibition of the Allotment of Indians]

Disorders in the treatment of the Indians have resulted from their being held in encomienda by viceroys, governors, vice-governors, officials of ours and prelates, monasteries, hospitals, houses, people connected with houses of religion as well as mints and the money thereof, officials of our treasury as well as others favored because of their offices. It is therefore our will and command that all the Indians such people hold, whatever their title, their reason, be placed immediately under our royal crown. [We refer to] people who were or are viceroys, governors, vice-governors, to our officials of whatever kind, of justice or of treasury, prelates, houses both religious and civil, hospitals, confraternities and such like, even though the Indians were not granted them in encomienda by reason of their offices. And even though such officials and governors should say they would prefer to relinquish their offices and governorships and thus retain their Indians, let this do them no good, let it not allow the avoidance of what we command.

Furthermore, we command that all those people who hold Indians without title, but have taken possession of them on their own initiative, should give them up and place them under our royal crown.

And due to information we have received that other people, though they have title, have allotments given them that are all out of proportion, we order the Audiencias, each in its own jurisdiction, to look into this very diligently and with all dispatch, then reduce such allotments to these people to an honest and moderate number, and immediately place those who remain under our royal crown, never mind any appeal or protest that may be lodged by the people affected. And the Audiencias shall send us a brief report of actions along this line that they have taken so we may know how our command is being carried out . . .

[Prohibition of the Brutal Encomienda]

In the same fashion, the Audiencias are to find out how the Indians have been treated by the people who have held them in encomienda. If it is evident to the Audiencias that the encomenderos should be deprived of their Indians due to the abuse and bad treatment they have meted out to them, we order that the Audiencias take the Indians away and place them under our royal crown . . .

Furthermore, we order and command that from this time on no viceroy, no governor, Audiencia, discoverer, or any other person may allot Indians by a decree of ours, or by giving them up or giving them away, by sale, by any other manner or form, neither those without owner nor those inherited, but rather, when the encomendero of said Indian dies, they are to be placed under our royal crown. And the Audiencias are to take pains to find out, right away, the particulars about the person who died—what kind of man he was, his merits, his services, how he treated the Indians he held, if he left wife and children or other heirs. And the Audiencias are to send me a report on their findings, and on the quality of the Indians and of the territory, so we may make provision for what is in our interest, and grant the favors we think best to the wife and children of the deceased. But if in the interim the Audiencia judges that provision for some support must be made for the wife and children, it may do so from the tribute the Indians will be required to pay, some modest amount for the wife and children, the Indians being incorporated under the crown, as stated above.

[Provision for Just Treatment of Indians]

Likewise, we order, we command that our above mentioned president and auditors take great pains to see that the Indians who are or will be freed from encomenderos in whatever way be well treated, and instructed in matters of our holy Catholic faith, as befits free vassals of ours. This is their main task, it is the one we will mainly judge them on, the one in which they can serve us best. And they shall see that the Indians are governed justly, in the way and manner used to govern those who are under our royal crown in New Spain.

[Regulation of Spanish Behavior in Discoveries]

One of the things we have been told about that has involved disorder, and will involve disorder in the future, is the manner of making discoveries. We therefore order, we command that the following procedure be adhered to: whoever wants to do exploration by sea shall request a license, he can explore and barter, but not bring out any Indian from the [islands] or mainland he may discover, even though he may claim they were sold him as slaves, and even though that may be true—make an exception perhaps for three or four interpreters—and even though the Indians of their own wills wanted to be sold, [he may not] under penalty of death. And he may not take or possess a thing without the consent of the Indians, only that which is through barter and in the presence of a person the Audiencia shall appoint. A discoverer shall keep the rules and regulations given him by the Audiencia under penalty of total loss of his goods, and his person shall be at our mercy. And a discoverer shall be told that wherever he goes he shall take possession of the area in our name, and he shall report back the location.

[Special Protection for Island Indians]

It is our express will and command that the Indians who are still alive on the islands of San Juan and Cuba and Hispaniola, for now, and for as long as we command it, shall not be troubled by the imposition of tribute or other services, public or private or mixed, any greater than those imposed on Spaniards who reside on the island. And they shall be allowed leisure in order to increase in number more effectively, and to be instructed in matters of our holy Catholic faith. For the latter, they are to be provided with religious personnel, those capable of achieving such a goal.

- 4 -

True Sovereignty Is from Consent

Prenote

The New Laws set up a gradual abolition of encomienda. That meant, for Las Casas, abolition of Indians before they could benefit. And the question concerning the right of the crown to allow such a system to go on arose in him again, and in his co-worker Andrada. In their joint letter of 1543, they returned to a basic theme—Indians are free, nothing justifies their conquest, therefore nothing justifies the disposition of them by way of encomiendas. Spain has a right only to serve as an agent of conversion, and that conversion can never justify the use of force.

To legitimize your royal claims to those peoples and lands, to make those claims legal and secure, and have them be lasting and beneficial, we ask Your Majesty to order the following procedure examined to see if it isn't the way to do this. [150] An agreement should be negotiated between the native chiefs, leaders, people, and Your Majesty by means of friars and of men designated by the royal audiencias—not just any men, but those of discretion and common sense, men of conscience. The Indians should all be asked to accept being subjects of Your Majesty, subjects according to a kind which obliges Your Majesty to rule and govern them as free people, free vassals. And their consent must be free, made of their own accord, since the decision affects them all and they cannot be deprived of something rightfully theirs by natural law, i.e., liberty. And some things have to be made clear to them prior to their choice, about tributes, about rights, about royal rents they shall have to pay, to earmark for Your Majesty in the future as a recognition

---

[150] From "Memorial de Fray Bartolomé de las Casas y Fray Rodrigo De Andrada al Rey," *Opúsculos* XV (BAE 110), p. 183 a-b.

of the sovereignty you hold over them. These have to be imposed honestly, all fraud removed, and fear, and ignorance, and imposed in accord with law and reason and justice. And must be proportioned to the actual or potential impoverishment of peoples, and to what they grow, what they gather, what they possess. It must be made clear to them that the tributes, the rents, the royal prerogatives they will agree to and obligate themselves to provide, do not prejudice their own liberty, nor the authority of their own leaders. But these impositions are always to be so minimal, so light, that people know they are better off—and are therefore more likely to accept our holy faith—for having placed themselves under obedience to Your Majesty's rule and governance, than what they were before in the time of their paganism when deprived of the knowledge of our God. Our Christian religion will thus be an easy and light and lovable thing, as well as the yoke, the burden of Jesus Christ. Neither will be heavy, harsh, hateful, horrifying, as they have been in the past, and are in the present, on those, all of them, who have been force-converted out in the Indies.

- 5 -

Anti-Slavery Tract

Prenote

During his presentation of material to the reform commission in 1542, Las Casas brought up the matter of slaves and enslavement in the New World, arguing there were none truly made so according to any norms then used, e.g., captives taken in a just war, purchase of such human beings later, etc. The commission asked him to write up his evidence and conclusions and leave the document with them. [151] He did this by early 1544, at least a draft, to which he later added material when he came to publish the tract in 1552. The nature of the oppression in the New World includes wars of conquest, parcelling out natives in encomienda, brutalization through overwork, and now enslavement on a massive scale. What Las Casas adds later are corollaries in which he appeals 1) to the conscience of the King, 2) the consciences of bishops, 3) the consciences of the religious, to stand between the oppressed and their oppressors—i.e., abolish slavery, abolish encomienda, abolish wars of conquest. In the following excerpt from the Anti-Slavery Tract, Las Casas argues from evidence, from law, from moral probity.

Spaniards in Bad Conscience

The basic moral principles just outlined prove the third part of my argument thusly: someone owns something in bad conscience when the owner has it from someone else who knows he gained it in violation of justice, of the divine and natural law, or was in doubt or had to doubt about

---

[151] See *Tratados*, vol. 1, pp. 559-595. I have placed all citations in footnotes to clear the text for easier reading. For the history of the manuscript, see Wagner-Parish, Catalogue # 23, pp. 270-1.

ownership. [152] But the Spaniards who own Indian slaves, who were bought as slaves or given as barter, or given as tribute, or as gifts, or had from other Indian in any other way, these Spaniards got them knowing that they were enslaved mostly in violation of justice, of the divine and natural law, or there was a doubt, or there had to be a doubt. Therefore Spaniards who own Indian slaves gotten from Indians themselves own those slaves in bad conscience. The major premise of the argument is clear and no one doubts the first part of it about someone who knows. Since the one from whom the present owner received the goods had no legitimate rights to the goods, he could not transfer ownership, nor make a gift of it, nor sell it to anyone else. The reasoning is that no one can transfer more of a right to a thing than the right he has, and if he has no right to a thing, he can transfer no right at all to it. [153] A man who knows that the goods he gets are not owned by the one who gives or sells them, the man who buys them or accepts them knowingly, becomes as evil as the one from whom he gets them; if the goods are stolen, he becomes a thief; stolen violently, he becomes a thug; run down the list of vices. That man is an owner in bad conscience. The reason is he is a thief and is in a state of mortal sin while he keeps hold of someone else's goods against the owner's will. And there is always thievery in delay. [154] Even if the goods pass through a thousand hands, a thousand people, they are all owners in bad conscience, as much as the first. [155] Whoever has his hands

---

[152] *Tratados*, vol. 1, pp. 501-641.

[153] This is proven in the law "Nemo" from De Regulis Iuris [*Sext*, lib. 5, tit. 12, no. 79 (Friedberg, 2:1124)]. Also in the law "Tradi[c]tio," from "De Adquirendo Rerum Dominio" [See Paul Krueger, rev. and ed.; ed. Theodore Mommsen and Rudolph Schoell, *Corpus Iuris Civilis* (Berlin, 1928, 15th ed. Hereafter, Krueger), *Digest*, lib. 41, cap. 1, no. 20 (Krueger, 1:693a)]. Also in [*Gratian*,] Causa I, Questio 7, [cap. 24,] the law "Daibertum" [Friedberg, 1:436-7]. And in the law "Nuper," from "De Donationibus Inter Virum et Uxorem" [*Digest*, Lib. 24, cap. 1, no. 42 (Krueger, 1:353b)]. No one can give what he has not got. See "Quod autem," from "De Iure Patronatus" [*Decretals*, lib. 3, tit. 38, cap. 5 (Friedberg, 2:610-1)].

[154] As is clear in the law "Qui ea mente," from "De Furtis" [*Digest*, lib. 47, cap. 12, no. 66 (Krueger, 1:822a)]. And in the law "Si res," from [*Gratian*,] Causa 14, Questio 5 [6, cap. 1 (Friedberg, 1:742-3)]. And in the rule "Peccatum," from "De Regulis Iuris," book 6 [*Sext*, lib. 5, no. 4 (Friedberg, 2:1122)]. See also the law "Si pro furi," from "De Condicione Furtiva" [*Digest*, lib. 13, cap. 1, no. 7 (Krueger, 1:207a)].

[155] See the law "Sed ubi," from "De Minoribus 25 Annis," [*Digest*, lib. 4, cap. 4, no. 15 (Krueger, 1:88a)]. And the law "Sed etsi," from "De Hereditatis Petitione," at the words "Si ante litem," a good text [*Digest*, lib. 5, cap. 3, no. 25 (Krueger, 1:115a, lines 23 ff.)].

on such goods is obliged to restitution. [156] He is not freed from bad conscience nor from being an owner in bad faith because some law or statute says whatever he buys on the open market he truly owns. The reason is that human law cannot abrogate the divine or natural law, nor work against civilized behavior which forbids theft or the possession and retention of another's goods against his will. The lesser authority, the kings on earth, cannot set a law against the law of God who is greater than all. In laws made by lesser powers, the laws of superior powers are always understood to remain in force. [157] The obligation to restitution is clear from a law already cited. [158] And restitution of profits made on stolen goods, as required by the same law. [159] The bad faith owner cannot demand back the price he paid for the stolen goods, even if law or statute should permit the opposite. The reason is the same, it is against civilized behavior. [160]

It is not only the one who knows he buys stolen goods that becomes a thief with the thief, but also the one who suspects or should suspect or is really obliged to suspect stolen goods—the other facet of our major premise—and makes no effort to resolve his suspicion before he looks at or buys said goods. That is pure negligence not to do what one must, what one

---

[156] As is clear from the law "Gravis," from "De Restitutione Spoliatorum" [*Decretals*, lib. 2, tit. 13, cap. 11 (Friedberg, 2:284)]. Also in the law "In re futura [read 'furtiva'] from "De Condicione Furtiva" [*Digest*, lib. 13, cap. 1, no. 8 (Krueger, 1:207a)].

[157] See [*Gratian*,] Distinctio 8, [cap. 2,] the law "Quae contra" [Friedberg, 1:13-4)]. And the final law from "De Presumptionibus" [*Decretals*, lib. 2, tit. 23, cap. 16 (Friedberg, 2:358-9)]. Also [*Gratian*,] Distinctio 9, cap. 1 [Friedberg, 1:16], and [*Gratian*,] Distinctio 10, cap. 1 [Friedberg, 1:19]. Also [*Gratian*,] Causa 11, Questio 3, [cap. 93], the law "Si Dominus." And the law "Iulianus" [*Gratian*, causa 11, questio 3, cap. 94 (Friedberg, 1:669)]. Also [*Gratian*,] Causa 28, Questio 1, [cap. 8,] the law "Iam nunc" [Friedberg, 1:1081-2)], and many another decree. Then the law "Ille a quo," at the word "Tempestatibus," from "Ad Senatus Consultum Trebellianum" [*Digest*, lib. 36, cap. 1, no. 13 (Krueger, 1:564b)]. Next, the law "Nam magistratus," from "De Receptis Arbitriis" [*Digest*, lib. 4, cap. 8, no. 4 (Krueger, 1:97a)].

See the law "Imperatores," from "Ad municipalem" [*Digest*, lib. 50, cap. 1, #38 (Krueger, 1:895b)], and the law "Imperialem," from "De Prohibita Feudi Alienatione," last paragraph, column 2 [*Codex*, lib. 4, cap. 51, no. 7 (Krueger, 2:183b)].

[158] "Si res" [*Gratian*,] Causa 14, Questio 5 [6, cap. 1 (Friedberg, 1:742-3)] and the rule "Peccatum" [*Sext*, lib. 5, no. 4 (Friedberg, 2:1122)], and in the entry "Gravis" [*Decretals*, lib. 2, tit. 13, cap. 11 (Friedberg, 2:284)].

[159] "Gravis" [*Decretals*, lib. 2, tit. 13, cap. 11 (Friedberg, 2:284)]. And in the law "Si navis," beginning with "Generaliter," from "De Rei Vindicatione." [*Digest*, lib. 6, cap. 1, no. 62 (Krueger, 1:124a)].

[160] As the cited entry "Quae contra" says [*Gratian*, dist. 8, cap. 2, (Friedberg, 1:13-4)].

can, courageously. [161] That it is also pure negligence when one fails to act because of gross ignorance, inexcusable ignorance to use another name, is proven in the fifth principle outlined above. There we argued that it is sinful for anyone to act on what might involve sin without first resolving his suspicions. Gross and inexcusable ignorance occurs when people in their dealings with one another accept certain norms, especially the more learned and to all appearances the more pious people who, it seems, do not have selfish motives, people one could reasonably trust, yet through carelessness or mindlessness do not desire or desire minimally to find out about the truth, or make no effort at all, behaving with the blankness of a beast. It is to have no doubts when doubts are absolutely necessary. Any owner who owns anything gotten through such ignorance or mindlessness or carelessness is an owner in bad faith and his conscience is bad. The effects of such ignorance equals the effects of malice and fraud as both canon and civil law hold. [162] Hostiensis also treats the topic. [163] And much to the point here is what Iason says. "If anyone has consulted an expert and receives bad counsel, his error is excused from the punitive effects of law." [164]

Iason sets up four cases in which there is no such excuse. First, no excuse if someone holds a position which requires that he know the law, someone who calls himself or is a doctor or a master. Second, no excuse for someone unless in asking advice or opinion he asks many experts, not just one. Third, no excuse except for someone who asks for counsel or opinion

[161] As stated in law 8, Title 16, first part [Reference is to *Las siete partidas*, Part 1, tit. 16, l. 8. See Alfonso X El Sabio, *Primera parte*, ed. J. A. Arias Bonet et al. (Valladolid: 1975), pp. 339-40. For similar material, see *Digest*, lib. 47, cap. 2, passim (Krueger, 1:814-24)].

[162] Cf. the laws "Latae culpae," and "Magna negligentia," from "De Verborum Significatione" [*Digest*, lib. 50, cap. 16, nos. 223, 226 (Krueger, 1:918b, 919a)]. And the law "Apostolicae," from "De Clerico Excommunicato . . . Ministrante [*Decretals*, lib. 5, tit. 27, cap. 9 (Friedberg, 2:832)]. And [*Gratian*,] Causa 12, Questio 1, the law "Que in humanis" [See "Qui et humanis, Causa 12, Questio 2, law 24 (Friedberg, 1:695)]. And [*Gratian*,] Causa 16, Questio 1, [cap. 5,] the law "Si cupis" [Friedberg, 1:762]. And chapters 1, final paragraph, and 2, from "De Ordinatis Ab Episcopo Qui Renunciavit Episcopatui [*Decretals*, lib. 1, tit. 13, cap. 1 (Friedberg, 2:125a].

[163] In his Summa, "De Penitentibus Et Remissionibus," under "Quid de praedam ementibus," at the words "Si vero emens" [See Henricus Cardinalis Hostiensis *Summa Aurea* (Lyons: 1568), lib. 5, 430v, cols. a-b, for "Quid de praedam"; and col. b, for "Si vero emens."]

[164] More fully on the law "Quamdiu," column 2, no. 7. And on the following law, no. 4, "Qui Admitti Ad Bonorum Possessionem Possunt." And in the third column, no. 9, "Ubi super," the gloss [*Codex*, lib. 6, cap. 9, nos. 5 & 6 (Krueger, 2:247b)]. [For Giasone del Maino, see *In digestum et codicem commentaria*, Milan, 1519-1520. 8 vols.]

from good, sound, learned, believing people, people he knows have no conflict or interest, no ax to grind, no side to take, not those he knows are the opposite. Fourth, no excuse for someone who asks advice or opinion from those he really should be suspicious of, for some reason. In these four cases someone is not excused should he err through learned counsel and do something against the law. And someone who doubts about a fact should come under the same rules. I wanted to make explicit these four qualifications because a sense of them will help us greatly to orient ourselves concerning doubtful transactions, especially in cases of conscience among those who feel the burden of doubt and want to be rid of their scruples and calm their consciences about affairs in the New World. The major premise is established.

The minor premise has two parts. First, in most cases, Indian slaves acquired from Indian masters were enslaved unjustly, in violation of both divine and natural law. This is clear enough both from the proof of the first part of the conclusion and from the third premise. It will be made more evident as we proceed. No one denies it, not the culprits themselves, not their agents. No one denies that if some do own slaves legitimately, they are mighty few, unknown to themselves or to others, so even they must doubt their ownership.

Secondly, when Spaniards bought and held slaves, they knew the slaves were unjustly enslaved, or they suspected, or they simply had to suspect, which amounts to the same. [165] The proof runs thusly: every Indian slave the Spaniards had from Indian masters was gotten through levies they were forced to pay, what with the litany of cruel and inhuman treatment visited on them, or gotten through the variety of deceits, unheard of, unjust, wicked deceits described earlier in the proofs of the first part of the conclusion. No human being who looked at the evidence would deny that the slaves were given and gotten unjustly and both giver and getter knew it. Thus the present holders of slaves are in bad conscience. They either bought them from Indians or got them through exchange—the Spaniards call it that. They used much the same methods either way. They coerced the leaders, the elders, to sell them slaves or swap them some by threatening to accuse the

---

[165] See the argument in the law "Si culpa," at the words, "si scire debuisti," from "De Iniuria Et Damno Dato," where "know" and "ought to know" are made equivalent [*Decretals*, lib. 5, tit. 36, cap. 9 (Friedberg, 2:880)]. And also, from "Pro Emptore," the law "Qui fundus," at the word "Servus" [*Digest*, lib. 41, cap. 4, no.7 (Krueger, 1:709)], and from "Si Certum Petatur," the law "Quod te mihi," at the end [*Codex*, lib. 4, cap. 2 (Krueger, 1:150a-1a)]. And from "De Liberali causa," the law "Filium" [*Digest*, lib. 40, cap. 12, no. 31 (Krueger, 1:687a)]. And from "De Episcopali Audientia," the law "Si legibus" [*Codex*, lib. 1, cap. 4, no.16 (Krueger, 2:41)].

leaders, the elders, of idolatry—before they ever thought of being Christian—to charge them in court with adoring and sacrificing to idols. And since the chiefs did not have as many legitimate slaves as the robber Spaniard demanded—see the materials in the 1st premise—the chiefs gave them free people from the villages, that is made evident in the proof for the conclusion of the first part. The situation was so lawless, so rotten—and everyone knew it—like a ruckus, it had to come to Your Majesty's attention. And you had to send notice that in no way would you condone anymore the swapping. There were some chiefs, some Indians who sold themselves into slavery of their own will. But it is certain that there were few who did so. But buyers knew the sale was suspicious, and if they didn't they ought to have, and therefore their traffic in slaves before examining the facts of enslavement closely makes them, then and now, owners in bad faith. They took, they take slaves, they held, they hold slaves in bad conscience. The conclusion is certain. The Spaniards knew that a huge number of Indians had been unjustly and wickedly enslaved, and that those who might have been enslaved justly were so few, so difficult to single out they could not be known for sure. Therefore the Spaniards had to cease from this traffic until they could be sure the slaves were justly enslaved. No one can put their soul in danger of hellfire for the sake of some worldly gain. The proof of this may be found in what was said in the fifth premise, a proof also from the fourth premise, that if one took as doubtful the definite evil done by pagans, he would end up approving evil. That the Spaniards should have suspected, and as a result, should not have trafficked in slaves—even if some slaves were legitimately so—is substantially proven by the foregoing arguments. Nonetheless, I want to add further evidence to prove the point.

First, every dirty trick we described the Indians using, in the third premise, to enslave other Indians was clearly known by the Spaniards there at least in a general way. They knew from the constant, intense sharing of information and of attitude they had among themselves, from the dealings they had with the Indians and the implicit recognition of the corrupt trafficking in slaves the Indians carried on while they were still pagans and even more after the Spaniards arrived. They knew because they valued slaves, sought slaves eagerly, and certain wicked Indians were eager to provide them and quickly turned into slave merchants, against all justice, to please the Spaniards or get paid for it. The Spaniards knew the process was suspect. They had to. It is obvious that common knowledge is on a par with scientific knowledge when it comes to raising a doubt in a case. Baldo argues this.[166] He states that common knowledge weighs the same as certitude.

Second, the very judges of the Royal Courts who heard and passed judgment on the issue of liberty, who looked into the truth of the matter, set many an Indian free in individual cases of being held as a slave. The Council said positively it found not one Indian anywhere who was a slave in any just sense. These were public statements, both the judgments in favor of Indian freedom and the reasons the judges gave for them. So the Spaniards knew the traffic in slaves was suspect, they had to know.

Third, the religious, many of them—preachers, confessors, men who knew the Indian tongues and understood their ways—took pains to scrutinize this business of slaves very closely, publicly, privately, and frequently. In the pulpit and out of it they stated that there was not one Indian who was a slave by any just title. The Spaniards were duty bound to believe this type of man who got nothing out of what he said, who wanted nothing else than the salvation of souls. The statements of such men ought at least to have raised some suspicion among the Spaniards. Such opinion we say has a probability to it. Probability occurs when the wisest, the most experienced people, people of integrity who obey God's law, who have little to gain, when they, or a large number of them, consider something harmful or dangerous. (Cf. Aristotle in 1° of the *Topical Analyses*.) People generally, and ignorant people specifically, people without schooling, ought to accept and to follow in doubtful cases what the wise follow and counsel in matters where there is no danger. Or if there is danger, it is a lesser one and involves a smaller risk than its alternative. If the advice leads to error, the error is due to the condition of probability and those who erred in the case are not culpable. Those who do not follow advice, who make themselves their own authorities, then make mistakes in probable cases, have all the subsequent damages charged to them. The principle is operative assuredly in cases where unschooled people must, in matters of conscience, follow the more prudent path, avoiding the path, the danger of sin. Therefore, it is again absolutely clear that the Spaniards were duty bound to suspect the justice of their traffic in slaves.

Fourth, the Spaniards were eyewitnesses unavoidably of their own complicity. They made fearsome demands on the Indians. They threatened them, they bribed them to hunt out, sell, or swap them slaves. The hunters were pagans with no knowledge of God, nor love, nor fear, and though they took baptism, they could easily believe it was not sinful since the baptizers

---

[166] Re: the law "Cum in antiquioribus," Quaestio 3, "De Iure Deliberandi" [Baldi Ubaldi Perusini *In primam et secundam infortiati partem commentaria*, 104a "Si servus," and 104c "Si quis"].

did it also. Through greed for what they got, for what was promised, or fear for what was threatened, they turned corrupt, became more fanatic than before at stealing orphans, at tricking any simple mind they could, at applying brute force. As a result, they made many slaves, they sold many slaves to the Spanish Christians. We see here the overwhelming reason why the practice of unjust enslavement was more vicious after the arrival of the Spaniards than before they came. Not only did the Spaniards spur them on to greater violations of justice, they approved of their mortal sins. The kind described in premise four. The Spaniards could not ignore their own influence on so much evil behavior, nor their own complicity in it, they had to suspect, they had to raise conscience doubts.

Fifth, the Spaniards dealt with dubious elements. They, in their right minds, ought to have been suspicious, ought to have presumed the traffic between them was not right, was wrong, i.e., the buying and selling of Indians as though they were rightfully slaves.

For one thing, pagans were involved, they had to be dealt with cautiously so as not to run the risk of complicity in unjust acts. See premise four above. For another, there were quite enough reasons to judge negatively on the slave business. For yet another, the Spaniards knew, the situation was public knowledge: the Indians practiced deceit of all kinds during their pre-Spanish days in making slaves of free people. For the reasons cited, everyone suspected the Indian of criminal activity, the unjust enslavement of free people, and on a large scale, as we argued in the third premise—we showed there that everyone knew. The upshot is that the Spaniards had to have doubts, doubts at least about slaves they purchased, that those slaves sold them were not truly slaves. Their minds ought to have raised the doubt, it was a moral obligation. Because common knowledge needs no proof, the way scandal needs no proof. And Baldo says: "Public reputation establishes the truth, the nobility, the quality of someone." [167] And a statement of Innocent supports this: "A reputation for good or bad can be known through hearing what most people say." [168] Someone who is suspected of or charged with a crime is considered criminal in that

---

[167] As noted in the law "Quia nos," from "De Appellationibus" [*Decretals*, lib. 2, tit. 28, cap. 32 (Friedberg, 2:420)]. [Baldo] on the law "Providendum," in the section "De Postulando" [See *Codex*, lib. 2, cap. 6, no. 7 (Krueger, 2:98a); and Baldi Ubaldi Perusini *In I. II. III. Cod. Lib. Com..* 130c]. Baldo holds the same on law 1, col. 1, "De Testamentis" As does Alexander on the law "De Minore," paragraph beginning "Tormenta," from "De Quaestionibus" [See *Digest*, lib. 48, cap. 18, no. 10 (Krueger, 1:863b)].

[168] In the law "Licet," from "De accusationibus" [Innocentii III *Opera Omnia*, lib. 1, lit. 277 (Migne, *PL*, 214:232)].

regard. [169] Because the Indians were suspected criminals in the slave matter, they should have been judged such simply to avoid doing business with them about slaves. The fish fouls the hands of the fisherman, and *Ecclesiasticus* 13:1 says: "Whoever touches pitch gets blackened."

The presumption of law favors this viewpoint. It runs: whoever does something bad on purpose is presumed bad when he does it again. [170] Someone who lies under oath is suspect thereafter and must prove the contrary. Someone excommunicated is presumed to stay that way. [171] This presumption in law is a clear proof of our point. [172] Since Indians made slaves unjustly, not once, but often—as we have already proven—one has to presume that they traffic in slaves all the time. For, "One can presume usury is going on when the lender is an usurer." [173] Equally, if the merchant is a thief, presume that the goods he sells are stolen. The Indians used to steal free people and make them slaves wrongfully—that is a slaver—therefore a Spaniard in his right mind should suspect that the slaves sold him are stolen, and the ones who sell them are slavers. So the Spaniards who did business with these men for slaves should have known, should have feared the slime on their souls from this rotten catch of fish. Therefore they should have doubted, in conscience. It is clear therefore that the Spanish slave owners are inexcusable, they own in bad faith for not having made beforehand a close scrutiny into whether or not the people sold them were rightfully or wrongfully enslaved. On this subject, there is an excellent clarification by Jason. [174] He says that someone who is not sure of the person he does business with has no excuse if he does not first ascertain the character of the

---

[169] As is proven in the law "Venerabili," from "De Officio . . . Delegati" [*Decretals*, lib. 1, tit. 29, cap. 37 (Friedberg, 2:181)]. And in the final law of "De Accusationibus" [*Decretals*, lib. 5, tit. 1, cap. 27 (Friedberg, 2:748)]. And in the law "Licet heli," from "De Simonia" [*Decretals*, lib. 5, tit. 3, cap. 21 (Friedberg, 2:760)]. And other Doctors on this topic.

[170] It is the rule "Semel malus," from "De Regulis Iuris," Book 6 [*Sext*, lib. 5, tit. 12, no.8 (Friedberg, 2:1122)].

[171] As in the law "Parvuli," from [*Gratian*,] Causa 22, Questio 5, [cap. 14 (Friedberg, 1:886-7)], and the law "Si cui," at the word "Isdem," from "De Accusatione" [*Digest*, lib. 48, cap. 2, no.7 (Krueger,1:842a)].

[172] As the text says, and the rule, and the Doctors on the law "Si tutor," from "De Periculo Tutorum" [*Codex*, lib. 5, cap. 38, no. 5 (Krueger, 2:225b)].

[173] As is noted in the law "Ad nostram," from "De Emptione et Venditione" [*Decretals*, lib. 3, tit. 17, cap. 5 (Friedberg, 2:519)]. See also the law "[Quod-]Si nolit," at the words "Quia assidua," from "De Aedilicio Edicto" [*Digest*, lib. 21, cap. 1, no. 31 (Krueger, 1:309a for "[Quod-]Si nolit, and Krueger, 1:310a for "Quia assidua"].

[174] On the law "Quam diu," from "Qui Admitti Ad Bonorum Possessionem," col. 2, no. 7. [See note 164.]

one he wants to deal with. If he does not take such pains, then any harm which might follow from the deal would rightly be charged to him. It is according to that judgment you know the Spaniards in the New World are in a state of soul little less than damned because of all that they have done.

So let me draw to a conclusion the foregoing material. Look at every Indian the Spaniards held as a slave in the New World, at least in New Spain, and in New Galicia, in the Kingdom of Guatemala, in the province of Chiapas, in the Kingdom of the Yucatan, in the provinces of Honduras and in Nicaragua, in every other area where slaves were brought from the areas cited, or acquired from other Indians, taken as taxes or as tribute, or as merchandise—leave out of consideration the Spaniards who knew what they did, we know for sure they sinned mortally—the rest suspected surely, or felt pressure to suspect the justice of their slave traffic, they surely knew what we described in the fifth premise. They should not therefore have dealt in the purchase of slaves without looking into the deal scrupulously. Not one Spaniard did this. They flung themselves into deals with blind avarice. The result, they did not know, they did not care, they did not ask, they did not doubt. They committed a mighty sin, a sin of malicious deceit. So they fell into the viciousness the slavers were in who trapped so many free souls. So they are owners in bad faith. In bad conscience they retain their slaves, exactly as described in the third part of the conclusion. The description is provided with proof in the fifth premise and supported by the rest of this treatise. And a pertinent text from law further supports the conclusion: Whoever buys regularly from thieves gets to be considered a thief himself. "It is unlawful if you desire not to return acknowledged stolen goods however they were gotten from their owners. Be wary of such deals lest you become suspect both in the deal and in the theft itself." [175] Those who wittingly purchase enslaved free men risk the death penalty or other punishment the law reserves for such criminal behavior. [176]

This is what I mean, what I affirm of those Spaniards who knowingly accepted slaves from others to whom the Indians had first given them, though the slaves given had already passed through a thousand owners. The reason is that no man of all the men in the New World does not know or does not suspect the vicious nature of the slave trade. If by a miracle someone is found who is in good faith, it would be well to free that Indian on the

---

[175] It is in the law "Incivilem," from "De Furtis" [*Codex*, lib. 6, cap. 2, no. 2 (Krueger, 2:238a)].

[176] As is clear in the law "Favia [Fabia]," and in the last law of "Ad Legem Fabianum De Plagiariis" [*Digest*, lib. 48, cap. 15, nos. 1 & 4 (Krueger, 1:859a, 859b)] And the whole section under that title. For parallel material, see what is said in section 1, "De Furtis," by the Doctors [*Digest*, lib. 47, cap. 2 (Krueger, 1:1224-5)].

principle that he was thought a slave one time, sinfully, but is not anymore, and there is no need to drag him through an examination by the Royal Court in order to set him free. The owner has to go much further. He has to investigate every way he can, he has to know if those he possesses were enslaved justly or unjustly. Even if the Courts should judge the opposite to be true, they can be deceived, still the owner is not in good conscience if he refuses to free his slaves. This point is well argued by Innocent and other experts. [177] Further, the owner cannot demand back the price he paid for those he freed, not from the former slaves, not from the slavers who sold them. Proof of the first point was noted earlier. [178] As to the second point, the first bad faith owner is bound in conscience to make good on the cost. [179] This is what I hold. I also think it is what one should hold concerning Indians captured in the wars the Indians fought with one another before their conversion, the ones they then made slaves.

I have many more reasons than one to say this. Firstly: no one knows, no one can prove it was the rightful side of the war who made the slaves. It makes sense for us Christians to presume they were taken by the aggressors. Perhaps then the pagans will not think we enjoy and use things indifferently, be they good or bad, especially if they know they got their slaves through an unjust war. We must do this out of zeal for the honor and glory of God, for the reputation and credibility of our Christian faith. We have argued this in the fourth premise and by the commandment of St. Paul, rather the commandment of Jesus Christ made known by St. Paul (1 Corinthians 10:31-3): "So, whether you eat or drink or whatever you do, do all to the glory of God. Give no offense to Jews or to Greeks or to the Church of God, just as I try to please all in everything I do, not seeking my own advantage, but that of many, that they may be saved."

Secondly, in doubtful cases, one has to take the safest option, not the more risky one, take the one that offers the least possible harm. One must presume the slaves were not taken in a just war. The presumption tells against the Indians, they were without faith, they sinned many times in this matter of illegitimate enslavement, as we outlined in the fifth reason a short way back. The truth cannot be known. Therefore, that one should not consider those held to be true slaves offers the way of the lesser harm, lesser danger, less than what someone suffers in an unjust captivity. Less surely

---

[177] See "De Immunitate Ecclesiarum," the law "Qui plerique" [*Decretals*, lib. 3, tit. 49, cap. 8 (Friedberg, 2:656)].

[178] It is found in the law "Incivilem" [*Codex*, lib. 6, cap. 2, no. 2 (Krueger, 2:238)].

[179] See the argument in the law "Si rem," from "De Evictionibus" [*Digest*, lib. 21, cap. 2, no. 29 (Krueger, 1:315a)]; and the final law of "De Emptione Et Venditione" [*Institutiones*, lib. 3, cap. 23 (Krueger, 1:39a-40a)].

for the Spaniard who owns a slave. There are so many strong presumptions of guilt against him, he has been found guilty of complicity so often, that he merits perhaps the loss of his soul forever. Thirdly, the difficulty is insurmountable of sorting out who is and who is not. No one knows, no one can ascertain, no man of conscience would dare affirm that even one taken in the wars, much less the Indian wars, was a slave, of the hundred thousand, five hundred thousand Indians, of the huge number the Indians gave the Spaniards as gifts, as taxes, as merchandise, as barter. The point being that if one knew there were some among that vast number who were made slaves in war, how would one know which, how would one spot them, sort them out?

Fourthly, if we want to halt the liberation process by saying we should put it off for the many until we investigated the slavehood of the few, that would be prejudicial to the many. To let this happen is not moral according to the laws of justice and charity—we proved rather, in the sixth premise, that one cannot do good for the few while harming the many. Especially if the harm to the many means the loss of their freedom, and the good so petty for the one who pretends to keep slaves—like the loss of property or money, far less than liberty. By contrast, one must do good to the many, must judge them all worthy of freedom, even though some few ought to suffer servitude. In order to punish one who is guilty, you cannot make the many who are innocent suffer—that was shown in the sixth premise.

Fifthly, just talking about who might be real slaves is talking about imposing punishment, great punishment, enslavement, without knowing who the punishment is to land on. Everyone ought to be judged as free, there is less harm done that way, as we have often argued before.

Sixthly, it is not at all the same thing to be a slave of the Indians or a slave of the Spaniards. We proved that in the second premise. To be an Indian and a slave among Indians is to have a freedom a little less than the freedom of sons in the household. The life a slave leads under his owners, the treatment he receives, is gentle and kind. The life of a slave under the Spaniards is life in hell, there is no relief to it, no stop to it, no time to catch a breath from it. The standard treament is durance vile, and at the end of a few days in it, it becomes like a lethal disease. Therefore, given such a difference between being an Indian slave to Indians, and an Indian slave to Spaniards, and given that the Indian-to-Indian enslavement is according to law and custom, just ones in this case, and thus valid in matters of slavery and freedom, it is clear, from both givens, that Indian owners cannot hand over to the Spaniards greater rights over slaves than they themselves have. [180] If the Spaniards use the Indians slaves given them by Indians with such uncontrolled cruelty—even if they knew for sure the slaves were gotten in a just war originally—that the end result of this bestial servitude is certain death, then it is absolutely clear the whole thing is robbery and the Spaniards must make restitution. It is beyond measure, the cruelty the Spaniards inflict constantly on their slaves, they destroy them this way utterly.

We know from experience that no law, no argument, no rule would be enough to make the Spaniards moderate the harsh treatment they habitually mete out to their slaves, so they would not use more power over them than did the Indians who handed them over. Therefore, when someone is discovered among the Indians to be a slave legitimately, he should not be left in the hands of a Spaniard, not with any justice. It is rather the judgment of good men that the Indian should grant him only that right which the seller or giver had and could sell or give, separating it carefully from all that excess which the owner has no right or power to demand from him unless unlawfully. When the master of a household denies the necessary food to a legitimate slave, denies it so there is no escape in a time of sickness, so that the slave is doomed, from that moment on, according to human laws, the slave regains his freedom completely. [181] How much more reason there is for the Spaniard to lose his right to the little service the Indian we spoke of owes him? And for the slave to be freed from a great evil? He would perish inexorably in that terrible state. A lesser evil is the one we describe, i.e., the legitimate slave should pay the owner in other ways, and the slave should begin to know what freedom is.

Seventhly, both civil law and canon law insist on fairness and kindness when they treat this subject of slaves; we are told to lean toward the more benign opinion, avoiding the more severe, and among benign opinions, we are told to follow the more benign of the two. "We should be more eager to acquit than convict." "We should be more quickly benign than harsh. It is better to argue for mercifulness than for mercilessness." "Avoid any implacable verdict." [182] We call that opinion more benign which lets stand

---

[180] See the law "Licet," and what is said there by the Doctors on "De Coniugio Servorum" [*Decretals*, lib. 4, tit. 9, cap. 3 (Friedberg, 2:692)].

[181] See "De Latina Libertate Tollenda," the law "Unica," at the words "Sed scimus" [*Codex*, lib. 7, cap. 6 (Krueger, 2:295b-297a, esp. 296a, no. 3)].

[182] Cf. the law "Arrianus," from "De Obligationibus Et Actionibus." [*Digest*, lib. 44, cap. 7, no. 47 (Krueger, 1:768a)]. And the law "Respiciendum [read Perspiciendum]," from "De Poenis." [*Digest*, lib. 48, cap. 19, no. 11 (Krueger, 1:866a)]. And the law "Ex literis," from "De Probationibus" [*Decretals*, lib. 2, tit. 19, cap. 3 (Friedberg, 2:307)]. And the final section of "De Transactionibus" [*Decretals*, lib. 1, tit. 36, cap. 11 (Friedberg, 2:210)]. And the only section of "De Rerum Permutatione" [*Digest*, lib. 19, cap. 4 (Krueger, 1:291b)]. And Book 6, the section "De Iudiciis," the law

a sworn oath, a will, a liberty, religion, the marriage bond. That is called more benign which frees rather than binds. [183]

Many things follow clearly from the above: the laws favor liberty strongly; when there is a doubt of law, one has to rule in favor of freedom; should it be proven that one cannot know whether or not some slaves were taken in a just war, or made slaves for other legitimate reasons, then every one of the slaves we speak about, those gotten from Indian masters, and held by Spanish masters, must be set free without delay and necessarily; it is surely the more certain choice to set the many free without knowing clearly which are true slaves, and how many, though if the truth were known, if that is possible, they ought rightfully to remain slaves—set them all free rather than damn one, who ought to be free, unjustly to the horror that slavery is. We explained the norm for this above about the group accused of homicide. It is even more true for those countless ones who were lawlessly, mindlessly enslaved, whose liberty was robbed from them, ones we are certain of, we have no doubt of. We find so few, we may find none who are lawfully enslaved, and even the few doubtfully, not one in a thousand, even if we look for them closely with all our energy. In this situation, the rules expressed in the sixth premise come into play, i.e., one can, one ought to admit, and justly, certain exceptions because of certain conditions or certain explanations which are offered. If the conditions cease, the exceptions cannot be tolerated further with justice. Thus we can tolerate with justice and charity a sweeping solution, as in the case we are now discussing, rather than one which falls short of the necessary, and in many other cases too, we can choose the least harmful way. We have explained all this in the fifth and sixth premises.

With all I have said, all I have argued, I think I have proven the conclusion and its parts: all the Indians who have been enslaved in the New World overseas from the day it was discovered until today were enslaved unjustly. The Spaniards who hold the living enslaved today are, with few

---

"Placuit" [*Codex,* lib. 3, cap. 1, no. 8 (Krueger, 2:120)]. And [*Gratian,*] Causa 26, Questio 7, [cap. 2,] "Tempora penitudinis" (Friedberg, 1:1041-2)]. And see [*Gratian,*] Distinctio 86, [cap. 14 (Friedberg, 1:300)], the law "Non satis" [& cap. 18 (Friedberg, 1:302) for "Melius est"]. See [*Gratian,*] Distinctio 50, [cap. 14,] the law "Ponderet" [Friedberg, 1:182-3].

[183] This argument is in section 2 of "De Cognatione Spirituali" [*Decretals,* lib. 4, tit. 11, cap. 2 (Friedberg, 2:693-4)]; and in the law "Sunt personae," at the end, from "De Religiosis" [*Digest,* lib. 11, cap. 7, no. 43 (Krueger, 1:190)]. And see the law "Odia," from "De Regulis Iuris" in Book 6 [*Sext,* lib. 5, tit. 12, no. 15 (Friedberg, 2:1122)]. Also in the cited "Arrianus," from "De Obligationibus Et Actionibus" [*Digest,* lib. 44, cap. 7, no. 47 (Krueger, 1:768a)].

exceptions, in bad conscience, even if they hold slaves gotten from Indian masters. . . .

Second Corollary

The pastoral activities which a Bishop must perform as part of his episcopal office, as part of the salvation of his own soul, have to include in scope the defense, the protection of the people from any harm to, or oppression of their bodily selves, especially if such bodily harm threatens or might threaten the soul-safety of his flock. [184] The Indians whom the Spanish tyrants have enslaved and oppressed exist in just such a dreadful condition. Therefore by divine law, on peril of losing their souls, every Bishop in the New World must plead before the King, before the Royal Council, that the Indians oppressed by such unjust enslavement should be restored, be reconstituted in their natural, normal state of freedom. To clarify further an already clear conclusion: there is no tyranny, no oppression greater or harsher than the loss of liberty itself. There is no human quality more precious, more priceless, than individual freedom—that is certain from earlier arguments—no human quality more important for conversion to the faith in those who are not yet converted. And in those who have received the faith, for their budding life, liberty is crucial, or the newly converted will never reach maturity of belief.

The first part of the corollary is further proven this way: natural law, divine law, both require people to lift the burden of pain and oppression from those who suffer under its weight. For all the more reason should bishops, etc. Take natural law first. Anyone trapped in a painful situation would yearn to have someone come and free him from it. So he should do the same for someone else. Notice the phrase from *Matthew* 7:12, "Whatever you wish that men would do to you, do so to them." So it is natural for humans to love one another. That love shows up in a certain instinct of nature by which someone will help someone else, even a stranger, in a moment of crisis, e.g., recalling him to sanity, pulling him out of an accident, such like; so everyone becomes both family and friend. Then take divine law, clearly stated in *Deuteronomy* 22:1-3, "You shall not see your brother's ox or his sheep go astray, and withhold your help from it; you shall take it back to your brother. And if he is not near you, or if you do not know him, you shall bring it home to your house, and it shall be with you until your brother seeks it; then you shall restore it to him. And so you shall do with

---

[184] See *Tratados*, vol. 1, pp. 605-35.

his donkey; so you shall do with his garment; so you shall do with any lost thing of your brother's, which he loses and you find; you may not withhold your help." And *Exodus* 23:5, "If you see the donkey of one who hates you down under its burden, you shall refrain from leaving him with it, you shall help him to lift it up." And *Proverbs* 24:11, "Rescue those who are being taken away to death; hold back those who are stumbling to the slaughter. If you say, 'Behold, we did not know this,' does not he who weighs the heart perceive it? Does not he who keeps watch over your soul know it and will he not requite man according to his works?" And *Ecclesiasticus* 4:9 "Free the one who suffers harm from arrogant power." And *1 John* 3:17, "If anyone has this world's goods—goods of bodily strength, or charm or any other temporal value—yet closes his heart against his neighbor, how does God's love abide in him?" We conclude from the authority of Scripture that all of us without exception are obliged by the law of charity and by divine law to help and defend our neighbor from oppression, from injury, from injustice, from any evil whatsoever so much as we can, bodily evil, and spiritual evil even more so. There are many texts on the topic in canon law. Apart from these, there is a clear text which says: "It is right for someone to come to the aid of a neighbor or kinsman in order to ward off harm. In fact, if he can and does not, he could seem to be an accomplice of the criminal and an accomplice of the crime, etc." [185]

All of us, therefore, great and small, educated, uneducated, ruler and ruled, public or private individual, all of us are bound unconditionally to help the oppressed, to help those suffering under violence, injury, any evil, with whatever power we have, official or personal. We are bound to free them both by the law of nature and the law of charity. This is even truer of prelates and of other leaders, both secular and sacred. It is clear: all people, especially Christian people, are held to act by the law of nature and the law of charity—we know this, we have proven this. Sacred and secular leaders are bound by the common obligation, but even more by the bond of justice. They bound themselves tacitly to protect and defend the people committed to them from every evil when they took office. Thus the

---

[185] [*Gratian,*] Distinctio 86, [cap. 21,] the laws "Pasce," and "Non satis" [Friedberg, 1:302, 300]. And [*Gratian,*] Causa 23, Questio 3, cap. 7, the law "Non in inferenda" [Friedberg, 2:897-8]. And the last law [cap. 11, (Friedberg, 2:898)]. And "De Sententia Excommunicationis," Book 6, the entry "Dilecto" [Sext, lib. 5, tit. 11, cap. 6 (Friedberg, 2:1095-6, esp. 1096, "liceat cuilibet . . .")]. Also in "De Sententia Excommunicationis," the law "Quantas" [*Decretals*, lib. 5, tit. 39, cap. 47 (Friedberg, 2:909)]. Also the law "Sicut dignum," from "De Homicidio" [*Decretals*, lib. 5, tit. 12, cap. 6 (Friedberg, 2:794-6)]. St. Thomas treats this amply in *Quodlibet Quaestiones De Veritate*, q. 3, art. 1, in the body. It is a doctrine commonly taught by the Doctors of theology and canon law.

obligation is greater for prelates, for leaders, who hold the dignity of office, sacred or secular, over other human beings, to defend the poor and the oppressed. This is the most telling argument for the minor premise: if an obligation exists for people of lesser rank, private persons, it exists even more so for public persons, those who hold the dignity of office, as the sources argue. [186]

It is as if ecclesiastics make a contract with the Church, and secular rulers with a people or realm. They take on something like a contractual duty to rule their people or realm justly the moment they accept and assume their power to rule. This is clear in the law. [187] The same principle applies to princes and secular rulers of the people. The obligation is there to seek the good of their subjects, to ward off, to banish harm from them. They are the watchdogs of justice, according to Aristotle, *Ethics* 5. And public authorities must give an account to their subjects of what they do. This is a requirement, a principle of justice itself; a ruler is like a guardian, he is automatically obliged, nothing more ado, to do whatever is best for his ward, to avoid doing anything that might be harmful or hurtful. [188] The obligation begins with the reception of power. [189] Therefore if leaders do not defend the people they rule from invasion or oppression, if the people suffer harm from their negligence, the leaders must make reparation on pain of serious sin. It is the same with mercenaries in the defense of a city. They must repay whatever the loss there may be to those who brought them in if the people do not receive proper protection. It is the same with the captain of a ship. If the ship founders due to his negligence, he is liable for both ship

---

[186] The argument is made in the law "Quuum in cunctis." from "De Electione" [*Decretals*, lib. 1, tit. 6, cap. 7 (Friedberg, 2:51)], and in [*Gratian*,] Distinctio 38, [cap. 3,] the law "Si in laicis" [Friedberg, 1:141)], and in other places.

[187] [See] "Nisi cum pridem," from "De Renuntiatione," at the words "cui, santae Ecclesiae, sponsae tuae" [*Decretals*, lib. 1, tit. 9, cap. 10 (Friedberg, 2:107)]. On this, an important counsel, 146, beginning with the words "Sanctissimus dominus noster" [Reference unclear.] And Panormitanus on the law "Ex literis," from "De Pignoribus," near the end [*Abbatis Panormitani Commentaria* (Venetiis: Apud Iuntas, MDXXCIIX [sic]), Tomus Sextus, "De Pignoribus & Aliis cautionibus," cap. 5, "Ex literis," p. 149a]. And Felix on the law "Quae in Ecclesiarum," column 14, from "De Constitutionibus" [For law, see *Decretals*, lib. 1, tit. 2, cap. 7 (Friedberg, 2:9)].

[188] See the laws "Pro officio," and "Sequenti," in the section, "De Admittendis Tutoribus Et Institutionibus," from "De Obligationibus Quasi Ex Contractu," at the words "Tutores quoque" [*Institutiones*, lib. 3, cap. 27, no. 2 (Krueger, 1:41b-42b, esp. 42b)].

[189] See the gloss on the cited law "Pro officio" [Reference is not clear.].

and cargo. [190] There is an inexhaustible series of texts. It is as clear as day
in them that all the suffering which leaders bring down upon the people
under them is to be blamed on those leaders. Simachus says there is little
difference between your killing someone and your letting someone be
killed. [191] A man who could prevent the death of helpless people and does
not is an accomplice. Likewise there is complicity in vile servitude or other
horrors if someone who can remove the servitude does not. "The error that
is not resisted is approved." "It is a wretched shepherd whom the wolves
adore." "You lay the blame for the faults of subordinates more on their
careless superiors than on them. The superiors often fuel the disease under
the guise of applying a harsh medicine." "No doubt he is as guilty as the
doer who did not repair the situation when he could, for it is written that they
are accomplices to a deed who consent to others doing it, etc." [192]

Therefore since the bishops of the New World are required by
divine law on peril of their souls' salvation to abhor, to refuse to be
accomplices in, the mortal sins that shackle the tyrants who hold Indians
enslaved, they are therefore by divine law required to plead before their
King and his Royal Council for the restoration of natural liberty to all those
Indians who were wickedly deprived of it.

There is some reasoning I can add briefly to prove this first part. It
runs in three stages. The bishops are required by divine law to halt every
mortal sin they can in the people committed to their care. And not just the
commission of mortal sin which then entails a penance. They are also
obliged to act fully before the commission of mortal sin, to halt it happening,
as if the Bishop saw someone on the brink of sin, ready to commit it. [193]

---

[190] This is proven by the law "Si culpa," from "De Iniuria Et Damno Dato" [*Decretals*,
lib. 5, tit. 36, cap. 9 (Friedberg, 2:880)],and the first law from "In Re Mandata," i.e.,
"Mandati," where all commission and omission in a charge one has accepted are not
free of moral responsibility [*Digest*, lib. 27, caps. 1-2 (Krueger, 1:247-62)]. And in
the Law "Sancimus," from "De Iudiciis" [*Codex*, lib 3, cap. 1, no. 145 (Krueger,
1:122b)]. And "Et insti." from "De Obligationibus Quae Quasi Ex Delicto Nascun-
tur," no. 1 [*Codex*, lib. 4, cap. 5, "De Condicione Indebiti" (Krueger, 1:151b-2a), also
Institutiones, "De Obligationibus," etc., lib. 4, cap. 1 (Krueger, 1:43a-44b)].

[191] See [*Gratian*,] Distinction 83, [cap. 3,] the law "Providendum," of Pope Simachus
[Friedberg, 1:293].

[192] See the law "Error." [*Gratian*,] Distinction 83, [cap. 3, (Friedberg, 1:293)]. And
the law "Consentire" [*Gratian*, Distinction 83, cap. 5, (Friedberg, 1:294)]. And the
law "Nihil" [*Gratian*, Distinction 83, cap. 6,(Friedberg, 1:294)]. See also [*Gratian*,]
Distinctio 86, [cap. 1,] the law "Inferiorum" [Friedberg, 1:298]. And the law
"Facientis" [*Gratian*, Distinctio 86, cap. 3, (Friedberg, 1:298)].

[193] As is clear in the law "Novit," from "De Iudiciis," [*Decretals*, lib. 2, tit. 1, cap. 13
(Friedberg, 2:242)], and the laws "Cum sit," and "Licet," already cited from "De Foro
Competenti" [*Decretals*, lib. 2, tit. 2, caps. 8 & 10, (Friedberg, 2:250, 250-1)], along

The aforesaid Spaniards who own, who hold the aforesaid Indians slaves, unjustly, oppressively, in servitude, are in a state of continual mortal sin. Therefore as a way of doing penance, of preventing sins in the future connected with the tyranny of slavery, the bishops of the New World are obliged to plead with the King to compel the slave-owning Spaniards to set free the Indians they hold under that tyranny.

Fourth reason. All the bishops are required by divine law to make peace, tranquility, unity the basis of their peoples' lives. They are required to punish disturbers of the peace, to make them adhere to peace. [194] The reason is this: to be occupied in the service of God, people need peacefulness—we know from the weight of the facts that it is only in peacetime that one can serve well the author of peace. [195] And peace means exactly a state of calm and quiet. Isidore says this in *Etymologies*. Augustine says it in *The City of God*, Book 19, chs. 13, 14. Peace is the harmony of order among human beings. Everyone knows that in war, physical war fought by physical weapons, spiritual war fought in the will using the passions of anger or hatred, in either war, no one can attend to God, or do so in a good and fruitful way. One can scarcely avoid sin in physical war, one can never in spiritual war. It is primarily for the bishops to bring people to the service of God. It is for them also to remove every hindrance, every disturbance to peace. They are by divine law the principle ones who must lead people to peace, to friendship with God. The states of peace and friendship with God come most certainly when all mortal sin has been excluded. This is the first purpose of divine law, to make people love God, through charity, as the words of 1 Corinthians [13] state, the goal of the law is charity, its effect is

---

with what else the Doctors say. See also [*Gratian*,] Distinctio 93, [cap. 11,] the law "Diaconi" [Friedberg, 1:322)]. And [*Gratian*,] Causa 23, Questio 11 [4 sic], [cap. 24,] the law "Ipsa pietas." And [*Gratian*,] Causa 22, Questio 5, [cap. 8,] the law "Hoc videtur" [Friedberg, 1:884-5)]. And [*Gratian*,] Distinctio 83, the entirety [caps. 1-6 (Friedberg, 1:293-4)]. On this point there is a good gloss, praised by the Doctors, on the law "Ex literis" [*Decretals*, lib 4, tit. 1, cap. 7 (Friedberg, 2:663). See *Decretales Gregorii Papae IX Suae Integritati Una Cum Glossis Restitutae* (Venetiis, 1595), pp. 1013-4]. And also no. 2 from "De Sponsalibus" [*Decretals*, lib. 4, tit. 1, cap. 2 (Friedberg, 2:661)].

[194] See the law "Treugas," and what the Doctors note there, from "De Treuga Et Pace" [*Decretals*, lib. 1, tit. 34, cap. 1 (Friedberg, 2:203)]. And [*Gratian*,] Distinctio 90, [cap. 7,] the law "Studendum est episcopis" [Friedberg, 1:314)]. And the laws "Placuit," "Si quis," and "Precipimus" [*Gratian*, Distinctio 90, caps. 9, 10, 11 (Friedberg, 1:315)].

[195] See the supplementary text "Super cathedram," from "De Sepulturis In Communibus" [*Extravagantes Decretales Communes*, lib. 3, tit. 6, cap. 2 (Friedberg, 2:1273). Refers to *Clementinarum*, lib. 3, tit. 7 "De Sepulturis" (Friedberg, 2:1161-4, esp. 1162 "Super Cathedram")].

peace. As Paul to the Galatians [5:22-4] also says, "The fruits of the Spirit are charity, joy, peace, patience, etc." Love of God does not exist without love of neighbor, as it is stated in 1 John 4:20-1, "How can one love God whom he has not seen, and not love his neighbor whom he has seen? We have this command from God Our Lord: 'Whoever would love God, let him also love his brethren.'" Therefore bishops must foster and preserve this inward peace in the people they have charge of, by divine law. They have to do more than preserve physical peace, that is the job of the secular ruler. The bishops must be larger in their care, concern, watchfulness, that their people one and all should have this love toward God and toward neighbor. [196]

Thus since peace is the harmony of order among human beings, that harmony is preserved, according to St. Thomas in a passage just before the one cited above, when each person is given his due. That is justice. It is the reason Isaiah says in ch. 32:17, "Peace is the work of justice." Our own Spaniards would take away, in fact do take away daily, something precious not theirs to take, liberty, from thousands of human beings. On this account there should be, there has to be on both sides, a great disharmony, a great hatred, an undying rage. Or it is that the oppressed Indians are by their very nature so patient, so gentle. Perhaps for this reason in most cases they do not sin on their side. Though they are in anguish. They do weep, beg, groan, they do mourn because of the weight of the injustice laid on them, the weight of slave labor. As for their oppressors, there is no doubt at all, neither love for God nor love for neighbor is preserved, no peace! And as a consequence, the Spaniards foster a great sin, not just because of their oppression, their tyranny, but also because they place an effective block in front of the oppressed, the wretched Indians, to the acceptance of the truths of the Christian faith. Therefore the bishops overseas in the New World must, by God's law, if they wish to save their own souls, plead before the King and the King's Council that they be set free immediately, to be as they one time were, all the oppressed who are unjustly enslaved by the Spaniards in what is most often a hellhole condition. The conclusion is clear: it is that on neither side is there true peace, true love, no harmony of order. There is great disharmony since there is no justice; no justice because liberty is denied those with a right to it; liberty so precious to those who have it, who have a right to it, who had it taken from them, torn from them against all reason, all justice. So, there is no love of God. A great mortal sin arises on

---

[196] See St. Thomas on this, *Summa Contra Gentiles*, bk. 3, chs. 117, 128, and Gay [Cajetan], 12, q. 99, art. 2, and 3. Cf. also [*Gratian*,] Distinctio 45, [caps. 12 & 13,] the laws "Tria sunt," and "Due sunt" [Friedberg, 1:165)], and [*Gratian*,] "De Consecratione," Distinctio 2, [cap. 9,] the law "Pacem" [Friedberg, 1:1317].

the side of the oppressors. And the oppressed have almost no life of grace because they lack the knowledge of the faith, lack the leisure to learn it. We must judge in all truth that the diagnosis and the cure of such ills of the soul belong properly to the office of Bishop. Divine law makes it certain.

There is a fifth and last reason, it is briefer than the preceding ones. It is this: every single Bishop is obliged by God's law to give an account at the Last Judgment not only for the small, the ordinary people of his diocese, but also for his kings and princes, for the laws and statutes of the same, since in the realm of the spirit, in matters affecting the soul, every earthly, secular power is subject to the spiritual power. [197] Pope Felix says: "It will surely help you in your dealings if, when the cause of God is involved, you are ready to prefer the will of the priests of God to the will of the King, not the reverse, etc." "Who doubts that the priests of Christ must be considered the guides and teachers of kings and princes and all the faithful, etc." "The influence of the priests is so much the greater when they must give an account at the Last Judgment for their kings and for human laws." [198] This it is that in matters which affect the soul, civil law imitates canon law respectfully. The Emperor submits to a canonical arrangement as he himself says. [199] And civil law is said to be subject to canon law. [200] Since bishops do have to render an account of those deeds which are the doings of a public person or a kingly power, it is clearly incumbent on the bishops the duty of supervising royal behavior in its temporal effect upon their dioceses. As a result they must plead before King and Royal Council, not every now and then, but every time the needs, the necessities of body and soul in their flocks require them to. That is exactly what we are talking about in this report, the need to liberate countless victims from the hell of such slavery. So divine law singles out the bishops of the New World as the ones to plead constantly for liberation before the King and the King's Council, and plead passionately. Therefore these bishops are under obligation to do so, or risk the loss of their souls. The first part of the corollary is thus established.

---

[197] As is evident in the law "Omnes principes terrae," and the law "Solitae," from "De Maioritate Et Obedientia" [*Decretals*, lib. 1, tit. 33, caps. 4 & 6 (Friedberg, 2:196-8)]. And [*Gratian*,] Distinctio 10, [cap. 3,] law "Certum est" [Friedberg, 1:20].

[198] [See *Gratian*, dist. 96, cap. 9 (Friedberg, 1:340); and *Gratian*, causa 22, quest. 3 (Friedberg, 2:875); and Gratian, dist. 96, cap. 10 (Friedberg, 1:340); and *Gratian*, dist. 63, cap. 3 (Friedberg, 1:235).]

[199] In [aut.] "Ut Clerici Apud Proprios Episcopos" [pe. cola. 6]. [Krueger, 3:409a-410ab]

[200] As in the law "Super specula," from "De Privilegiis" [*Decretals*, lib. 5, tit. 23, cap. 28 (Friedberg, 2:868)].

Now for the second part, that the bishops, in order to bring about this liberation, i.e., to have his Majesty and the Royal Council free or order freed the Indians who were unjustly enslaved, the bishops should risk their lives if necessary to do so. It is proven by expressing it in terms of all the dangers, all the physical evils involved. At work here is the effect of spiritual death, eternal damnation, for the slaveholders, the Spaniards. They are in habitual mortal sin. The oppressed are also in danger of damnation, the Indians. They are bound in an unjust tyrannical enslavement and thus are denied the path to salvation. Therefore the bishops must expose their very bodies to any danger, even danger of death in order to free the souls of both masters and slaves. This conclusion is proven through the citation from St. John, ch. 10:11, "The good shepherd gives his life for his sheep." And the reasoning is as follows: in every obligation one must consider first the purpose of the obligation. The bishops take on the pastoral office for the purpose of saving the souls of their flocks. Thus when the salvation of the flock demands the presence of the pastor in person, that pastor cannot abandon his flock for any reason of temporal welfare or physical injury possible to himself—a good shepherd must even lay down his life for his sheep. [201]

We have now to prove the qualifying words expressed in this corollary. The bishops are obliged to plead for, to work for the liberty of the wretched, suffering Indians, in season and out, that is to say, their care and concern must be magnanimous. It is enough to quote St. Paul here to the Romans, ch. 17 [i.e., 12:8]: "Be the first one to care," and 2 Corinthians [i.e., Timothy 4:2], where he speaks especially to a bishop about bishops: "Preach," he said, "in season, out of season." And further on: "Be watchful, work hard at everything, etc." [4:5] All the Doctors strongly condemn neglect of the faithful by a Bishop as mortal sin. [202] There is no excuse for the shepherd whose sheep are eaten by the wolf if said shepherd says he did not see, did not know. It is his duty to see, to put every ounce of his strength into guarding his flock. The rule of law is: "No excuse for the shepherd if the wolf devours the sheep and the shepherd does not know." This is proven

[201] See St. Thomas, $2^a 2^{ae}$, q. 185, art. 5, corp. And [*Gratian,*] Causa 23, Questio 4, [cap. 12,] the law "Tres personas" [Friedberg, 1:902-3].
[202] See the treatment in the law "Ea quae," from "De Officio Archdiaconi" [*Decretals*, lib. 1, tit. 23, caps. 1-10 (Friedberg, 2:149-53)]. And in the law "Irrefragabili," from "De Officio Iudicis Ordinarii" [*Decretals*, lib. 1, tit. 31, cap. 13 (Friedberg, 2:191)]. And in "De Regularibus," last law [*Decretals*, lib. 3, tit. 31, cap. 24 (Friedberg, 2:578)]. And in "De Statu Monachorum," the law "Quum ad monasterium," at the end [*Decretals*, lib. 3, tit. 35, cap. 6 (Friedberg, 2:599)]. And in "De Accusatione," the law "Qualiter et quando," 1.2 penult. [*Decretals*, lib. 5, tit. 1 "De Accusationibus," cap. 17 Friedberg, 2:738-9. "1.2 penult." not clear.].

by the similar example of the bondsman Solomon gives in Proverbs 6:1-5. It seems to be the fuller meaning intended by the Holy Spirit. St. Gregory understands it this way in his comments on Ezechiel, Homily 11. He says as much in the third part of the pastoral letter, fifth admonition: "My children, if you have stood bail for your friend, you have given your word to a stranger. You are bound by your own words, you are held to them. Do what I tell you and free yourself because you have fallen into the clutches of the stranger; hurry, quickly, get hold of your friend, before you go to bed, before your eyes close, rescue the deer from the trap, the bird from the fowler's snare, be busy as an ant, etc." [Proverbs 6:1-6] If someone who stands bail for someone else in debt for money or property has to be very careful as the bondsman for that other, how much more careful must he be who stands bail for human souls, obliged himself to pay for their sins, their everlasting spiritual debts, with God to collect what is owed. [203] Genesis 31:40 writes about Jacob who had the duty of being a good shepherd. "By day the heat consumed me, and the cold by night, and my sleep fled from my eyes." Gregory argues from these words in Registro, Book 7, ch. 74: "So did Jacob watch and work to keep the flock of Laban. What watch, what work must there be for the one who keeps the flock of God, God's people." [204] The reason for burdening prelates with this watching and working for the care of souls is this: when one knows where the greatest danger is beforehand, there, most certainly, one must exercise the greatest watchfulness, the greatest care. [205]

[203] [For homily 11, see Migne, *PL*, 76:905-919; for 5th Admonition, see Migne, *PL*, 77:54-6.]

[204] [Migne, *PL*, 77:980-1 (Epistle 49)]

[205] See the law "Ubi periculum," from "De Electione," Book 6 [*Sext*, lib. 1, tit. 6, cap. 3 (Friedberg, 2:946-9)].

Part IV.

Defending
Pro-Indian Law

- 1 -

Rules for Confessors

Prenote

*Las Casas was named bishop of Chiapa in late 1543.[206] He accept-
ed in order to be able to enforce the provisions of the New Laws from an
exempt position. As a friar he was under obedience. He arrived in Chiapa
in 1545, and the place was a hornet's nest of resistance, both from settlers
and ecclesiastics. Las Casas' main strategy was to use Church sanctions to
back state policy, i.e., refusal of absolution to those who refused to
surrender their encomiendas or their slaving practices. After many a
fracas, Las Casas realized he could make no progress against the settlers'
intransigence, a crown official would have to manage the battle. So in
1546, he went to a meeting of the Bishops of New Spain in Mexico City.[207]
There he managed to have a second meeting of religious and confessors to
discuss the forbidden topics of encomienda and enslavement. For he knew
the law abolishing encomienda, the Law of Inheritance, had been revoked
in 1545. So during this time, he composed a set of rules for confessors, to
be used in his own diocese by trusted priests, and in the rules, he outlines
what was for him the true conscience position of Christians, and the
classical doctrine of restitution required of all who exploited and oppressed
other peoples. The rules were to be kept secret by the confessors, but they
were soon leaked and became a source of outrage among his opponents.
Their ultimate charge against him was treason—he denied the right of the
King of Spain to power over the Indies. At this point, Las Casas wrote a
Latin treatise,* De exemptione, *in which he defended ecclesiastical*

---

[206] See Helen Rand Parish, *Las Casas As A Bishop* (Washington: Library of Congress,
1980), pp. xi-xxiii, esp. xi-xiv.

[207] For a dramatic account of this period, see Helen Rand Parish's Introduction to *The
Only Way*, pp. 41-6.

*immunity, the right of clerics to maintain conscience positions and remain
free of coercion by secular power.*[208] *I do not think Las Casas really held
that Indian souls were damned to hellfire because Christians took away
their chances to be converted. Such a view was a traditional doctrine, and
Las Casas uses the doctrine on people who believed in it. His own
viewpoint is that God saves, preferably through sacraments and the Church,
but in default of these, through the inner law of charity inscribed in the
human heart. According to that norm, he saw many more conquered
Indians being saved than conquering Christians.*

For Confessors: A Manual of Rules and Regulations

Prologue

Confessors should keep to and judge by the following twelve rules
when they hear confessions of penitents in the Indies, or elsewhere of
penitents from the Indies, those who have been conquistadors overseas, who
have held or now hold natives by allotment, or had a share in the wealth
made from natives or through natives.[209]

The first rule, for present purposes, deals with three kinds of
penitents who come to confession: 1) conquistadors, 2) settlers who have
allotments of natives, those otherwise called *comenderos*, or those who
control *encomiendas*, 3) merchants, not every one, but those who transported
arms and provisions to the ones doing the conquering, the ones making war
on the natives, merchants warlike themselves in their cooperation. If it is a
conquistador, one who, close to death, wants to go to confession, call a
notary public or an official of the King before the penitent begins. The
confessor should make the conquistador declare, ordain, and grant the
following things: First, he is to agree and say that he chooses so-and-so for
his confessor, a secular priest or religious priest of x order. Then that the
conquistador is a believing Christian and wants to depart this life free of
offense to God and with clear conscience, thus to stand before the judgment
seat of God in a state of innocence. He gives his confessor complete power
over all those matters the confessor judges to pertain to his salvation—insofar as the penitent is able and is obliged to by divine and human
law in the discharge of his conscience. If the confessor should think, should
judge it necessary for the man to give back all he owns in the manner the
confessor judges best, leaving nothing at all to his heirs, the confessor is free
to do so. It is what the sick man, penitent man should do, would do freely,

---

[208] See *Las Casas en México*, pp. 65-68.
[209] *Opusculos*, XXVI, pp. 235-49.

if he were still alive, for the safety of his soul. As a dying man, he submits all he owns to his confessor's best judgment, without condition, without limit of any kind.

Second, the writer declares, admits he took part in this or that conquest or those wars against the natives in the Indies, was responsible himself or helped commit the robberies, the violences, the devastations, the murders, the enslavements of natives, and that the destruction of many cities and towns was done for that express purpose.

Third, the writer declares, admits that he brought no wealth from Castile. Everything he owns he owns from the natives, or through them, though some possessions come from his own labor. He admits how much the wealth is that he has from the natives, how much he owes them, what the damages are he has done them, or cooperated in doing since he came out to the Indies, and that far greater wealth than his would not suffice to pay them back. And therefore it is his wish, his final wish that the confessor he named should give it all back, should make total satisfaction, at least insofar as all his holdings could do it, as the confessor shall see fit for the man's soul, and to that end he binds the confessor in strict conscience.

Fourth, if the penitent should hold any Indians enslaved, whatever the way or the title by which he got them or keeps them, he is to give them their freedom instantaneously, and irrevocably, no ifs, ands, or buts. He is to beg pardon from them for the harm he did in making them slaves, in taking their freedom from them, or helping to do so, or in being an accomplice in the slave making, and if not in the slave making, pardon for having in bad faith purchased them, held them, used them as slaves. . .

Fifth, that the penitent revoke any other will he has made, or codicil to a will, affirming this will to be the only one he wants to have stand as valid and sound, and that it be obeyed as his last. . . . .

Sixth, the penitent is to make a solemn oath, in legal and binding form, an oath he will keep and fulfill, concerning all his goods, furnishings, holdings, that he consents to the disposition his confessor shall command to be made of all his material goods, nothing at all excepted. Should it happen that the penitent recovers from his illness, he will not revoke this will, in whole or in part, while he lives, nor at the end when he dies. . .

. . . After the penitent makes and signs the will as described above, the confessor then hears the confession. The confessor urges the penitent to have a deep, deep sorrow and regret for his enormous sins. They are the sins he committed, doing terrible damages and evils himself, or aiding them to be done, harrassing the natives, robbing them, killing them, depriving them of their freedom, of their authority, of their womenfolk, of their children, of their living, making countless widows, countless orphans of them, blackening their name by calling them beasts, extremes of cruelty committed or promoted against the natives. . .

The penitent must regret not only what he committed with his own hands, he must be sorry as well for all the evils, all the harm done by those others he came out with. Each of them is responsible for the whole. The reasoning is this: every one of them who came out knew well why they came—to conquer, they all had exactly that purpose. And they brought no authorization from the King to do the evils they did. And even if they had such authorization, it would have been worthless as an excuse, no reason could justify the horrible wars they waged against the natives. The only reason they had was their own ambition, their insatiable greed. And therefore each one of them is obliged to have remorse for the offenses all committed. . . . Each one is required to make restitution for what everyone stole, what everyone acquired so wickedly, for the damages all did, even though a particular person did not gain or spend a cent of the fortune made. Each one is obliged to restore the fortune.

Third rule: the confessor, once he has a reckoning of all the goods of the penitent, should learn broadly which were the places where the penitent did the harm, the evil to the natives, he and his accomplices. And if the injured parties are alive still, or their offspring are, the confessor shall order them paid what he thinks just, and shall make known in a public way what he has worked out and made mandatory. If there are no survivors among said natives, restitution shall be made for the good of their villages, if the villages were not entirely destroyed. Natives from other areas nearby may be brought in to restore said villages. They are to be given their livelihood, or sources of livelihood, or provisions to start them off. Or restitution may be made by freeing natives who were enslaved during the time when tyranny reigned and fear of the Lord and of eternal damnation impelled no one who held slaves to set them free. . . .

Fourth rule: Even if the dead man has a hundred legitimate sons, he may not leave them a cent, nothing is owed them by law, nothing by way of inheritance, they have no right to that estate. Out of charity he may leave them what the confessor thinks is enough to feed them. Though he can give enough of a livelihood so they can become settlers. . . . He can even give them preference over strangers, all other things being equal, but beyond that nothing. The explanation for the first part of the rule is this: Not a one of those conquistadors has a single cent that is really his. . . .

Fifth rule: If the penitent is not in danger of death, but would confess in a state of health, the confessor should talk to him beforehand, should ask him if he wishes to be rid of all doubt and set his conscience completely at rest. If the penitent's answer is a sincere yes, the confessor is to require him to provide a public document by which he obliges himself to consent to whatever disposition of his whole estate the confessor shall ordain and deem most suitable for the man's conscience, even if the confessor gives the entire estate away. Then, to be sure he holds to it, that he is firm about fulfilling what the confessor shall arrange and prescribe, he shall put all his goods under a legal obligation in the same way as described in the first rule, giving power to the Bishop of the diocese and to ecclesiastical justice, such that they can force him in ecclesiastical court to comply with his own promise. . . .

Sixth rule: Once the guarantee is made, and the juridical obligation spoken of is set, the confessor shall look to see if the penitent is rich, if he owns native villages that pay him taxes, and what income he has, if it is income on income (as they say) and sure, distinct from taxes or income from production. With a penitent of this type, the following must be adopted and made mandatory. One, budget him for the normal cost of food and drink, for clothing himself, his wife, the children he has, only the necessaries, no more, it is not a matter of all or nothing. Arrange his household and the dowries of his daughters to match the quality of his person, if he was of low social rank. The same process if he was of noble lineage, place him on a modest scale of living. It is not right for him to live with pomp and circumstance off what belongs to someone else, to live off the sweat of fellow human beings who owe him nothing. And see to it that each year he has enough for a moderate life, only the necessaries as stated earlier, no more, and let him know he is to make good use of it. And everything over and above the income he has, not derived from natives nor from the taxes they pay, but derived from some other holding or the fruits of labor, the confessor, or some other trustworthy agent who is suitable, shall use to make the restitution with, in the way the third rule prescribes. The best agent would be the Bishop to whom the penitent gave the power of disposition. And it is legal for him so to act. . . .

Seventh Rule: There are penitents who were not conquistadors. They were settlers. They held once or now hold allotments of natives. If they are at the point of death, the confessor shall order them to make total restitution to the very people they took taxes and services from, if they are still alive, or to their offspring, or to the villages where they lived. The result intended being that all the natives of the village or villages share in the restitution. This is to be understood of taxes he thought honestly taken because he took no more than they had formerly paid. Even if rightly taxed [before the Spaniards], they were never rightly taxed [after], it was always unjust, excessive, coerced. . . .

Eighth rule: If the penitent, the encomendero who is to confess, is not at the point of death, but healthy, and poor in the sense that he possesses no more than what the natives give him in taxes, if meantime the condition of the natives is debased, as it is now, whether they are taxed a lot or a little, then the confessor shall tax in turn the estate and the expenses of the penitent in the same way as described in rule six. He shall order the penitent to take no more than stated there. He shall set up other rules about the situation that seem wise to him, e.g., that the penitent should try as hard as he can to provide schooling and instruction in the faith for the natives by the Friars, and that he, the penitent, personally, to the best of his ability, shall instruct them, look out for them, care for them, fend for and foster them, and in sum, give them aid and comfort in their necessities.

Further, the penitent should be ready to accept what the King has come to command, and shall not provoke a resistance, directly or indirectly, to a law, a provision, an order which the King shall provide in a given case. He shall, on the contrary, induce others to accept and obey. For the Spaniards to resist the good, the peace, the preservation, the freedom of the natives, who are their neighbors, is not done, cannot be done, without great offense against God. To do so is expressly against the divine command that we love our neighbor, and that what we want not done to ourselves, we want not done to other human beings. They are in no debt to us. The support given natives is justifiable because it is a policy that populates the earth and consorts with Christianity. Had there been order in the Indies, had the Spaniards not wrought such ruin, such mortal harm, on the natives, they could have helped the natives live off the land, with the one goal in mind, stated earlier, to nourish the faith, and good could have come about for the natives because of the presence of the Spanish Christian. . . .

Everything stated in these seventh and eighth rules concerning comenderos should be applied also to mine owners and ranch owners, Spaniards who are called calpisques in New Spain. But they ought to be judged more severely, held more severely to contrition and restitution. They were the most barbaric towards the natives, the most cruel and soulless, they were the executioners, the instruments of utter damnation for the natives who died and still die in the mines and in the other jobs they do.

Ninth rule: The confessor shall order a penitent who holds slaves to set them free immediately. This refers to natives who are held in slavery, whatever the way they were enslaved or bought or inherited or had from other natives in lieu of taxes. The confessor shall order this with no doubt or scruple or hesitation, and the penitent shall do it by a public act before a notary. And he shall pay the freed natives everything they earned by their services or labors, judging by year or month. The penitent shall do all this before he comes to confession. Likewise he must beg the natives' pardon for the harm he did them, the way the first rule states it. For it is an absolute, proven fact, to anyone who knows the situation, that not one single native was enslaved for just reason anywhere in the Indies from the moment the Indies were discovered down to the present day. And the same judgment is to be made of slaves bought from natives. There is scarcely a one who could be proven to be a slave, and could therefore be passed on as one certainly and according to law. Even if it could be proven that someone is truly a slave, or made so in wars between natives, or according to just laws, that is no excuse for the penitent I am describing.

If one of the Spaniards who holds native slaves has sold some, he is obliged as a penitent to buy them back whatever the asking price may be, e.g., if he sold them for two and can only buy them back for a thousand. If he has not the resources to buy them back, he is obliged to become a slave and take the place of the one he sold unjustly in order to free him. . . . The penitent should make great efforts to discover the whereabouts of the slave he sold so as to free him. If the slaves are dead, he shall give up what he received for them plus what the work they did was worth. And he shall grieve for the rest of his life over his terrible sin, over the harm he did his neighbor. The restitution is made for the good of the penitent's soul, or the souls of those he sold, if they were Christian, or for the good works described above.

Tenth rule: If the penitent is married, man or woman, and if the natives they hold as slaves are held half and half, as the two may have arranged it to be when they married, then the confessor must make it obligatory on the penitent, if it is the husband, to cast lots and determine for himself which are his. He is to set them free in the manner described. And the confessor shall urge him to urge his wife to do the exact same thing in turn. If it is the woman who is the penitent, she cannot be required to free her half while her husband is still alive. According to law, the husband is the one to administer the estate, even if it is all the wife's, while the marriage lasts. But she must be of the mind to set free all those belonging to her half should her husband die. Should she die first, she should make the same provision in her will, and also command that those freed be paid for their services and labors. But prior to all this, should it seem possible, she shall urge her husband to do the freeing while she is still alive. Meantime she shall try to lighten their load, and treat them as the free beings they really are insofar as she can. The confessor is to act the same way toward married couples in matters concerning taxes taken from natives, if held by allotment and half and half, or even if all are held by her. But if they are all his, i.e., under his control, the confessor should make him obey and keep to what is contained in the above stated rules.

Eleventh rule: Those merchants sinned mortally who imported war matériel such as firearms, gunpowder, bullets, lances, swords, and the worst weapon of all, horses, while the Spaniards were in the act of conquering and subjugating the natives—as they are now doing in Peru, have been doing all along, as they did in New Spain and Guatemala, Santa Marta, Venezuela, and other places. They are guilty of all the evils, of all the damage done by those things, they are bound to restitution for whatever they stole, for whomever they terrorized, killed, destroyed.

The reason for the rule is this: They were participants, causes along with the actual doers of the evils, the plunderers, the devastators, because of the aid they gave them through the matériel of war. They knew, more or less, those wars, those conquests, were unjust. At the very least they were in doubt or were obliged to doubt the justice of them. And that is quite enough to put them in bad faith. They are guilty of the whole thing. So, in like manner, they are obliged to make restitution of the money they made selling arms to the conquistador, though they wielded no weapon themselves. Since the robbers, the thugs, had nothing they had not stolen, they paid the merchants in stolen gold and silver, so were unable to give the least bit of that back, while the wine and clothing they had were luxury items and useless for other than gifts. What we say supposes the merchants were not in good faith. . . .

Twelfth rule: The confessor must dispose the penitent to keep a firm purpose, in the future, about two things. First, that he never again participate in a conquest or war against the natives. Spaniards will never have a just cause for war against the peoples of the Indies of the Ocean Sea, no matter the passage of time or years. Second, he will not go to Peru while the thugs there are in rebellion against the King. And even if they should return to obedience, he will not go while they continue to slaughter natives and make our faith a thing of mockery to them.

"These are hard words and who can take them? The one who would follow the straight and narrow path that leads to eternal life."

- 2 -

Anti-Defamation Stance

Prenote

There was another attempt in the late 1540's, early 1550's, to justify Spain's use of violence against the Indians of the New World. Such violence, argued Juan Ginés de Sepúlveda, was biblically warranted and made rational sense—Indians were peoples immersed in sin, especially in idolatry, and were barbaric in their cultures, especially in the practice of human sacrifice and of cannibalism. Therefore a superior people, Spain, had the right and obligation to subject such people to civilized control and remove obstacles, by force, to the acceptance of Christianity. Las Casas got wind of Sepúlveda's manuscript proposing these ideas, and moved to stop him from publishing it.[210] The two eventually ended up before a junta expressly called to consider conquests and slavery. Sepúlveda presented his arguments briefly. Las Casas then took five days to respond with a massive document, the Apología.[211] Fray Domingo de Soto, a member of the junta, was asked by it to summarize both positions. Sepúlveda replied to the summary and Las Casas replied to the reply.

We have, in the following excerpt, an example of the exchange De Soto's summary caused.[212] But it is important to remember that Las Casas thought that Spain was in the New World for anything but the good, the conversion of the Indians. Though that was the only valid reason it could adduce. So the argument with Sepúlveda is an argument with insincerity, but one that had to be made if conquests and slavery were to be kept at bay. It is one thing, Las Casas knew, to toss around scripture and Aristotelean texts in proof of a position. It is another thing to know the facts of the case

---

[210] See Wagner-Parish, ch. 15, "Casas Versus Sepúlveda," pp. 170-82.

[211] See Wagner-Parish, Catalogue # 45, pp. 278-9.

[212] See *Tratados*, vol. 1, "Aquí se contiene una disputa o controversia," pp. 217—459. Sepúlveda's 11th Objection runs from p. 315-21; Las Casas' reply runs from p. 395-415.

the proof texts are supposed to illuminate. Sepúlveda does not know the facts of the Indies, nor the facts of Christianity, so Las Casas makes a frontal assault on him, revealing his misuse of scripture and his ignorance of Indian existence, and thereby nullifies Sepúlveda's position. The prohibition against conquests and enslavement remains on the books.

Eleventh Objection

Sepúlveda:

[The Bishop Las Casas] claims that war was allowable to save innocent lives that were being sacrificed, but ought not to have been made because one must choose the lesser of two evils. Greater evils than the death of the innocent followed from that war. His Lordship has the figures all wrong. In New Spain, we are told, by all those who return and took care to find out, that twenty thousand persons a year were sacrificed. Multiply that number by the thirty years since that sacrificing was brought to a halt and you have six hundred thousand. The total deaths caused by the Conquest did not surpass the number sacrificed in one year, so I calculate. What is more, the war halted the loss of those countless souls who save themselves by converting to the faith, now, or later on. As St. Augustine says in Letter 75: "The greater evil is to have one soul lost through death for lack of baptism. Not to have thousands of people slain, however innocent they may be." To want to explain away the sacrifice of human victims is utterly alien to Christianity. It was alien also to pagans who were not barbaric and inhuman, they thought it an abomination. Pliny writes of it in Bk. 30, chapter 1: "In the year 656 (A.U.C.) the Senate decreed that a human being should not be sacrificed and open celebration of that bizarre rite in temples ceased." A little further on he says: "We cannot appreciate enough what we owe to the Romans who banned the monstrous rites in which it was an act of religion to sacrifice a human being." Quintus Curtius says in Bk. 4: "Certain authors were for starting again a sacred rite—which I would think was little to the liking of the gods—one suspended during our era, the sacrifice of a young child to Saturn, which would be sacrilegious, not sacred, etc." Plutarch also, in Apothegmatis, writes that Gelon, the tyrant of Sicily, having conquered the Carthaginians, demanded that they no longer sacrifice human beings or else he would make further war on them and wipe them out; they promised to comply. St. Augustine writes also about the same topic in his book Questions about Judges, q. 49. So to hold that ignorance excuses in such a beastly, abominable sin, makes no sense at all. In a city of people that permits human sacrifice by public authority, everyone is guilty, since everyone agrees to it. Yes, it is a common occurance in war that the guilty and innocent alike suffer evil consequences. But that is an accidental result, it is not intended by the leader. And so, when there is a just cause, when the goal is good, when the intention of the prince is good, he excuses as much as he can the sins of the soldiery done against his will. They injure their own souls, those who offend God, they do not injure the leader nor the cause. On this topic Gerson, a respected author, says the following in his rules of morality, the chapter "De Avaricia": "When waging war which is filled with evil effects to innocent people on both sides, only the common good excuses from mortal sin, or the avoidance of an evil to the common good greater than the harm that comes from the war to the individual good." In a war of this kind, whether waged to stop idolatry, or for that and further to stop the sacrificial killing of human beings, the evils avoided by waging it are much greater than the evils incurred. More than anything else, the deaths of many souls from among those who were converted or will one day be. This is a far greater effect than any other which derives from war, as St. Augustine says in Letter 75, i.e., it is a greater evil to lose a soul to death without it being baptised than it is to kill countless people, however innocent they be.

And I repeat, the claim that ignorance excuses people who sacrifice humans to their gods is not tenable in Christianity and still have Catholic and Christian truth respected. One could excuse all the idolatry in the world for the very same reason. All were blind that way, all who intended to honor mere creatures as gods by offering them sacrifices, inexcusable sacrifices, as St. Paul says: "Though people knew God, they did not glorify God, but changed the glory of the incorruptible God into the likeness of a corruptible man, bird, etc." And if it is right for those barbarians to defend their religion, their idolatry, as I am given to understand in the synopsis of the Bishop's book, and as his Grace claims clearly in the Confesionario, it follows that they are right to approve and consequently to honor their idols and do so without sin, though the approving of a crime is a greater sin than the doing of it. Approval is not permitted to Catholics. For idolatry is the worst of all sins. So say all the theologians. It violates natural reason. Ignorance of natural law is no excuse for anyone. Theologians and canonists agree on this. As to the claim that the opinion that it is good to sacrifice humans is probable because the wisest men among the natives agreed on it, a claim supported by a quote from Aristotle, I reply that the Philosopher thought no barbarian wise or prudent. He thought such types came from developed and humane peoples. It is what he says in I Politics where he speaks of the barbarians. And the reference to Abraham works against the Bishop because God did not allow Abraham to sacrifice his son. The same is true about the sacrifice of the firstborn where God commands the sacrifice of animals, not of human beings. Rather the one should stand for the other, as St. Augustine concludes in the work cited earlier. For someone to claim they need not accept what faith in Christ and natural law both condemn is an open attack on the Gospel text of Mark 16: "Whoever believes and is baptized will be saved. Whoever does not believe will be condemned." For God does not condemn anyone for something he is not obliged to do."

Eleventh Reply

Las Casas

Take what he answers to the eleventh objection. To my statement: if the means of freeing oppressed, innocent people has to be by war, it is more the innocent who will perish, so where it is a choice between two evils, the lesser has to be chosen. The Doctor says my figures are off. For in New Spain more than twenty thousand people a year were sacrificed, and in the thirty years one has to count, six hundred thousand have disappeared. My first answer is, let us do some real counting, the Doctor and I. My second is, it is not true to say in New Spain twenty thousand people a month were sacrificed, nor a hundred, nor fifty a year, for if that were so, we would not have found the huge numbers of people we did find. It is the voice of tyrants speaking, to excuse, to justify their own tyrannical violence, to continue their oppressions, to plunder the Indians, to keep them slaves for the profit they make from them, to lord it over them. It is also the voice of those who want to back the tyrants, like the Doctor and his followers. My third answer is the Doctor has counted the wrong column. It is truer by far to say the Spaniards have sacrificed more to the god they love and adore, greed, in each year they have been in the Indies, from the moment they entered each province, than the Indians sacrificed in a hundred years to their gods throughout the Indies. The heavens cry out the fact, the earth, the elements, the stones, they are witnesses. Even the perpetrators do not deny the fact. For it is clear how populous all those places were at the time we entered each one. They are empty on us today. The people destroyed, erased. We should be utterly ashamed, disgraced beyond words—since the fear of God does not affect us—to want to gloss over or excuse such brutal, beastly deeds. We had before our eyes land as broad and wide as the whole of Europe and part of Asia. And because it had goods and riches, we wiped out its people with consummate cruelty, injustice, tyranny, theft, seizure, we made a deserted ruin of it in the work of forty five, forty eight years. I saw how full of human life those places were. And if the Reverend Doctor will consider this with any feeling, any charity, he will know I made a more accurate tally than he. And it would be fine if he answered that he wept for those who died without baptism among the Indians sacrificed, whether there were ten or a hundred, whether there were a thousand or ten thousand. But it is not true. For his conscience does not trouble him, and his stomach does not upset him, and his heart does not break over the twenty million souls who have perished in the intervening time, without faith, without baptism. They could have been saved since God disposed them for the faith. Instead, they were damned by losing the time and space for their conversion and penitence because the Spaniards cut them to pieces against all reason and justice solely to rob and enslave them.

My fourth answer is, the Doctor puts words in my mouth. He says that I want to give reasons excusing the sacrifice of human victims. He says pagans who were not beastly barbarians considered such sacrifices abhorrent. And he cites Pliny, Bk. 3, ch. 1. What I say does not excuse them before God. I do not know how God judges them. God's judgment is inscrutable. But I wanted to show by evidential argument that they suffered from ignorance, from understandable error for not believing at the first outcry the Christians made to them, nor later reproaches, that it was against the natural law, a sin, to sacrifice human beings. Therefore they could not justly be punished for it by human beings, by human judgment. And I said more, they will never be required to believe any preacher of our faith who comes in the company of tyrants, warriors, thieves, killers, the way the Doctor would want to send them in. To say what he says is more alien to Christianity than what I say. What he says is the opposite of it, as any intelligent Christian will recognise, will admit. I further say it is not easily proven that it is against the natural law to offer human victims in sacrifice to the true God. Rather, one can argue persuasively the contrary, using good, cogent, almost unopposable reasons. I laid them out extensively in my *Apología*. I read them in the presence of many lawyers and theologians. And certain barbarians convinced the Romans themselves. When they saw themselves beaten and harried all over by Hannibal, they sacrificed a Frenchman, a Frenchwoman, a Greek man, a Greek woman, in the cattle market, to appease the gods they thought were angry at them. Plutarch recounts it, and Titus Livius, in Bk. 2, 3rd. Decada. And in Italy, people were persuaded to give the first fruits of human birth in sacrifice as a result of the tribulations they suffered from hunger and other calamities, even though it did them damage. Dionysius Siculus of Halicarnassus narrates this in Bk. 1 of his History of the Romans. And the French employed such sacrifice, especially when they saw themselves plagued by some disease or in other mortal dangers like those of war. And the reason they gave was that they judged if they did not offer the lives of human beings in order to cure or save the lives of human beings, the immortal gods would not be placated. Julius Caesar testifies to this in his Commentaries, Bk. 6, On the War in

Gaul. He says: "People in the whole of Gaul are deeply influenced by religion. For that reason those who are affected by serious illness, and those exposed to the dangers of war, offer human beings in sacrifice, or vow to offer themselves. They judge that the spirit of the immortal gods cannot be placated toward the life of humankind unless the life of a human being is sacrificed. They have established public sacrifices of that kind." There is no nation on earth, or little short of that—Spain included, as Strabo shows, Bk. 3, De Situ Orbis—that did not offer the gods a sacrifice of human victims, led to do so by natural reasoning. For this and more is owed to God by all humankind. And though the Doctor should spend more days studying the topic than he already has, there will be no evidence that human sacrifice to the true God—or false God if thought to be the true—is against the natural law, "a crime, by all positive law, divine or human."

The Reverend Doctor adds that to kill the innocent in a just war is "by accident." Or if the intention of the leader is just, the sins of his soldiers shall not be blamed on him, etc. To that I respond that when innocents are killed in a just war, that is "by accident." And for it to be "by accident," and excusable, the situation must be such that the war cannot be concluded in any other way, the victory cannot be had unless that action be done in which the innocent are going to die or get killed along with the guilty. Example, when it is necessary to attack and destroy a fortress, and there are some small children within who will perish. But if it is not necessary to attack it in order to win it, especially if one has sure or probable knowledge that there are innocent people inside, their deaths are no longer "by accident," but "on purpose," and it is on purpose that those who die inside are killed. And likewise, the prince, should he give the order, and those who carry out the order, would sin mortally, would be, in fact are, obliged to restitution for all the damages, and would not save their souls without true repentance. The reason is that war, and the acts usually done in war—killing, stealing, and the rest—are intrinsically evil things. War must never be waged unless one can do nothing else and it is a pure necessity. Augustine says it: "Peace is the product of choice, war the product of necessity."[213] And Pope Nicolaus, in the same Causa, says: "One must abstain from war not just during Lent but all the time, unless necessity requires."[214] Necessity is the only excusing circumstance for those acts not to be mortal sins which are "per se" evil and otherwise destructive. For, as in the example given, if there is no need to attack the fortress, then it is clear there is blame for the death and damage

---

[213] Cf. "Noli," from Causa XXIII, Questio VIII. [*Gratian*, causa 23, q. 1, cap. 3 (Friedberg, 1:892)].

[214] For "Si nulla," cf. *Gratian*, causa 23, q. 8, cap. 15 [Friedberg, 1:956].

done not just to the innocent but to the guilty as well. From that moment on the warfare is unjust according to the sure opinion of many sound theologians. That is exactly the case in the Indies, there is no necessity whatever to wage war. To stop, to root out the vice the Indians have of killing through human sacrifice, which went on in a few areas—but even if in many—is easily done through the preaching of the Gospel alone and not through vicious wars. Therefore it is not possible to wage war for the reason the Doctor gives since there is moral certitude that there are countless innocents among the Indians, countless children, women, adult men who do not have such vices and do not approve of the same. Not possible without committing the most mortal of sins, without incurring the obligation to restitution. The text he cites from Gerson goes counter to his argument, and if one looks at it calmly, works much more in favor of what I say against him. Gerson says: "Only the good of the state excuses from mortal sin, or the avoidance of damage to the common good markedly worse than the damage to individual good stemming from the war." It is clear what is far worse damage—a bad name for the faith, a horror of Christian religion—which results from the thoroughly wicked wars the Doctor wants to precede the Gospel, a block to salvation of so many, the damnation they then incur whom the tyrants cut to pieces and kill, the deaths of countless innocents who are not guilty of the alleged sins, even in the kingdoms where they are committed, that is, the children, the women, the peasants, the others who do not do these things, and many another who would also not do them unless they were chosen and ordered to by priests and leaders.

Further, there is the opportunism, the arrogance, the hatred that again rises in the tyrants so they can continue to rob, enslave, oppress those peoples. They itch to make war on them, with no pangs about committing sin, the result being they live and move in a state of mortal sin. And it is clear what a great common good this is, that many innocents perish because many innocents are sacrificed! As we have proven beyond cavil in our *Apología*. What happens to the Reverend Doctor commonly is this: that the texts he cites on his own behalf, twisting them against a correct and proper meaning, come back, step by step, to their proper sense, and stand in opposition to his mindless ideology. As to the Doctor's further argument, that if those idol worshippers, those pagans, justly defend their religion, their idolatry—as he says I say, and I do, clearly, in my Confesionario—it follows that they justly and without sin honor those idols, etc. I answer by saying again: On the supposition that the idolaters are in error, have an erroneous conscience in holding that their gods are the true God, then they not only have a just, or to put it better, a probable cause to defend their religion, but they are required by natural law to defend it. And if they do not do so to the point of losing their lives, should need be, to defend it and their idols or gods, they sin mortally and will go to hell for that sin alone. And the explanation is, to take one of the many set out in our Apologia, that every human being is obliged by nature to love and serve God above him or herself, and therefore to defend God's honor and service even if it includes death, at a given time or place, as the passage from Romans 10 says: "One acknowledges the faith publicly in order to be saved." This is the interpretation of the doctors and St. Thomas, 2ª 2ᵃᵉ, q. 3, art. 2. And the deaths of all the martyrs substantiate this. As far as the obligation is concerned, there is no difference between those who know the true God, as we Christians do, and those who do not, provided they hold or believe some god to be the true one. As there is no difference between a man who flees carnal knowledge of a woman not his wife in order not to commit a sin of adultery against the sixth commandment, and the man who believes, who thinks he must have carnal knowledge of the woman, and if he does not he breaks the divine command. And though the latter is mistaken, he clearly sins mortally if he does not know her. The explanation is that the erroneous conscience binds, obliges equally as the right conscience, "though not in the same way." Because right conscience binds simply and of itself. The erroneous conscience "by accident," and by way of a certain similarity. Insofar as it perceives as a good that which is an evil. If it acts, it does not avoid sin. If it does not act, it incurs sin.[215] Thus the idolaters make the judgment that their idols are the true God, or that in those idols the true God is served, adored, or ought to be served and adored. And in all truth, the universal concept of God is oriented toward the true God and does not rest until it reaches Him, according to St. John Damascene and Gregory Nazianzen and Boethius and St. Thomas and all the fathers who deal with this subject. And the idolaters know by natural reason the first principles of moral actions, which pertain to sinderesis, i.e., God must be obeyed, honored, served, and pagans understand this fully. So it follows from their false judgment, the error spoken of, the bind upon their conscience, that they are obliged to defend their god or their gods which they think are true, and their religion. Just as we Christians are obliged to defend our true God and the Christian religion. If they do not, they sin mortally. Just as we would sin not defending it should the need arise. The similarity breaks down at this point: we, defending ours, merit heaven; they, defending theirs, merit eternal damnation. They act against a divine command whether they defend it or not. This is what Cicero says, who thinks all people are obliged by natural

---

[215] Cf. St. Thomas *1ª 2ᵃᵉ*, q. 19, art. 5 & 6. And 2 *Sentences*, Dist. 39, q. 3, art. 3, the whole of it. And other citations.

law to defend their God or gods, thinking them the true God, as he speaks of the blasphemy of the Gauls in the 11th speech he made for Marcus Fonterus, Gauls who had degenerated were different from all other nations in that they did not make war in the defense of their gods. "Are we to think that those nations of the Gauls are influenced by belief in an oath on the fear of the immortal gods in giving their testimony? They differ utterly from the nature and practice of the rest of the world. The rest wage wars in defense of their beliefs. The Gauls, counter to the custom of everyone else, etc."

Thus the Doctor's line of reasoning does not follow, that pagans can justly and without sin honor and serve idols, can be idolatrous, because they can justly, in all probability, defend them, or be obliged to defend them. So because the Doctor does not recognise the nature of the error the idolaters suffer from, nor recognise what erroneous conscience is all about, he draws an erroneous conclusion. . .

- 3 -

Defense of Indian Civilization

Prenote

*In the aftermath of Sepúlveda's denigrating description of Indian
civilizations, Las Casas separated out a mass of material from the* History
of the Indies, *formed a new manuscript around it, and named it* Apologética
historia sumaria *[A Defense of Indian Civilizations].*[216] *He took basic
Aristotelean categories denoting what civilization entailed and showed that
Indian peoples matched European ones in all the categories, and in some
cases surpassed them. There was some personal experience behind his
knowledge, but he mainly depended on a wide variety of sources which he
himself sought out—missionaries, reports, documents—so what he forms is
an early ethnological treatise of great probity.*

*His attitudes, however, are present to the material, especially that
concerning Indian religious ideas and practices. He had a basic medieval
sense that right reason could arrive at some understanding of the true God
and of the moral order. But such right reason in everyone was subject to
distortion by the enemy of human nature, the demon. The only preservation
from such distortion lay in revelation, God communicating the truth about
human beings through Jesus Christ, and through the Church which was the
guardian of that truth. But Las Casas also saw that the demon could distort
Christianity. Much of what Spain did in the New World was demonically
inspired and worthy of damnation, he thought.*

*Demon, demonic, the terms mean, in modern parlance, a turning
of the powers of a self and group into life-destroying ways, powers which
were intended for life-creating ways—mind, will, imagination, emotions,
sociability. What causes those powers to turn is a modern problem too.
How are free will human beings brought to pitches of inhumanity? Through*

---

[216] *Apologética*, Bk. 3, ch. 120, passim. For the story on the formation of the
Apologética, see Wagner-Parish, ch. XVII, "Historian of the Indies," pp. 195-208,
esp. pp. 200-4. See also Catalogue # 64 for a history of the manuscript.

nationalism, ethnicity, religion, past sufferings? Throughout Las Casas'
writings, particularly the History of the Indies, *a set of principles appears*
which are clearly akin to the United Nations Universal Declaration of
Human Rights. These are the detectors of the turning. In the paradoxical
way of Christianity, Las Casas has translated biblical, symbolic material
into philosophical, rational, legal expression. He is aware of how strange
the Bible sounds, both in itself and for people hearing it for the first time.
He fears symbolic expression if it is taken literally.

In his descriptions of religious beliefs and practices, Las Casas is
accurate in what he knows. And where he can see life-creating beliefs, or
openness to belief, he is very appreciative, unlike his contemporaries,
particularly Bernardino de Sahagun, who saw everything pagan as
damnable.[217] *The description Las Casas gives of Quetzalcoatl is positive*
and clear, it well matches modern descriptions of the same. Sahagun places
Quetzalcoatl in hell. Las Casas sees the demonic as something that can turn
Christian and non-Christian religion into negative forces. This is doubly
tragic for the Christian who has such a clear example of holiness in Jesus
Christ, such a defense against the demonic. Las Casas ultimately thinks that
in default of true Christianity, Indian ways of altruism, as represented, say,
in Quetzalcoatl or Inca sun worship, bring believers to eternal life and
acceptance by God.

Religion

Note at the start, there was a kind of common religion and almost
no idolatry, though there was some, among the peoples of Hispaniola, Cuba,
the island we call Jamaica, all the Lucayos, all the islands that run in a row
from mainland Florida to the point of mainland Paria. . . . Not many places
had temples. The temples there were had little to recommend them, they
were huts of straw like the other dwellings, though set somewhat apart.
They rarely housed idols. The idols were not for adoration as gods. But
certain priests put them there—and the demon was behind the priests—on the
pretense that the idols could do some good, i.e., give children, bring rain,
and other useful things. There were not physical rites involved, nothing

---

[217] See Fray Bernardino de Sahagun, *General History of the Things of New Spain*, tr.
from the Aztec by Arthur J.O. Anderson & Charles E. Dibble (Santa Fe: University
of Utah, 1950), pp. 39-40. The passage about Quetzalcoatl is worth quoting: "And
though a man of saintly life, who performed penances, he was not to be worshipped
as a god. The things which he did [which were] like miracles, we know he did only
through the command of the devil. He is a friend of devils. Therefore he must needs
be accursed and abominated, for our Lord God hath caused him to be thrust into the
land of the dead. . . And his soul our Lord God damned and caused to be thrown into
the land of the dead. In that place it is. It will forever suffer in the flames."

really visible, though some exceptions, and these were conducted by priests the demon used as his agents. They did some fake things, were fooled themselves. Basically, religion in the region rested on the awareness, the sense that there was a god. Religious practice was based on that, though some error got mixed in due to the tricks the demons played or the seductions they worked.

The people of the island of Hispaniola have a belief, a sense of God as one and only, an immortal god, invisible, no one can see him, he was always there, his dwelling place is in heaven. They named him Yocahu Vagua Maorocati. I do not know what they meant by that name. I wasn't attentive back then when I could have known. The errors that got mixed in with this true and universal knowledge of God were these: God had a mother, her name was Atabex; God had a brother Guaca, etc. The people were headed for the truth but had no guide, had instead those who misguided them, who clouded the light of natural reason that could have kept them on track.

According to a letter the Admiral, Don Christopher Columbus, wrote the Kings, the Hispaniola natives had certain wooden statues inside which they placed the bones of their ancestors—in all likelihood those of their kings and lords. These statues were named after the people whose bones were enclosed.[218]

The story goes that since the statues were hollow, a man was put inside and from there spoke out what the king or lord would tell him to say to the populace. It happened that two Spaniards entered a hut that had one of those statues. It gave a grunt, so it seemed, and said a few words. But Spaniards are not easily frightened by voices coming from wood statues, they are not stupid enough to fall for such a trick. A Spaniard came and gave it a kick, knocked it over and discovered the secret of what was inside. It was this: in the corner of the house there was a hollowed out space covered with branches. The person who spoke was concealed inside. He had a trumpet device stuck into the hollow statue so when he spoke the statue seemed to speak. The Admiral goes on to say he tried to discover if the people of the island had any religious belief that had the clear smell of idolatry about it, but he was not able to find out. For that reason he ordered someone to search out all he could about the rituals, the beliefs, the traditions of the people of the island and put his findings in writing. The someone was a Catalan who had taken the garb of a hermit, people called

---

[218] For Columbus' letter, see *Vida*, p. 184-86.

him Fray Ramón, a simple, well-intentioned man who knew the Indian tongue somewhat.[219]

From what he could manage of the languages, Fray Ramón inquired as he could. There were three languages on the island. He knew just one spoken in a small area I said was called Lower Macorix, and knew it incompletely. The language spoken generally he did not know much. Nor did other Spaniards, though he knew more than the rest. For no Spaniard—priest, brother, layman—mastered any Indian language, except maybe the mariner from Palos or Moguer whose name was Cristóbal Rodriguez. . . . The non-knowledge of the island's languages was not because they were very difficult to learn. It was because neither cleric nor layman had the least intention to educate these people in the knowledge of God, but intended only to use them, every one. So cleric and layman alike learned no more of the Indian languages than the words for "Give me bread!" "Go to the mines!" "Dig gold!" and other phrases needed for carrying out the will of the Spaniards . . .

What Fray Ramón learned was that the Indians had idols, statues, the kind described. As a rule, they called such idols Cemí . . . The people believed the Cemí's gave them the water, the wind, the sunlight, when they needed them. Same way with children and other things they wanted. Some idols were made of wood, some of stone, Fray Ramón records how they make the wooden ones. Some Indian is on a journey and sees a certain tree that is more agitated by the wind than the others. Apprehension takes hold of the Indian. He approaches the tree and asks it, "Who are you?" The tree replies, "Call a bohique, he will tell you who I am." A bohique is a priest, a seer, a sorcerer. I will explain later. When the bohique arrives, he goes to the tree, sits near it, performs a certain ritual, then rises, tells it the rank and titles of the most important chiefs on the island, then asks, "What are you doing here? Why do you want me? For what reason did you order me summoned? Tell me, do you want me to cut you down, do you wish to go with me, how do you want me to carry you? Am I to make you a house and garden?" The tree then answers that it wants to be cut down. It indicates how its house should be constructed, its garden, and the rites that must be performed during any year. The bohique cuts down the tree and carves an idol or statue from it—an ugly face, idols usually have the look of old, sour-puss monkeys. The bohique constructs the house and garden, and each year performs certain rituals for it. He turns to it as to an oracle, asking and finding out about things in the future, the good, the bad, then he communicates this to the common folk.

---

[219] For Fray Ramón's report, see *Vida*, pp. 186-201.

* * * *

Blessed be God who freed me from the ocean of sacrifices pagan peoples welter in without a clue, ignorant for ages of what true sacrifice is . . .[220]

Let me begin with Hispaniola. It is according to the knowledge people have from the past and present that they serve, honor, venerate God. They set up temples, priests, rituals, sacrifices, all based on the primary source, knowledge. We have seen this to be true through the wide range of explanations and examples we have given. The people of Hispaniola and all the neighboring islands have a knowledge of God. It is spare, weak, jumbled, though it is clearer, cleaner of the tripe of idolatry than the knowledge many other people have. As a result, they do not have idols or many gods. They have few, almost none. They have no temples, no priests, or nearly none, just the kind we earlier called witch doctors. Therefore there were very few sacrifices, though they did have some. I will say of them what I saw and knew, and what others experienced.

We find that, when the time comes to harvest the fields they have planted, they set a certain amount aside—the bread which is made from roots, the peppers, the sweet potatoes, the grain. They are like first fruits, given in thanksgiving for benefits received. But since they do not have temples as such, nor cult houses . . . they put the first fruits in the store-houses of the chiefs, the caciques—places called caney—and they offer, they dedicate this food to Cemí. They say Cemí is the one who sends rain, provides the sun, creates the fruits of the earth, gives them children and all other good things in abundance. All that they set aside remains stored until it rots, or children steal it, play with it, toss it away, waste it, and so it disappears.

I began to recognise it was a natural law obligation to set things apart for God well before New Spain, before the regions of Naca, Honduras, Peru were discovered. I did so just by watching the care the Indians took—especially on Hispaniola and Cuba—to set aside as first fruits a portion of the harvest they gathered, and this way surrender use of it. I had read about this working of the natural law, but not seen it in action . . . What people do everywhere without being taught to, what they do of their own accord, argues clearly to the working of natural law . . .

I used to ask the Indians from time to time, "Who is this Cemí, as you call him?" They would tell me, "He makes it rain, he made the sun, he gives us children, he gives us the goods we need." Then I would add, "The Cemí who does this, I bear him in my soul." Then I would take the opportunity to teach him something about God, though back in those

---

[220] *Apologética*, lib. 3, cap. 166.

times—I say this to my shame—God had not yet granted me the great grace
He later did, giving me to understand the severe need those people had for
temporal and spiritual transformation, and due to that need, the amazing
eagerness they had to be drawn to Jesus Christ. I did not grasp then the
obligation we Christians had, who came to the islands, to help a neighbor in
such severe need. From my description of them, the island peoples seem to
know just one God, though their knowledge was vague.

I said earlier that they had a kind of statue on the island, though
these were rare. Our interpretation was that the devil spoke through these
statues to the priests who were called behiques, spoke also to chiefs and
leaders when they presented themselves to hear, so that the statues became
their oracles. The next step was a sacrifice or ritual to please the demon, one
the demon had to have shown them. It developed this way: they had ground
to powder certain herbs, very dry, very fine powder, the color of cinnamon
or henna dust, tawny. They put the powder on a circular plate, one not flat
but bowl-like, carved out of wood, very beautiful, thin, graceful, it would not
be lovelier if it were made of gold or silver. It was jet black and shiny. They
had an implement made of the same wooden material, beautiful, graceful
also. The implement was fashioned much like a small flute, completely
hollow the way a flute is. Two thirds of the way along, the tube divides into
two further hollow tubes, like our hand when we part the first two fingers
after folding in our thumb. The two tubes are placed in the nostrils, and the
one tube, the mouth of the flute, so to speak, is put into the powder lying on
the plate. Then they draw in their breath, absorbing through their nostrils
the amount of powder they had laid out. Once they took it, they lost
rationality, as if they had drunk a strong wine, and they stayed that way,
almost drunkards. The powder, the ceremony associated with it, they called
"cohoba" . . . and while in that state, they spoke a kind of gibberish, or spoke
like foreigners, who knows what words. In "cohoba," they were fit for
colloquy with statues and oracles, or, to name things more properly, fit for
colloquy with the enemy of human nature. That was the way hidden things
were revealed to them, they way they prophesied, read into things. In that
state, they heard or divined what the future was going to bring, something
good, or something bad and damaging. . .

* * * *

[Gods of the Mexicans]

The Mexicans adored and treated as gods men who had done some
remarkable deeds or who had fashioned something new to foster the growth

of the people.[221] Or men who had given the people laws, customs to live by, or taught them rituals or sacrifices. Or men who had done other things worthy of being honored by acts of thanksgiving. They had a great god in Mexico City. His statue stood in the largest, most important temple there. Uichichibichtl they called him . . . we simplified the name down to Uichilobos. His two sons were with him—or, as other people say, his two brothers. One was called Texcatepócatl. He was the ruling deity in the city of Texcuco. The other son or brother was called Camachtl. He was ruler in Taxcala. They considered him a god there. The Taxcaltecans imagined that the wife of this ruler changed herself into the mountainous area where the city of Taxcala was founded.

These man-gods came from the west, the offspring of the Chichimecas, the story goes. The Chichimecas were mighty warriors, there were brave men among them, they took over by force or surrender all the provinces of Mexico, Tezcuco, and Taxcala. The native, the aboriginal peoples of the areas they seized were called Otomiés. . .

Uichilobos was the first to name Mexico Theonustitlán. The reason was his ancestors were Chichimec *thehules*, a word describing *thehuthiles*. It is the fruit of a plant we call prickly pear . . . a staple food for the Chichimec thehules. Uichilobos had the prickly pear on his shield and today Mexico has it on its coat of arms by royal grant. He enlarged the city, and ordered the causeways built over the lake, so access to the city could be over dry land, thus avoiding the need for canoes or boats. He organized the temples, the sacrifices, the rituals of divine worship. He was the first to devise and carry out human sacrifice. Prior to him, it was not seen or done ever before anywhere. The story on him is that while still alive he demanded to be honored as a god, though not with the same arrogance as Nabucodonosor—perhaps with no arrogance at all . . .

Over the altars of the great Temple there were two gigantic idols. They were statues of Uichilobos' two brothers, I think. Uichilobos' statue was set in the chapel above the brothers. And it was huge and frightful . . . The two brothers had built the city of Tezcuco and Taxcala, they had organized the rituals and sacrifices there. After they died, the people took them as gods and venerated them as such. They tell the story of the god of Tezcuco, the one called Texcatepócatl, that while still alive he plunged into the volcano of the Sierra Nevada which was close by, and from there sent his people his thigh bone. They placed it in their main temple for their main god. It is the great boast of the people of Tezcuco. And the volcano is named after the god who entered it—Popocateptl. The second brother,

---

[221] *Apologética*, Bk. 3, ch. 122.

Camachtli, founded and ruled Taxcala and its environs. He was a great huntsman. They say that with his bow he shot an arrow skyward and on its path up then back down, it killed a lot of birds and animals, with which he then fed his people.

But of all the gods, the most honored, the best, the most worthy in everyone's esteem was the great god of Cholula, a place two leagues distant from the present city of Puebla de los Angeles. They called him Quetzalcoatl. According to the stories about him, he came to Cholula from somewhere in the Yucatan. He was white-skinned, large in body, broad of brow, large eyed, with hair long and black, and a great full beard. People made of him their supreme god and had great love for him, reverence, devotion, and the sacrifices they offered him were gentle and generous and willing. For the following three reasons. The first, he taught them the art of working silver, something they had never even heard of in that region. That art is, was, the boast of the peoples native to Cholula. The second, he never allowed blood sacrifices of man or beast, only sacrifices of bread, of roses, flowers, perfumes, incense. The third, he forbade, he blocked, and with great success, the wars people inflict on one another, the robberies, the murders, the destruction. Whenever, in his presence, mention was made wars or murders or other evils that did harm to humankind, he turned his face away and closed his eyes so as not to see or hear of them. They say in praise of him that he was utterly chaste, utterly honest, someone of great moderation in many things.

This god was the object of great reverence and devotion, vows were made to him, visits, all throughout that region, and because of the qualities just listed. So much so that even enemies of Cholula made promises to come there on pilgrimage, to keep vows they made and to express their devotion. And they did so unmolested. And rulers of other regions or cities kept in Cholula their chapels or oratories, representations of their gods. And this god, alone among all the other gods was called Lord because of his excellence. So it was that when someone took an oath and swore by "Our Lord," people understood it meant "by Quetzalcoatl," not by any other god. Even though there was many another god around, and highly esteemed at that. All this was done for the great love people had for Quetzalcoatl, and for the three reasons given above. But the overarching reason was that truly his authority was a gentle one, and he asked in service only light things, nothing painful, and he taught people the virtues, forbade them the vices, the things that were harmful, damaging. He taught them to abhor such like.

In the light of the above, it is clear, and will be clearer later, that the Indians who, in the past or present, performed human sacrifices, did not, do not do so willingly, but out of the great fear they had of the demon, because of the threats the demon made against them—he was going to destroy them, bring bad times on them, a mass of misfortune, if they did not supply him with the ritual service which they owed him as tribute to his sovereignty. He based this on the pretended right he had acquired over them from long years past.

The Cholulans say Quetzalcoatl spent twenty years among them. After the years were up, he returned back where he had come from, taking with him four young men outstanding for their virtue, all from the city of Cholula. He sent them back from Guazacualco, a province some hundred leagues or more away, towards the sea. He gave them some further instructions. One was that they should tell the Cholulans they could be certain that in a future time there would come over the sea from the direction of the rising sun, with the help of the stars, some men of white skin, with white beards, like unto him, who would rule these lands. They were his brethren. The Indians kept on waiting for the fulfillment of this prophecy. As soon as they saw the Christians, they called them gods, sons, brethren of Quetzalcoatl. But after, when they knew through experience the deeds of these beings, they mistook them no more for heavenly. Because it was right in this city that a massacre was performed by the Spaniards. It was so bad there was nothing ever the like of it in the Indies, maybe nowhere in the world.

Others tell the story this way: the people of Cholula kept the belief that Quetzalcoatl was going to return and govern and console them. So when they saw the sailing ships of the Spaniards, they said their god Quetzalcoatl was back and had brought across the sea the temples in which he was to live. But when the Spaniards landed, the people said, "There are a lot of gods—tequeteteuh, in their language—not our one god Quetzalcoatl. . . ."

Quetzalcoatl, in Mexican, means a certain kind of snake which has a small feather on the top of its head. The place where it flourishes is properly the province of Xicalango, which is near where the kingdom of Yucatan begins, on the route from Tabasco. None or few of the snakes have ever been seen, so we are told, outside Xicalango. The Indians affirm that at certain times, these snakes are transformed into birds, birds with green plumage. There are many such in the province of Xicalango; the Indians consider them very precious. This transformation could possibly happen naturally. The snakes would decompose first, would corrupt, then from the corruption the birds could be generated, the way many things are generated out of corruption . . . Or the transformation could occur through diabolical craft, illusion . . . in order to deceive those God allows to be deceived.

* * * *

[Gods of Peru] . . .[222] Two groups of Peruvians were highly religious, very devoted to the Gods, much more so than other groups—those who lived high up in the mountains, those who lived down along the coast. The mountain people's reason concerned crops, which often failed, sometimes for lack of rain, sometimes from an excess of snow or ice; the reason for the coastal people was their fishing. Both groups had gods who governed these things, and they turned to those gods with devotion and sacrifice when they had to. One group had temples for their gods up on mountain crags difficult of access, the other out at sea on certain islands. They believed also that everything which had a distinctive quality, enough to set it apart from its kind—the shape of a mountain peak or of some rock—and seemed to them specially placed or unusually shaped or hollowed out in some way, they believed such things participated in divinity somehow, so they showed the things great devotion, they worshiped and sacrificed to them.

Back before we came, people in the province of Manta considered as a god a very rich emerald. It was displayed in public for brief periods and simple people adored it. When some were sick, they went and prayed to the emerald, and brought other emeralds to offer it, influenced to do so by the priest who gave them to understand that through the offering their health would be restored to them.

Peruvians also had lords who governed them well and justly, with love and concern, lords who had been sources of culture for their peoples, who thought of them as more than human. Gradually, the people came to esteem them as gods, to offer them sacrifice, to turn to them and ask their help in times of crisis. So the people of that region held in veneration the kinds of things just described, during the whole time that preceded the sovereign rule of the Inca kings, especially the first of them, one they called Pachacuti Inga, which means "Changer of the World." He brought them a culture wider and deeper than they had before, and this wider and deeper culture made them think the world had passed from night to day. This king and his successors had a quite refined, quite accurate knowledge of the true god, because they held that it was God who had made heaven and earth, the sun, the moon, the stars, the whole cosmos. This God they named Condici Viracocha, which means, in the language spoken at Cuzco, "Creator of the Cosmos." They said this God existed at the apex of the world and from there watched over it, ruled it, provided for it. He was God and ruler and they offered their main sacrifices to him. They further said that this God had an evil son, very, before God created anything, and the son had the name

---

[222] *Apologética*, Bk. 3, ch. 126.

Taguapica Viracocha, and he acted against his father in everything, i.e., if the father created good human beings, he turned them bad in body and soul; if the father made mountains, he made plains, if plains, he made mountains; the springs his father made, he dried up. He was the contradiction of his father in everything. For being so, his father finally, in a fit of rage, pitched him into the sea so he would die a bad death, but he never died. This fiction, this invention may mean the fall of the first angel to go bad, a son of God through creation, but turned evil forever through rebellion against God who created him. He was pitched into the deep, Book 20 of the Apocalypse says. Peruvians also say the sun was the primary creature of God, and it is the sun which reveals that which God commands. And the Peruvians are not far from the truth in this, for no creature—with the exception of angels and humankind—represents as well as the sun does the attributes, the perfections of God. Since the sun is the source of such excellent and varied effects, what other created thing could reveal as clearly the way the creator works in and through all things? That is why Peruvians serve the sun, honor it, offer it sacrifice. Though prior to it, and more fundamentally, they serve Conditi [sic] Viracocha, "Maker of the World," as lord of all.

When King Pachacuti started to rule the realms of Peru, many regions were already united . . . The first matters he set in order were those concerning divine worship. To do this, he needed to know about all the gods each people or province or household had. When subjects came to affirm their allegiance to him, he asked them what gods they had, to whom they offered sacrifice, to whom they turned in need. Each one told him, some saying they held the sea to be god, i.e., the fishermen; others saying high peaks were god, high mountains, hills, i.e., farmers, folk from the sierras; still others saying birds, or this or that bird; still others trees, or wood they had worked. There were people who revered foxes, lions, tigers, to keep themselves from harm, or duped by the demons who spoke through those beasts or effigies of those beasts in answer to the petitions of the priests. And there were people who worshiped their former rulers because these latter had governed them with kindness and gentleness, so people had come gradually to believe their rulers were more than human.

The story goes that during the time when each one was recounting what gods they served and worshipped, the king laughed at and made a mockery of many of the said gods, making it understood that certain objects were not worthy to be considered gods. And the king said as much, that it was ridiculous to consider and adore as gods such base and crude things, people should not worship them, not offer them sacrifice. However, in order not to harm those who spoke to him, he gave them permission to go on believing as they had believed, if they wished, but on condition that also they serve and worship the sun as supreme over all other gods. Because, he said, the sun was the greatest of all things, it brought the most good, most life to humankind. So humanity was obligated to serve and worship the sun as god and lord, and do so before any other god. And to help them to accept and honor and worship the sun as something most to be adored after god, he gave them the example of himself—he converted palaces he held in the city of Cuzco, inherited from his father and grandfather and further forebears, palaces where his father, who was still alive, and he lived at that moment, into temples of the sun. He and his father gave up residence and made there that stately, rich, remarkable temple we mentioned earlier. Those dwellings, palaces, had been named Chumbichuncha up to that point, but from then on were called Coricancha, which means "clad in gold," because within it he had build a lot of rooms which were larger than those made out of marvelously worked stone, and these rooms were clad in sheets of gold and silver, some just in silver . . .

In one richly clad, remarkable room, he placed a sculpture of the sun, a bust, solid gold, the face of a man, rays of gold out from it the way we depict rays. They brought this sculpture out into the open on occasion, saying that the real sun would thus communicate its own power to the effigy. Within this chapel-like, richly decorated room, they made important sacrifices, and every day. He ordered made, out of the finest gold, many ears of corn, to rest before the sun. Behind the temple or complex of buildings, there was a fair sized garden, still in use today. Rich loam had been brought a long distance to be put in it, and for irrigation, water was run a long distance through marvelously made tubes, and they still supply water to that garden today. Every year corn was sown there, plus other food producing seed, and the produce was offered the sun in sacrifice. The garden was tilled and planted by the king himself, Pachacuti Inga, his brothers, his closest officials, with their own hands, and they all deemed it a great honor and privilege to do so, not just doing the planting, but the harvesting as well. Both times were cause for great festivity—banquets, gatherings, good times.

He staffed the temple, to serve the sun, with a great number of women and girls, daughters of lords, and some, the most important, were consecrated as women of the sun. Then others were to be their servants, others servants of the servants. The women of the sun and their women served it by fashioning clothing that was rich to the point of marvel, making wine, preparing food, all of which they offered. These women and their servants were virgins. They kept chastity with such rigor that if there was a violation, it was considered as an unpardonable fault, and it was punished only with the cruelest of deaths. Our own religious affirm—and they are

shrewd and knowledgeable in the language—that they heard the elderly say
often there was never a fault of that kind to be found among those women.
And it was a priceless honor and dignity for those named to be among the
women of the sun. They were called mamaconas, which, in the native
tongue, means lady mother.

   In that temple, the king also placed priests to conduct liturgies and
play a role in the cult of the sun. And he furnished the temple with vessels
richly fashioned out of gold and silver for use in worship. So, in sum, he
supplied for the cult the buildings, the vessels, the men and women
ministers, and he did so with the opulence and largess befitting a king and
lord who was prudent and religious and pious and generous. This king had
been so zealous, so attentive concerning the cult of the sun, and with such
quality, making the sun almost a god, though a false one, that our own
people took a lesson from it, saying it would please the true God if,
following the example of those who were ignorant of the true God, we were
as zealous and devout in God's service, we who know God for his gracious
ways to us. The way the King was towards the sun. Who thought, though
mistaken in his thought, that the sun was a little less than God, or maybe the
equal, though the King did profess that the sun was a creature of the the true
God.

   The King sent an edict throughout all his realms. It ordered the
local authorities, both those who were subject to him in the past, and also the
new ones, those who submitted themselves more recently, drawn by
laudatory reports about him, to construct a temple to the sun, each local
authority, for the villages under their control, and scaled to the size of the
various villages. And they were to furnish it, and staff it sufficiently with
priests and other ministers, following the pattern of the temple he had set up
in the city of Cuzco. And though he permitted each one to retain the ancient
gods they had, that was not to admit they were gods, but it was out of respect
for the people, to keep them receptive. And yet, though the people could
retain their local gods, they must accept the sun as the highest God and lord,
and should build temples to him as such, should adore and serve him as such.
He set this policy going throughout the entire realm over which he ruled, and
that covered a thousand leagues, give or take some.

   So, though in each region there were temples dedicated to local
gods, the main one, the richest one, the one most used, was for the worship
of the sun, built to imitate the one the King had made in the royal city of
Cuzco. Most of that temple structure still stands, though not with the
richness and personnel it formerly had. A convent of Dominicans is there
now. But still alive are some old men who were assigned to service there,
and some old women from the group of virgins called mamaconas.

The matter is worthy of deep consideration. One man, with no faith, no knowledge of the true God, no more than anyone else from all evidence, just by the use of natural reason, recognized that those objects others prized and worshipped as gods were not worthy of the reverence and service which was owed to God. And even though he too erred, at least he chose as God the most worthy of all creatures. He understood and professed, though tacitly, that the best of all things would, did, merit being God. And even further, as I mentioned above, he knew, and expressly, that the sun was a creature of the true God. We should go on and think what the temples would have been like if he had had faith in and knowledge of the true God! And what the ministers, the riches, the ceremonies, the sacrifices he would have instituted to honor the divine name, to celebrate the Christian religion! We can at least think that if he were unable to improve on what he did for the sun, he would have done the same with greater certitude, a greater sense of reward, a deeper, gentler devotion. . .

- 4 -

Defense of Indian Sovereignty, Peru

Prenote

From 1547 onwards, Las Casas was back in Spain to defend the laws he had caused to come into being. After thwarting Sepúlveda's attempt to justify conquests and slavery, he had to handle another menace, this time from Peru and the encomenderos thereof. In 1556, at the accession of Philip II, due to the abdication of his father, Charles V, the encomenderos of Peru recognized that Philip was suddenly a debt-ridden man desperate for money, so they offered him eight million gold ducats for the rights to permanent encomiendas. Philip was in England at the time. Las Casas got wind of the offer and wrote a Dominican friend, Carranza, a small book showing how lacking in conscience and legality such a sale would be, and he asked Carranza to make Philip aware of the true state of things. But Philip pressed ahead, so Las Casas resorted to a bold maneuver. He had friends gain a power of attorney for him, from the Indians of Peru, to make a counter-offer to Philip. The Indians would pay more than the encomenderos and thus purchase their freedom. Las Casas made the offer, Philip pursued it, but his commission tangled itself up in such corruption that the whole venture failed.[223] But in the process of defending the Peruvian Indians, Las Casas hones his major arguments to a sharpness no one can ignore. The King's sovereignty is needed in the New World, but only for the sake of converting the Indians, never for the sake of worldly power. All sovereignty must proceed from the freely given consent of the Indians. Within that sovereignty freely granted, all Indian authority remains intact, except for some token recognition of the King of Spain. The latter's purpose is the preservation of Indian sovereignty over a broad scale of territory. No

---

[223] The best summary of the entire tangled situation is found in Helen Parish's "Introduction," *The Only Way*, pp. 50-1.

312

King may alienate subjects without the subjects' consent. Sale of subjects is immoral, illegal. All violations of Indian sovereignty must be redressed by the King. The hold Spain has on the Indies, through the conquistadors and encomenderos, is illegal and immoral, so Spain must change and seek legal and moral ways of being present to the Indies. That is only done through consultation with the Indians, with their will on the matter being definitive. The conscience of the King must be made right first, then other consciences will follow. That is the burden of the first selection which follows.

The theoretical foundation for Las Casas' confrontation of the King in the first selection is found in the second. The third selection, from 1560, contains the counter-proposal in fully authorized form, a remarkable piece of political dealing to try to reverse a bad situation. The fourth selection, "The Twelve Doubts," places on the plane of conscience all the problems connected with the conquest of Peru and Spanish self-enrichment therefrom. Whatever may or may not be possible on the political realm, everyone who believes in conscience must face the tribunal of conscience and purge themselves of sin before death, or death is a damnation. Las Casas lays out the classic norms for conscience and applies them to the situation on the ground in both Peru and Spain. A confessor who does not determine for himself what right Spain and Spaniards have to be in the New World, what right they have to the goods thereof, will become an accomplice in all the sins he forgives. The Jesuit missionaries who went to Peru in 1568, two years after Las Casas' death, had to face this problem. Unfortunately, the problem was basically suppressed by two Jesuit generals, Borgia and Mercurian. But some Jesuit confessors remained troubled, and continued to counsel total restitution as a condition for sacramental forgiveness. The later Jesuit solution, 1609 onwards, was to remove Indians from contact and control by Europeans and risk the accusation of founding independent Indian republics. Those republics, called reductions, were truly products of Las Casas' kind of thinking. They were suppressed in the 1760's by a wicked complicity between the Church and certain European states concerning the absolute power of monarchs over peoples at home or abroad.

a. Memorial to Philip II (1556)[224]

My sovereign Lord and King:

You have often been gracious and kind enough to accept the information I offered Your Majesty concerning matters of the Indies. There is a crisis now in the offing. And I beg Your Majesty to bear with my refreshing your memory, and briefly, about things I made known to you in

---

[224] *Opúsculos*, XLI, pp. 453-60.

requests before now, when I asked you to receive what I said as coming from a loyal subject and servant of Your Majesty and of past kings of Castile. I have no other motive than to tell you the truth and thereby prevent unimaginable, irreparable harm from happening, both to these realms as well as to the royal standing of Your Majesty.

I have known the Indies, have been involved in them for over sixty years. I have been eyewitness to all the early events out there, I have reflected on them deeply. I sense my obligation as a Christian and as a loyal subject of the kings of Castile to make visible to them what they could not see from their distance, and what their advisors should have made plain. For lack of this advice, I saw that those vast realms overseas were being devastated. And I saw it was impossible that graced and Catholic kings would ever permit this if the devastation I spoke about was brought to their attention. So I decided to return to Spain—difficult journeys by sea and land, at great personal expense for I was then a cleric—and return I did in the year 1515 to let your great grandfather know and ask him to provide a solution. So I told him, and he decided to remedy the devastation of the Indies, which was not so bad then as it later was, due precisely to a lack of remedy. He decided to draw up the remedy in Seville, but on his way there he died, as God would have it. After his death, I gave a lengthy report to Don Fray Francisco Jiménez, the Cardinal of Toledo, who had assumed authority, and asked him to send the remedy out. But due to the failure of those he sent, the situation remained as before.

During the Emperor's time, I informed him repeatedly about how the Indian peoples were perishing, and repeatedly His Majesty convoked commissions of lawyers and people expert in other knowledges. I was at the one in the city of Madrid, then in Valladolid, in Zaragoza, in Barcelona, each at a different time. I was absent from others the Emperor convoked, i.e., the one he ordered the Royal Council to hold the year he came to be crowned at Barcelona, 1529, when Cardinal Don Juan de Tavera was Council president. In every one of these meetings, those I attended, those I did not, the decision was that in no way, for no reason, under no pretext, none whatsoever, was the parceling out of Indians to Spaniards allowable—encomiendas, they called them, "entrustments," to hide the poison, the wickedness, these "entrustments" were in actual fact. His Majesty saw the worth of these judgments, decisions, coming from such qualified people. So he ordered annulled, revoked, all parceling out, all encomiendas, backing his commands with a complex of laws and penalties, thereby giving them a weight, as though they had been issued by the Cortes General. He thereby recognized the encomiendas as pernicious plagues that had devastated, wiped out broad stretches of land and the people thereof. Which was and still is an unforgiveable offense against God, this devastation, this wiping out of such a large portion of the human race. And was and still is a defamation of the Catholic faith, a block to it, countless souls dying without faith or sacrament. The damage from this, the loss, to the kings of Castile and to the whole of Spain, has been greater than ever loss has been in the whole world to any king or ruler, to any region or realm. Despite what I have tried constantly to propose, to push, these past forty one years, right to this minute—we are in 1556—and everybody knows my efforts. In these efforts I have come and gone back and forth from the Indies to inform His Majesty of the fact that his policies, his orders and commands were not being carried out, and how that whole overseas world was perishing away.

Now that Your Majesty has come to be ruler, now that God has given you the Indies totally under the control of Spaniards, the ones who bashed and broke to pieces what was there—tyrants, then traitors who rebelled against the Emperor, betrayed him when he wanted to put his remedy in place—I have learned that someone named de Ribera has offered Your Majesty seven or nine million ducats. He does so on behalf of the Spaniards who tyrannized and destroyed the regions of Peru. It's clear how openly and often they intended to secede with them, on some pretext, but didn't manage. The ducats are to have Your Majesty grant Spaniards perpetual allotments of Indians—princes and chiefs and people alike—to be their vassals, to have them under civil and criminal jurisdiction for things major and minor, under authority that is both judge and jury. Your Excellency, by the fidelity I owe to God and to Your Majesty, I have felt obligated according to divine and natural law to beg you please not to grant this. For the following reasons.

First. This business is fraught with difficulty and importance, and with risk, should there be a mistake, more so than any faced or decided on ever in this world by a prince, Christian or pagan. By not yielding, Your Majesty can gain greater service and greater satisfaction than heretofore; by yielding, Your Majesty can gain greater sorrow and remorse if things do not go the way the petitioners say they will. By rights, Your Majesty should be in Spain for the deliberations, should order the procurators of the Cortes and all the estates thereof into session. Because it is of the utmost importance to our realm that sovereignty over the Indies should remain firmly and permanently with the kings of Castile, no danger of losing it should be allowed. This will be clear to any prudent person who looks at the matter in moral terms and without bias. The loss of sovereignty will begin, it is obvious, with exactly this deal those overseas would like to work out with you. And surely, noble sir, you should consult more than a few experts, however shrewd they may be, when at stake is the alienation of more territory than there is from Valladolid to Rome, to Germany. Especially since it's clear that those who counsel, who persuade you that the sale, the alienation, can or ought to be made, have never seen the Indies, do not know them, do not know what they are or what they are worth, or what perpetuity, what preservation of the Indies means!

Second. Your Majesty, precisely as Christian, should recall to your royal consciousness that the Indies did not belong to the Kings of Castile. The Indies owe nothing to the Kings of Castile. It is only by the will of God and donation of God's Vicar and the authority of God's Church that the lands overseas and the countless peoples throughout them were given into the care of the Kings of Castile. Who were to convert them, gain them for Jesus Christ through the preaching of the faith. Who were to preserve them in their dignities and properties, providing a court of appeals for them as their overall, international sovereign. And according to divine and natural law, they have to be summoned, and informed, and advised, and listened to, and instructed about what best serves their rights. Because this deal means enormous damage to them, if Your Majesty were to sell them for money to those who have been from the start their mortal enemies, who have destroyed them, a fact notoriously well known.

There is natural law, divine law, there are the laws of Your Majesty in this realm. But not one judge great or small, upper court or lower, who, according to those laws, would condemn a man, no matter how low his class, to pay a hundred maravedis—less, much less—for the total loss of his liberty, nor a noble his estate for the loss of his liberty, never mind his life, without that man, that noble first being summoned, being heard, being defended, and at the end convinced that he should pay. If the Indians are thus summoned, thus heard, they will know that Your Majesty really wants to do them the favor of plucking them out of the captivity, the tyranny they now suffer in the grip of the Spaniards, and they will provide you with greater treasure, greater income than those others promise you who want to buy them in such a wicked, corrupt way.

Third. These peoples are free and never gave cause for captivity. The Catholic Kings have said as much, and the Emperor declared the same many a time and often, basing himself on his Councils and legal advisors. And these peoples want to be subjects of Your Majesty. It makes just and reasonable sense for Your Majesty to accept them, and not to sell them to local powers. It is obvious how much happier the lives of these people would be, how much more love they would have for their ruler, how much more ready to put their lives, their wealth at his service, these latter would be, than those who lived under the control of local powers.

Fourth. It is utterly false, noble sir, the excuse, the pretext those *encomenderos* use to persuade Your Majesty, i.e., that if you give them the Indians in exchange for money, your hold on the land will be secure and permanent, and the Indians will be preserved because held under vassalage to them in perpetuity. Those who propose this argument are worthy of severe punishment for wanting to fool Your Majesty with falsehoods quite injurious to your royal well-being. And that is clear just from what they say about the secure and permanent possession of the land. There are in Peru, plainly, eight, maybe ten thousand ruffian Spaniards. The only reason they put up with the hardship, and do not rebel or riot or cause trouble, is the hope they have that some allotment will come free, and Your Majesty will make them a grant of it, on the grounds of their service. Now say the land and the allotments thereof, not more than four hundred, are given to four hundred, five hundred, make it a thousand, and given each one for himself and his heirs. The seven thousand, once they see their hope dashed, will they remain so meek and mild as to accept this for the love of Jesus Christ? Isn't it a certainty they will get desperate, rebel, kill the *encomenderos*, scoff at Your Majesty's Viceroy and Audiencia, do a thousand thuggish things? Especially since those now with no bread to eat will be gentlemen who fought against treachery to Your Majesty? And those who have Indians and are rich, or a good many of them, are those who have been most guilty in the past of that treachery? Is this, noble lord, what will secure and pacify the land? Or lose it quicker? Wipe the Indians out quicker?

And the argument they give that they will treat the Indians better if their own property, that is devilish counsel, mightily bad! Because their pride and ambition is enormous, and they have risen to states in life so beyond their wits that neither the Indians they have, nor double what they have, are enought to satiate their wastrel, wayward lives and needs. They look only to keep up their present level, whether it kills Indians or not. But in addition to this, they do see that this sale they want Your Majesty to make is in fact a violation, irrational and unjust, and they have to be afraid that Your Majesty, or the king who comes after you, pressured by conscience, will want to remove them, exclude them from what is now being sold to them. So they will have one preoccupation only, to get rich, through the suffering and death of the Indians. Then put down roots back in this realm of Castile. Thus, in a brief stretch of time, they will efface all those Indians as they, and those like them, did when they depopulated two thousand leagues worth of islands and three thousand leagues of the main.

Two lies, most noble Lord, that look very reasonable, calculated by those pure tyrants and their backers to fool Your Majesty and anyone else who does not know them or their works or their purposes (all out in the open, nothing hidden)—two lies when they say the land will be secured and the Indians preserved like personal property if they are given to the *encomendero*s in perpetuity.

Fifth. After Your Majesty shall have sold the Indians and the Spaniards shall have bought them, along with jurisdiction over them both civil and criminal, the right of judge and jury, why would they allow Your Majesty to tax them, or discipline them when the defenseless Indians are brutalized by them, exhausted by them, stripped clean by them? Because all the laws, the orders, the penalties the kings and the Emperor in the past have laid down have been useless to halt the massive Indian deaths, the ruination of countless places and the peoples who filled them—all derived from those allotments, those evil, brutal, plague like things they call encomiendas. And the Emperor had not the power to force moderation of those unbearable tributes that flattened and finished off those peoples—and the royal tribute was only 1/1000 of income, but the Spaniards would have none of it, they rose in rebellion against their King, traitors now for a second time.

Sixth. How will the Indians dare complain to the Audiencias a hundred leagues away, two hundred, sometimes five, Indians over whom their *encomendero*s have civil and criminal jurisdiction, and can as judges unabashedly hang them? Right now, the *encomendero*s do not have civil and criminal jurisidiction, the right of judge and jury—they haven't needed it to kill. Right now the frightened, fearful Indians do not dare go to Your Majesty's justice officials to lodge complaints about the robbery, the harassment, the terrible brutalities, the irreparable damages inflicted on them every hour. That is because of the torture, the beatings, the whippings they get—even the chiefs, their natural leaders, under whom they could easily live—so they have a deep seated fear, a horror.

Seventh. How are the Audiencias of the Indies to bring relief to the Indians when some are as far away as Rome from Valladolid, some further than is Belgrade from Seville, and Your Majesty three or four thousand miles across the ocean? What justice, what relief will an aggrieved Indian get? Say the Audiencia of Valladolid is ten leagues away, and the Court is there or close nearby, and the Royal Council and Your Majesty also near, say all is within the space of eighty leagues at the farthest. And say some men in Spain dare bring a complaint, make them the simplest of farmers, they introduce a complaint against the lords who hold them as vassals. As a general rule, these men continue to be overworked and depleted by their masters. A good third of all complaints in chancery occur between lords and vassals—and there are a lot more which people do not dare bring—and they never succeed in halting the grievances people endure.

Eighth. How is it, most noble Lord, the *encomenderos* will allow religious in to preach? They will have given nine millions to buy the Indians as vassals, as slaves in perpetuity, and Your Majesty will have granted them civil and criminal jurisdiction, the right of judge and jury. And how will Your Majesty fulfill the command you have from God to convert the Indians, to draw them to Christ? The *encomenderos* hold allotments of Indians even now by permission of Your Majesty. And every day the governor removes those Indians from them, for trivial reasons, or because they have angered him. Thus they do not allow religious among the Indians in order to preach in the villages so the preachers do not find out about the robberies, the oppressions, the barbarities they inflict. Because the religious would alert the Audiencias and those who govern, the religious would write to the Council, and the Council alerted would send inspectors. The Viceroys and the Audiencias have been in continuous combat with the *encomenderos* about not impeding the preaching of the faith.

Ninth. When the children, the heirs of these *encomenderos* are the rich ones, are the owners, they will know their forebears conquered the land and bought it from Your Majesty for some millions. They will not have known a king, nor known that fidelity, obedience to a king must be kept like the light of one's own eye. They will have been brought up in riches, in exemption, in authority, without belief, without Christianity, with no fear of God. Why should they have anyone preach to the Indians and show them the way of salvation? Why not rebel, why not get rid of, forget the little name Your Majesty has in that region, abjuring and abhorring to hear the word king? In all truth, if Your Majesty permits the sale, those *encomenderos* who have no fear of God now or ever will take it as a superb and ripe occasion to flout and cross you.

Tenth. It is against divine and natural law to hand innocent peoples and places over to their mortal enemies. That is what the Spaniards are. And for proof, look at the cruel, unjust wars they have waged, the fearful slaughters, the unheard of ways of killing they have fashioned in those wars, the captivity and brutal enslavement they have imposed on the Indians. Look at the kings and lords they have tortured to death, the kingdoms, the titles, the estates they have seized and usurped. And the nobility they have spared, they have plunged to the lowest level of life possible, human beings have never seen themselves so cheapened. What the conquerors have always wanted, what they are after now, is to be given these peoples in perpetuity. It is an easy thing to prove, that the Spaniards are deadly enemies of the Indians. So it is not a fitting nor a licit thing for a Catholic sovereign, born of such Catholic stock, to sell so many innocent people to such cruel, guilty aggressors.

Eleventh. The Emperor reigned for a long time. During the whole of it, because he had to be absent outside the realm in multiple affairs of state, and because people who were obligated to tell him the truth kept him in the dark, the Indian peoples overseas suffered enormous evil and destruction and loss of numbers and loss of soul. But when, in 1542, the Emperor found out, he decided to bring the Indians relief, acting as a most compassionate king. He ordered summoned a host of notable people from his various Councils, and on the strength of them he created many just laws, and by means of those laws he made it that all the Indians overseas were to be free, and the plague of encomienda cut out, gotten rid of, because basically unjust and tyrannical. But all this had no effect. The Emperor succeeded only in making the treacherous *encomendero*s rebel against the Royal Audiencia. They killed the Viceroy in defense of their own tyranny and insurrection.

Now the preaching, the word of the religious, had heretofore given them hope—I am speaking of the Indians—that Your Majesty would grant them relief. But the *encomendero*s see that Your Majesty, at the very start of your reign, when the Indians ought to have an increase in confidence—you being the son of such a father—the *encomendero*s see that not only do you not grant the Indians liberty, nor relief from the burden of such hopeless suffering, harsh servitude, but you sell them anew instead, and sell them in perpetuity, with jurisdiction over them both civil and criminal, authority pure and simple. So if the *encomendero*s have, up to now, beaten and murdered the Indians on the sly because they feared punishment, it will happen henceforth out in the open, on a much greater scale, the *encomendero*s being judges with nothing to stay them, nor anyone bold enough to tell them, "What you do is evil!" Nor anyone to keep them lawful.

What consolation will they get, which is to say what desperation will ravage them when they learn that for so many millions Your Majesty has sold them to their sworn enemies who are now to consider them slaves in perpetuity with no hope ever of escaping that hellish life? What are those trapped Indians to do?

Twelfth. I beg Your Majesty to recognize you are going to do something awesome, something that will be broadcast and passionately discussed wherever people meet. It will be caught by Turks and Moors, Indians and Christians, and that you do it right at the start of your reign. And recognize that to sell such huge areas, even for the greatest price in the world, is clearly damaging to your royal name, to the preservation of your future reputation and authority. And recognize that all those who counsel you to do this—though they have official standing—do not grasp the negative results really in the offing, do not see what is really at stake. They do not see what it really is they think can be put up for sale.

Thirteenth. It would be a good thing, my noble Lord, if those who counsel you to sell on the cheap something of enormous worth, could give you their explanation, whether they think we find those realms overseas filled with human beings or filled with cattle. If they say people, rational, human beings, let them answer if they think or believe that Your Majesty has more of a right over those there than those here in Spain. If they say more or greater right over people there, I do not accept it because proof to the contrary is quite available. If they say the same, then it's clear you cannot cause harm to your successors, which is to say here, in these realms, the king cannot give away free peoples or royal income. They are inalienable, they cannot be surrendered, alienating, surrendering them would cause harm to a king's successors. So you cannot give away those overseas. And I affirm to Your Majesty that I can state, without veering one point from the truth, that you have even less right to give away the free people, kings, lords, subjects, in the Indies.

Fourteenth. If Your Majesty has pressing needs stemming from realms here or other regions under his sovereignty, he must draw on them for the means of solution, and not sell free peoples overseas who were not the cause of the needs, and who never owed us a thing. It is the other way around—what we owe them we could not pay, no matter how long the world lasts, it is too much ever to pay. And the laws called "Partidas," written in Spanish, say that when the king has needs he should get help from his subjects, yes, but never by daring to sell them. That is the law of these realms, it is based on just and basic reasoning. Because what is sold can never again help us, support us. It is the difference between a felled tree, and a tree we get fruit from year after year, one we tend.

Fifteenth. Though the Kings, for some grave crisis, are allowed to alienate something—for the well being of the realm—they are not allowed, they may not alienate something major, a great city, say, or the equal, without violating the natural law. The reason is that such alienation results in damage to the realm, to the common good, to the welfare of all. And against that common good, there is no power on earth, spiritual or temporal, that is free to act. Never mind that Your Majesty is going to decide on alienating forever—so the talk goes here, and if a rebellion does not occur there first—more land and kingdoms and peoples than there are from Valladolid to Rome and from Rome to Germany and from Germany to France, and the whole of Spain included, in all more than six times the donation Constantine the Great made to the Roman Church, and there cannot be any greater damage done to all those kingdoms and against their common good, their very life. Those who urge, who counsel you to do it first ought to recognize there isn't a reason big enough, urgent enough, nor will there be from here unto a thousand years, to warrant the alienation of even one single free Indian of the Indies.

Sixteenth. Even though it could be proven that Your Majesty could alienate what those tyrants want to purchase, Your Majesty should by rights find out if they are malicious in the deal they offer you, or just blind—they are telling you that something worth a hundred, two hundred millions is worth seven millions at the most.

Seventeenth. It is well known in Spain and in the world at large that Spain was recovered in a series of just wars, from Arabs, Moslems, who had conquered Spain earlier—and all the goods taken from them were rightly taken, and those many, strong, military men from whom the noble houses of Spain derive, deserve great gratitude for their remarkable deeds and struggles. But there cannot, there will not be found a king, from the first one, Don Pelayo, right down through all the kings who have handed the kingship on in succession right up to Your Majesty, who gave away even one-one hundredth of what Your Majesty now wants to give away, and to tyrants, my noble Lord, who have done more to offend and do damage to Your Majesty and past Catholic kings than any man born, ever in this world, has done to his sovereign.

Eighteenth. It is not on record that any past king of Spain, however great the emergency was, who ever sold a subject, or a place, large or small—though there were always great emergencies, therefore the kings levied taxes, they increased tribute requirements and their right to them. And all those kings were needy and beset by a thousand worries and conflicts. Your Majesty is a powerful lord and master. It makes no sense for you to consider selling anything in the Indies, be it great or small. God is mighty, and can pull you out of this or any other need in a thousand different ways.

Nineteenth. If Your Majesty is bent on gaining relief from the goods of the Indians for immediately pressing needs, order the Indians to be told about it. Then set them free, restore the caciques, the native rulers, to their possessions and authority. They will buy themselves. They will supply the millions that man Ribera so wickedly offers for their purchase. This way, Your Majesty will resolve a great deal of your present crisis, at least within the time frame Ribera asks for, which is four years, so people here say. This way, the regular tributes ordinary free subjects are required justly to pay remain for Your Majesty. A perpetual, a major source of income is not sold away. And it is clear that those about to buy those realms do not have the millions they promise. They have to get them out of the hides, the lives of the Indians, whom they must kill off in the process. The religious can get the money better than anyone. We will all lend a hand in doing so, even from here [in Europe].

As for securing the land, not against the Indians but against the Spaniards, Your Majesty should set a garrison up—to be paid for by the income from thirty holdings those tyrants now control—then everyone not of the right mind will sense the threat. And I beg Your Majesty not to think lightly of this proposal. Instead, order someone who knows Indian affairs, who truly wants to serve Your Majesty, to look it over. He will find there is no other sound way to secure the Indies, or for your royal position to maintain its power over them.

Twentieth. This is the last, the main of all the reasons present-ed—Your Majesty has more need for the light, the help of God than any other king in the world right now, at the start of your reign. You are immediately in more trials than perhaps any of your predecessors, trials kings are not usually freed from by quantities of money. Especially not by suspect money. But only by the help, the grace of God. Therefore Your Majesty should be terribly careful not to do something that will unleash God's anger against his royal person. And even if this material were a matter of opinion—which it is not, not to me, I have spent long years searching out the truth of it—Your Majesty should follow the opinion I am arguing here, it is the surest, it involves fewer drawbacks, fewer risks, even if it should be erroneous. So anyone will judge who has their eyes open. In fact, they will find this opinion certain, its opposite doubtful, dangerous, damaging beyond repair. And I hope before God that Your Majesty, sooner or later, comes to realize that I have always presented the truth, and I am now, that I follow a path that is straight and narrow, unlike those who affirm the opposite decision.

May it please Almighty God to favor the noble and royal position of Your Majesty the way Your Majesty desires it to be—to the glory and honor of God, to the good, the well-being of both the Church universal and these your realms. Amen.

b. The Limits of Royal Power

I

The human race, at the start, and the entire earth, and all things on it, all were free and unowned, by the law of nature and original law of nations, all were free, not subject to any servitude.[225]

II

Inanimate things—land, goods, and the like—were free in the beginning according to the original law of nations, this must also be said.

III

Therefore, no king as king, no emperor as emperor, has power, according to legal experts, over the goods of individuals, over the possession of those goods, or provinces, or territories inherent in those individuals, nor does king or emperor have power over the use of those goods, nor over control of them.

IV

No subjection, no servitude, no burden was ever rightly imposed on a people unless that people gave their free consent to the imposition.

V

The power, the jurisdiction of rulers exist only to procure the common good of their people, and this power, jurisdiction implies no interference with liberty, nor any suspension of it.

VI

Say a king or a prince happens to have many principalities, many cities. One of these suffers damage from war, or, for other reasons, has severe needs. Even though the other principalities or cities ought, out of charity or natural compassion, to come to the aid of the one in need, this has to be done without serious damage to themselves and only after their own needs are met. And the aid should be given voluntarily, and not so as to avoid some evil or loss. Nor, in order to promote the well-being and growth of another city, are they obliged by any law to expose themselves to such danger that it verges on their serious damage or total destruction.

VII

From the preceding, it will be clear what one is to say about the help a city or realm is to offer another realm in need, when the several realms are under the same king. The answer is easy enough, the obligation is less on

---

[225] Bartolomé de las Casas. *De Regia Potestate,* Eds. Luciano Pereña, J.M. Perez-Prendes, Vidal Abril y Joaquin Azcarraga. Madrid: Consejo Superior de Investigaciones Cientificas, 1969. For a brief description of its place in Las Casas' struggle, see Helen Rand Parish's Introduction to *The Only Way,* p. 52.

the part of a city than of a realm, and the realm is to help another realm only if it wishes to do so voluntarily—apart from obligations of charity, etc.—even though it has great resources in gold and silver, has other riches in plenty.

VIII

No king, no ruler, no matter how sovereign, can order or command anything within the realm, concerning the whole of the realm, which is to the damage or detriment of the people or subjects, unless the people or subjects agree to it, through legal and formal agreement. If this process is not observed, whatever is done has no legal standing at all.

IX

Likewise no ruler, king, prince, of any kingdom or community of people, however great his sovereignty, has the liberty or the power of ruling his people as he pleases, in pursuit of his own will. He must rule according to laws. And the laws have to be fashioned so as to be useful to everyone, not injurious to the people. In fact, the laws must be made for the people and the public welfare, not the people for the laws. So no one has the right of legislating anything prejudicial to the same.

X

Thus, there are scriptural texts which prove that all things done to the detriment of subjects, all things prejudicial to them, are blameworthy and damnable.

XI

Concerning the possessions of subjects, or potential damage to subjects, it is not permitted a prince, however sovereign he is, to make donations, make grants, make treaties, make changes that risk them, without first asking and receiving due permission of said subjects.

XII

No prince or king however sovereign may alienate, by gift or sale or transfer or any other mode, a city, a town, a fortress, however small, that is under his rule, to any other ruler, nor may he enter treaty negotiations concerning the right of sovereignty, unless the citizens or townspeople or inhabitants of that city, town or place, voluntarily agree to that alienation. If in fact the king does alienate them against their will or through forced consent, he sins mortally, and the alienation, the treaty, the shifted sovereignty is worthless in law. And the receiver, the buyer also sins mortally and cannot hope for salvation unless he makes it known to the king, every way

he can, that he renounces the gift or that the contract for the sale, the alienation is abrogated, is dissolved.

XIII
A prince may not do anything that violates the natural law or the law
of God. But to sell sovereignty is against the natural law and the law of God.
Therefore a prince may not sell sovereignty.

XIV
Public offices that carry jurisdiction with them cannot be sold.
Public offices that are simply administrative can be sold.

XV
A prince who sells jurisdiction with public offices acts against
justice, both contractual and natural. Therefore he sins mortally. A king
who sells such offices is held to restitution for any resulting oppression of
people.

XVI
Those who buy jurisdiction, and public offices that have jurisdiction
or a like power attached by which citizens or people can easily be harmed,
sin mortally.

XVII
No prince may sell or give away or alienate in any other way what
is properly called the national treasury. If he does he sins mortally and is
obliged to restitution for the damage such alienation brings on the realm or
the commonwealth. He may alienate his own property.

XVIII
The king cannot, without legitimate cause, exempt the provinces
from payment to the national treasury, nor exempt possessions, border
provinces, fortresses from payment destined for the maintenance of the
military. If this cannot be done by right of office, it cannot be done by right
of privilege, because right and privilege in a king amount to the same thing.

XIX
A prince, or any prime administrator, is bound by natural law to
distribute gratis official positions of state, both those for times of war and
those for times of peace, and along with these positions, their perquisites,
their privileges, their salaries. He may grant them something from the

national treasury or the patrimony of the realm for a limited time, never perpetually.

XX

What a prince possesses as private patrimony, as personal wealth, he can alienate, or give to someone else as theirs, as he pleases. But this is to be done in moderation.

XXI

A prince, however sovereign, has no power over the private property of citizens, unless to protect and regulate the same. But in time of public crisis, his power is great, even over private property.

XXII

A kingdom cannot be alienated, neither in whole nor in part, because it is not within the king's power to do so.

XXIII

To alienate a kingdom, the consent of all in it is required.

XXIV

A master cannot give over to someone else the right he has over a vassal or servant against the will of that vassal.

XXV

Each prince must make prosper his own realm, not someone else's.

c. Joint Memorial to Philip (1560)

of Bishop Fray Bartolomé de las Casas
and Fray Domingo de Santo Tomás

against the sale of the Indians of Peru in perpetuity, and in their name. They offer to pay the same sale price as the Spaniards, plus one hundred thousand ducats. If that is not a good match for the Spanish sum, they offer two millions more, to be paid over four years, but on condition.[226]

We are Bishop Don Fray Bartolomé de las Casas and Master Fray Domingo de Santo Tomás, Provincial of the Order of St. Dominic in the Province of Peru. We speak in the name and on behalf of the *caciques*, the native rulers, and their people in the provinces of that realm, or realms commonly called Peru. We speak in virtue of the powers we hold from a group of them who represent the remaining *caciques* and Indians living in that region. It is this group that speaks, representing a common cause, guaranteeing what they promise. For them we ask the following of Your Majesty, the King.

First. A matter has come to the attention of the *caciques* and people of Peru. Your Majesty, up in England or in Flanders, is considering acting on the false information and urgent argumentation of some people interested only in their own selfish purposes. Or Your Majesty has already yielded and decided to grant in perpetuity whole villages in that region, with their *caciques* and Indian inhabitants, to the Spaniards who now hold them in allotment or encomienda. For this perpetuity, the *encomendero*s promise to pay a certain sum in gold and silver. A sum so excessive, it will be impossible for them to supply it. When the *caciques* and people heard of this deal, they thought it horrible. Should Your Majesty really do this, they saw as a certainty their own perpetual captivity, their reduction from being free villages and people to the state of slavery. They saw their doom, their total loss of self.

There is no doubt they are right, and that can be well known, well verified now. For all the laws and commands and prohibitions the Kings of Castile have issued for their good treatment, the Indians are practically gone already when compared to the huge numbers of mortal beings once teeming in those regions. They will be treated much worse, finished off faster, if their *encomendero*s own them as purchased goods. So many people will perish. The evils that will follow those losses, for Your Majesty's interests out there, will be readily apparent. We cannot mention them all, but at least

---

[226] *Opúsculos*, XLVI, pp. 465-468.

five great, irreparable harms will result for Your Majesty's estate in those realms.

First: You will lose, you will be bereft of a great number of productive subjects—the *caciques*, the Indians—that is what they are now, and will remain. Second: You will lose all income, or the most of it, at least that amount the *encomenderos* get from the Indians, if the Indians stay alive. So nothing remains for Your Majesty to give as a reward to those who serve you, even less to mount an armed force if some of the tyrants rebel. Third: There will be no funds to maintain a justice system in the area, nor will the Audiencias be stable, nor able to exercise justice. Fourth: When the *encomenderos* recognize that they have subjects, grow proud as a consequence, presumptious, powerful, they will have a thousand motives an hour to rebel. Rebel they have already without this much of a motive, or even any. They will see Your Majesty retains lordship only over the roads, and they will take that away also. Fifth: If Your Majesty grants perpetuity, you fail in the duty you have of maintaining justice for those peoples, of procuring their growth and prosperity. But especially in the duty of creating an ordered society through which the Indians can be converted and become Christian. Without this, no Christianity.

The *caciques* and people, informed in Peru by people who see how badly damaged those realms will be, want to prevent those terrible, irreparable evils, those losses, from happening. They want good things to happen instead, and Your Majesty to have those good things. So they have sent us their power of attorney, as we said above, so that we, speaking for them and in their name, could lay the whole situation out for Your Majesty. And if we judge it right, to offer to pay you, in their name, all that they need to, in keeping with their capacity. We now use those powers, we, the Bishop and Master Fray Domingo de Santo Tomás, to the limit we can according to the law. So, in their name, we state to Your Majesty that those *caciques* and their peoples will pay you whatever the Spaniards offered to pay that can be verified as in good faith and without fraud. Then the Indians will top that price with one hundred thousand ducats Castilian. And if that is not a good enough match for the Spanish sum, they will pay Your Majesty two million ducats Castilian, over a four year period, in gold and silver.

They will pay the said sum over the said time if Your Majesty, as a just and Catholic king, will promise a series of things, and keep to those promises inviolably, yourself and your successors, ordering drawn up and given to the said *caciques* and people all the documents, the necessary provisions, with all signatures, witnesses, solemn oaths, that just and Christian kings are wont to provide when entering a contract. The things to be promised are the following:

First. Your Majesty must promise and grant that once the lives of the *encomendero*s who at present hold Indians, once the time they have to profit from said Indians is over, you do not give now or ever, do not consent to or permit one single allotment to be given or sold, of all the ones there are now throughout the entirety of Peru. Meaning those which are under your royal crown at the moment, and all those granted to Spaniards. Meaning no kind of subjection or alienation whatever—vassalage, encomienda, feudal subordination, allotment, no kind, if there is another kind. Meaning the Indians should always be, remain, immediately under the crown of Castile, the way the cities, the crown subjects are in the realm of Spain.

Second. The Spaniards are always counter to the good of the Indians, for reasons of self-interest. They will be especially counter in this matter of a negotiated agreement. They must block the Indians, every way possible, from paying Your Majesty a price they themselves cannot pay. It is necessary, therefore, to forbid any *encomendero* for any pretext, for any reason, to enter those Indian villages they hold in encomienda, forbid any of their wives—who are the cruelest, the most destructive—any Black, any servant, any other agent. Those Indian villages should place their tribute in a place that should be designated for their taxes. The reason is the *encomendero*s rob and harass the Indians more than by means of tribute. They will do so even more to block this payment.

Third. The Indians and villages that are now or were under the King, and those also that will be, should pay Your Majesty no more than half the tribute they now pay. And that will be quite an income for Your Majesty, quite a boon for your royal estate. Because the payment the Spaniards offer to make you will be robbed from their subjects, and from the rents the Indians are supposed to pay you. But in the Indian offer, you retain them all as subjects, you retain half the rents, and you remain Lord, with the capacity to reward those who serve you and to punish those who do not obey.

Fourth. If any village or villages among those held by Spaniards in encomienda should find themselves overburdened because the tribute requirements are too high, if that were the real situation—either because there was a dry year, or Indian numbers were down due to death—the demand on them should be lowered. They should be required to pay only a reasonable tribute.

Fifth. As the villages, the allotments, come free, the lesser ones should be brought under the greater, reverting to the order that prevailed in the time of the Inca kings. That is the way to preserve the whole, it cannot be preserved any other way, and that is quite clear at this date.

Sixth. When issues are not general and touching the well being of states as a whole, then delegates from various groups and their communities should be brought together so they can weigh and agree on the usefulness of the proposals, or they can argue against them, a process that used to occur in the time of the Inca kings, and used to occur with the Cortes here in Spain.

Seventh. Your Majesty should see fit to grant the principal rulers of that realm privileges they actually hold from natural law, that they be free and exempt, that they pay no taxes, nor be obliged to other service—the way knights and gentlemen are here in Spain. That is the way those principle rulers lived in the time of their Inca kings. And they should be allowed their symbols and insignias. And allowed to retain their possessions and rights of inheritance so their ancient lineage is not lost.

Eighth. From this time on, it should not be permitted, the taking of lands, water resources, other things specific to communal life, from a community or from individual Indians. It is mindless to do so, against natural justice. Up to this time, Indians have been seriously harmed by this practice. And those common fields and structures which are called *chacaras* there, and have been taken from them in the past to their great disadvantage, these *chacaras* should be returned to the villages and the Indians thereof. And also those holdings whose loss was less harmful—those that had bounds set to them along lines determined by the first governors or justices as if by way of concession or grant. That was the ploy those governors used to expand their control. It was bold-faced usurpation.

With these grants made by Your Majesty, their acceptance by the *caciques* and people, the five bad effects, the loss of sovereignty sketched above will be avoided. Instead, good effects will follow. Firstly, Your Majesty will gain a great number of subjects, not just those alive at present, but multiples of them due to the good treatment, the favors Your Majesty extends to them, due to the peace and happiness and joy they will draw from that treatment, i.e., they will be freed from those who destroyed them, almost to the point of annihilation.

Secondly, Your Majesty will acquire half the rents they have to pay anyway. Take them away from the Spaniards and the Spaniards cannot siphon off any of the rents. We have shown that.

Thirdly, Your Majesty, as king and lord of those regions, will be able to exercise, to administer justice both to Indian and Spaniard. You will be able to hand out rewards to those who deserve them, deserve to remain in the realm, and be able to inflict punishment on those who, for the crimes they commit, must be removed from the realm by death or exile.

Fourthly, the motives for rebellion on the part of those Spaniards who hold Indians will cease, those brutal, evil motives, those swollen prides, those ambitions that exist and fester in them every hour. Because every one of them thinks himself king because of the utter liberty he has gotten out there, far beyond the reach of their own king. To prevent that danger, it is crucial that there be no Spaniard in power out there. Those who know the region well recognise this, and also the designs on the region that suffuse the Spaniards.

Fifthly, incorporating the Indians under the royal crown will be a more pacific, less odious procedure to the Spaniards, because giving Indians in perpetuity to the *encomenderos* would satisfy only them, and they are a small number. The rest would be disturbed, seeing themselves with no hope of getting encomiendas or any other wealth because the King would have no more income or Indians they could acquire. But if Your Majesty retains half the rents, even more retains subjects, you have sources and positions to dispose of for the benefit of the Spaniard. And also for a garrison in the region, something very necessary to maintain a royal authority and the exercise of justice there.

Sixthly, Your Majesty will have the opportunity to fulfill without hindrance the obligation you have towards good government, towards the preservation and the conversion of the Indian peoples. If they are under your royal crown, with the good treatment provided them, the liberty at their disposal, they will have more time, more chance to listen to preaching, and to consider the things of God, what everyone else must have and do who professes Christianity.

There are in the region many tombs which contain great treasure. The *caciques* do not want to uncover them lest the Spaniards seize the riches thereof. So Your Majesty should, by public edict, order that no Spaniards seize treasure uncovered by the Indians. They desire to give Your Majesty a third of the gold, the silver, the precious stones. Two-thirds will remain with them.

We say all this, we offer all this, we ask all this, speaking for those peoples, rulers and subjects alike. And we sign it as it stands.

Bishop Fray Bartolomé de las Casas
Fray Domingo de Santo Tomás

Addendum: Your Majesty must grant authorizations and all the backing required to the person or persons who are to conduct the Indian negotiation on the Indian side, and before a notary whom these persons shall select. The reason is the Spaniards are bound, as said earlier, to block the deal, by fear, by threat, every way they can.

Bishop Fray Bartolomé de las Casas
Fray Domingo de Santo Tomás

d. Twelve Problems of Conscience (1564)
Reason for the Tract

. . . A religious of the Order of St. Dominic, a learned man, concerned about Christian faith and conscience, went out to the Indies, to Peru in particular, for the purpose of helping to convert the native peoples of the region.[227] He worked at preaching the Gospel for some years, and with good success. But he saw the oppression, the servitude those peoples suffered. He learned about the invasion of the region initially made by the Spaniards, then about the way they subjugated the people. He tried to think what reason they had or could have had for doing this, tried to think about the appalling unawareness that possessed every rank of our society out there. No one brought up, no one understood the danger, the damage to conscience they all were living, not even the prelates and religious who were the most required to be on watch, to look into, to know, to say aloud to the people what was the truth: prelates because of their office, religious because of their education. There were many, many problems of conscience, many pros and cons. He reduced them down to twelve—not an easy task—with that same concern for faith we spoke of above, i.e., conscience, and the desire to help the Indians who were suffering the evils, and the Spaniards who were inflicting them. He decided to return to Spain and put these problems to scholars in the various university faculties. He wanted from them, if it was possible, some consensus on the problems, some witness to the truth.

The first one he posed the problems to was the lord bishop of Chiapa, Don Fray Bartolomé de las Casas of the Order of Preachers. He did so because the bishop was reputed to have a great understanding of this material due to years and years of experience. The bishop responded to the problems posed with the following tract.

---

[227] For the manuscript, see Wagner-Parish, Catalogue #74, pp. 295-297; for the importance of the work, see Parish's Introduction to *The Only Way*, pp. 52-3. I have placed problem and solution in close proximity to one another for easier access to Las Casas' thinking. I have omitted the principles of solution since they occur abundantly in previous selections from Las Casas' writings. And I have left out the references to canon law since, again, the same canons occur earlier and abundantly.

Reply of Don Fray Bartolomé De Las Casas to Problems Posed in 1564 Concerning the Moral Consequences of the Conquest of Peru

I.

First Problem: It concerns the treasures of Caxamalca.

The areas that comprise Peru are vast. What we call Peru stretches from the area of Quito to the border of, but not including Chile. It is a thousand leagues long, and in width, sometimes five, sometimes six hundred leagues. All the Indians of the area were pagan peoples. Some worshipped the sun as God, some worshipped stones, and some the mountains. These Indians had never harmed a Spaniard before the Spaniards came, not a one, had never harmed the Church of God, nor any Christian, never. The areas were simply unknown. There was not a word about them until the Spaniards arrived there. They are peoples south of the equator.

The Spaniards went to the realms of Peru in 1531, they wanted to get hold of gold and silver and become rich as rich can be. Once into Peru, they seized the native ruler of the place, Atabaliba, and he gave them no cause for doing so. They seized him in order to kill him and thereby get control of the realm with less of a struggle, and possess it for themselves without opposition. But the captive Atabaliba promised to give them a house filled with gold and silver if they would free him. The Spaniards promised to do this if he kept his promise. Atabaliba did just that, he gave them a house filled with gold and silver artifacts. The Spaniards split this treasure among themselves and set aside a fifth of the lot for the King of Spain. But the Spaniards did not keep their word to Atabaliba, they strangled him to death, then burned his body, spreading the story that he, from where he was kept, had ordered his people to mass together and murder the Spaniards.

So, with this for background, here is the first conscience problem: Is each Spaniard involved in the capture and killing of the said Atabaliba—not quite two hundred of them—bound in conscience to restore all the gold and silver taken by them all? Or is each bound only to restore the amount he took? Or bound to restore nothing?

II.

Second Problem: It concerns the time of non-limitation of tribute.

At the time the Indies were discovered, Pope Alexander VI entrusted them to the Kings of Castile and León so that, as Christian rulers, they could send missionaries to attract and convert the peoples out there to faith in Jesus Christ. The Emperor—may he be with God—sent his captains to the Indies with good, sound instructions aimed at making the Indians Christian. But the captains and the people with them did not obey the instructions—they were after all the gold and silver they could get, whatever they had to do, so they could come back to Spain rich.

So after Atabaliba—the primary ruler in Peru—was murdered by the Spaniards, some of them did come back rich from what they got from that ruler's death. Some stayed there in Peru in order to become richer, there are a few still alive today. A lot of Spaniards went out to Peru on the strength of the reports about riches. Those there headed inland and subjugated the Indians by force of arms, making them tribute payers, almost slaves, in order to take everything they had to the last grain of wheat. And they parceled out the Indians in the following way: the captain gave each soldier an allotment of villages as he saw fit. He gave twenty Indian villages to one man, thirty to another, and so on through the rest. The result was that some soldiers took in ten thousand pesos a year from the Indians the Captain gave them; others took in thirty; others fifty thousand. And each one took whatever else he could squeeze from his Indians. There was no limitation at all on tribute. This was the way the Spaniards went on subjugating the whole of Peru and splitting it among themselves. It is happening in Chile the same way, and in other regions as each is discovered. If some Indians try to defend themselves, the Spaniards kill them, since the Spaniards are far more powerful, and the rest of the Indians submit, little else can they do. All the Indians of Peru are subjugated at this time.

The soldiers who held Indians required tribute of them, as I just said, but without limitation, throughout Peru, for thirteen or fourteen years. Are the holders of Indians obliged, every single one of them, to give back everything they took from the Indians during that period of time? And is each one of them obliged for all the rest, to give back what they all took then, or can they retain it?

III.
Third Problem:
It concerns the period when limits were first imposed on tribute.

After the initial period, some religious and some other people who saw the threat to God's honor caused by the enormous cruelty going on in those realms, persuaded officials of the King to put some kind of limit on tribute exacted from the Indians so they would not be oppressed that severely, but would be able to keep a cloak to cover them and a bit of corn to eat. As a result, a limitation was imposed throughout the area, this way: controllers ordered that each allotment of Indians should supply their *encomendero* with everything he needed for his household. What was needed was left up to the *encomenderos* themselves, they could require, as necessary for their individual households, whatever they could think up. And that was what the controllers granted them, allowed them to exact, unable to do otherwise—there would be a rebellion all over if the controllers did not yield to the soldier *encomenderos* and give them what they demanded. So the controllers ordered given, in each exaction, a lot of gold, of silver, a lot of clothing, hats, mantles, sacks, horse blankets, a lot of grain, corn, sheep, lambs, pigs, chickens, partridges, fresh and salted fish, sandals, tallow, matting, chairs, boats, and a lot of coca, and many, many things else. So the controllers, ultimately, gave the *encomenderos* everything they wanted. . .[228]

Is each one of those soldier *encomenderos* obligated to restore to the Indians everything they took from them, given that the tribute the soldier *encomenderos* could exact was limited? Or obligated to restore only some, not all? Does the reply have to distinguish between the *encomendero* who supplied a chaplain for his Indians and the one who did not?

IV.
Fourth Problem:
It concerns the present day limitations on tribute exaction in Peru.

Most *encomenderos* have, up to the present moment, kept to the limitations just described. The Viceroy, the Marquis de Cañete, and the Audiencia have readjusted some of the limitations, removing some requirements so as to unburden the Indians, though the tribute is still excessive. Some *encomenderos* retained a cleric for their Indians, some two, some none, nor a layman capable of catechizing them. Some *encomenderos* had a sufficient program of catechetics. Some half what was needed, because in a number of allotments of Indians there was but one cleric or brother, and three priests were necessary. The *encomendero* paid the priest

---

[228] . . . Those who set the limits, as I [Las Casas] said, did not do so justly in order to avoid a rebellion. A repartimiento which gave thirty thousand, they limited to twenty thousand, not because twenty thousand was the right sum, but so the Indians' load would be lightened by ten thousand, that's what these people kept saying over a long time.

Something to note here—encomiendas, though officials of the King granted them, were against the King's will, and against the officials' will too, because both King and officials allowed encomiendas and limitations on tribute so the Spaniards would not rebel and rouse the whole territory in rebellion.

Something further to note—in the documents of encomienda given to soldiers, those who set the limits ordered them to provide religious instruction for their Indians. Some encomenderos had a cleric for the purpose, some none at all.

some three or four hundred pesos and kept the rest of the tribute for himself, ten thousand in some cases, more and less in others.

In some of the allotments, half the Indians were pagan, they were not baptized nor did they want to be, but they paid the *encomendero* the tribute as well, just as did the baptized Indians. Among the *encomenderos* are ones who hold encomiendas due to the express will of the Viceroy or the Audiencia, not from earlier governors. So there are many soldiers who hold what they hold due to the will of the King's officials. But others do so without the consent of the King or of royal officials, and such like are allowed to keep what they hold and no one says a word, so these soldiers think they have a King's grant for services they have rendered him. This situation is allowed in order to avoid a widespread rebellion. Such is the situation in Peru today.

The question is, are all these *encomenderos* obliged to restitution? And can the *encomendero* who has a sufficient catechetical program for his Indians keep the total tribute? Or if a part, how much of a one?

V.
Fifth Problem: It concerns those who profit from *encomenderos*.

Nearly all the gold and silver in Peru derives from these *encomenderos*. The merchant gets two bars from them for his cottons and silks; the lawyer one bar for legal services; the scribe for writing; the doctor for healing; the tailor a hundred pesos for making clothes; servants five hundred pesos in salary; religious two hundred pesos for saying masses, plus other stipends. Remember the first four problems, and also that the lands of the *encomenderos* belonged to the Indians. The *encomenderos* seized those lands, and with Indian labor they planted their vineyards on Indian soil. The herds they had they grew with Indian labor on Indian territory. Thus the tribute belonged to Indians, as did the homes and estates the *encomenderos* had.

So this is the problem: are the people who made money off the *encomenderos* obliged to restore the money they got this way? Can we accept that there were many officials in Peru who did not know the tribute exacted by the *encomenderos* was ill-gotten, did not know the estates of the same were ill-gotten also? Even though the truth was that nearly every other Spaniard in Peru had some doubts concerning the holdings of the *encomenderos* due to what they heard from preachers in the pulpit and from common talk? Or can we absolve merchants, doctors, lawyers, tailors, servants, scribes, religious, etc., who got their money from *encomenderos*?

VI.

Sixth Problem: It concerns mines, silver and gold.

When the Spaniards went to Peru, there were mines already known in the realm, those at Porco, many elsewhere. Some belonged to Guainacáp-ac, who ruled the land. Others belonged to specific Indians who drew from them the gold and silver they paid as tribute money to Guainacápac. After the Spaniards came to Peru, many more mines were discovered in the region, both gold and silver, some by Indians, others by Spaniards; some by accident, some by design, the result of search.

The Spaniards have seized for themselves any mine, worth anything today in Peru, ones found before them, ones they found after. Those not owned by specific people are owned by the King of Spain. And they own them in such way that neither the specific people nor the King of Spain permit anyone else at all to work them for ore. And concerning those mines found after the Spaniards came, some are old, twenty five years, some quite recent and quite good, like those at Guamanga.

Every mine the Spaniards work, discover, have worked, have discovered, right up to the present day, must be considered done in violation of the Indians' will. For two reasons. One, the mines are in their territories, and therefore are, and must be considered to be, theirs, though they cannot profit from them. And note there is not a handsbreadth of land which isn't divided up among the Indian villages, according to people who have investigated the matter. Two, it is in violation of the Indians' will because all the gold and silver dug is dug by Indians—the Spaniards force them into the mines. The Indians feel this as a terrible grievance, an intolerable burden. They do not refuse because they are unable. The Spaniards in Peru, past and present, are there against the will of the Indians. This must be noted, even though today there are twenty Spanish towns in Peru, some large, some small, and not counting those in Chile. The Indians allow this because they cannot do otherwise.

The King of Castile and León has a Bull issued by Alexander VI. In it the Pontiff grants him the Indies and their discovery, as noted in the Second Conscience Problem, so that the said King of Castile and León should see to the preaching of the faith out there, and to the administration of justice. For which services the Indians pay a huge, even excessive amount in tribute. But the mines they have on their own lands are taken from them, mines from which they must draw the wherewithal to pay the huge tribute, and pay for whatever else they need.

Three conscience problems stem from the above. First, can the King of Spain own any mine out there from which he derives gold and silver for his own profit? Second, can Spaniards out there own mines? Third, can the King or Spaniards keep any metal from any mine that existed in Peru before the Spaniards came, or are they obliged to give back to the Indians all the gold and silver taken up to the present day, plus the mines themselves?

VII.
Seventh Problem: It concerns the tomb treasures.

The Indians of Peru had the custom of burying their riches with themselves, at least those who were important people—this was before they were Christian and still in their pagandom. So, riches like gold, silver, the finest robes they had, emeralds, jugs, vases, pitchers, other utensils all made of gold and silver. There were two reasons for doing this. First, they thought it was an honor, both for the living as well as for the dead, to have rich and splendid tombs. Second, they thought they would retain possession of those things in the afterlife. So, in their view, someone who took a lot into the grave with him would be highly honored in the hereafter and considered wealthy, whereas someone who took nothing with him into the grave would be poor and oppressed in the hereafter. This is why there are rich tombs, tombs of parents, grandparents, great grandparents, etc. There have been found more than five hundred thousands ducats worth of wealth, between the year 1554 and the present day, in the tombs of just one city called Trujillo. The Spaniards have appropriated more than four hundred thousand of those ducats.

Some tombs have owners, those whose children or grandchildren are still alive and set great store by said tombs. Others are so ancient that the Indians do not know whose they are, but only know they were leaders of that people and all memory of them lost. The Spaniards hunt out those tombs, against the will of the Indians, and take everything they contain. This very day, they are out after them eagerly.

The conscience problem is this: are the Spaniards obliged to restore everything they take from those tombs? Do we distinguish between those which have owners and those which have not, to the effect that Spaniards can keep the treasures taken from those which have no specific owners? But if Spaniards are obligated to restitution, to whom should it be made?

VIII.
Eighth Problem: It concerns offerings in sacred places.

The Indians of Peru call "guaca" any place where they adore something. So a "guaca" is the hill that has a stone they adore as a god. It is the well where they wash before sacrificing to the demon. Sometimes a part is given the name of the whole, i.e., they call "guaca" the object they adore, the stone, the fountain, the tree, etc.

The Indians of Peru, while they were still pagan and unconverted, made at these "guacas" offerings of gold aplenty, of silver, of precious stones. The most important of these sacred places in Peru was the Temple of the Sun in the city of Cuzco. That place is today the monastery of Saint Dominic. In the Temple of the Sun was a great wealth of gold, silver, other things of great price, dedicated to the worship of the Sun. It was God for the Incas, the principal people of Peru. The Spaniards took all that wealth, plus huge treasure from other sacred places like the one at Pachacámac. Such sacred places are found in every Indian village; the riches in them are incredible!

The conscience problem is this: are the Spaniards who plundered the riches of these "guacas" obligated to give back all they took. And if so, to whom do they make restitution.

IX.
Ninth Problem: It concerns land set aside for the Inca king.

The Inca Guainacápac, King of Peru, set aside for himself, in each village, a stretch of good ground strictly his. The ground was called "chácara"—it is called that today—because the word means reservation. The king was called the Inca, though the people of the region, past and present, were also called Incas. It is like the ancient Egyptians calling all their kings Pharaoh.

The Inca designated these lands for growing the maize the Indians then paid to him as tribute. And that maize was either carried to the Inca's court in Cuzco, or stored in the villages that grew it for disposition later at the Inca's command.

Inca Guainacápac, whose grandchildren are still living, was the native and legitimate ruler of some of the regions of Peru, Cuzco, for example. But not of many others, people say. Those others he conquered by tyranny and force of arms, and made them tribute-paying for no good reason. People say further he did this just to dominate, and in every region he conquered and ruled, he designated a stretch of ground for his own purposes, as noted above.

When the Spaniards took over Peru, they divided up among themselves all the reservations of the Inca—the best ground in an area—and these reservations today are the Spanish holdings, on them the Spaniards have built their homes, planted their vines, walled their orchards, etc.

The conscience problem is this: are the Spaniards obligated to restitution? And to whom should it be made?

X.
Tenth Problem: It concerns the capture of Cuzco.

When the Spaniards went to Peru, they crossed the country conquering the Indians, as described in the Second Conscience Problem. At Cuzco, the Indians put up a defense against the oncoming Spaniards, but were unable to succeed, so they abandoned the city, the most important one in Peru, and fled away from it. When the Spaniards entered, they despoiled the city of the great riches found there, especially in the Temple of the Sun, as described in the Eighth Conscience Problem, but also in the Temple of the Moon. They divided up among themselves the best houses of the place—ones whose walls are still standing—ones which would be the stoutest because made of stone. Many Spaniards afterwards built fine structures right into those walls or right on top of them. Because the homes of the Indians had straw roofs, and were simple things. So the Spaniards put on tile, doubled the size of the places, built corridors and porches. Though many Indian homes are still standing today, and will stay so because they are sound. The Spaniards have lived in the city of Cuzco now for twenty five years.

The Spaniards took also the land the Indians owned in that valley of Cuzco, and did not leave the Indians a foot of ground anywhere, they split it all up among themselves. These are the lands—worth so much—the Spaniards in that city retain to this day. And have not restored a whit to the native dwellers of the place, who must live up in the hills that encircle the city, and work them for their livelihood, deprived as they are of the valley floor. The houses the Spaniards seized from the Indians belonged to King Guainacápac, to the people of his court.

This is the problem: are the Spaniards obligated to give those houses, those valley floor lands back to the Indians, or can they retain possession of them? They feel no scruple. They think that since a cathedral church has been built on the house sites, since there is a bishop, four monasteries belonging to the four orders, it is quite all right to retain possession.

XI.
Eleventh Problem: It concerns the sovereignty of the Inca.

Guainacápac was the ruler of Peru. His realm stretched from Chile all the way to Quito, a distance of a thousand leagues. He died when the Spaniards entered Peru. Two of his sons were alive at that time, Atabaliba and Guáscar, plus further [family]. In addition to Atabaliba and Guáscar, there were other rulers at the time of the invasion. They were at war among themselves, either for the whole kingdom or just part of it, the province of the "canares." The two principals and all the children of Guainacápac are now dead, though a lot of the latter's grandchildren still live. Many of them, when they experienced how badly the Spaniards treated them, simply fled somewhere into the mountains and set up in a province they named Andes, it is behind lofty peaks, and there, this day, they adore the sun, adore it as god, just as they did before the Spaniards arrived.

The Indians recognize one of the Inca's descendants as king over the Andes—his name is Tito—and king over the rest of the country as well. Tito has his own court, has his own military guard. He keeps to the mountains, along with the rest of Guainacápac's descendants, so as not to be subject to the Spaniards, as are the rest of the Indians of Peru. The ones in the mountains want to be Christian, to leave where they are. That is if the King of Spain would provide for their livelihood once they came out and were in among the Spaniards. And they would be satisfied if the King of Spain gave them an allotment of people, the way he did to Spanish *encomenderos*. Tito wrote many letters to the authority in Cuzco, over a two year period, and in them he asked the authority to pay him a visit in the Andes, and said he needed to work things out with him. The authority did go see Tito, and had him set up many crosses in the area. Tito asked him to request the Viceroy to grant him a livelihood, he wanted to come out of where he was and become a Christian.

The problem is this: is the King of Spain obligated to bring this Inca called Tito out of the mountains, grant him the kingdom of Peru, but retain ultimate and overall power to use force on Tito and crush him should he rebel? Or can the King of Spain, in good conscience, allow Tito to stay as he is in the mountains, deprived of his authority?

Some object that it would not be a good thing to give Tito authority over his kingdom. They give two reasons. One, he and the whole region would rebel. Two, he would prevent the Indians from becoming Christian. Others argue that it would be a good thing to have him out. They answer the negatives of the first group by saying Tito could not rebel along with the whole region. There are more than six thousand Spaniards in Peru today. A hundred of them are enough to kill every Indian on the ground. A little more than a hundred, certainly less than two hundred Spaniards conquered the place to start with. They answer to the second objection that the opposite is true, for if the Inca comes out, all the Indians of the Andes who are now pagans would become Christian, and those outside the Andes would become better Christians than they are now. And this is the reason: the Indians are very obedient to their native rulers, and very inclined to imitate them. If the Inca were to become a good Christian, the rest would be also, and better than they are now. Many, though baptized, are still heathen. Because they see themselves heavily oppressed, bereft of their own king, and their king is heathen right now, and all the Indians look to Tito for their lead.

But something further must be known about the situation, and it is that Guainacápac, grandfather of this Tito, was legitimate ruler only over some sections of Peru. His ancestors were kings over the same. But Guainacápac conquered some other provinces and made them all subject without real cause, the same way that the Spaniards conquered all Peru and made it subject without real cause.

XII.
Twelfth Problem: It concerns soldiers who claim good faith.

The Spaniards who went out to Peru, especially those who found the place, committed great crimes there, like the murder of Atabaliba and seizing of his wealth, like burning many Indians alive, loosing attack dogs on them, cutting off their heads, making them all pay tribute money, slaves right from the start, even though they were not sold as such, yet slaves in everything but name. And Spaniards did this unprovoked to it by the Indians. And in sum, did many other abominable things to them.

The problem is this: can there be any Spaniard among them all who could have acted in good faith and been invincibly ignorant about the sinful nature of the evil deeds done? So their good faith would excuse them from the necessary restitution required as a result?

Some Spaniards claim they acted out of good faith and out of ignorance. They claim they did not sin when they killed the Indians and took their territory and made them subject, etc. Because, they said, the Indians were heathen pagans, enemies of God, and to be treated like the dogs they were. But really, there cannot be ignorance about the ten commandments—i.e., murder is a sin, even if it is a non-Christian who is murdered; robbery is a sin, even if it is a non-Christian who is robbed; burning people alive without cause, without reason, is a sin, even if it is a non-Christian who is burned alive. . .

Response to First Problem

All the Spaniards involved in seizing and killing Atabaliba committed grave mortal sins of injustice. . .

These same Spaniards—upwards of two hundred—who were in on the murder are bound in conscience to restore the realms of Peru to the heirs of Atabaliba, or to the one who succeeds him according to their law or custom. And bound under threat of eternal damnation. . .

These same Spaniards involved in seizing and killing Atabaliba are obliged to restore all the gold and silver they got in the operation, i.e., the gold and silver he paid to ransom himself, then the rest of the riches they got along with the gold and silver. . .

These same Spaniards . . . are obliged to make restitution for all the robbery and ruin done by the rest of the Spaniards who came afterwards to that region. For they despoiled many of the important leaders of their honor, their dignity, their authority, their riches, their subjects, their estates, and took from every Indian else their land and liberty, putting them in servitude under the allotment system. . .

These same Spaniards. . . plus the nearly two hundred others in Peru at the time, are all bound individually for the whole, each must restore Peru to its rightful ruler, and must restore the ransom of Atabaliba, and make up for all the damage done at the seizure and after in that country. I say each one is bound to restore the whole if he knows the others have not done so, though they could have, for there is no individual salvation without total restitution. . .

These same Spaniards involved in seizing and killing Atabaliba were out of their minds when they did so, they were immoral, they were lawless. . .

From the minute these same Spaniards seized Atabaliba, his sons and heirs acquired the right to make just and lasting war against every Spaniard as against a public enemy. And that right to wage just war will last until Judgment Day. Unless it is interrupted in one of four ways: by peace, by truce, by satisfaction where possible, by forgiveness of the debt on the part of those who suffered the damage, but forgiveness freely made, not through force or fear—that can come only after the oppression, the tyranny going on now over there ceases. . .

Even if the realms of Peru were to have recognized the sovereignty over them of the King of Castile and León—something they never actually did, never recognized that sovereignty—nevertheless, it would be right for them to make war against the Spaniards, their enemies, and against judges, governors, officials of the King, right to kill them and through war make up for the damage, the harm they had suffered from such Spaniards. . .

Response to Second Problem

All the Spaniards referred to in this second problem committed grave mortal sins when they exacted the tribute they did, after they had completed their invasion and conquest. . .

All the Spaniards referred to here are bound to restore the gold, silver, precious stones, clothing, cattle, food, everything they took from the Indians, during the course of conquest by war, or as they call it, entry. . .

All the Spaniards referred to are obliged to restore the entire tribute they exacted, to the last kernel of corn, prior to the time they were limited by law on what they took. . .

All the Spaniards referred to here are obliged to restitution for everyone else—in solidum—concerning what they took in the wars they made on the Indians. . . And the obligation extends to every one of them to make restitution for everyone else concerning the tribute they all exacted. . .

All the Spaniards referred to are obliged to restore whatever lands they seized from the Indians, lands they call *chácaras,* even though the Spaniards have built houses on them, planted vineyards, orchards, or used the lands to profit otherwise.

Response to Third Problem

The Spaniards who were controllers of the tribute acted well, and before God meritoriously, if they acted in good faith and limited the tribute exacted to what they thought the tyrant *encomenderos* would accept short of mutiny. They could not do otherwise. They permitted the tribute to be exacted, they did not order it. . .

The reasoning is this: when they set the limits they did, they did what they could, and helped the Indians by relieving them of a third of their burden, or whatever the proportion was in terms of what the Indians carried before the limitation. Because to remove an evil or diminish it in some way is a good deed according to the Philosopher in his Ethics. As a consequence of this principle we could talk someone just about to do a great evil into being satisfied with doing a lesser one. Example: if someone is intent on killing a cleric, we could beg him to be satisfied with beating up that cleric. We could urge a usurer not to demand as much interest from a poor person as from a rich one.

The reasoning depends on the controllers acting in good faith. Because if appeal entered their decisions, or friendship, or personal, family, group interest, the controllers sinned mortally and were bound to restore what they might with the least provocation to those tyrants whose exactions they could and should limit. So, for the controllers to escape mortal sin and the obligation to make restitution, they had to have in mind only the prevention of the greater damage that could fall on the Indians if the Spaniards were ever to rebel against the King. . .

Once the tribute was limited by the controllers, the *encomenderos* could not exact one grain of wheat more than the amount fixed. But in reality, they are obligated to restore everything they took, within the limits, or outside them.

The principle involved is this: the invasion of the Indies by the Spaniards was in violation of divine and natural law, and the invaders were absolute tyrants . . . Thus everything they did was null, nothing, of no validity. As a result, they had no right to exact even a kernel of corn due to their violent, tyrannical invasion. . .

Encomiendas, allotments of Indians . . . were always against the will of the Kings of Castile who considered them bad ways of governing, from the moment they were started on the island of Hispaniola without any authorization from the Catholic Kings. . .

The *encomendero*s who had clerics or religious teach religion to their allotted Indians, are not obliged to pay back the amount they gave to the said clerics or religious, nor the further expenses paid for the same. . .

Response to the Fourth Problem

Whether the *encomendero*s had a sufficient or insufficient program for teaching religion, whether or not the Indians reverted to paganism once or often, the *encomendero*s are obliged to give back all they are taking, have taken, except for what they paid the people who taught the Indians. . .

Response to the Fifth Problem

All the people included under this problem—those who did not ex officio help the Indians or who did not profit from Indians in any direct way, but profited only from Spaniards—sin mortally and are obliged to give back to the Indians everything the *encomendero*s gave them by way of salary or wages or gift or settlement or handout. . .

The wife and children of the men who robbed what they hold, cannot feed and clothe themselves from such holdings without incurring the obligation to pay for the food they ate, the clothes they wore. And further, they are obliged to look for another source of livelihood, in every way they can. If they cannot find one, they may take from the holding only the bare necessities of life. . .

Those who feed and clothe themselves with what is not theirs, but have no other way to survive, are nonetheless obliged—should they ever inherit something, or come to possess something in any other way—to make restitution, satisfaction, for the food and clothing they once needed. . .

Religious, preachers, can eat and have the strict necessities of life if in their sermons they warn people who hold what is not theirs to give it back and do penance. And warn people in confession and in personal encounters. . .

But if such religious, such preachers do not argue and urge those who keep what they stole to give the same back and do penance, if they are not arguing and urging this day in, day out, they cannot take food, cannot take a single maravedi without being obligated to restitution for every bit they ate or took. . .

A tithe is owed the Church from the property of Christians, whether it is in the owner's hands or someone else's, and ministers of the church can receive the tithe licitly. . .

But tithes on things people possess unjustly cannot be accepted without committing theft. Like things from an unjust war, from a robbery, from usury, from simony, from unjustly imposed tribute, from an unjust verdict, and from things similarly acquired unjustly. A tithe cannot be required, cannot be accepted. Much less anything as an offering, a stipend for a church ceremony. . .

The Church cannot exact tithes from the property of pagans, even though such property is in the hands of Christians. The proof of this lies in the fact that one cannot give alms from stolen goods, nor give them away, nor pay them in tithes, without the consent of their real owner. Since such property has been stolen from pagans, one cannot use it to pay Church tithes. . .

Religious and ecclesiastics commit mortal sin when they accept from *encomendero*s any alms at all, any donations, whether for church buildings or monasteries, or for silver, gold, alhajas altar vessels, or to found chaplaincies or construct chapels or tombs for their burials. . .

Prelates of cathedral churches, pastors, religious superiors, must appoint godly people to evaluate the cost of building churches and monasteries, the cost of the grounds, the sites on which they were built, the worth of the labor and matériel the Indians put into the same. They must pay the Indians restitution for the entire value of the land used, and for the labor doing the building. . .

All religious and all others who asked alms from *encomendero*s for the purpose false or true of helping their parents, family, friends, and who sent these alms home, or brought them, sinned mortally. They are obliged to restitution. It is no excuse that they had the permission of their superiors.

Response to the Sixth Problem

The King of Spain and the Spaniards possess the mines of Peru against the will of Indian kings and people. . .

The King of Castile and León cannot possess mines for gold or silver or any other metal, for emeralds or anything else in Peru unless by the voluntary permission of the Peruvian kings or their successors. And the King of Castile cannot give such mines to anyone else. . .

Individual Spaniards, living in Peru today, cannot possess mines in that land, mines for gold or silver or anything else, without permission of the Kings of Peru. What they have mined to date, Spaniards are required to give back and completely. . .

As to the mines for gold, silver, or any other precious metal or stone, discovered when the Spaniards invaded the kingdoms of Peru—or indeed those discovered after the invasion, whether discovered by Indian or Spaniard, whichever—Spaniards took them, stole them, and are obliged to give back all the gold, silver, precious metals and stones they dug from said mines, or run the risk of eternal damnation. . .

The King of Castile and León is obliged by divine and naural law to provide fit people to preach, to teach, to administer the sacraments to the Indians, to both converted and unconverted. He is obliged to construct places of worship, churches, to support the personnel needed for divine worship. But for such service, tithes may not be required of the Indians, for the time being, nor should they pay tribute, not a pennysworth of anything else if the Indians do not wish to give it willingly.

Response to the Seventh Problem

Whoever takes or orders taken the tomb treasures the Indians of Peru hold by heredity, or anything of value from the same, commits robbery, and is obliged to give back whatever was taken. . .

Spaniards who took treasure or precious objects from the tombs in Peru that did not have owners or family, are obliged to give it all back to the last maravedi.

Response to the Eighth Problem

Spaniards who live, or have lived, in the realms of Peru, are obliged to give back all the gold and silver and precious objects they took or got from the temples and shrines of the Indians—shrines called guacas in the language of Peru. And give it all back to those who placed such treasure there, if they are still alive, or to their inheritors. . .

Treasure that has no owner or inheritor, and all other riches, jewels, robes, precious stones, must be given back to the Indians. Spaniards cannot retain possession of such goods. . .

Response to the Ninth Problem

The Spaniards are obliged to restore to the Indians all the land they took from them. If they do not, the Spaniards will not save their souls. . .

For the Spaniards to say that Guainacápac was a tyrant, and that he had taken over many parts of the Peruvian realm by force, does not excuse them from giving back the lands called *chácaras*. They are now in the possession of tyrants. . .

Response to the Tenth Problem

The Spaniards involved in the seizure and control of Cuzco, in the parceling out of houses and buildings among themselves, the lands also and the estates, sinned mortally. They are obliged for restitution to the Incas and their successors, as well as to individual Indians whose houses and fields were taken. And each Spaniard is obligated for the whole, though he got only part of what was robbed. Likewise those who build houses in Cuzco must hand over what they built. . .

Response to the Eleventh Problem

The noble and most Christian King of Castile and León is obliged—if he wishes to save his soul—to seek every way, every means possible to draw the king, the legitimate heir of Guainacápac, down into Christian territory where he and his people might be converted to the Christian faith. He and his whole army fled into the Andes mountains. . .

The Catholic King of Castile, our ruler, is obliged—if he wishes to save his soul—to give back the realm of Peru to the Inca nephew of Guainacápac. I mean the one who is the heir to the realm. And our King is obliged to give back to all other rulers there the power that belonged to them. . .

If, when the King of Spain should restore the Kings of Peru to their realms, the *encomenderos* should rebel against the King of Spain, refusing thereby to give up what they gave each other, then the King of Spain is obliged to make war on them, and die in war if that is what it takes to free those innocent peoples the Spaniards hold in subjugation. . .

[STEPS TO DRAW THE INCA, KING OF PERU, OUT OF HIS MOUNTAIN FASTNESS]

First, let the cleric who was the provisor at Cuzco, the one who already knows the Inca, plus some religious, good and prudent ones who can speak the native language, go see the Inca with letters marked with the seal of His Majesty, and some gifts sent in the King's name. Then, speaking for the King, they tell the Inca the King knows about the evils, the harm the Spaniards have done him, his predecessors and his people. And this has troubled the King greatly. So he has decided to remedy the situation, insofar as he is able, all that can be remedied, as the Inca will see from the King's actions. The cleric and religious are to promise the Inca, in the King's name, absolute safety, freedom, for his person, for his family, for everyone else with him. A certain area is to be indicated where the Inca may settle, may have certain villages of Indians to serve him, ones that would be the most acceptable. The same should be offered lesser rulers who are with the Inca, according to the dignity of their status. His Majesty should promise the Inca that all this will be his, and the more His Majesty intends to give.

Once they are on Christian ground, the people are to be presented with our holy Catholic faith, quickly but thoroughly, according to the manner left us by Our Lord Jesus Christ. Once they accept it freely, they will readily see why we believe, as intrinsic to our faith, that Jesus Christ Our Lord gave to His Vicar, the sovereign Pontiff, a position of overall authority and godly power. The next step for the preachers is then to persuade the Inca and his people to grant their consent, to accept the designation, the status of overlord that the Holy See provided the Kings of Castile and León. This step demands that something be made clear: it is in the Inca's power to accept or reject this status. All fear, all deception is out. If there is either, no matter how little, we will have nothing, nullity will suffuse everything. And because we are in this process to provide a good conscience for the Kings of Castile and León, and to have Spain begin to receive from the Indies something rightfully gained, it is utterly necessary that the whole process be carried out with absolute sincerity.

Once the religious goal has been accepted, the other conditions and agreements should come into play—as described in Principle 7, i.e., the King, our ruler, promises those people good government, promises to maintain their laws, their procedures, their customs, the ones not adverse to faith and the Christian way of life, promises to give back to them all the villages now under His Majesty's authority and in the possession of *encomenderos*, but only as the *encomenderos* pass away. Further, the boundaries of Spanish towns and villages, their common pastures, are to be kept strict and narrow in so far as it is possible to do, not allowing them to expand beyond what is necessary. The same thing with church areas, monasteries, places for pious uses. All other land shall be given back into Indian control, it was their land or *chácaras* on which those buildings were constructed. If the Indian owners are not alive, the restoration shall be made to their heirs. If they are not alive, then to the king, Tito Inca, so he may parcel the land out to those he thinks best suited. His people can set up house there, work the fields, graze cattle. Further, the value of the construction sites must be paid back, the value of the labor it cost the Indians, even the value of the buildings not made with Indian work, but which the

Spaniards erected with Black or other than Indian hands, though it would be a miracle to find even one. The reasoning is that those structures do not belong to the Spaniard, but to the Indians. The structures were built on someone else's land, their supposed owners have no right to them. . .

For their part, the Inca and the people must promise to the Kings of Castile and León a permanent respect and fidelity and loyalty. And the Inca and his successors shall give token gold and silver every year as a recognition of the international authority [of the Kings], token in terms of what is right according to natural law demands. Once all these conditions and agreements have been worked out, both parties shall swear to them with absolute sincerity, with religious integrity. The Indians shall perform certain juridical acts whereby they show they accept his Majesty as overall ruler and protector, and also his successors in Castile and León. But apart from that, the Indians are to retain their entire freedom. It is from that freedom that they grant the Kings a peaceful presence in their realms. It is from that freedom that they recognize the Kings thenceforward as overall ruler.

The Indians can be persuaded by the religious not to ask back the treasure taken from the Indies and kept by the Kings of Castile, and it can be a free act on their part. The difficulty would be extreme of hauling back there and handing over all those boatloads of gold and silver that went to Spain. And the Indians can be given to understand that from this point in time onwards the small amount the Kings of Spain do return should be considered restitution, and though small what they return, it is nonetheless significant and intended.

The Indians can likewise be persuaded to forgive the insult, the injury, the deaths, the wicked treatment the Spaniards have meted out to them, the wreck and ruin, etc. No amount of money could ever repair for that. After this, the Spaniards could begin to feel safe in Peru and get free of the anxiety and disorder abroad in that area.

The above are the steps that ought to be taken by the Kings of Castile and León, according to divine and natural law, so as to become the supreme authority over the Indies, this is the way to have juridical possession, and have an actual jurisdiction out there. What has been done, what is being done now, what will be done, without taking the steps I have laid out, has no jurisdictional value of any kind, nor ever will. There will be just the bare title. Up until now, our King has only the right to receive the title, not actually have it, i.e., he has the potentiality for being lord over those realms, but he does not have the right to actual rule over them because consent on the part of the kings and the people out there is lacking him. And the tyrannical invasion and occupation by the Spaniards blocks [that consent].

What I have left to do is reply to the two arguments the 11th Problem contains. It is about those who do not want the Inca king restored to his power. One argument says that with Tito Inca restored, the whole country will rebel. My reply is, first, that those who make the argument are themselves involved in tyranny, and they do not want to surrender their ill-gotten goods. Second, how can they possibly think there will be a rebellion? With one hundred and seventy men, more or less, the invaders had enough to capture King Atabaliba who had at his side more than forty thousand men, so the story goes. And the same few, afterwards, were sufficient to subdue the huge number of people there were in that country. Today there are in it more than six or seven thousand Spaniards and as many horses and rifles and all manner of weaponry, and there are half as many Indians as there used to be!

The tyrants present a second argument, they say Tito Inca will block or distort on his people matters of Christian belief. I maintain he will instead help them. If it is just a question of the spiritual good which is to follow, then restoring him to power is quite enough. He will persuade his people to become Christian. But until the time he comes out of the mountains, becomes a Christian himself, Peruvian Indians will never be really Christian, they love him, revere him, obey him that much, even up there in the mountains. If he is not Christian, they are not Christian. By the same token, if they see their King is one, and restored to his power and dignity, they will begin to have an affection for the faith, for the things of our religion. They will see the troubles of the past now stopped.

But if that land stays in the condition it is now in, it will take a miracle from God to convert a single Indian. Because they see in us the exact opposite of what we preach, of the faith we teach. They see we are lords over their property, their estates, their rulers, over their persons. That is the only interest we have in their realm, the only one.

Response to the Twelfth Problem

All the Spaniards meant under this problem lack good faith, they never had it, any more than did those pagans who killed and cut to pieces the martyrs, any more than do the Turks today when they persecute the Christian people. The ignorance is culpable.

- 5 -

Last Will and Testament

Prenote

Las Casas expressed the meaning of his whole life spent for Spaniard and Indian in the few words of his last will and testament—it was to save both, body and soul, from the death caused by the one—Spain's immoral, illegal behavior in the New World—on the other, innocent, defenseless peoples. There is an agony over both right to the end, for even on the day he died, aides of his were presenting a proposal to the council about calling a meeting to reform behavior in the New World, and someone he sent to Rome was presenting a petition to the Pope asking for a formal condemnation of conversion by conquest.[229] But it is the thirst in the man for the truth, founded on evidence and reason and faith and law and compassion, that is the most remarkable feature of his last words, it is like an eternal flame burning within them, for he saw the connection between truth and freedom, and he wanted Indian and Spaniard to be free, in this life, and in the next. The principles he worked out are capable of producing that freedom, even to this day.

From Las Casas' Last Will and Testament

The profession of faith.[230] In the name of the Most Blessed Trinity, Father and Son and Holy Spirit, one God and true. I, Bishop Fray Bartolomé de las Casas, knowing that every believing Christian must lay bare his soul at the time he comes to die, insofar as he can by the grace of God, and knowing that many things can prevent this at the hour of death: I wish to say solemnly before I see myself at that point that I will live and die as I shall

---

[229] See Helen Rand Parish's Introduction to *The Only Way*, pp. 53-4.

[230] *Opúsculos* [BAE, 110], doc. 52, 539a-40a; captions and pars. added. Reprinted with permission from *The Only Way.*

have lived, in the Holy Catholic Faith of the Most Blessed Trinity, Father, Son, Holy Spirit, believing and holding, as indeed I do, all that the Holy Church of Rome believes and holds. I wish to live the rest of my life in that faith, right up to and including death, and I want to die in that faith.

The call. And I testify that it was God in his goodness and mercy who chose me as his minister—unworthy though I was—to act here at home on behalf of all those people out in what we call the Indies, the true possessors of those kingdoms, those territories. To act against the unimaginable, unspeakable violence and evil and harm they have suffered from our people, contrary to all reason, all justice, so as to restore them to the original liberty they were lawlessly deprived of, and get them free of death by violence, death they still suffer, they perish still the same way. Thousands of leagues of land were thusly depopulated; I witnessed a great deal of it. For almost fifty years I have done this work, in the court of the Kings of Castile, back and forth between the Indies and Castile, Castile and the Indies, often, since 1514. I have done it for the sake of God alone, out of compassion at seeing the deaths of so many human beings, rational, civilized, unpretentious, gentle, simple human beings who were most apt for accepting our Holy Catholic Faith and its entire moral doctrine, human beings who already lived according to sound principles. As God is my witness, I had no other motive.

The Prophecy. What I say next I hold as certain doctrine, I judge it certain, it is what I think the Holy Roman Church holds and values as a norm of belief for us. All that the Spaniards perpetrated against those [Indian] peoples, the robbery, the killing, the usurpation of property and jurisdiction, from kings and lords and lands and realms, the theft of things on a boundless scale and the horrible cruelties that went with that—all this was in violation of the holy and spotless law of Jesus Christ, in violation of the whole natural law, and a terrible blot on the name of Christ and the Christian faith. It was all an absolute impediment to faith, all a mortal damage to the souls and bodies of those innocent peoples. And I think that God shall have to pour out his fury and anger on Spain for these damnable, rotten, infamous deeds done so unjustly, so tyrannically, so barbarously to those people, against those people. For the whole of Spain has shared in the blood-soaked riches, some a little, some a lot, but all shared in goods that were ill-gotten, wickedly taken with violence and genocide—and all must pay unless Spain does a mighty penance. And I fear it will do so too late or not at all, because there is a blindness God permits to come over sinners great and small, but especially over those who drive us or are considered prudent and wise, who give the world orders—a blindness because of sins, about everything in general. But especially that recent blindness of understanding which for the last seventy years has proceeded to shock and scandalize and rob and kill those people overseas. A blindness that is not even today aware that such scandals to our faith, such defamations of it, such robbing and injustice and violence and slaughter and enslavement and usurpation of foreign rule and rulers, above all such devastation, such genocide of populations, have been sins, have been monumental injustices!

Bishop Fray Bartolomé de las Casas

Bibliography

Albornoz, Nicolás Sanchez. "La población de las Indias en Las Casas y en la historia," *En el quinto centenario de Bartolomé de las Casas.* Madrid: Ediciones Cultura Hispánica, ICI, 1986.

Baptiste, Victor N. *Bartolomé de las Casas and Thomas More's Utopia: Connections and Similarities.* Culver City, CA: Labyrinthos, 1990.

Boethii Consolationis Philosophiae Quinque Libri, E. Gegenschatz and O. Gigon, eds. Zurich: Artemis Verlag, 1949.

Casas, Bartolomé de las, *The Only Way*, ed. Helen Rand Parish, trans. Francis Patrick Sullivan, S.J. Mahwah: Paulist Press, 1992.

_____. *Historia de las Indias.* Introd. by Lewis Hanke, transcription and index by Agustín Millares Carlo. 3 vols. Mexico City: Fondo de Cultura Económica, 1951.

_____. *Apologética Historia Sumaria quanto a las cualidades, dispusición, descripción, cielo y suelo destas tierras, y condiciones naturales, policías, repúblicas, manera de vivir e costumbres de las gentes destas Indias Occidentales y Meridionales cuyo imperio soberano pertenece a los Reyes de Castilla [Defense of the Indian Civilizations].* Ed. by Edmundo O'Gorman. 2 vols. Mexico City: Universidad Nacional Autónoma de México, Instituto de Investigaciones Históricas, 1967.

_____. *Obras completas.* Madrid: Alianza Editorial, 1989-1990.

_____. *Conclusiones sumarias sobre el remedio de las Indias.* Portfolio containing three separate items: a complete facsimile of the newly acquired manuscript and commentaries by Isacio Pérez Fernández and Helen Rand Parish. Madrid: Biblioteca Nacional, 1992.

_____. *Tratados.* Mexico City: Fondo de Cultura Económica, 1965. 2 vols.

_____. *Apologia [adversus Sepúlvedam].* In Juan Ginés de Sepúlveda/Fray Bartolomé de las Casas, *Apologia.* Ed., introd. and Spanish trans. by Angel Losada, appending full facsimiles of Latin texts. Madrid: Editora Nacional, 1975.

_____. *Opúsculos, cartas y memoriales.* Ed. by Juan Pérez de Tudela Bueso. Madrid: Ediciones Atlas, 1958.

Charles V, *The New Laws of the Indies for the Good Treatment and Preservation of the Indians, promulgated by the Emperor Charles the Fifth, 1542-1543:* Facsimile of original Spanish first edition, literal English translation, and Introd. by Henry Stevens and Fred W. Lucas. London: Chiswick Press, 1893.

Colón, Hernando. *Vida del Almirante,* trans. and ed. by Ramon Iglesia. Mexico: Fondo de Cultura Económica, 1947.

Corpus Iuris Civilis. Rev. and ed. by Paul Krueger; ed. Theodore Mommsen, and Rudolph Schoell. Berlin, 1928, 15th ed.

Corpus Iuris Canonici. Ed. by Emil Friedberg. 2 vols. Leipzig, 1879-81.

DII: *Colección de documentos inéditos, relativos al descubrimiento, conquista y organización de las antíguas possessiones españolas de América y Oceanía, sacados de los archivos del reino, y muy especialmente del de Indias (Documentos inéditos de Indias).* Madrid: Impr. de Manuel B. de Quirós, vol. 1, 1864.

Aristotle. The Basic Works. Trans. by Richard McKeon, New York: Random House, 1941.

Gutiérrez, Gustavo. *Bartolomé de las Casas: In Search of the Poor of Jesus Christ.* Maryknoll, NY: Orbis Press, 1993.

Hanke, Lewis. *La lucha por la justicia en la conquista de América.* Buenos Aires: Editorial Sudaméricana, 1949.

_____. *All Mankind Is One: A Study of the Disputation Between Bartolomé de las Casas and Juan Ginés de Sepúlveda in 1550 on the Intellectual and Religious Capacity of the American Indians.* DeKalb: Northern Illinois University Press, 1974.

Keen, Benjamin, "Approaches to Las Casas, 1535-1970." Introduction to Juan Friede & Benjamin Keen, *Bartolomé de las Casas in History: towards an understanding of the man and his work.* DeKalb: Northern Illinois University Press, 1971.

Migne, Jacques-Paul. *Patrologiae Cursus Completus, Series Latina. 221 vols. Paris, 1844-55.*

Migne, Jacques-Paul, *Patrologiae Cursus Completus,* Series Graeca, 161 vols. Paris, 1857-1866.

Nicholas of Lyra, *Bibliorum Sacrorum cum Glossa Ordinaria,* Lyons, 1545.

Parish, Helen Rand. *Las Casas as a Bishop: A new interpretation based on his holograph petition in the Hans P. Kraus Collection of Hispanic*

American Manuscripts in the Library of Congress. Washington: Library of Congress, 1980.

_____. *Las Casas: The Untold Story.* Berkeley: University of California Press, 1995. (In preparation.)

_____. ed. *The Royal File on the administration of the Indians: Restored and edited from the Kraus Codex in the Library of Congress (plus added documents from Spanish archives).* Introduction, discursive notes, and bibliography. Washington: Library of Congress, 1995. (In galleys.)

Parish, Helen Rand, with Weidman, Harold E. *Las Casas en México: Historia y obra desconocidas.* Mexico City: Fondo de Cultura Económica, 1992.

_____. "The Correct Birthdate of Bartolomé de las Casas." *Hispanic American Historical Review* 56 (1976): 385-403.

Pedro Mártir de Anglería, *Decades de orbe novo.* Alcalá, 1530.

Perez Fernandez, Isacio. *Bartolomé de las Casas Contra los negros? Revision de una leyenda.* Madrid: Editorial Mundo Negro; México: Ediciones Esquila, 1991.

Provost, Foster. *Columbus: an annotated guide to the scholarship on his life and writings, 1750-1988.* Detroit: Omnigraphics, for the John Carter Brown Library, 1991.

S. Anselmi Opera Omnia, ed. Franciscus Salesius Schmitt. Stuttgart, 1968. 2 tomes.

Santa Cruz, Alonso de. *Cronica del emperador Carlos V.* Madrid: 1920-19-25. 5 vols.

Taviani, Paolo Emilio. *Christopher Columbus: The Grand Design.* London: Orbis, 1985.

Thomas Aquinas. *Opera Omnia.* 2nd ed. Parma: Pietro Ficcadori, 1852-1873.

Varela, Consuelo. *Cristóbal Colón: Textos y documentos completos.* Madrid: Alianza Editorial, 2nd ed. 1989.

Wagner, Henry R. and Helen Rand Parish. *The Life and Writings of Bartolomé de las Casas.* Albuquerque: Univ. of New Mexico Press, 1967.

Glossary of Terms

Baptism: The sacramental ritual which provided entry into the Church and its means of salvation, the other sacraments. It was considered a sine qua non of salvation. But that depended on the behavior of the Church, i.e., forced baptism was null, though many Christians thought Baptism worked automatically, never mind the quality of the minister or the dispositions of the person being baptized. In the real order of history, people recognised that God would have to save the non-baptised by other means than a defaulting Church.

Capacity: The power in individuals and groups to understand and accept or reject the presentation of human or revealed meaning by those who already possess that meaning. The meaning can be theological, philosophical, legal, cultural, historical. The power to receive meaning implies the prior exercise of that power in fashioning meaning, i.e., a mature use of intellect, will, imagination, emotion, senses. Difficulties in communicating meaning do not reveal a disparity in levels of being, i.e., differences in experience, language, culture, etc.

Catholic Faith/Church: The community in which conversion to the life of charity modeled on that of Jesus Christ is fostered by means which transmit that life, i.e., sacramental re-enactments of the words and deeds of Christ intended to foster what is loveable to God in human beings. The Catholic Church considers itself a necessary means of salvation. But some in it have known it cannot reach everyone or reaches people badly. So these Christians fall back on the deeper truth that God wishes the salvation of all and will accomplish it through other means.

Confession: A sacramental action whereby someone in sorrow for a sin or sins tells a duly authorized minister of the Church the nature of the sin or sins and asks that the minister, in the name of Christ and the Church, grant him or her absolution from the sins so that his or her soul will be in a restored relationship to God. Absolution depends on sorrow, but also on making amends for wrongs done which may have harmed other people. Making amends is called restoration, restitution. E.g., sorrow for a theft and absolution depend on restoring what was stolen, if that is possible without public self-inculpation, in which case restitution may be occult, but it must occur.

Conscience: An awareness in the human being of the conformity or non-conformity of an action with some norm of behavior, i.e., natural law, divine law, law of nations, law of charity. The awareness is the result of a judgment, so truth and error may be involved, i.e., the norm of behavior may itself be disordered, in which case it may induce disordered behavior in a sincere conscience.

Conversion: A turning of the human being from a condition alien to God to a condition loveable to God. The turning can have many causes, but all are considered the results of divine prompting. The condition loveable to God is spelled out for Christians in the life of Jesus Christ and all conversion is a movement towards that model. The preaching of the truth of Christ has, as its goal, the conversion of the human being to the ideal so salvation (of the behavioral kind) will occur, and damnation (of the behavioral kind) will not. Since the human being does not know the mind of God about who is to be saved, who not, the human being must presume that all are destined to be saved on the behavioral model.

Damnation: A state of separation from eternal bliss with God, and a consequent pain of loss. Damnation is also either gratuitous on the part of God or caused by the evil behavior on the part of the human being who is punished by God for his or her behavior.

Decimation [devastation]: Reduction of a population in an area as a result of recognisable causes, war, enslavement, forced labor, malnutrition and consequent disease and death, splitting of families, removal to other areas. It is the abuse of a population in order to achieve some goal, i.e., personal enrichment.

Demon: In religions of revelation, a counter-force to God, allowed by God, to test the sincerity of goodness in the human being, and thus reveal if they are fit for relationship with God. The demon is a real person in religions of revelation, but often also is a symbol of what humans do along destructive lines.

Encomienda: A condition of unfreedom forced upon New World Indians. They were given in numbers to individual Spaniards, to serve the will of the individual Spaniard—work in mines, in fields, in households—without any conditions being laid upon the will of the owner except that he train in Christianity the Indians he held. It was a condition worse than slavery and death was the only way out.

Enslavement: A condition of unfreedom forced upon a human being by other human beings for cause considered legitimate by those doing the forcing. The condition of unfreedom had many levels, from the temporary with light requirements, to the perpetual with heavy, even brutal requirements. Laws concerning enslavement were worked out from the time of the Greek city states, through Roman times, into the Christian, and their purpose was to preserve a certain level of humane treatment. People captured in a just war were considered to be justly enslaved. Slaves could generally achieve their freedom under existing laws. Spanish enslavement of New World Indians had no legitimating cause. As it was practiced, it had only the facade of legality and was inhumane in the extreme. Natural law, divine law, the law of nations condemned unjust enslavement, and condemned enslavement based upon "inferior nature" arguments.

Innocence:

moral: A condition of non-culpability in an individual or a group vis-a-vis precepts of natural law, divine law, law of nations. It concerns free will acts. Indian peoples are innocent with respect to European peoples because they have never harmed them, usurped their territory, demeaned their religion, been in debt to them, in fact never knew they even existed.

physical: A condition of being apart from free will acts, the nature of something as it is received. Theological traditions quarrel about innocence in being: some affirm it; some see it as affected by a primal sin in the first parents of humankind, affected either partially or wholly. The condition is relative to God, not to humanity, the latter may not act punitively towards physical conditions of being.

Law: natural: Norms for behavior derived from an understanding of human being in its individual as well as its social nature. The norms are built into the nature by the creator of that nature.

divine: Norms for behavior, individual and social, derived from an understanding of revelation as it addresses human beings, revelation being from God through various media, i.e. prophets, priests, chroniclers, evangelists. The norms both reinforce natural law and add greater requirements. To the natural law of justice is added the divine law of mercy.

of nations: Norms for behavior, individual and social, derived from the practice of peoples in their dealings with one another. These norms are practical and intended to smooth relationships by common consent.

canon: A body of precepts used for the governance of the church in its internal as well as external relationships. It is a mixture of divine and natural law plus elements taken from the law of nations as these are used to resolve concrete problems. Canon law exists in codified form to make access and application easier.

of charity: Norms for behavior, individual and social, derived from revelation which indicate an ideal God wishes human beings to practice. The primary example for Christians is the life of Jesus Christ as it is recorded in the New Testament.

Paganism: Religion based on what humans can discern about the divine through the things of the cosmos. Religion based on revelation considers paganism to be derived from demonic distortion so the truths of revelation can be blocked and the demon can prevail against the true God. But some, in religions of revelation, respect the basic symbolic truth of paganism where those truths create harmony and peace and promote a cultural life which is salvational.

Papal Donation: An action of the papacy towards the Kings of Spain whereby the papacy empowers Spain to act in the name of Christendom and be in charge of the evangelization [conversion] of the New World. The papacy did not have the material resources and wanted to avoid having Christian nations in conflict over the task. The pope was supposed, in one theory, to have power over the world in temporal as well as spiritual terms. In another theory, only spiritual power, and only upon the consent of peoples to the Christian faith.

Salvation: A state of eternal relationship in bliss for the human being, deriving from God who grants the relationship gratuitously or on the fulfillment of certain conditions. The gratuitous granting is called predestination by theologians. The conditional granting is called the judgment wherein a person's behavior is weighed prior to the granting of the eternal relationship.

Sovereignty: Rulership derived from the people and invested in a ruler for the good of the people. The good of the people is their freedom to act as their lives require, and to be protected in their activity. There are similar principles involved which affect the different groups, principles of right and obligation. The ruler is the guarantor of these principles among the various groups. The sovereignty of the King of Spain over the Indies exists only on this level, it is not to profit the King or Spain, but to serve the various peoples as a guardian of their rights and obligations. But the King must be chosen as such by the various peoples.

War: just: A use of violence by a people against another people in order to defend against destruction or damage by that other people. For a war to be just, there must be a cause that is morally right (i.e., self-defense) according to natural law, divine law, the law of nations, and there must be authorization by duly constituted authority. The violence employed must be proportioned to the threat and must cease when the threat has been halted, though punishment and recuperation of loss is allowed, but in proportion.

  unjust: A use of violence by a people against another people who are innocent of any harm against the warring one. Unjust war carries with it the obligation of restitution on the part of the warring force.

Name Index

Subject Index